The Man Who Saw The Future

The frontispiece of the bound journals of 'The Company of Scotland Trading to Africa and the Indies' – 1696–1698. It proudly displayed the newly devised coat of arms. In the vision of the artist the native peoples of Africa and the Indies would welcome the Scots. Note the symbol of the rising sun that reflected the optimism of the promoters. The Latin motto, loosely translated, means: 'As the world is revealed, in unity we shall have greater strength'

Reproduced by kind permission of The Royal Bank of Scotland Group

The Man Who Saw The Future

Andrew Forrester

Australia · Canada · Mexico · Singapore · Spain · United Kingdom · United States

The Man Who Saw The Future
Andrew Forrester

COPYRIGHT © 2004 by Andrew Forrester.
Published in 2004 by TEXERE, part of the Thomson Corporation. TEXERE, Thomson, and Thomson logo are trademarks used herein under license.

ISBN: 1-58799-143-8
Printed and bound in the United States by Edwards Brothers
1 2 3 4 5 6 7 8 9 07 06 05 04

For more information, contact TEXERE, 300 Park Avenue South, New York, NY 10010, or find us on the Web at www.etexere.com.

This publication is designed to provide accurate and authoritative information in regard to the subject matter covered. It is sold with the understanding that the publisher is not engaged in rendering legal, accounting or other professional services. If legal advice or other expert assistance is required, the services of a competent professional person should be sought.

Project managed by: Macfarlane Production Services, Markyate, Hertfordshire, England (e-mail: macfarl@aol.com).

A CIP Library of Congress Cataloging in Publication Data Requested.

The names of all companies or products mentioned herein are used for identification purposes only and may be trademarks or registered trademarks of their respective owners. TEXERE disclaims any affiliation, association, connection with, sponsorship, or endorsements by such owners.

Contents

To the memory
of
Robert L. McLaughlan
who brought me to history
and showed me what it meant

Acknowledgements

This book would have been impossible had it not been for the help and assistance given to me by archivists and librarians everywhere. There are too many to list in full, but I would like to single out for special mention Ruth Smith, the archivist at The Royal Bank of Scotland in Edinburgh. The minute books of the Company of Scotland passed to the bank when it became the successor company in 1727. In a few hours they showed me that all previous accounts of Paterson's role within the Company of Scotland, once it moved its operations to Edinburgh, gravely underestimated his contribution to the successful launch of the company.

The collections of company records and personal correspondence known as 'The Darien Papers' and housed in the National Library of Scotland, is immense and worthy of much more detailed research. But, with the help of the staff, I was able to examine in detail the period from October 1696 to May 1697 when Paterson and three others scoured Europe looking for funds, and supervising the building of the new ships required for the first and second expeditions. The correspondence between Edinburgh, London, Amsterdam and Hamburg, gives a real sense of the size of the undertaking, and the confusion and the bitterness that arose between the company accountants in London and the continental agents engaged by Paterson and the others. The letters throw into stark relief the difficulties a multinational company, such as the Company of Scotland, faced in a world when it could take up to a month for a letter from Edinburgh to reach Amsterdam.

The University of Glasgow, as befits an institution whose Principal sat on the board of the Company of Scotland, holds the Spencer Collection, a remarkable library of contemporary tracts and such later material as Eliot Warburton's *The Merchant Prince*, and Dr Cullen's survey of the Isthmus. Working with the ever helpful staff there was a pleasure.

In London, the bulk of the materials dealing with the Bank of England and the Darien Scheme are found to be in the British Library. For 18 months the staff catered for my every request, helping to locate volumes and pamphlets that could not be easily found in the catalogue; my thanks to them.

Through the Internet, I located a small collection of original documents and other works dealing with the Darien project in the University of London Archive. A phone call alerting them to my needs was enough to produce for my inspection not only the original sailing orders prepared by Paterson for the first expedition, but – even more remarkably – a 'petition' from William Paterson, dated February 1699 and written from Darien, suggesting it was time he was paid the money he was owed! How it came from the forests of Darien to be lodged in the University of London Archive appears something of a mystery. I want to thank them for posting such information on the Internet, and so readily letting me look through the material they hold.

The Bank of England Archivists proved extremely helpful, helping me to locate the early papers relating to the founding of the Bank. The minutes of the Society and the letter sent by William Paterson proved to be particularly useful in establishing Paterson's real role in the enterprise. Their willingness to arrange for documents kept in the Bank of England Museum to be brought in for me to peruse was much appreciated.

The City of London Archive, kept by the Corporation of London, provided another fascinating journey of exploration, especially into the curious business of the Orphans' Fund, and the founding of the Orphans' Bank by William Paterson. There was much original material here, and many secondary works, including the very valuable account of the financial repercussions of the Chamberlain's mismanagement of the Orphans' Fund. I would like to thank them and the staff of the Guildhall Library, who produced at very short notice the pamphlet written by James Smith on the subject.

I live close by the Public Record Office in Kew and dipped into the vast hoard of documents dealing with the whole Darien adventure, seen through the eye of English ministers. The service was brisk and cheerful.

I am particularly indebted to the help and advice given to me by Dr D.W. Jones of the University of York. His work on the merchants of London and their relations with the East India Company gave me an invaluable insight into the mercantile politics of the time. That, and his longer work, *War and Economy in the Age of William the Third and Marlborough*, provided the information that allowed me to link William Paterson and the Company of Scotland and the leading opponents of the old EIC.

I would like to make a special mention of the Dumfries and Galloway Natural History and Archaeological Society who replied so promptly to my queries about William Paterson's burial place, and on the matter of the Dumfries Election. Mr James Williams, their secretary, was particularly helpful, sending me several articles that proved useful.

I want also to thank the many friends who encouraged me to pursue this task and who gave me succour when I came to visit Scotland. Chief among them are Ken and Elizabeth Munro, constant pillars of support, and Vanessa Coulter who was so kind as to drive me all the way to Prestwick to take advantage of a Ryannair flight to Stansted. Such little gestures will never be forgotten.

On the home front, I need to give a very special thank you to Lis, my wife, who has endured my two-year obsession with this book with remarkable equanimity and good humour. I also want to thank Mairi Campbell Mackinlay, my mother-in-law, for the keen and informed interest she has taken in the progress of the book. I hope that she will find it more than worth the wait.

As something of an innocent abroad in the world of publishing I will be forever grateful to my agent, Pat Lomax of Lomax-Bell, for her constant support and encouragement.

Lastly, I must acknowledge my deep debt to David Wilson. He was my editor at TEXERE from inception until submission of the final manuscript. He played a vital role in the conception of this book, and provided an ever-dependable sounding-board for testing my developing views on such issues as the role of James Smith as Paterson's right-hand man, or the critical part played by the currency crisis of 1696 in discrediting the Company of Scotland in Hamburg. His encouragement kept me going, his editing helped make the book the one I always wanted to write. To him, and to all the staff at TEXERE, I offer my sincere thanks.

Without the help of all these people and organisations, the story I tell could never have been told in the way that it has. Errors in fact and interpretation, with their help, I have striven to keep to a minimum. For any that remain, I have to accept full responsibility.

Andrew Forrester

A Note on Money Values and Dates

Money Values

It is impossible to make any true comparison between the value of money in the 17th century and today's values. The pattern of consumption and the nature of the balance between private and public expenditure have changed too much. But we can say that the sums involved in William Paterson's more ambitious plans were huge. A subscription to raise £1.2million to launch the Bank of England may seem small beer today, but in 1660 the English parliament considered that such a sum was quite enough to fund a year's government expenditure, including the upkeep of the army and navy, the maintenance of law and order, and the conduct of foreign affairs.

Again, Adam Smith reckoned that the entire wealth of Scotland in 1700 amounted to just £1 million. So the plan to raise £400,000 in Scotland to fund 'The Company of Scotland Trading to Africa and the Indies', involved tying up some 40% of the country's assets. Another way of looking at comparative value is to consider that the directors of the Company of Scotland assumed that £25,000 would be sufficient to pay for five or six ocean-going ships and all necessary equipment, including armaments.

Dates

During the period covered by this story, Europe was divided over the question of how to determine dates. Since 1582, Catholic Europe had adopted the new Gregorian calendar (named after Pope Gregory XIII who had introduced it). The aim was to restore the relationship between the sun and the chief religious festival of Easter. From then on Catholic Europe ran 10 days ahead of the rest of the continent. To complicate matters, under the old Julian calendar the new year began on 25 March

(Lady Day) while the new calendar began the year on 1 January. This meant that 21 January 1689 in England was 31 January 1690 in Spain and France. To make the issue even more complex Britain itself had more than one way of reckoning dates under the Julian calendar. From the year 1600 Scotland had chosen to start the year on 1 January.

Since most of the events related in this book took place in England and Scotland and in the English colonies, the dates throughout have been stated according to the old style calendar, modified only by using 1 January rather than 25 March as the first day of the year.

Introduction

Most people travelling north into Scotland from Carlisle find it easy to miss Dumfries. The road and rail links speed past the little border village of Gretna, where runaway lovers from the south used to be married at the blacksmith's anvil, and head directly for Lockerbie and the pass of Beattock. Beyond them lies Glasgow and the distant highlands. Dumfries lies off to the west, sitting all square on both banks of the River Nith, a historic county town, associated with the poet Robert Burns and with the great hero of Scottish history, Robert the Bruce. It bears its historic importance with dignity, its older buildings handsomely dressed in the rich red hue of the local sandstone.

This is Paterson country. It was just north of Dumfries, in the parish of Trailflatt, that the remarkable but largely forgotten William Paterson was born over 300 years ago. For those who have never heard of him, it will suffice for the moment to say that he achieved the remarkable feat of marrying both triumph and disaster in the course of a varied career. In 1694 he laid the foundation stone of Britain's future commercial and industrial might when he founded the Bank of England. Just a year later, he had turned his back on the Bank and thrown all his energies into an even more ambitious project to transform the way the world did business. Three years later we find him sailing into a great natural harbour on the Isthmus of Panama (then known as the Isthmus of Darien) with a fleet of five heavily armed ships, and a plan to open up a new route across the Isthmus to open up trade with the Pacific. This was to be a first step on the road to the globalisation of world trade, with each region of the world supplying what it could best produce or provide, on the basis of free trade. In this, William Paterson was some 250 years ahead of his time. But the grand plan came unstuck, leaving his native Scotland burdened with debt and in the throes of an economic crisis that was resolved only by Scotland accepting union with England in 1707.

Just how the grand plan for Darien came about, why it failed, and what its failure meant to the thousands of enthusiastic young Scots involved in it, and their many supporters in America, is the subject of this book.

Paterson, when he was alive, was a master of the art of self-efface-ment. It extended even to making a mystery of his birth, a mystery that took 200 years to clear up. The first mention of his link to the Dumfries area arose only some 70 years after his death when, in 1791, the Reverend James Lawrie, minister in the little hamlet of Tinwald made the claim that:

> The famous Paterson who planned the Darien Scheme and the Bank of England, &c, was born at Skipmyre (now in my parish) about the year 1660.

Even then not everyone agreed. In 1853, John Burton Hill, the Scottish historian who collected and printed the first set of documents to throw light on Paterson's business ventures, was adamant that:

> There is no visible authority for the statement that Paterson was a native of the parish of Tinwald, and no means of knowing that he was a native of Scotland.

The mystery was eventually cleared up by some good detective work. In 1865 another Scottish historian, William Pagan, came to Dumfries to search the local church records – for the Church of Scotland had long obliged its parishes to keep a register of births, marriages and deaths. The search failed to turn anything up. But then he was directed by a local man to an old burial ground in the ruins of the old church of Trailflatt, a church abandoned in 1662 when its congregation amalgamated with the church at Tinwald. At Trailflatt, among a tangle of overgrown graves and fallen headstones, Pagan found three graves, belonging to the Patersons of Skipmyre, a small tenant farm on the uplands some five miles north of Dumfries. One of these appeared to be the grave of William Paterson's father. Then Pagan saw the name Mounsey on two of the stones, side by side with Paterson. He knew from the will of William Paterson, drawn up in London in 1718, that one of the banker's sisters had married into the Mounsey family. On closer examination, one of the graves held the remains of William Mounsey, Janet's son, a man to whom William Paterson had left what was then the princely sum of £200.

The only contemporary portrait of William Paterson. The Latin motto can be translated 'Thus you strive but not for yourself' (By permission of the British Library, Add. 10403, folio 1).

So from 1865 it was at last clearly established that William Paterson was indeed of Scottish birth, and that he had been born in Skipmyre. The date of his birth, 1658, had already been established from statements made in the will.

This story is instructive in highlighting one of the great challenges facing any biographer of Paterson. He was, in personal terms, a secretive man. He left no diaries, no self-justifying memoirs. And the personal letters sent by him to others, with few exceptions, have not survived.

Fortunately, there is a wealth of material buried in the archives in Edinburgh and London that allow us to reconstruct his career in great detail and to correct the false view of Paterson that has grown up, that he was only a minor player in establishing the Bank of England, and that later he became a self-deluded confidence trickster who contrived to lead a whole nation astray.

Before considering how Paterson came to be most unfairly misrepresented in the average history book, if mentioned at all, it is worth taking a look at the only contemporary portrait of him that has ever come to light. It is a rather crude pen-and-ink drawing made in 1708 when he was 49 years old. The lean man staring at us across 300 years of time is formally dressed, his head crowned with the mark of a gentleman, the powdered periwig. But the drawing gives away little of his character. The gaze is cold and there is not a trace of a smile on his lips. It inclines us to accept the verdict of Sir John Dalrymple, given in 1771, that Paterson was a buttoned-up teetotaller: 'one of the very few of his countrymen who never drank wine, and who was by nature void of passion'.[1]

This is to go too far. Paterson did indeed have passion, revealed in the one or two letters from him that have survived, and to a much greater degree in his actions. A man without feelings would not have walked out on the Bank of England in the way he did, nor dedicated much of his life to the relentless pursuit of his own vision of the future. It was just that he did not believe in letting such feelings show.

The portrait puts a face to the man and gives some impression of the status he held in 1708, when he was much respected as the accounting genius whose arithmetic had settled just how much England should pay to Scotland when the two countries united in 1707. Much of that was to be paid as direct compensation to Paterson's Darien shareholders, an oblique acknowledgement that England had some part to play in the failure of Paterson's grand scheme. 1708 was also the year Paterson stood for election to parliament, a contest that he both won and lost, a result that pretty much sums up his whole career.

Below the portrait appears in Latin: '*Sic Vos, non Vobis*'. This is best rendered as 'Thus you strive but not for yourself' and suggests something of the fierce commitment of the man, a man driven by an inner belief that he had been put on earth to make the world a better place. But we would be wrong to imagine him as a selfless saint, bound by a vow of poverty. He sought a fair financial reward for all that he did. His persistence in demanding it irritated people. Often, the reward never came.

The lack of Paterson diaries and memoirs, and of any personal detail of his character that comes from his own pen or that of his friends, has left historians with a major headache. The great banker and projector left behind a vacuum of personal information about himself. And into this vacuum rushed a classic piece of character assassination.

In 1700, when Paterson was still deeply involved with the *Company of Scotland Trading to Africa and the Indies*, the Darien company, a scurrilous pamphlet appeared on the streets of Edinburgh written by a man nursing a grievance against the company. The author was Walter Herries, a disreputable ship's surgeon, spirited out of the Royal Navy after stabbing his commanding officer. By 1700 he was in the pay of the English secret service. For all the ugly side of his character, he had a brilliant way with words. His memoir on Paterson and the Darien project ridiculed the Scottish company in general and Paterson in particular. The man who had so brilliantly founded the Bank of England was now caricatured as a roving 'Scotch pedlar' who dreamt up his idea of a Scottish trading company principally to take revenge on the English for the way he had been treated by his colleagues in the Bank. This Paterson, a conceited fool of a man, had straightaway gone to Edinburgh and caught the entire people of Scotland in his net. They were mesmerised by his talk of warm lands and of the gold and silver that could be found in them. They were transfixed by his promises that all who subscribed to his company would die rich men. Herries laid it on with a trowel:

> Nay, some persons had such a conceit of the miracles he could perform, that they began to talk of an Engine, to give the Island half a turn-round, and to set the Orkneys where the Isles of Scilly stand.[2]

Paterson became, in short, the snake-oil salesman to end all snake-oil salesmen. A confidence trickster *extraordinaire*.

The vivid account of Paterson's life supplied by Herries was denounced by the Scots at the time as an utter travesty but surprisingly it was not countered by any action on Paterson's part. He issued not a word in response. This was unfortunate since the Herries pamphlet became the first point of reference for those who afterwards wanted to tell Paterson's story. Chief among these was the great English historian, Lord Macaulay. Macaulay's depiction of Paterson as a hopeless dreamer with an extraordinary power of oratory, leading his countrymen sleep-walking to disaster, all based on Herries, has stuck ever since. For good measure, Macaulay lifted from Herries the myth that the Scots took nothing but thousands of bibles and hundreds of periwigs to trade with the Indians. It was a perfect way to ridicule both Paterson and the Scots. Where Macaulay led, others were to follow. Notably the historian of the Bank of England, Sir John Clapham, who in 1944 dismissed Paterson as a 'Pedlar turned Merchant',[3] and questioned his role in the founding of the bank.

Nearly 300 years after his death it is time to set the record straight. Though Paterson wrote little about himself, the archives in Edinburgh, Glasgow, London, and elsewhere bulge with the records of his activities. To this can be added many printed sources, and much new research into the period when William Paterson played an important part in London life and London business. With the help of the Internet it has been possible to trace collections of Patersonia never before scrutinised, and to find much reliable research on such matters as the buccaneers of the West Indies and the great currency crisis of 1696. The posting on the Internet of entire books out of copyright, and the coming of newly published electronic books have also been an unexpected boon.

With the aid of this research, we can now discover the real Paterson. The picture that emerges is far removed from the Herries caricature. Here was a businessman of great experience, with a vision that was always subject to the limits of practicality. His track record in launching new projects ranged from meeting the needs of Londoners for running water, to a lavish scheme to open up Nova Scotia as a source of timber for the Royal Navy. He was known and respected in Amsterdam, and in Boston, and inspired merchants in New York to attempt to come to the rescue of his great scheme in Darien. All this was achieved by a man of lowly Scottish origins who played the field brilliantly in rallying people of all social classes to his support. Above all, this is a story of a man, utterly convinced that his schemes would benefit mankind, who could not be deflected from the task in hand, no matter what tragedies and hardships came his way.

There was some talk of raising a monument to William Paterson in 1865.[4] It was to be built on the summit of Pendicle Hill, overlooking his boyhood playgrounds, to stand as a 'thing of beauty'. But the Scottish amnesia (or Macaulay-induced embarrassment) on the subject of Paterson, meant that it was never built. Perhaps it is time to think again.

Chapter 1

The Doors of the Seas

... But open these doors of Tubagantee and Cacarica, and through them will circulate all the wealth and rich commodities of the spacious South Seas.

William Paterson 1700[1]

December 1679. The day dawned with tropical suddenness over the calm waters of Port Royal harbour, the first rays of the sun catching the sails of a little fleet of armed sailing ships, flashes of white against the deep azure sky. The small fleet slid quietly passed the harbour fortress and set sail east, tacking into the freshening easterly breeze. There were four ships, two barques and two sloops,[2] carrying a small and irregular force of fighting men, about 300 in all, hardened seadogs and fresh new recruits set on adventure. Few knew exactly where they were going but all expected to come back rich, their purses full of the fruits of piracy.

Port Royal had witnessed scenes like these before. In its twenty-five-year history it had grown from a few fishermen's huts to become capital of the new English colony of Jamaica. Eight thousand people now lived here, making it the largest English-speaking town in the Americas, out-growing its nearest rival, Boston. The two towns could scarcely have been more different. Boston was a hard-working, god-fearing community, Port Royal notorious as a dissolute and godless place. Writing only a little later, an anonymous visitor to Jamaica memorably summed it up as:

> The dunghill of the universe, the Refuse of the whole Creation, ... The Place where Pandora filled her box ... The receptacle of Vagabonds, the Sanctuary of bankrupts, and a [chamber pot] for the Purges of our Prisons. As sickly as a hospital, as dangerous as the Plague, as Hot as Hell, and as wicked as the Devil.[3]

Port Royal seems to have taken pride in its reputation as 'the Wickedest City in the World'. Crowded along the waterfront were

1

around a thousand taverns[4] doubling as gambling dens, and innumerable cheap boarding houses offering more than just a bed for the night. Here, it seemed, people lived only for the moment – if life was 'nasty, brutish, and short' as Thomas Hobbes had written in 1651 – why shouldn't the seadogs of Port Royal make the most of it while they could?

Despite its reputation for sin, Port Royal was by all accounts a finely built little town with broad streets and grand four-storey buildings of stone and brick, standing on a tiny triangle of land. The site sat like a fist at the end of a long arm of sand and rock that jutted out from the mainland, enclosing one of the great natural harbours of the world. The little triangle was barely a thousand yards long and only five hundred across at the widest point. Yet for all the crushed intimacy of the site Port Royal was a town divided against itself – a place where the lawless old days of piracy lingered on even as the plantation owners and merchants strove to transform it into a centre of legitimate trade and commerce.

The pirates were out-and-out hedonists, the ultimate practitioners of conspicuous consumption. When not at sea in search of fortune they were digging deep into their purses. One observer recorded:

> They are busy dicing, whoring and drinking so long as they have anything to spend.[5]

The pirates and those who lived on the immediate fruits of piracy – such as rum-sellers and brothel masters – frequented the seedy taverns of Thames Street, the main thoroughfare that hugged the waterfront and looked north across the harbour to the Blue Mountains on the mainland. The rising merchant class preferred to meet in the respectable establishments of High Street and Queen Street, back from the waterfront. There a man could dine or take coffee, and exchange information on prices and on the latest movements of shipping.

Anyone looking for William Paterson that December, would have been wise to begin the search in the more respectable part of town. Paterson had been born in Scotland, raised in Bristol, and was at this stage of his career just twenty-one years old. We know remarkably little about his early life, but it seems he had come to Jamaica by way of Old Providence Island – a small rocky outcrop in the Caribbean lying about 500 miles to the south-west of Jamaica seized from Spain by a buccaneer fleet in 1670. This island, we are told by Walter Herries, Paterson's first biographer, was a lawless place: '[A] sanctuary for Buccaneers, pyrates and such vermin'.[6]

According to Herries, whose assertions must be treated with some caution, Paterson's earliest inclinations may have led him towards religion rather than trade, and he would scarcely have found such a place to his liking.[7] At least in Port Royal legitimate trade was granted the importance it deserved, and men of trade whiled away their evenings discussing how it might be improved. It was here that Paterson was to learn the art of being a merchant.

Although much of what he did in Port Royal has to be in the nature of conjecture, it is hardly possible that people would have guessed on meeting him that before them stood the man who was one day to found that cornerstone of London's financial power, the Bank of England, and even less that he would then attempt to revolutionise the manner in which the world conducted business. He was to become a prophet of free and fair trade, urging states to cast aside their practice of rigging the rules of trade to favour their own merchants. They should open up their harbours to foreign merchants on an equal basis, whatever the grumbles of those threatened by such competition. He later made plain that he believed free and open trade would have the effect of benefiting everyone and bringing prosperity where only poverty prevailed:

> Trade will increase trade, and money will beget money, and the trading world shall need no more to want work for their hands, but rather want hands for their work.[8]

He was to become a man of advanced ideas, many of them 200 years ahead of their time. But he was also, first and foremost, a man of action. In his fertile imagination he conceived of a way to demonstrate the practical benefits of this 'free trade' through the construction of a great market (an 'emporium' he called it) on the site he identified as the natural centre of global trade the Isthmus of Panama.

Here, in a region still today known as Darien, the great Atlantic was separated from the Pacific (then popularly known as the South Sea) by as little as forty miles. Paterson proposed building a great highway, part road, part canalised river, across the narrow neck of land, linking two great natural harbours found on the opposite shores, each capable of holding a thousand ships or more.[9] In these harbours jetties and warehouses would be built, and merchants encouraged to sail from all over the globe to meet here and exchange their products and commodities on a 'duty free' basis, both within the harbours themselves and across the Isthmus. As he envisaged it, this was to be the first world trade centre, and the benefits of opening up global free trade would soon be apparent to all.[10]

Had Paterson not been in Port Royal at the time of the last great flourishing of piracy he may never have developed his grandiose scheme, a project that was destined to swallow up vast fortunes and leave nothing to show for it in the end but a few sad overgrown remains on a peninsula in Darien known to this day as 'Punta Escocès' – the Cape of the Scots. The pirate expedition that set out in December 1679 proved to be the catalyst that ignited his revolutionary ideas. It brought back a wealth of information on the little-known lands of Central America. It also showed how much could be accomplished by comparatively few men. And Paterson was there in Port Royal when some of them returned to tell their remarkable story. It was a happy accident that Port Royal was one of the few places in the world where legitimate merchants and lawless pirates could rub shoulders and even become intimate friends.

Jamaica had been home to pirates since its first days as an English colony, when it had been wrested from Spanish control by Oliver Cromwell in 1655. The island lay just south of the route taken by regular convoys of Spanish treasure ships, sailing out from the armed citadel of Portobello on the north coast of the Isthmus to make the hazardous trip across the Atlantic to Cadiz. Spanish gold and silver attracted pirates like blowflies to a dead horse. The pirates, or 'buccaneers', as they preferred to be called,[11] were of many different nationalities, French and English, Dutch and Danish, Scots and Welsh. They needed secure bases, places where they could restock, maintain their ships, and plan their next exploit. And, in this respect Port Royal was ideal, close to the route taken by the Spanish treasure fleet, yet sheltered and safe from all but the most severe tropical storms.

In the early days the buccaneers were made welcome in Port Royal. This was a time of almost continuous conflict in the Caribbean, with the leading European maritime powers intent on establishing colonies or 'plantations' on often neighbouring islands. Although the English Royal Navy was already growing mighty, it was simply not feasible to provide the all-the-year-round protection that the colony needed. The English governors of Jamaica[12] turned to the buccaneers as an unofficial defence force, the bargain they struck nicely judged to benefit both sides. It worked like this. The pirates would be given a letter of authority, a 'Commission', from the governor, which gave them the right to fly the royal standard and attack enemy shipping and harbours with the blessing of the King of England. In an instant they were transformed from criminals who could be hunted down and hanged, into 'privateers', respectable servants of the king, with a licence to steal. The governors in return claimed a right to a share of any treasure or cargo seized by these new servants. The resulting booty defrayed the costs of government, and left something over for their private enrichment.[13]

By the time William Paterson arrived in the Caribbean, probably in the early 1670s, the name of Henry Morgan was on everybody's lips. In 1668 this Welshman, the most famous of all the privateers, had been elevated to the post of 'High Admiral' by the then Governor of Jamaica, Sir Thomas Modyford. These were desperate times, with rumours sweeping the island that the Spanish forces in Cuba were about to mount an assault on the island. Following the adage that attack is the best means of defence, Modyford had sent Morgan off to plunder Spanish ships and Spanish ports along the Main.[14] Then in 1670, after a Spanish force landed on the north coast of Jamaica, killing some Englishmen and carrying off others into slavery, Modyford replied by issuing Morgan a fresh commission – by so-called 'letters of marque' – authorising him to raid the great harbour of Havana in Cuba. The Governor's instructions were nicely open-ended, concluding with the following words:

> ... many things may happen in this Action which cannot be by me foreseen and provided for in these Instructions, therefore all such matters are left to your well known prudence and conduct ...
>
> I remain your faithful Friend and Servant
> Thos. Modyford[15]

Modyford had no sooner issued Morgan's new commission when word arrived from London that an English delegation had been sent to Spain to negotiate peace between the two countries. He was instructed to stop all further attacks on the Spanish Main. But putting a leash on Morgan and his men proved difficult. When told of London's wishes, the Welshman simply replied that it was up to the Spaniards to be the first to honour the peace.

It was clear that even then Morgan was hatching his great plan to hit the Spanish hard, where they least expected it. Tucked away on the south side of the Isthmus, facing the South Sea, was the jewel of the

Spanish empire, the old city of Panama. Here the Spanish treasure ships regularly sailed in, laden down with the silver of Peru and the gold and precious stones of Mexico. Here the treasure was stored until it could be taken by mule at six-monthly intervals north across a cobbled trail – known grandly as the *Camino Real* (or Royal Road) – to the Caribbean coast at Portobello, from where the Spanish treasure fleet would carry it back to Spain. Morgan planned to attack Panama, not by way of the *Camino Real*, but by a route further west, using native canoes to carry the buccaneers south up the Chagres River, and then across country to the South Sea.

This was no easy task, since the route was guarded by a fortress at the mouth of the Chagres, and by a number of Spanish fortified settlements along the river. But fortune favoured the brave and Morgan and his band of 1,200 murderous buccaneers struck terror into the Spanish forces. In January 1671 Morgan defeated a Spanish force of 2,000 men and cavalry at the gates of Panama and took the city.[16]

His part in the subsequent destruction of the 150-year-old city, which boasted the oldest cathedral in the Americas, is disputed. The fire may have been started by the retreating Spanish forces. But whatever its cause Panama was left a smouldering ruin, never to be rebuilt on its old site. From what we can tell, Morgan's biggest disappointment was to find that much of the Spanish treasure had been removed to safety before his forces reached Panama. After a stay of four weeks he had to settle for a booty that consisted largely of silver coins – 250,000 pieces of eight. These were loaded on mules and carried back to the River Chagres and from there north to the waiting buccaneer fleet.[17]

Morgan's exploits are well enough known to those with an interest in buccaneering history, including the fact that he kept much of the booty for himself and left many of his seamen furious. What is less well known is the effect his expedition had on the psyche of the buccaneers who were to profit by his example. Until then, crossing the Isthmus had been seen as too difficult and dangerous to attempt. Now Morgan had shown it was comparatively easy, even in the face of Spanish opposition. If a route could be found that did not involve taking on Spanish forces it would be even easier. The new pirate expedition that set sail on that fine morning in 1679 was to find that route, 200 miles east of the *Camino Real* in the land of Darien. Travelling with these pirates were two remarkable men, men curious about everything they saw in this strange land, William Dampier and Lionel Wafer. Their maps and records were later to provide William Paterson with some of his strongest evidence when he boldly proposed turning Darien into the trade crossroads of the world.[18]

Herries account of Paterson's short stay in Old Providence Island helps us to date Paterson's arrival in Jamaica fairly precisely. Paterson, he wrote:

> was one of those who settled the Island of providence, a second time: But meeting some hardships and ill luck there, to wit a governour being impos'd on them by the King of England, which his conscience could not admit of, [he decided] to shake the dust from his shooes and leave that island …[19]

Old Providence Island had first been settled by Europeans in 1629 when it had been chosen as a site for a colony for English puritans – men in the mould of the Pilgrim Fathers. But, unable to turn their labour to profit, some of them at least had chosen a life of piracy instead, preying on passing Spanish ships. In 1641 a Spanish force had driven them out.[20] The island was then seized in 1670 by Morgan himself before his assault on Panama (legend was to tell that he hid some treasure there) and the second settlement followed. The first English 'Governor' arrived some three years later,[21] suggesting that Paterson came to Port Royal in 1673 or 1674, around the middle years of the decade.

He would have arrived to find the fate of Henry Morgan very much on the lips of the citizens of Port Royal. The 'High Admiral' had returned in triumph in April 1671, the hero who had avenged the bloody Spanish attack on Jamaica in a way that the Spaniards would not quickly forget. But, in his absence, word had arrived of the new peace signed at Madrid in 1670, a treaty designed to bring 30 years of conflict with Spain to an end. King Charles II of England – in return for a Spanish recognition of the right of England to hold on to the Caribbean islands of Barbados and Jamaica (seized from Spain by English naval forces in 1639 and 1655) – had agreed that England would stop the islands being used as bases for piracy against Spanish ports and Spanish treasure fleets. It had been unfortunate to say the least that the ink had been scarcely dry on the treaty when Henry Morgan had descended with his sea wolves upon Panama. Charles II had been gravely embarrassed by the destruction of the old city, and was determined to make

Morgan pay. On his order, the hero of the Port Royal waterfront had been summarily arrested in 1672 and taken back to London to stand trial for piracy.

Perhaps, Paterson may have speculated, a new era was about to dawn, one in which honest labour and honest trade would offer Jamaica a more settled and prosperous future. For Morgan had not been the only casualty of the new peace. Thomas Modyford had been removed from office, the price to be paid for having turned a blind eye to the worst excesses of the buccaneers once too often, and his place taken by a new governor. Thomas Lynch, himself a merchant and planter, offered a free pardon to all buccaneers who gave up their trade. To their captains he offered land on the island. Almost all the captains accepted, trading adventure for respectability.

Then all progress came to an abrupt halt. In 1675 Henry Morgan sailed back into Port Royal, bearing the new title of 'Sir Henry' Morgan. Astonishingly, he had been cleared by a London jury of all charges of piracy and had then befriended people at court. In a perfect illustration of the cynicism of the age, Charles II had been persuaded that Morgan was much too useful a man in the Caribbean to remain in permanent disgrace.

From the moment of his arrival Jamaica slid back into its old ways. From the Governor's house above Port Royal harbour, Morgan played a double game. He sent a fleet of Royal Navy frigates to hunt down pirates, and indeed had a few of the most desperate of them hanged on the gallows set out along the Palisadoes, the sand spit that connected Port Royal to the mainland. But at the same time he continued to loiter in the taverns on Thames Street, drinking and gambling with his old colleagues. Indeed, one of the most notorious pirates, John Coxon, actually shared a house in Thames Street with Morgan's brother-in-law, Robert Byndlass. Worse, Coxon and Byndlass were co-proprietors of a trim little pirate ship.[22] When the time was ripe, a new pirate raid on the wealth of Spain could easily be organised, with Henry Morgan looking studiously the other way. Paterson almost certainly got to know some of these colourful figures. Byndlass, with a foot in both the respectable and disreputable camps,[23] must have been hard to avoid in the streets of Port Royal. And among the buccaneering captains there was a fellow Scot, a man called Robert Allison. Paterson and Allison were later to become business partners. It is tempting to imagine that he and Paterson met for the first time on the bustling quays that faced Port Royal harbour.[24]

Four years after Morgan's return, the time for the next great expedition in search of Spanish gold and silver had come. There was now a new governor lacking Lynch's determination to suppress piracy. Charles Howard, the Earl of Carlisle, had quickly run into trouble with the elected Jamaican assembly. He had come from London in 1678 determined to establish the principle that the King could tax citizens without the consent of the council and the assembly had replied by blocking the collection of all the local taxes. It was a case of 'no taxation without representation', a slogan invented in the West Indies a hundred years before the revolt of the American colonies.[25] As a result, Carlisle was now in desperate need of cash to fund his administration.

Carlisle knew that the potential for profitable piracy was still there. He must have known that John Coxon had himself seized a Spanish merchant ship with a rich cargo of Indigo that very summer and had smuggled the cargo into Port Royal, beneath the noses of the frigate patrol.[26] Carlisle now sounded out Coxon and the other buccaneering sea captains in Port Royal and struck a deal. He offered to allow them to mount a fresh raid on the Spanish Main under the cover of a 'commission', with a goodly share of the profits to go to him. Of course the 'letters of marque' did not spell out the details. Coxon and his friends were simply granted the right to sail to Honduras, on the coast of Spanish Central America, to cut 'logwood'.

This 'logwood' was in fact a very valuable tree found in the forests of Honduras and Nicaragua,[27] a bushy shrub related curiously to the garden pea, much sought after for the rich dyestuff it yielded, a powder that brilliantly enhanced colour. Like most exotic dyestuffs of the time it fetched a pretty price in the great cities of Europe. The commission made no mention of attacks on Spanish treasure ships, or of attacks on the Spanish Main. Since groups of buccaneers had been harvesting logwood from the coastal forests of Honduras and Nicaragua for years,[28] it seemed a plausible enough plan. But Carlisle must have known all along that this was a cover story, since the true objective of the expedition was well enough known to the other sea captains and sailors who signed up for the voyage in the taverns of Thames Street.[29]

At the end of December 1679 it was these selected pirate captains and their crews who had quit Port Royal on the first leg of the great adventure. In January they assembled their small fleet at Port Morant on the

south-east tip of Jamaica, 20 miles east of Port Royal and John Coxon
was elected leader, with another famous buccaneer, Bartholomew Sharp,
as his right-hand man. Sharp was a veteran of Morgan's sacking of
Panama, although he was still only 29 years old.

In mid-January 1680 they set off from Port Morant, not for Honduras
but with their eyes set once again on the Spanish treasure ports of
Portobello and Panama City. Other ships were to join in, making the
fleet the biggest buccaneering armada to have been assembled since
Morgan himself had sailed on the high seas.[30] To avoid the attentions of
the Royal Navy pirate hunters, they did not all set off at once, but
arranged to rendezvous on the north coast of the Isthmus. Thus, a few
days after Coxon and Sharp had set sail, two small ships were to be seen
quietly slipping past the fort that guarded Port Royal harbour and setting course to the south-west. Aboard one of them was Lionel Wafer, a
young Scottish seaman and educated adventurer. Wafer had been born
in the Scottish highlands 19 years before. (He was later to claim that his
knowledge of Scottish Gaelic helped him make sense of the dialect spoken by the Darien Indians, a claim that surely should have made people
doubt his account.) He had come to Port Royal to visit his brother, serving as a ship's surgeon on the voyage out from London. No-one challenged him to prove his claim to competence, and indeed the trade was
easily learnt. A ship's surgeon had no medical qualifications. He simply
had to know how to bleed a man (the most common cure-all) and how
to supply traditional remedies designed to purge the bowels or make a
man vomit. Only *in extremis* would he ever have to apply the knife.

On his arrival in Port Royal after the tedious six-week passage from
England, he had set off to find his brother who was working as a man-
ager on a sugar plantation owned by none other than Thomas
Modyford.[31]

> I had a Brother in Jamaica, who was imployed under Sir Thomas
> Muddiford, in his Plantation at the Angels: And my chief Inducement in
> undertaking this Voyage was to see him. I staid some time with him, and
> he settled me in a House at Port-Royal, where I followed my Business of
> Surgery for some Months. But in a while I met with Capt. Cook, and Capt.
> Linch, 2 Privateers who were going out from Port-Royal, ... [who] took me
> along with them.[32]

Cook and Lynch knew what Coxon and Sharp had in mind, and were
set on joining them. For Wafer it was a thrilling prospect, altogether

more exciting than doctoring to the sick in Port Royal and he was not to be disappointed. Within weeks, he was to watch in some awe as the Scottish captain, Robert Allison, led an advance party and successfully stormed Portobello.

In other ways, the assault on Portobello was less exciting. For all the bravado, the takings proved disappointing and Coxon and company now turned their minds to other targets. Three days after taking Portobello, they encountered a lone Spanish despatch boat on the high seas and it quickly fell into their hands. Aboard they found a wine jar crammed with 500 gold coins, which excited some interest. But it was a packet of letters sent from the Spanish port of Cartagena on the north coast of South America to the Spanish Governor in Panama that had the greater historical importance.

A week was to pass before the significance of the find was fully appreciated. By that time the fleet had gathered in a sheltered bay called Bocas del Toro to repair their timbers. This meant beaching the vessels to remove the growth of barnacles and sea-weed, and to repair timbers attacked by the wood-boring *teredo* 'worm',[33] a process known as 'careening'. In these lazy and sunny February days the sea captains had time to consider the letters and to discuss their next move. They had been joined by William Dampier, who had reached Bocas del Toro aboard a small buccaneering vessel he had encountered by chance at Negril Bay in Jamaica. Dampier was to go on to become one of the world's most famous explorers, sailing round the world and landing on the coast of Australia. He had been born in Somerset in England, and was 28 years old. Like Lemuel Gulliver of *Gulliver's Travels* (a character modelled in part on Dampier[34]) he was subject to a constant urge to go to sea and to indulge his passion for writing and recording his adventures.

With Lionel Wafer to assist, he was to become the chief recorder of the journey from now on. The two met at Bocas del Toro and found they shared an inexhaustible curiosity about the unexplored world, its exotic wildlife, and the customs and practices of primitive peoples. Their diligence in recording what they saw and experienced meant that the pirate exploits of 1680 were to become as well documented as any that had ever taken place.

Dampier was with the sea captains when the Spanish papers were read over and recorded the extraordinary effect. One of the letters voiced the fears of the Spanish authorities in Cartagena that 1680 was destined to produce a rerun of Morgan's terrible visitation of 1671. But this time the pirates could well pose an even greater threat to the Spanish treasure ships coming from the silver mines of Peru. 1680 might be the year, the letter predicted, when 'The English pirates would make such great discoveries as to open a door into the South Seas'.[35]

The letter may have been cryptic, but Coxon and his fellow sea captains interpreted it to mean that the Spaniards knew of other possible routes across the Isthmus not guarded by Spanish forces, offering a door into the Pacific that, once found, would allow the buccaneers easy pickings. Inspired by the letter, Coxon and his fellow captains determined to go and seek the crossing, there and then. One of their number even had a suggestion where they should look.

Michel Andresson, a Dutch buccaneer, had been in the land of Darien but a few months before. The Cuna Indians who lived there had offered to act as guides to anyone wishing to reach the Pacific and indeed seemed anxious to ally themselves with any fighting men who might help them in their war against the Spanish. So, with the careening complete, Coxon led the fleet on a voyage some 300 miles east along the coast to a spot called Golden Island, and dropped anchor there on 2 April 1680. Everything that Andresson had told them proved to be true. On arrival, they were enthusiastically welcomed by the local chief, a man called Andres (or Andreas). He wanted to revenge himself for a recent Spanish attack that had left 20 of his tribesmen dead. If the buccaneers wished to pass to the Pacific, he would gladly show them the way.

Of course, to take up his offer, they would have to leave their ships behind. But it was common enough for buccaneers to leave a fleet at anchor with a skeleton crew in charge – Morgan had himself done it. As it happened, two of the commanders, Robert Allison and Thomas Maggot, were unwell and volunteered to stay behind in their sloops with a few men, to act as guards and await the others' return. The ships were to be tied up in safe water in the lea of Golden Island, facing the coast of the Spanish Main within a couple of miles of a great natural harbour. Later, when Allison and Maggot had time to explore the harbour, they would have found it ran inland for two miles, sheltered by a wooded peninsula on its north-eastern side. At its widest point it was a mile across. There were few, if any, harbours in England that could match it.

The adventures of Coxon and Sharp, and the others, would fill a book on their own. They successfully crossed the Isthmus and seized a fleet of Spanish ships lying off the newly rebuilt Panama City. Many of the buccaneers then spent a year cruising south along the Pacific coast of South America, attacking Spanish treasure ships and Spanish harbours. All this was achieved with a force of less than 350 men. Led by Sharp they then became the first sailors to sail round Cape Horn from west to east.

When the story of the new 'door' to the Pacific eventually reached Jamaica, there were three particular details that had a significant influence on William Paterson's thinking. The first was the claim made by the Cuna Indians that they had never been ruled by the Spanish, but were a free and independent people, a claim supported by the fact that they went largely naked and had not been converted to Christianity. Secondly, they appeared to be subject to a supreme prince, referred to variously as 'The Emperor of Darien' and 'The King with the Golden Cap', a man that Coxon and his fellow buccaneers swore they had met. Here was a man who could grant the right of settlement to Europeans. Paterson was not alone in accepting this story at face value, although he was later to be ridiculed for his naivety in believing it to be true. And of course the Indians showed how relatively easy it was to cross the Isthmus. Even in the rainy season it took only ten days to cross the divide by the pass of Toubacanti and sail by canoe down the winding river Chucunaque to be met by a great natural harbour looking on to the Pacific. This was even larger and more extensive than the harbour on the north coast.

One further detail is important – just how this information came back to Jamaica to reach the ears of Paterson. After the capture of a small fleet of Spanish at Panama, Coxon fell out with his fellow commanders and announced on 6 May that he intended to re-cross the Isthmus and return to the Caribbean. With a party of 100 men and with the Cuna chiefs and warriors to guide him, he made the journey back, returning to Golden Island without great difficulty to rejoin the waiting Allison and Maggot. Coxon and his 100 men then sailed back to Jamaica in the captured Spanish despatch boat with Allison and Maggot following in their wake. In early July they reached landfall at Negril Bay.

The trio of buccaneer captains could not have chosen a worse moment to return. Governor Carlisle, faced with mounting Spanish protests about the earlier attack on Portobello, had been forced to send out his frigates to hunt down the very men whose voyage he had secretly sanctioned. Coxon and his three ships were the first to be sighted, amazingly by Carlisle himself. The Earl had chosen this very moment to depart for London. As his ship beat west along the south coast of

Jamaica the two erstwhile allies encountered each other. In no mood for reconciliation Carlisle sent the Frigate *Hunter* in hot pursuit, and Allison and Maggot, hard-pressed to match the chasing frigate for speed, opted for prudence rather than valour. They abandoned their ships and joined Coxon in his dash for safety.

Coxon escaped capture and waited until Carlisle was well on his way before applying to Henry Morgan, now once again the acting governor, for a pardon, a request made all the more palatable by the offer of a sum of £2,000 – a considerable fortune for the time. Morgan hesitated. He sent a letter to London recommending that the offer made on Coxon's behalf by Byndlass and other leading citizens should be accepted.

Although there is no direct evidence that Coxon took up residence in Port Royal while Morgan awaited an answer from London, it is hard to imagine that he went sailing off for the four months or more it would have taken for the reply to reach Port Royal. We must assume that Coxon and Allison were for a while made welcome in Port Royal and that Paterson had a chance to talk to one or both of them about the great expedition. Allison in particular had spent some three months among the Indians, and would have been able to inspect the land that lay around the great harbour. He would have seen the turtles in the bay, and the sea-cows (or manatees) lolling around the shores. This appeared to be a land of plenty, a place where disease was unknown. And although it rained heavily at times, there was much sunshine and a cooling north-easterly breeze that sang in the palm trees. Much of Paterson's early vision of Darien as a sort of paradise on earth may well have come from his conversations with Allison.

From Coxon, or from the men who had crossed the Isthmus with him, Paterson would seem to have picked up the rest of the detail that made his vision of a great port in Darien so beguiling. The idea of an 'Emperor of Darien' for instance, and the evidence that, though the Spanish may claim this land, they had certainly never conquered it, or done anything to change the native way of life. Paterson himself never envisaged a conquest of such a land, merely a treaty of friendship with the Indians and the lease of land to allow the harbours to be built and the road and water link to be put in place.

From these conversations arose Paterson's grand plan for Darien, a vision described many years later, in language that echoed the words found in the captured Spanish letter:

seated between two great oceans, furnished on each side with excellent harbours, with easy and convenient passes between one and the other sea … these doors of the seas and the keys of the universe … [will enable] their possessors to give law to both oceans and to become the arbitrators of the commercial world.[36]

It may have been from Coxon that Paterson also heard of Dampier and Wafer, and of the records they had been keeping of the journey. It was enough to make Paterson seek them out in later years when they returned to London.[37]

Coxon did not stay long in Jamaica. Morgan's proposal that the buccaneer should be pardoned in return for a promise of good conduct in the future was rejected. Instead, London ordered his immediate arrest. Given Morgan's closeness to Coxon it is perhaps not surprising that this was an order never to be carried out. Before he could be clapped in irons Coxon set sail to the Bahamas where a grateful English Governor there soon put his services as a fighting man to good use. He was finally pardoned in 1688.

Not much is known about Paterson's early years. He was born in the parish of Skipmyre in Dumfriesshire, Scotland, in 1658, the year Oliver Cromwell died. His childhood years coincided with years of religious unrest. That flamboyant dilettante of a prince, Charles Stuart – the eldest son of Charles I – had been welcomed back as King Charles II by both Scotland and England[38] in 1660. Anxious to vindicate his father's stance on religion, a stance that had helped take Charles I to the scaffold in 1649, the dutiful son was determined to restore bishops to the Church of Scotland, a symbol of hierarchy totally unacceptable to devout Scottish Presbyterians who held all men to be equal in the sight of God. Those who resisted the king's demands became known as the 'Covenanters' – supporters of the 'Covenant', the great petition drawn up and signed in Edinburgh in opposition to Charles I a generation before. The greatest concentration of these new Covenanters lay in south-west Scotland, the very district where Paterson's family lived. On Sundays many of them held secret church services in the hills rather than cross the door of a church run by government-appointed bishops. They risked fines and imprisonment.

The Patersons may have been active Covenanters. We do not know. But we do know that William's father was summoned by the local magistrates to face charges for refusing to swear the prescribed oath of loyalty to bishops. With such threats in the air, it was perhaps understandable that he decided to send his son south to Bristol, to be safe in the care of an aunt who lived there. It was in Bristol that the young William entered his adolescence and emerged as a devout god-fearing man with a very strongly developed sense of right and wrong.

Of his schooling we know nothing, but he was certainly a highly educated and widely read individual. Perhaps he attended a Quaker school in Bristol, a district where Quakerism was already strong. With the Quaker emphasis on 'useful education' – with arithmetic and practical maths taking pride of place at the expense of Latin and the classics – there was certainly no better preparation for a life in trade.

In the parlance of the time, Presbyterians like Paterson formed part of the larger pool of 'dissenters' found in England, people who 'dissented' from the doctrines of the Church of England, not just on the issue of bishops but on matters of doctrine and on the form of church service. As things stood, dissenters could not enter the professions, the universities or politics. So they turned to business instead, often embracing it with a fervent passion that derived from their religious beliefs and their attitude to living.

About this time a dissenting minister, the Rev. Richard Steele, published a pamphlet that could have served as Paterson's business bible. It laid great stress on the moral virtue of honest work:

> God doth call every man and woman to serve him in some peculiar employment in this world, both for their own and the common good.[39]

To Steele there were four Christian virtues when it came to living the good life – diligence, moderation, sobriety, and thrift. For the dissenters, it was a fortunate accident that these were the very virtues most conducive to success in starting and running a business.

Dissenters also believed that vice of any sort was ruinous to human happiness and to business. Some vices were singled out for particular condemnation by Steele. He railed against speculation, gambling, and politics, by which he meant the corrupt and self-seeking politics of the time. At all costs, a man should also shun bad company, and avoid alcohol, a danger occasioned by the 'frequent and needless frequenting of taverns.'[40]

Paterson certainly was a life-long teetotaller, unusual in an age of excess. He was also diligent in his habits, moderate in his life-style and clearly thrifty. He was a man of his time in believing that God intervened in the world to punish men for their sinfulness. The earthquake that destroyed Port Royal in 1692 and the fire that burnt down a large part of old Edinburgh in 1700 were part of that pattern. Hardship and disease, too, were a sign of divine displeasure. He also saw life as something of an obstacle race. God placed hardships and discouragement in the way of men to test their resolution and persistence. This belief gave Paterson a remarkable optimism in the face of adversity. Just one more push and success must follow. Few of his associates shared this resolve.

Paterson was untypical for his time in refusing to condemn men for their religious beliefs. At a time when religious persecution was the norm, he was quick to see that the remarkable success of the Dutch in business – a success clearly demonstrated in the Caribbean of his time – was due in part to their relaxed attitude towards people who held religious views different from theirs. Paterson was to make religious toleration a key element in his plan for Darien. A strong belief that virtue would ultimately be rewarded and a willingness to avoid discriminating against people on the grounds of religion were strong weapons in Paterson's business armoury. But he had weaknesses too. He trusted people whom he should not have trusted and he lacked any sense of humour. In everything he wrote there was a deadly serious tone, the tone of a man who put frivolous things behind him. There is no record that he ever told a joke or a funny story. To some people he must have seemed an insufferable prig. What Paterson made of Port Royal and its wild and dissolute ways he never committed to paper. We can only guess that he would have found its hedonism, its lawlessness, and its disdain and contempt for honest business a highly distasteful and disgraceful combination.

Given his serious turn of mind and his interest in business, it is hard to imagine he ever frequented the taverns of Thames Street, even in the company of Robert Allison. That was not to say he was totally against relaxation and fine living. Quite the contrary. In 1690 he specifically condemned the view that luxury corrupted good men:

> some men ... look upon the ornaments and delights of life as baits to vice and occasions for effeminacy, [if they] but partially examine the truth of matters they would discern them to be true issues of virtue, valour, and elevation of the mind, as well as just rewards for industry.[41]

So Paterson was no puritan, but someone who believed a man should enjoy the fruits of his labour if it meant a more comfortable life, a more varied life, and – above all – one that gave him intellectual satisfaction and more than a veneer of civilisation. He believed that an entrepreneur deserved ample reward for his vision and hard work in setting up a company. As we shall see, others did not always share this view.

Where Paterson found employment in Jamaica no one has yet been able to say for sure. With his Bristol connections he would probably have found it easy to get a job as a merchant's clerk. We can imagine him passing from ship to ship along the length of Thames Street, soberly dressed in his dark frock coat, his face sheltered from the ferocity of the sun by a broad-brimmed hat, his buckled leather shoes tapping out his footsteps across the decks of merchantmen. We can see him bent over his clerk's desk, his periwig topping his thin face, his eyes deep set above high cheekbones, scrawling out bills of lading and invoices in his bold copperplate handwriting.[42] Certainly by the time he came to be noticed in London in the 1690s he had acquired a formidable understanding of accounting practices, making him the foremost banking expert of his day. But the years he spent in Jamaica served to introduce him to more than just the nuts and bolts of the merchant's profession. With his philosophic turn of mind, he could not help but observe how government policy decided in London was so often at odds with the best instincts of the commercial trader.

The job of the good merchant, as Paterson was increasingly to see it, was to find ways of bringing together the producer and the consumer to the best advantage of each. Merchants were midwives to prosperity since, without their intervention, suppliers and customers might never find each other, and might never release the potential for profitable exchange. In a world that regarded even the most humble jobs as a 'calling' from God, he saw the merchant as the most noble calling of them all:

> The whole produce of nature and art would be dead matter without a proper motion to convey it to its true end, consumption; all other callings receive their vigour, life, strength, and increase, from the merchant. Commodities rise in esteem or value as they are rightly distributed. And lose their very nature, as well as worth, when they perish for want of use. [43]

He came to believe that progress depended on giving the merchant free rein, letting him get on with his job without unnecessary burdens and restrictions. To that end, laws should be designed:

> never in the least to discourage or check any endeavour of the adventurous merchant, to whose extravagant and hazardous undertaking, the nation chiefly owes its wealth and glory.[44]

These views were totally at odds with the accepted wisdom of the time. But they grew out of Paterson's experience of trade in Port Royal and across the Caribbean. There the 'adventurous merchant' was locked in a long and unrelenting battle against policies originating from London that seemed designed to make life as difficult as possible.

For instance, Bristol men in Port Royal – and Paterson would have been very much seen as one of their number – found themselves excluded, officially at least, from what they considered legitimate trade, a fact all the more galling because it was one that they had played a part in developing. This was the traffic in human beings, the African slave trade. Paterson was typical of his age in seeing no particular moral dilemma in such business. Indeed he commonly referred to the 'Negroes' as though they were a commodity, to be bought and sold in the same manner as a sack of English flour. Paterson developed the view that the great problem with the slave trade was not the nature of the trade itself, but the unfair restrictions placed upon it. London had decreed that only certain privileged merchants could take part in it.

The slave trade in Jamaica had grown quickly after the arrival of Thomas Modyford in Jamaica in 1664. Modyford had come from Barbados – where the sugar trade was already well-established – bringing with him some 200 sugar planters and the machinery needed to process the crop. Just six years later, there were already some 70 of these 'sugar works' on the island. The rise of King Sugar is one of the great business stories of the 17th century. It was more or less responsible for shifting the economic balance of power in global trade from the East to the West and from the East Indies to the Caribbean and South America.

At the beginning of the century the eyes of European princes and merchants looked east to India, the East Indies and China. Shiploads of pepper and nutmeg, of mace and cinnamon, made fortunes for the East India merchants of Amsterdam and London. Nutmeg was so valuable and so sought after that the great Dutch and English East India Companies fought to exclude each other from the trade.[45] While they struggled for supremacy, the West Indies lay poor and undeveloped. Then, quite suddenly the enterprising Dutch discovered the magic of sugar cane. The plant had been known in the east for centuries, but never cultivated on a wide scale. Columbus had introduced it into the western hemisphere, but its development had to wait until Dutch genius found a way to produce the crop commercially, with the help of the processing plant they invented. By 1640 they had opened up great sugar plantations in what is now Brazil. From there, sugar spread to the West Indies where the climate and the crop seemed perfectly matched.

In Europe, the new substance was at first sold by apothecaries, not by grocers. But as production built up, sugar transformed the diet of Europeans, ushering in the age of cakes, sweetmeats, puddings, patisseries and confectionery. By 1650 the business of importing sugar to grace the tables of first the wealthy and then the not so wealthy across Europe had overtaken the spice trade in value, and was still growing. Jamaica was soon to surpass even Barbados in the production of sugar. When Paterson arrived, new plantations were being laid out all over the island and the demand for plantation labour was rising fast.

Working on a sugar plantation in the tropical heat of Jamaica was about as unpleasant as any job could be. The tall canes had to be harvested by hand during the dry season – hot, dusty and physically demanding work. Transforming the sugar canes into raw brown sugar was, if anything, even worse. Temperatures in the 'boyling houses' – humid hell-holes – could reach well in excess of 40 degrees Celsius (over 100 degrees Fahrenheit). It is not perhaps surprising that the average European proved incapable of working in these conditions.[46] The first plantations were manned by 'indentured servants', many of them Irish and Scots, who often did not live to see out their contract. For production to grow apace, a new source of labour had to be found.

The answer to this dilemma was the use of slaves brought from the West Coast of Africa. The Portuguese were first to begin this grim trafficking in fellow human beings, but it was the Dutch who played the leading role in the mid-17th century,[47] first building a huge sugar empire in Brazil, and then exporting it to the Caribbean. Dutch slaving ships were soon a familiar sight on the Guinea Coast of Africa, but English merchantmen, many from Bristol, soon joined the fray. Clashes between Dutch and English ships competing to buy up slaves for the

Caribbean market, were not uncommon, and indeed were a major cause of the Anglo-Dutch War[48] of the mid-1660s.

The first sugar planters in Jamaica had looked to the Dutch to supply most of the slaves they needed but soon slaving ships from both Bristol and London were a common enough sight in Port Royal harbour. The competition for trade kept the supply up and the price of slaves down, and the early Jamaican planters were grateful for it, but in 1672 this benign trading situation came to an abrupt end. In London Charles II, much influenced by his brother James, Duke of York, launched a plan to turn the slave trade to the advantage of a few privileged London merchants and to his own pocket, while striking what he hoped was a deadly blow at the Dutch. The Bristol merchants, however, proved the biggest losers. In that year King Charles granted a charter to the new Royal African Company (the RAC), giving it powers to build forts on the African coast, and to equip a large fleet. It was not the first such English company, but the first to be granted powers in the English colonies of the Caribbean and North America. From then on, to pay for the operation and guarantee good profits for its shareholders (the biggest of whom was the Duke of York himself), the RAC was to have a monopoly on the supply of slaves to these lands.

The Royal African Company went on to make money although not as much as hoped; its arrival on the scene added immensely to the problems faced by the Jamaican planters. Between 1672 and 1689 the Company was to ferry 90,000 slaves to the West Indies. Such was the pace of expansion in the industry, and so high the death rate among slaves, that the number fell far short of what was actually required.[49] In the case of Jamaica the RAC performance was woefully inadequate, delivering only about half the slaves needed.[50] The shortage forced the planters to bid the prices higher, at a time when the price being paid for sugar was going through the floor as a result of over-production.

There could have been no disguising the air of crisis that hung over the planter community when William Paterson first arrived in Jamaica. The evils brought by monopoly would have been rehearsed daily over the Port Royal dining tables. The remedy seemed obvious. When Captain Robert Portin gave evidence to a parliamentary committee some years later, while the RAC monopoly was still in place, he was voicing a view held widely across the English West Indies when he claimed that 'the Plantations would be much more plentifuller served with Negroes, by an open Trade'.[51] There was one saving grace. The monopoly could

never be fully enforced. There were always free-wheeling Bristol merchants, and Dutchmen too, willing to risk sailing into Port Royal hoping
that the telescopes of the customs officers were looking the other way, or
trusting that bribery would suffice to let them ship their cargoes of slaves
ashore. Were they caught, these 'interlopers' stood to lose their ships and
have their cargoes confiscated without compensation.

Monopoly did not come alone; it brought with it those unlikeable
bedfellows, arrogance of office, disdain for the customer, and poor value
for money. But it was the slaves themselves who ultimately paid the
highest price, forced by plantation owners to work even harder than
before. Like most Bristol men, Paterson certainly thought little of the
Royal African Company monopoly. But whereas many Bristol men
thought monopoly a bad thing only in the hands of others,[52] Paterson
came passionately to oppose it on principle. The best way to organise
trade was to release it from such restrictions and leave it to the free market to find ways to supply what was needed at the best possible price.

A whole mish-mash of regulations governing colonial trade had been
in place long before Paterson ever came to the Caribbean. They were
unashamedly aimed at the Dutch, that small and resourceful nation
which had thrown off Spanish rule and with surprising speed had
become the leader in world trade. Oliver Cromwell had already tried to
curb the growth of Dutch commercial power in the Caribbean by excluding them from English ports. Then the restored Stuart kings had
resolved to squeeze the Dutch orange until the pips squeaked. In 1660
Charles II won the backing of the two houses of parliament in London
for an even tougher measure, a law that officially aimed at 'the
Encourageing and increasing of Shipping and Navigation' but was really
designed to discriminate against Dutch shipping. It became commonly
known as the Navigation Act and solemnly decreed that:

> noe Goods or Commodities whatsoever shall be Imported into or Exported
> out of any Lands Islelands Plantations or Territories to his Majesty belong-
> ing … in Asia Africa or America in any other Ship or Ships Vessell or
> Vessells whatsoever but in such Ships or Vessells as doe truely and without
> fraude belong onely to the people of England … under the penalty of the
> Forfeiture and Losse of all the Goods and Commodityes …

By insisting that only English ships could use English ports, the Act
hoped to ruin many of the Dutch merchants dabbling in the English
colonial trade. Excluding the Dutch would mean more business for

English ships and more work for English shipyards. In the long run, the government hoped it would boost English sea-power at the expense of the Dutch. But many colonists in Jamaica and elsewhere had come to depend on Dutch merchants to supply the everyday essentials of life, and to provide a ready market for crops such as sugar and ginger.[53] Such relationships could not be terminated overnight without some real pain.

Three years later the screw had been turned even tighter. A new law laid down that all sugar, tobacco, and cotton grown in the colonies must first be despatched to England, whatever the ultimate destination. If the Dutch wanted to buy these goods they would have to come to London or Bristol to buy them and pay the hefty customs duty on the re-exported products. But not only the Dutch were hit by such rules. It meant that sugar being sent from Jamaica to American colonies like Virginia, or New England now had to make the long roundabout trip to England and back. Equally tobacco grown in Virginia could be sent to Jamaica, but only by way of London. This was a patent absurdity.

The effect of this Act was to lead to smuggling on a massive scale. Dutch ships would slip into Port Royal and take on a cargo of sugar bound for Europe. As a result, nine years later in 1672 there came a further blow to Jamaican trade. To catch the smugglers a new law insisted that duty must be paid on cargoes before they could leave harbour. In the case of refined sugar, increasingly produced in the island's refineries, this amounted to a whacking five pounds a ton.[54]

This was the regime just newly set in place when William Paterson arrived in Port Royal. Of course, merchants had found ways to circumvent the rules where they could; smuggling was more rampant than ever, and bribery a daily occurrence.[55] It is more than likely that Paterson found himself caught up in a cat-and-mouse game being played out between the Jamaican colonists and the royal officials. He had become involved in the trade between Jamaica and New England and was apparently a regular enough visitor to Boston, Massachusetts, to meet and marry his first wife, Elizabeth Turner, widow of the Rev Thomas Bridge, a dissenting minister there.[56] Boston had become a notorious centre for the contraband trade, typified by the Hutchinson family who regularly despatched New England provisions and cattle to the Caribbean, where they traded it for sugar and molasses, the basis for the rum-distilling industry in New England.[57]

As the decade reached a close – just at the moment when John Coxon left to make his startling trip across the Isthmus – a mood of despondency had cast itself over the Port Royal mercantile community. Sugar prices were depressed and indeed had been steadily falling, year on year, as more and more of the Caribbean islands had moved into the sugar business. It was good news for cake eaters, but left many of the planters on the verge of bankruptcy. And while smuggling had increased to relieve the burden of the Navigation Acts so also had the chances of getting caught. Ships found in breach of the regulations became the property of the crown, and all cargoes confiscated. Such an outcome was an even more certain road to financial ruin.

Sailing between Jamaica and Boston, and very probably on shorter voyages around the Caribbean, William Paterson found himself with time enough to reflect on the trials facing the honest merchant reluctant to break the law. There had to be a better way of doing things. One common port of call for merchants out from Port Royal was the Dutch island of Curaçao, a barren and rocky outcrop just off the coast of what is now Colombia. Paterson certainly knew the place.[58]

It was an island of striking contradictions. It was not suitable for cultivation in the way that Jamaica was, and it had no gold and silver deposits. Nor was it part of a larger Dutch empire in the Caribbean.[59] Yet it enjoyed an opulent standard of living, with fine buildings that gave it an air of Dutch grandeur. Apart from its people, its one asset was to be blessed with a good natural harbour. Trade seemed to be the sole source of its wealth.

Certainly its harbour was crowded enough, sheltering a fleet of 80 barques, many owned by the Dutch Jews who made up half of the mercantile community. About 4,000 sailors were regularly based here, and the streets of the capital Willemstad, swarmed with humanity.[60] Much of its trade with the Spanish colonies was by means of shallow-draught long-boats ideal for the harbourless and shallow coastal waters of Venezuela and New Granada, carrying cargoes of everyday household supplies, linen clothing and furniture. The long-boats returned with sugar, cocoa and tobacco, duly sent on to Amsterdam. Curaçao also thrived on the slave trade to the Spanish plantations. It found business where it could, looking to the English, Spanish and French West Indian colonies, and further afield to the English colonies in North America. On the island there was no Navigation Act and no ruinous duties paid on imports and exports. Traders of all friendly nations were welcome, coming from Boston and Jamestown, as well as Jamaica and Barbados.

As a result, Curaçao had developed as an entrepôt, a depot where goods could be unloaded from an ocean-going ship and packed into the equivalent of a modern-day tramp steamer to be distributed to many different destinations. The cargo ships of Willemstad were common sights in Barbados and Jamaica returning with cotton and indigo, tobacco and ginger, dyewood and sugar, and sending them on to Europe.

Entrepôts, as Curaçao showed, attracted not only merchants, but financiers and insurers, ship-builders and tradesmen of every type.[61] Such a place depended for its prosperity not on imposed monopoly or on cunning restrictions on trade, but on the ethos of the traditional village market. The Dutch were no paragons, they embraced monopoly where it suited them, as in the East Indies Trade; but alone among the European states they were resisting the siren attractions of protectionism. They were positively prepared to put their faith in their own ability to compete.[62]

The lessons of Curaçao came to be deeply engraved on the mind of William Paterson. Its remarkable prosperity shouted out the message – set trade free and prosperity will follow. This became the 'Patersonian' orthodoxy, repeated again and again in the years to come, even finding their way into contemporary ballads, the popular music of the time:

> trade by sea
> Needs little support than being free:
> Freedom's the polar star by which it steers
> Secure its freedom and it nothing fears;
> No mighty power it needs, no fertile lands
> No gold. No silver mines –
>
> Free trade will give – and teach us how to use,
> Instruct us what to take – and what refuse.
> Trade has a secret nature none can see
> Tho' ne'er so wise, except they traders be.[63]

In Curaçao there seemed to reside the living proof that it was trade, and not gold or silver or fertile soil, that brought wealth. And it provided food for thought in another respect too. It had opened up a trade route to the Pacific coast of South America, using the Rio de la Hacha and

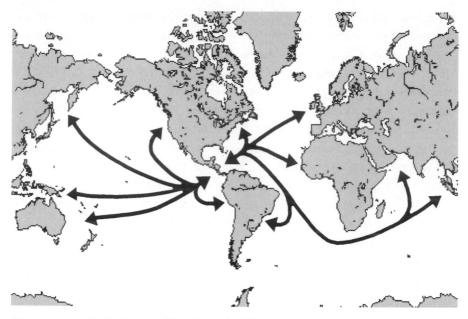

Paterson saw the Isthmus of Darien as holding the key to the growth of global trade. He was not the first to advocate trading with China and Japan by sailing westwards. Lord Macaulay pointed out that his plan was 'the original project of Christopher Columbus, extended and modified'.

mountain passes in the Andes. The route was about 400 miles long, difficult and dangerous, through tropical forest and then over challenging mountain terrain. Despite this, one historian has described it as: 'one of the most crucial connections in the Dutch world-trading system, the channel whereby Dutch manufactures and Dutch cinnamon flowed to the heart of Spanish South America'.[64]

It did not take too much wit to realise that other parts of the world were much better placed than Curaçao to trade with the Pacific Coast of South America and across the great 'South Sea'. The first mass-produced maps and globes were flowing from the Amsterdam workshops of Mercator and Blaeu. As Simon Schama relates, Blaeu made 'beautiful and exact globes without which no gentleman could have expected to be regarded as cultivated'.[65] They were not entirely accurate, since sailors still lacked a way to determine longitude, but they all made clear that the Isthmus of Panama was ideally placed to serve all the five known continents as well as the one yet to be discovered in the South Pacific. The great 'unknown continent' was thought to exist somewhere out there in the unexplored Pacific – without it the earth would be unbalanced. Its indisputable existence was graphically projected on these early maps and globes.

It was thus the happy coincidence of Paterson's knowledge of Dutch trade and his meeting with the returning buccaneers in 1681 that gave him a sudden insight into the great potential of Darien. Here he could create an entrepôt for world trade that would soon outshine Curaçao by far. Which is not to say that the idea emerged fully developed, since its final form depended on information yet to be brought back by William Dampier and Lionel Wafer. They did not re-cross the Isthmus until 1681, and then did not return to Jamaica. Instead they joined a group of buccaneers anchored in Chesapeake Bay and set off on a series of new adventurers. It was not until Dampier had his book ready for publication in 1695, and Lionel Wafer had prepared the first manuscript describing the magical land of Darien in 1696, that the final pieces of the plan could be slotted into place. By that time Paterson had been trying to float his great project for an entrepôt in Darien for at least ten years. But by then of course he had become a famous man.

Chapter 2

Selling Darien – The First Offensive

In the 1680s London was the wonder of the Western world, in a class of its own as a metropolis. It had long outgrown the bounds set by its Roman founders, and now occupied some seven square miles mainly on the north bank of the River Thames. With a population of over 600,000 souls, it far outreached the other great European capitals of the day. It was half as big again as Paris and three times larger than Vienna. In England the next biggest towns, Norwich and Bristol, were in comparison mere villages, with just 40,000 people in each.[1]

Approaching the great city by way of the Thames estuary was perhaps the most exciting way to experience the size and grandeur of the place. At Deptford, a full three miles down river from London Bridge, came the first jumble of wharves and shipbuilding yards. Soon a forest of masts loomed ahead marking the start of the port proper at Blackwall. From this point ships might queue for days before making their last short journey, on an incoming tide, right into the pulsing heart of the port. Despite the fact that it did not as yet have any man-made docks London already handled more than three-quarters of all English trade.[2] On opposite shores, more than 30 busy shipyards wrestled with wharves for a toe-hold on the river bank, for shipbuilding was a boom industry, justifying in the minds of many the restrictive Navigation Acts[3] that had decreed that only English 'bottoms' could serve the English colonies.

Just downstream from the city proper the largest ocean-going ships would drop anchor in midstream. From here city-bound passengers would be carried by smaller and nimbler river boats that could dodge and weave their way past the coastal sailing vessels and the lighters that served them until they broke free into clear water and the city lay stretched out before them.

The eastern outpost of the old city was still marked by the Tower of London, that great monument to William the Conqueror, a man who had done more than anyone to bind England to Europe when he had come with his Norman armies to subdue London in 1066. The Tower's days as a royal residence were long over and Londoners could now go there to see the lions or visit the museum.[4] But it still stood as a symbol of royal authority, a last dreaded prison for those judged traitors to the state, although some – like the diarist Samuel Pepys – did survive to tell the tale.[5]

Once beyond the Tower a first-time visitor would next see the great bulk of London Bridge looming up ahead. This was a remarkable structure – a solid phalanx of eighteen sturdy stone arches topped by tenement buildings, five stories tall. Passing under the arches at certain stages of the tide was highly dangerous, with river currents buffeting the bow, forcing the steersman to wrestle with the rudder to control the boat. For those who cared to look up, there was the unnerving spectacle of convicted criminals gazing down with eyeless faces from a row of spikes above the bridge. Then, once through the arches, the new City of London opened out.

In 1666 most of the old town had been destroyed by the 'Great Fire' and had been rebuilt in a remarkably short time. The old timber heart of the city swept away by the blaze had been replaced by elegant houses and warehouses in brick and stone that gave the illusion of having stood there for years, their brickwork already mellowed by the grime of the city. Only the rebuilding of St Paul's Cathedral, a work still very much in progress, betrayed the last hint of that dreadful event. Its massive cliffs of white Portland stone reared up behind heavy scaffolding, but the great dome that gives it today such a serene air of superiority had yet to be started. Indeed it was not to be finished for another quarter of a century, a delay blamed equally on the incompetence of the building contractor (the expression 'as slow as a St Paul's workman with a bucket of mortar' had come into popular use)[6] and the stubborn determination of astronomer-turned-architect, Christopher Wren, to have his way with a committee of surly churchmen.

Over the whole scene hung a tenacious pall of smoke, the outpouring of thousands of coal fires, the acrid smell making the nostrils twitch. Barges bringing sea-coals from Newcastle had been supplying the city since the days of Shakespeare and before. And the revenue brought by taxing this coal was, much later, to be turned into a novel way of paying off the City's debts to its orphans – based on a scheme devised in part by William Paterson himself.[7] And indeed there were many orphans in London. The city had the highest mortality rate in England, about one person in every 25 dying each year. But despite its obvious unhealthiness – as a result of bad sanitation rather than foul air – it continued to attract more than enough newcomers to keep the population growing. Every year they came in their thousands, in search of fortune, or fleeing from persecution. Death was a commonplace event. Men put their trust in God's mercy and hoped the grim reaper would not come calling too soon. In the meantime fortunes were there to be made.

William Paterson, an optimist by nature, came to London late in 1681 determined to lay the foundations of his future fortune. This he intended to do, not by engaging himself to work for one of the city merchant firms – where his talents as a book-keeper and accountant would have been much appreciated – but by persuading the wealthy merchants of London to invest in his grand project for a great new trading complex on the Isthmus of Darien. This might seem like a Herculean task, since investors could not expect to see a return for many years to come, but Paterson was never one to shirk such a challenge and was determined to find enlightened and wealthy people who, he hoped, would see immediate sense in the idea. It offered not only personal gain, but a way to change the way the world did business. But first he had to find a place to live.

His first wife, Elizabeth Turner, appears to have died before he came to London, and any property or money she had inherited from her first husband would have given Paterson a nice little nest-egg with which to acquire a house.[8] For those who could afford it, the west end of town, where fresh air blew in from the fields of Kensington, was the best and healthiest location. Just off the broad new avenue of the Strand lay the fashionable new suburb of Covent Garden with its elegant piazza where gentlemen and ladies liked to parade themselves like peacocks in a country estate. Beyond Covent Garden to the north and west was another new neighbourhood called Soho. There, the builders were still in the process of carving out new streets. Here or hereabouts, William Paterson was to make his base of operations for the most fruitful part of his life, finally taking up residence in a terraced house in Denmark Street, a stone's throw from the parish church of St Giles in the Field.[9]

The City of London prided itself on its ancient institutions. It had its own government, its own lord mayor, and its own agents of law enforcement, the city militia. The venerable livery companies (the trade guilds) had regulated trade in the city for centuries, and the Royal Exchange, where the great merchants met daily to finalise business deals, had an air of respectability that the dining rooms of Queen Street in Port Royal found impossible to match.[10] The first Exchange had been destroyed by the Great Fire. Its replacement was a rather splendid building, with fine arcades and spacious meeting rooms, topped by a tall spire that announced its importance to the world. Below it was a fine new open piazza where great merchants and financiers came and went on their daily business. Here a variety of men would gather, hoping to catch the eye of this or that merchant. Some of those advertising their wares were goldsmiths – offering the safe keeping of gold and silver coins and plate in their vaults in Lombard Street: others were 'stock-jobbers', buying and selling stocks in the very few companies that issued them; a third group were men attempting to raise fresh capital for some scheme or other. These men were what today would be called 'entrepreneurs'.

'Exchange Alley', as the district close by the Exchange came to be called, was scarcely the place for Paterson to set his pitch. His idea was too grand and too complicated to be sold casually to any passer-by. A new word was coming into use to describe people like him. Such men were called 'projectors'. Projectors were almost by definition men who would have to struggle to win the backers they needed, as Daniel Defoe was to explain:

> the true definition of a project, according to modern acceptation, is ... a vast undertaking, too big to be managed [by small concerns], and there-fore likely enough to come to nothing.[11]

Paterson's plan would seem to fit this description exactly.

According to Defoe, perhaps as many as nine out of ten of such grand projects amounted to little more than moonshine. Those who peddled them, unscrupulous rogues who resorted to 'private methods of trick and cheat, a modern way of thieving ... by which honest men are gulled with fair pretences to part from their money'.[12] This hardly made the task of an honest projector easy, as Paterson was soon to learn. In addi-tion, Paterson suffered from the twin disadvantage of being an outsider and a Scotsman, the latter a class of person held in little respect in London.[13] Trying to sell his grand plan to merchants on the cold paving stones of the piazza would clearly be a waste of time. So Paterson took the sensible step of first taking up membership of the 'Merchant Taylors Company' – one of London's ancient livery companies – as a 'member by redemption', a polite way of saying he had bought his way in.[14] Once on the inside he could then hope to make the contacts that might open the door to the grandees of the city, men of sufficient vision and sufficient means to make the whole thing possible.

His first soundings may have been encouraging. His arrival in London coincided with a renewed controversy about how trade should be organised, and there was a clear shift of opinion away from the old ways of managing English overseas commerce. There was much talk in the coffee houses of 'free trade', a growing belief that the days of the great trade monopolies were numbered. At the centre of the debate was the greatest monopoly company of all, the English East India Company. And in 1680 and 1681 its monopoly was being seriously challenged by rival merchants intent on breaking into the East India trade.[15]

The great trading monopolies had had a good innings. They had been established almost 100 years before, at a time when the Spanish and Portuguese had grown rich on the fruits of the new trade routes opened up by the discoveries of Christopher Columbus and Vasco Da Gama in the 1490s. In 1493 Pope Alexander VI had famously divided the world into two hemispheres, awarding the ownership of all new discovered territories to just Spain and Portugal. Spain was to have the western and Portugal the eastern hemisphere.[16] However, the legitimacy of this arbitrary division of the world and its spoils did not survive the Reformation that convulsed Europe in the 16th century when most northern countries adopted one or other form of the Protestant faith. Challenging the Pope's right to make such decisions became an article of Protestant faith.

Towards the end of the 16th century London merchants – and Dutch and French merchants too – had begun to explore ways by which they might challenge the Portuguese grip on the rich trade of India and the East Indies. Voyages to the east round the southern tip of Africa were then just too long and hazardous to be undertaken by any single merchant. And establishing trade relations with eastern princes and potentates could be a tricky business. It involved an elaborate courtship and considerable diplomacy. Should a trading post (or 'factory'[17]) be permitted, it had to be big and grand enough to impress both the local prince or potentate and the local population, as one writer made clear:

> Wherever the English or any Europeans settle a Factory in India they must presently build them large Houses, Ware-house, etc. take many Servants, and maintain the appearance and splendour of a petty court: and in many places where the company have not fixt Garrisons, they are forced to fortifie their Houses, or else they will be despised and trampled upon by the Natives.[18]

For all these reasons merchants needed to be brought together to provide the funds and spread the risk associated with each and every voyage. But provided this were done, the rewards could be great, since cargoes brought back from Asia – exotic spices, precious stones, lavish silks, richly woven carpets, or just plain saltpetre[19] – were in great demand across Europe and would fetch high prices. Out of this set of circumstances arose the idea of the great chartered monopoly company: a privileged group of merchants granted the sole right to such trade for a fixed period of time.

The English East India Company had its first charter granted in 1600. All trade between England and a vast zone of territory stretching from the Cape of Good Hope all the way east to the tip of Cape Horn – more than half the known world – was reserved for ships belonging to the company. Any English merchants who dared break the company monopoly were branded as 'interlopers' and faced having their vessels and cargoes confiscated if caught. Any foreign vessels attempting to trade in their 'factories' would be driven off by force.

The right to grant such monopolies in England rested firmly with the monarch, and the Stuart kings took full advantage of this power to their own advantage. Each time a charter came up for renewal a delicate piece of royal blackmail extracted extra money from the company coffers.[20] And the bounty arising from such companies did not stop there. There was also considerable revenue to be raised from the levying of customs duties, a power residing not in parliament but with the king. As a result, the whole question of monopoly companies and their powers became one of the great issues of 17th-century England. The most potent lever of power held by parliament was the ability to withhold extra taxes when a king needed them. If he could depend on the monopoly companies to fill his coffers there might be no need for parliament at all. It was not an academic point.

The struggle between king and parliament had by William Paterson's time already led to the execution of one monarch, Charles I. There was now in London a real fear that his son, Charles II, restored to the throne in 1660, might not limit his revenge to desecrating the corpse of Oliver Cromwell and sending those most closely involved in his father's death to a gruesome end on the scaffold.[21] He might dispose of his own parliament when the time was ripe. Charles II had already raised alarm in this regard by his decision to set up the new Royal African Company in 1672. A large percentage of the shares of the company had been kept in royal hands and his brother James was appointed to run it as Governor. This principle could one day be extended to the East India Company monopoly too. This explains the peculiar passions surrounding the East India Company, passions that had risen to new heights just as Paterson arrived in London.

The company had been doing particularly well in the 1670s. Imports from India and the east had increased by around 15 per cent every year.[22] The share price had risen steadily until, by 1681, a £100 share was worth as much as £500.[23] The wealth of the Company had become legendary. On the Thames at Blackwall it had an impressive dockyard, its waters bustling with ships recently arrived from the Orient, its dockside warehouses groaning with cargoes of silk and fine cotton, spices and coffee, commodities that were sold not only in England but to much of Europe and to the English colonies in America.

In the dock could be found some of the finest ocean-going ships of the age, weighing up to 500 tons, with holds capacious enough to bring back the riches of the east in huge quantities. Samuel Pepys has left us his vivid impressions of just what the holds of these ships contained. He was shown round an East Indiaman (admittedly a Dutch ship captured as a prize of war) in 1665 and was amazed by:

> the greatest wealth ... that a man can see in the world. Pepper scattered through every chink, you trod upon it, and in cloves and nutmegs I walked above the knees, whole rooms full. And silks in bales, and boxes of copper-plate, one of which I saw opened ... as noble a sight as ever I saw in my life.[24]

Such riches had helped produce the profits to fund the building of the company offices in Leadenhall Street at the heart of the city. Half-timbered in the Elizabethan style, the grand old building had miraculously escaped the Great Fire which had reduced many similar structures to smouldering ruin. It stood there, exuding tradition and prestige. Below the red-tiled roof, a huge wooden sailor gazed down on a striking wall painting of the Company's fine ships riding the high seas, framed at each side by a pair of great timber dolphins.[25] When wealth ostentatiously displayed itself in this way, jealousies were bound to be aroused. But in London jealousy went hand in hand with anger – the anger of the wealthy have-nots, those who wanted to buy East India Company shares but were unable to do so. Their anger was directed, with some good reason, at the Governor of the Company, the clever but arrogant Sir Josiah Child.

Child had been born into a poor family in 1631 and some people still remembered the days when, as an apprentice, he had swept a counting-house floor. During the Civil War period, when King Charles I was being publicly executed on a scaffold outside his own Banqueting Hall, Child had shown a radical turn of mind and championed the cause of republican rule, to his great personal advantage. He was a food merchant by profession, a victualler. In the year after the king's execution in 1649, Oliver Cromwell had planned to send an English fleet to assist the Portuguese in their war with Spain. Child had won the contract to supply the fleet with food and drink and had not looked back since. This was despite the fact that the Stuart line of kings had returned in the shape of Charles II in 1660, and men who had had any association with Oliver Cromwell could now face ruin. It was here he first displayed his remarkable ability to ingratiate himself in high places.

We find him in 1665, the year of the plague in London, already presiding over an expanding business. He had met Samuel Pepys, who combined his role as diarist with being first secretary at the Admiralty, a man who had shared Child's republican sympathies but had cleverly jumped ship to place himself in the royal service. Pepys obliged by recommending him to Charles II.[26] This had smoothed the way for Child to move into the timber business, importing timber from New England to meet the insatiable demand of the Royal Navy for good oak.[27]

This was a trade that allowed him to emerge in 1670 as an exceedingly wealthy man, with an eye turned to profitable investment. The flourishing East India Company had a special appeal. It was an early example of a joint-stock company. Rather than invest in a single ship and a single voyage – the original practice – investors were able to spread the risks by owning shares in the company, which in turn owned a fleet of ships. The losses incurred when one or more ships were lost at sea were more than balanced out by those who returned safely. This made business sense, but it also opened the way for Child to gain a large stake in the company. There was as yet no formal stock market but, by keeping an ear to the ground and picking up shares as they became available through death or misfortune, Child steadily built up his holdings. By 1671 he owned shares to the value of £12,000, making him the largest shareholder in the Company. Three years later he was invited to join the 'Court of Directors', a springboard that took him to the very height of power.

Child was a ruthless and unscrupulous operator. Most of the East India Company shares were traded within the Company, rather than on the open market, meaning that he had prior intelligence on would-be sellers.[28] And there were ways to manipulate the share price to make it easy for him to pick up shares. He was a natural 'stock-jobber', another breed vividly denounced by Daniel Defoe, men who could turn the lack of reliable news on how the Company ships were faring to personal advantage. Defoe reported on such practices:

> letters have been written from the East Indies, with an account of the loss of ships which have [in fact] arrived there, and the arrival of ships lost ...
> It was thought proper to circulate these rumours for the raising and falling of stock ... to buy cheap or sell dear.[29]

Though Child may not have been so blatant, he steadily built up his holdings until by 1680 he was sitting on some 15 per cent of all the company stock and had been elected Governor. He ruled from his Leadenhall Street offices like a prince, and was probably richer than most of the princes of Europe. To his enemies he had become the 'despot of Leadenhall Street', one of the most hated men in London.

The fiercest hatred came from the growing group of powerful London merchants who felt unfairly excluded from any share in the Company's good fortune. These were people who would have jumped at a chance to buy shares in the Company had any come their way. But they never did, thanks to Child's cornering of the market.[30] It was the resentment of those on the outside, forced to stand by helplessly as Child's fortune multiplied, which did more than anything to produce the great crisis of the early 1680s.

Just as William Paterson arrived in London, news arrived from the east of an organised trespass into the company's monopoly territory. Some 73 merchants, most of them London based,[31] had joined together and chartered ships to round the Cape and bring back the riches of the east. In doing so, they proved that such trade could now be successfully carried on by private merchants, even in matters of elaborate eastern 'diplomacy'. One of them was a certain Captain Alley, who turned up off the coast of Bengal and sailed up the Hughli river (the future site of Calcutta) to present himself to the local potentate with all the trappings of a company agent. The Company's own Bengal agent, William Hedges, was taken aback. He reported that Alley arrived in a 'stately barge' complete with a musical quartet, and was rowed ashore by ten English seamen decked out in 'blew capps and coats edged with red'. Once ashore he was carried in style on an ornate litter, preceded by his own flags, his dignity bolstered by the presence of 80 servants. It all made a splendid impression. Hedges admitted that: 'A gaudy show and great noise adds much to a public person's credit in this country'.[32] It was particularly galling to people like Hedges that many of these interlopers were working in collusion with the company's own 'factors' or agents who had shown themselves happy enough to make some extra cash on the side.

This created the greatest crisis of Child's long career. His fall from power was daily expected as the value of the company shares tumbled. But he was saved when his opponents within the company overplayed their hand. The leader of the opposition to Child was an important timber merchant of Huguenot descent, by the name of Thomas Papillon. Papillon had been a leading figure within the company for more than ten years and had been instrumental in bringing Child on to the board: he had lived to regret it ever since. Papillon was a City man, who knew the strength of feeling out there against Child. So he adopted a simple strategy aimed at pleasing the London merchants and disposing of Child at the same time. He proposed that the existing company shares should be withdrawn, and replaced by a much broader share issue, opening the doors of the company to all who wanted to subscribe. The new shareholders would then force Child to resign. Papillon may have had an even more radical agenda, hoping to replace the narrow old company with a new loose grouping of merchants, each of whom could trade freely with the east.[33] But before he could take the idea any further he found himself outmanoeuvred by Child.

Papillon's great weakness stemmed from his political connections. He had been the elected member for Dover in the recently dismissed parliament and had supported those who had wanted to prevent James, Duke of York – and Charles's brother and legitimate heir[34] – from ever coming to the throne. James was a known Roman Catholic and there were many who feared he might return England to the Catholic fold should he ever get a chance.

Papillon had voted in the House of Commons for James' formal exclusion from the succession in October 1680 and had seen the measure approved, only for it to be blocked in the House of Lords. The so-called 'Exclusion Crisis' was a pivotal moment in English political history, giving birth to opposing factions in parliament to be known ever after as 'Whig' and 'Tory'.[35] The Whigs supported exclusion, the Tories bitterly opposed it. By the summer of 1681 the immediate danger to James had passed and a reaction had set in. This gave Josiah Child the perfect opportunity to turn the tables on Papillon and the interlopers and thereby sink all hopes that the age of monopoly might be drawing to a close.

The governor began by persuading the board to reject Papillon's scheme for broadening the shareholder base. Since he already owned or controlled a quarter of the votes,[36] it was not such a difficult task. With his power-base secured, he then resorted to naked bribery. The coffers of the Company were opened and money disbursed in great quantities to government ministers, judges, and civil servants. King Charles II himself received a secret personal donation of £10,000. His brother James was presented with company shares and invited to sit on the board.[37] In an age where bribery of this sort was commonplace, Child took the art of corruption to new heights.

He could now use the courts to crack down on the impertinent interloping merchants. Twenty-five of the ships were seized and 48 merchants subjected to restraining orders, among them Thomas Pitt, the unruly ancestor of two future British Prime Ministers. While Captain Alley seems to have evaded the law, one notable London interloper, the merchant Thomas Sandys, was spectacularly hung out to dry. His was chosen as a test case – *The East India Company* v. *Sandys* – with the proceedings conducted before the notoriously partisan Judge George Jeffreys.[38] The judgement triumphantly reaffirmed the Company's monopoly and those who dared to challenge would henceforth have to pay dearly. Sandys had his ship and cargoes seized and was left a ruined man.[39] And that was not the end of the story.

In 1685, when the Duke of York came to the throne as James II of England, one of the first acts of the new king was to reissue the East

India Company charter, with strengthened powers. It was now permitted to raise its own armies, and to fly the standard of the Royal Navy on its ships, turning the company into what amounted to a privately owned arm of the state. As long as James was on the throne Child seemed untouchable. In the midst of it all he married his daughter to a Duke (it cost him a quarter of his fortune)[40] and climbed to the top of the social tree. Not bad for a man who had begun with nothing.

By that time Thomas Papillon had retired from the scene, lucky to have escaped with his life. The king's ministers had ordered his arrest for 'sedition', the crime of plotting against the state. He had been dragged before Judge Jeffreys and fined a hefty £10,000. At this point he decided, for his own safety, to flee across the North Sea to the Dutch city of Utrecht. He waited there for a change in the political climate in London. When that might come no-one could tell.

We do not know if Paterson ever met Papillon, but it would not be surprising if he had. Paterson almost certainly met some of the London merchants implicated in the 'interloping' offensive of 1681, for in later years he was intimately associated with some of the best known of them, men such as James Bateman and Samuel Sheppard.[41] The victory of Josiah Child may not have threatened Paterson's life, but it had closed off any chance there had been of floating his scheme for Darien in London. Like Papillon, he too then chose to go to live and work in the Dutch provinces, but for very different reasons. Paterson was as determined as ever to find the financial backing he needed. What was not forthcoming in London might reasonably be raised elsewhere.

Paterson may have passed through Rotterdam when he first landed in Holland.[42] That city had become the centre of a group of Scots exiles, people who had fled from their homeland to escape religious or political persecution under Charles II and then James II. He certainly seems to have known and met the Scottish community there, for he was to come back in the autumn of 1696 to raise capital for his new 'Company of Scotland',[43] by then established as the vehicle for the great Central American project.

His real target, however, was always Amsterdam, by far the largest city in Holland and the centre of Dutch international trade. Such a place had a fascination for many observers of the day. It had survived as a boom-town in the middle of war-torn Europe. For any man anxious to fathom the secrets of Dutch business success, Amsterdam was the obvious place to begin. It helped that there were active business ties between London and Amsterdam. Dutch capital had after all largely financed the rebuilding of London after the Great Fire[44] and many London merchants and financiers had business associates in the Dutch city.[45] As a result Paterson almost certainly came bearing very useful letters of introduction to this or that merchant living in one of those fine canal-side town houses that still grace the city today.

Amsterdam was the only port in Europe to rival London, and yet it lacked easy access to the open sea. It was approached by way of the Zuider Zee, that long and shallow arm of the North Sea which today has been dammed and reclaimed.[46] At the head of a muddy channel called the Ij, lay the burgeoning port, an impressive man-made structure that stretched the entire length of the northern flank of the town, offering protection from the buffeting north-east winds behind a double row of wooden palings, crusty with barnacles and green with seaweed.

At first glance – as with Venice in the Adriatic Sea to which it is so often compared – there was nothing remarkable about the site of Amsterdam to explain why the city had grown and flourished. It had begun as a small settlement around a dam built on a tributary river, the Amstel, and on ground so soft and waterlogged that piles had to be driven deep into it to support even modest buildings. Its rise to fame had come with the rebellion of the Netherlands – the lands that today encompass both Holland and Belgium – against Spanish rule, an uprising that had begun in 1578. One effect of that war had been to close the River Scheldt to navigation, cutting off the great mercantile port of Antwerp from the North Sea. Antwerp's loss had been Amsterdam's gain.

But it was not quite as simple as that. Visitors to Amsterdam in the late 17th century were impressed by its energy and its rich mixture of tongues and people. Amsterdam was an immigrant town, swollen initially by a flood of refugees from southern Netherlands which had been left in the hands of the Spanish. The tradition of welcoming outsiders had continued ever since. Freed from Spanish control and driven by a new humanism that put material progress at a premium, Amsterdam had taken off, powered by the new creed of 'money, money, and more money'.[47]

The Dutch economy has been described as 'the first modern economy'.[48] Its success was based on an unusual freedom from regulation, largely due to the happy chance that the 'United Provinces' (as the new Dutch state was known) was a loose confederation where central authority was treated with great suspicion, allowing two Dutch societies to co-exist, the strict Calvinist society of the countryside and the small town, and relaxed humanism of Amsterdam.[49] In Amsterdam where commerce and industry were the chief gods, all religions were tolerated and foreigners generally welcome, the more so if they brought trade and valuable skills. So the Sephardic Jews of Portugal had settled here, with their trading connections with the East Indies, Africa and South America. Many had merged into the Dutch way of life, wearing Dutch clothes, eating pork and even dispensing with male circumcision.[50]

More recently had come a flood of French Protestants, the Huguenots. The growing religious intolerance of the French monarchy[51] had presented Huguenots with a stark choice between country on the one hand and freedom of conscience on the other. If you believed devoutly that Catholicism was the religion of the Anti-Christ but preferred life to martyrdom, there was nothing for it but to seek refuge in neighbouring countries where your religion could be freely practised. Amsterdam had attracted more than its fair share of Huguenot refugees, talented craftsmen who gave a significant boost to the economy, bringing their skills as weavers, glass-blowers and papermakers.[52] Even so, it was the maritime trade and its related industries that gave Amsterdam its character. By 1685 the town had become the greatest shipbuilding centre in the world, its yards stretching along the broad tidal waters of the Zaan River. So great was Amsterdam's fame that Peter the Great, the new Czar of Russia, was to come here to work in an Amsterdam yard to learn the basics of shipbuilding. Later he was to take what he learned back to Russia where he was to establish the first modern shipyard in his new capital of St Petersburg.[53]

Amsterdam must have been all that William Paterson expected and more. Prosperity broadcast itself from its fine new buildings, its twin harbours crowded with ships from all corners of the globe, and its towering warehouses crammed with merchandise – spices from the East, timber and grain from the Baltic, sugar and tobacco from the West Indies, and Brazilwood and other exotic dyewoods from South America.

It found expression in the grand new merchants houses proudly lining the new canals that embraced the old town, the Herengracht, the Kaisergracht and the Prinzengracht. Most of all the brimming self-confidence of the merchant city expressed itself in the new town hall on the Dam. A rich confection in the classical style, the *Burgomeisters* declared it the 'eighth wonder of the world'.

Paterson's years spent in Amsterdam are poorly documented. We do not even know where he stayed. But we have the direct evidence of a fellow London-based Scottish merchant, by the name of Robert Douglas, that Paterson spent some of his time in the city canvassing support for his project for a world trade centre in Darien among Dutch merchants. Douglas tells us that in 1687, when he spent some six months in Amsterdam, he chanced upon Paterson. Perhaps he sat in on one of Paterson's 'presentations' of his grand project. Or he may merely have had a first-hand report of what was said. He wrote that:

> I heard accounts of his design, which was to erect a commonwealth and free port in the Emperor of Darien's Company, as he was pleased to call that poor miserable prince, and whose protection he pretended to be assured of for all whom would engage in that design.[54]

Douglas was to be no friend of Paterson, bitterly opposing his plans for Darien when he was in Edinburgh in 1696. So the hostile tone of his report is to be expected. But his reference to the 'Emperor of Darien' rings true. As we have seen, Paterson may have heard of this grand chief of the Darien Indians from Coxon himself. But it was equally possible that he may have read about him in a newly published account of the great buccaneering adventure. In 1684 Bartholomew Sharp, one of the captains involved, had given his own version of the story in the *Voyages of Bartholomew Sharp*. We know that Paterson had a copy of this book in his extensive private library.[55]

In fact Paterson did more than just canvass for the support of Dutch merchants. He formed a partnership with three Dutchmen – Heinrich Bulen, Wilhelm Pocock and James Schmitten – and attempted to raise funds to form a company to exploit the potential of Darien. During 1687 and 1688 he and the three others unsuccessfully tried to win support, first in Amsterdam, then in Hamburg, and finally in the east

German city of Berlin.[56] And Paterson was very much the prime mover in this exercise as events were to show.

Paterson was a man who respected people as human beings regardless of their origin.[57] He held no prejudice against foreigners and probably felt more at home in Amsterdam than ever he did in Edinburgh. He certainly seems to have had a good command of Dutch[58] and an ability to do business in the Dutch way. But for all that, the response of those he met in the Amsterdam coffees houses was disappointing. It may be that his scheme was not as eye-catchingly radical as the one he was to present in London and Edinburgh in 1695.[59] A scheme for a new entrepôt on the model of Curaçao would not have been enough to set the Dutch imagination on fire. For the Dutch saw themselves as already providing the greatest world entrepôt of all. This was, of course, Amsterdam itself.

One only had to take a stroll around the harbours of Amsterdam, looking at the ships and their cargoes, and where they were coming from and going to, to see the truth in that. The Dutch were bringing in raw materials, such as wool and flax, and re-exporting finished work of great craftsmanship to the world. They also imported spices, tea and coffee, from the East and freighted it on, packed and branded, to most of Europe and America. They did the same with American tobacco and American sugar and cocoa beans, Amsterdam being famous for its cigars and chocolate, which they exported to wherever a market could be found. If Amsterdam was already as great an entrepôt as anyone had ever seen there hardly seemed the need to build a new one in America.

It was the way that Paterson reacted to his Amsterdam rebuff that gives us the measure of the man. He was already showing signs of that remarkable energy and perseverance that were to become his trademark. Instead of giving up on his hopes of continental European backing, he set off in early 1688 with Bulen, Pocock and Schmitten to canvass support in Hamburg. Hamburg was a city that could claim to rival Amsterdam in importance, sitting on the broad waters of the Elbe 50 miles inland from the North Sea. Ships had come to Hamburg for centuries from the Baltic ports – Danzig, Konigsberg,[60] Riga and Stockholm among them. It was the point where, in European terms, east met west. The timber and furs of Russia came here, alongside the grains from the open farmland of Poland, and iron and steel products (such as ships' guns) from Sweden. In return the fine woollens and linens of western Europe, and the exotic imports from the Far East and America were shipped through the Baltic or up the Elbe. It was also home to a considerable colony of Dutch and English merchants. The Merchant Adventurers (or Hamburg) Company was the very first English trading company established under Royal Charter.

At some time early in 1688 the four men arrived in the town and met with some interested merchants but again they drew a blank. The merchants of Hamburg were fixed in their ways. They had no personal experience of trade with America or the East. It is perhaps not so surprising that the four travellers could not find the backing they needed there. They now set their sights on Berlin, capital of the increasingly important state of Brandenburg (soon to be known as Prussia) where the ruler – Frederick William, 'The Great Elector' – had already shown himself an enterprising man anxious to gain a toe-hold in America.

The story of Frederick William's interest in the Caribbean can be traced back to 1677 when he had been approached by a Dutch merchant from Flushing, an enterprising sea captain called Benjamin Raule. Raule had suggested that Brandenburg should become involved in the African trade, and especially the associated slave trade to the Caribbean. This was followed by the launch of the Brandenburg African Company two years later. In 1680, with money raised from shareholders in Emden and Konigsberg, two bizarre expeditions had set sail from the Baltic, buccaneering fleets armed with the Elector's 'letters of marque' authorising them to attack Spanish ships. Frederick William had no navy of his own, and gathering a fleet of mercenary ships had served as a quick way to create one. He had the excuse that the Spanish still owed him money in return for his military support some six years previously and this was one way of collecting the debt.

In December 1680, the same year that Coxon and Allison had returned to Jamaica from Darien, Sir Henry Morgan had reported that a fleet of four ships under the 'Duke of Brandenburg's flag' had arrived off Jamaica looking for Spanish ships to seize in compensation. But expeditions had not been successful, the value of a few Spanish 'prize ships' being too small to cover the costs. Some put the failure down to the simple fact that 'the Elector had no harbour in America and therefore the fleet was forced to return with its mission unperformed'.[61]

Both Frederick William and Raule had looked for such a harbour but without success. They had managed only to lease a base on the Danish island of St Thomas for a Brandenburg 'factory', an arrangement that had pleased no-one. There had been a succession of quarrels, chiefly because the Brandenburgers were thought to be dabbling in piracy. Thus, in 1688, when Paterson set his sights on Berlin, the offer of a good base in the Caribbean would have been hard to resist.

So was Paterson's decision to travel to Berlin an inspired guess? Of all the rulers in Europe Frederick William was the man most willing to give the plan serious consideration, the more so since the site at Darien appeared to offer a secure base for the Elector's African trade – within easy reach of the sugar plantations and of the slave markets of the Caribbean and the American mainland.[62]

It now appears that Paterson in fact knew very well what he was doing when he decided to travel to the Elector's court at Berlin. One of his partners in the enterprise was the young Dutchman, James Schmitten. It cannot be a coincidence that Schmitten's father was already established in the Caribbean, as a merchant working for the Brandenburg Company in St Thomas.[63] In effect, Paterson and Schmitten could offer Frederick William a solution to a long-standing problem. The plan was to travel from Hamburg to Berlin by way of the Elbe and its tributary, the Spree. But before they could set off they received the news that Frederick William had been taken ill suddenly and died. This seems to be have been the first example of the bad luck that dogged Paterson throughout his life. But as always he appears to have shaken off the momentary gloom and to have gone ahead with the journey as though nothing had happened.

On 25 October they were received in Berlin. The Brandenburg clerks described the four as 'English Merchants' a sure indication that Paterson dominated the proceedings. He produced from his travelling bag a grand scheme – or *Octroi*[64] – for 'An American Company'. The new Elector listened politely enough, but Frederick III (soon to become King Frederick I of Prussia) was a man determined to strengthen Brandenburg's place in Europe, and was not likely to be much interested in Caribbean adventures. The four left Berlin with nothing to show for their prolonged travels. Still, there was one positive outcome for Paterson at least. He found that Schmitten shared with him a sense of adventure and a good grounding in accountancy. Schmitten – who also used a French version of his name, Le Serreurier (or locksmith) – threw in his lot with Paterson, and from thenceforth took the name of James Smith. He was an accomplished linguist (it was said he had command of seven languages) and his English was impeccable. When he came back with Paterson to London in 1691, he soon found work at the very heart of the business establishment. It seemed he was a man who would go far. He was certainly to play a dramatic role in Paterson's story.

Paterson returned from Berlin to Amsterdam just in time to hear the astonishing news that William, Prince of Orange, Stadhouder of the United Provinces,[65] had descended upon England with a fleet and a smallish army. He had now been installed as King William III with his consort, Mary, eldest daughter of James II, as queen. Her father had fled to France. But for the moment Paterson decided not to return to London.

Since 1686 he had been involved in the American trade, probably with Dutch merchant partners although we have no way of knowing for sure. But he was a man given to great precision and the fact that in 1715 he told the British parliament that he had been 'concerned in business and trade' for 29 years suggests his career as a businessman began in its own right in 1686. Given the months spent travelling across Europe it was now time to pick up where he had left off and spend some time developing his business. It was one of the better decisions of his life. By staying on in Amsterdam he had time to discuss with Dutchmen just what it was that made them the richest country in Europe, when it had few natural assets other than people. Like another man who had studied Dutch methods – Josiah Child himself – Paterson found that part of the answer lay in the Dutch approach to education, very different from what was found in England. In Amsterdam education was seen as a practical matter, preparing boys for a life in business, and more surprisingly for the time, girls too. There was much emphasis on the skills required by business, especially accounting. Child observed that:

> A skill in arithmetic ... makes people more aware of costs and expenses ... they grow up with a delight in and aptitude for commerce. They also know that benefits [of a girl's education] will pass on to the family, whereas in England a merchant with a considerable estate, frequently withdraws from trade, fearing loss of one-third of his possessions through inexperience of his wife to carry on the business.[66]

Paterson's library as listed in 1703 contained 57 books devoted to finance and banking with many of a practical nature, a further 22 devoted to navigation, and no less than 10 to mining and hydraulics.[67] He clearly took the Dutch philosophy of education to heart. But the great lesson he learnt in Amsterdam was that much of the current thinking about trade was simply wrong-headed. Child himself took the view that the volume of trade in the world was finite, that one nation's expansion in trade could only be at the expense of another country. This might seem absurd today, but it was then the prevailing orthodoxy at the heart of the emerging science of economics.[68]

It was from the Dutch experience that Paterson developed his view that trade begat trade. Give trade its freedom and everyone would be better off. In an essay published in 1708 he put it more eloquently:

> Foreign trade is of such a chemical nature and virtue, that it can extract the finest metals out of the basest, convert the worst commodities into the best, turn a barren land into fruitfulness, and make a contemned and slighted people a formidable and awful nation.[69]

Paterson learnt from the Dutch that trade produced wealth exponentially, and that the best and fairest societies left trade free, raising the money they needed to fund government, not by customs duties, but by taxes on consumption.[70]

While in Amsterdam he reflected on more than just the mysterious power of free trade. Compared with the chaotic state of affairs in London, where stockbrokers met in streets and coffee houses, where banking was in the hands of private goldsmiths who all too easily could go bankrupt, the Dutch had established the public institutions needed to fire up a modern economy. Paterson noticed that Amsterdam had a publicly run stock exchange, and, even more important, a publicly run bank that accepted deposits and eased the pressure on the availability of liquid cash – gold and silver coins – by accepting 'paper-money' in the form of bills of exchange payable to its own clients.[71] He almost certainly had reason to make use of both these institutions and could see in practice just how much they smoothed the path of business.

Paterson took a particular interest in the Bank of Amsterdam. Modern banking may have begun in Italy, with the first private bankers coming from there to the Low Countries 300 years before Paterson's time. But it was the Dutch genius to see that private banking had its limitations. If a bank was privately owned who was to stop the owners absconding with the deposits in the event of a financial crisis? If security could not be relied upon, many people would prefer to keep their savings in a box under the bed, or at least demand the right to inspect their cash held by the private banker. This made money unproductive when it could be better used funding other business. Money would create money just as trade begat trade.

The merchants of Amsterdam had solved the problem overnight by creating a public bank guaranteed by the City Council. The Bank of Amsterdam, the Wisselbank, had flourished since it had been founded in 1609 and was now playing a vital role in oiling the wheels of commerce. It used 'bills of exchange' and paper 'promises to pay' as a form of paper money that could fund business. Instead of the money being tied up in the bank, it was now free to generate more work, and more wealth. The key ingredient was trust – every merchant believed the bank would keep their money safe and honour the notes and the bills of exchange in gold and silver if ever asked to do so.[72]

Again, Josiah Child described the Dutch system well. In Amsterdam, he wrote:

> The law allows them to transfer bills for debt [bills of exchange] from one man to another in foreign trade – unlike in England where a bill has to be settled in cash before the merchant can buy again to his advantage. As much as six, nine or 12 months can be spent recovering debts here.[73]

But Paterson noted something else. The Dutch had developed a means whereby huge sums could be raised by the government simply by setting aside a sum to cover the annual interest on such a loan. So Paterson's stay in Amsterdam sowed the seeds of his most famous idea, a plan to give London traders the benefit of a public bank that would also be the means of raising loans for the government – the basis of the Bank of England. When he drew up his first ingenious plan for such a bank he gave away the origins of the idea by using the phrase 'yearly rent' instead of the more usual annual interest. In Dutch, the phrase for interest meant precisely that – *jaarlike rente*.[74]

Paterson was no mere imitator. His plan for a bank took the whole concept much further. His remarkable scheme for a Bank of England gave him the right to be hailed as a financial genius to rival any in human history.

For the next eight months or so Paterson concentrated on building up a business as a merchant trading with America. He may have been based in Amsterdam, or he may have been based in Boston. We simply do not know. But we do know that by the time he came to settle in London for the second time his apprenticeship as a projector had been successfully completed. He was ready to assume the mantle of the Great Projector.

Chapter 3

The Great Projector

In March 1686, while William Paterson was busy in Amsterdam working on his plan for 'An American Company', a weather-beaten sea captain from the port of Boston in New England, a certain William Phips,[1] came cap-in-hand to London in search of a backer for an interesting business proposition. He had fixed his sights on a suitable candidate in Christopher Monck, the Second Duke of Albemarle.

Until recently Monck had cut a dashing, if slightly scandalous, figure on the London social scene but had now fallen on hard times. His father, George Monck, one of Cromwell's generals, had played a key role in securing the throne for Charles II in 1660 and had reaped a rich dividend by his change of allegiance. Honours were heaped upon him. He had been granted a great landed estate in England and the title of Duke of Albemarle. He had also been gifted a sixth share of the vast new territory of Carolana, carved out of the coastal lands of North America immediately south of Virginia.[2] A Duke required to live grandly, and to this end Monck had purchased the finest home in London. So grand indeed that it put the king's rambling Whitehall Palace to shame.[3] Albemarle House stood in its own grounds off the fashionable new street of Piccadilly and commanded a fine view of Westminster Abbey and the distant River Thames.[4]

When George Monck died in 1670 the young Christopher had set about dissipating his inheritance and shaming the family name. He was a foppish drunkard who had come to see life as one long round of house-parties, hunting, and horse-racing. Whatever he did not spend on entertaining princes and ambassadors, he frittered away on the racecourse or at the gaming table. Within ten years he was all but bankrupt and had been forced to sell the great mansion. But he determinedly kept up appearances as best he could, finding sufficient means to attend the king at Windsor Castle and Whitehall, and praying daily that good luck might come his way.

Phips may have heard of Monck through the Duke's Carolana connection and thought him the sort of man who might be persuaded to put his money on a safe bet. The proposition he had to offer certainly seemed to be in that category. According to the Boston man, there was a great hoard of treasure lying in shallow water in the Caribbean, and he alone knew exactly where it was.

Phips related the tale of how, 50 years earlier a great Spanish galleon, the *Senora de la Concepcion*,[5] had gone down in a storm off the Bahamas at a spot called *Abrojos*, carrying her cargo of gold, silver and precious stones to the bottom. Treasure hunters had come looking for it over the years but it had only now been located, by Phips and a small team of divers. They had already brought up a small fortune in 'pieces-of-eight'. Phips was showman enough to have brought some of the silver coins with him in his purse and would have produced them to maximum effect. The straitened Duke must have been suitably impressed. But this, Phips assured him, was only the beginning. Much more wealth lay at the bottom of the sea. All that was needed to recover it was a team of good divers, supported by the new diving machines that could now be purchased. Such machines were nothing more sophisticated than an upturned wooden vessel, or 'diving tub', that trapped air inside as it descended to the depths. Crouched within, the divers sat on a plank and burnt candles for illumination. Primitive as it now seems, such a device would give the divers a chance to stay on the bottom for up to an hour and conduct a thorough search for the signs of any wreck. Phips had come to London to get backing for such a new expedition.

Not surprisingly, Monck gave the plan his enthusiastic support. He could find the money from wealthy friends, and use his influence with James, Duke of York, who now sat on the throne as James II, to secure Phips a king's commission. This would at least give him some protection against arrest by passing Spanish ships. Within a matter of months, Phips and his team sailed from England aboard an elderly ship (dutifully renamed the *James and Mary*[6] in honour of the king and queen), with the all-important diving engine and enough dried codfish, pickled beef and flour on board to allow them to spend four months or so scouring the sea bottom. The destination was for obvious reasons kept a closely guarded secret. The fortunes of Christopher Monck and his business partners were riding on its success.

It was the nature of the business deal that Phips had struck with Monck that made this great treasure-hunting expedition more than merely a tale of adventure and derring-do. It was to be financed through the issue of shares in what had become known as a 'joint-stock' company. Dividends, if there were any, were to be paid on the basis of the number of shares held. Monck, as the chief sponsor of the project, had been granted a generous quarter of all the shares, the king a tenth, and the remainder had been divided between the investors who put up the money and William Phips. Phips's shares were allocated to him in recognition of his role as the originator of the whole scheme. The award of such so-called 'maiden shares' to the lead entrepreneur in a business venture was soon to become the norm.

In October the *James and Mary* dropped a tentative anchor off what are now the Turks and Caicos Islands, near the spot where Phips had found the first hoard of treasure, as best as he could establish it, given the poor charts and the primitive navigational aids of the time. Then the diving bells were made ready and the first divers plunged expectantly into the depths. But search as they might, nothing was found. The wreck had mysteriously vanished. Perhaps it had been swept away in a storm. Perhaps he had simply chosen the wrong bay. Whatever the truth, after weeks of fruitlessly scouring the seabed, Phips decided in January 1687 to call a halt, wondering no doubt quite how he was to break the awful news to Monck and the rest.

On that last day, some of the divers went looking for mementoes of the trip. As they explored a relatively shallow reef close to the shore they chanced upon a spectacular plume of coral reef in relatively shallow water. It was a treasure of sorts and they decided to take pieces of it home. But when they dived to look more closely they saw beneath it the unmistakable shape of a large cannonball. Further dives revealed masts, a carved figurehead, and then the encrusted timbers of a great ship. At the last possible moment, the *Senora de la Concepcion* had been found.

The discovery of the vessel and the huge quantities of undisturbed treasure in its holds snatched triumph from the jaws of disaster. The crew spent the next 58 days bringing up the hoard. Altogether they raised silver plate and coins to the value of £176,000 sterling, nearly a match for the fortune Josiah Child had taken a life-time to amass. Then, with much of the wreck still to be explored, Phips wisely decided to call it a day. Rumours of the fabulous wealth they had been dredging up from the deep had spread along the coast, still the haunt of buccaneers and other adventurers.[7] In March 1687 the order was given to sail for England.

It was June when the *James and Mary* dropped anchor below London Bridge and immediately became the subject of frenzied speculation. John Evelyn and Narcissus Luttrell, the most celebrated diarists[8] of the time, picked up the tale that swept the city and expressed it in similar terms. This modest ship, their diaries recorded, had come home laden to the gunwales with 'a vast treasure'.[9] The actual value of the find remained a secret shared only by the six partners, William Phips and King James.[10] But the story circulating that the dividend paid out on the investment was an unprecedented 10,000 per cent (put more simply, for every pound invested a hundred pounds were paid back) was apparently accurate. For Monck's investment of £325 he received back more than £30,000, a fortune that he did not sadly live to enjoy.[11]

Still, the good fortune of the treasure seekers set tongues wagging among the merchants and financiers on the piazza of the Royal Exchange in Lombard Street. There was a sudden rush to invest in new companies devoted to treasure hunting and the production of diving machines,[12] creating a short-lived bonanza for the despised 'stock-jobbers'. But the expedition was to have a more lasting, more profound effect on London as a business city. Daniel Defoe, that sharp and prescient observer, spotted that it had made men think of making money through launching new companies and funding them entirely with other people's cash. William Phips's 'strange performance' – as he quaintly termed his bonus share arrangement – had: 'set a great many heads on work to contrive something for themselves'.[13]

Defoe's disapproval did not stop joint-stock companies from becoming all the rage. Previously the 'joint-stock' approach to business had been the preserve of the really large long-distance trading monopolies, the corporate giants of the day, like the East India Company. From now on, the joint-stock principle was applied enthusiastically to much more mundane and much less expensive undertakings. Before Phips brought the *James and Mary* safely to anchor in the port of London in 1687 there were barely 20 such companies in the whole of Britain. Eight years later the number had risen dramatically to reach 150. To historians this was a turning point in English history, the moment when London began its spectacular climb to become the financial capital of the world, first overtaking and then leaving Amsterdam far behind.[14]

The world of the West Indian merchant was a small one, and it is perhaps not surprising to discover that William Paterson and Phips knew each other.[15] Phips had gone back to Boston in 1687, carrying a small fortune in his purse and the light touch of a royal sword upon his shoulders. As a tribute to his achievements, King James had made him a knight of the realm, and he could now call himself 'Sir William'.[16]

Paterson, for his part, had long-standing Boston connections. Indeed, as we have seen, he had married a Boston woman. This match could only have been solemnised between 1676 and 1680.[17] While the marriage had ended with her early death, Paterson had maintained a range of contacts over the years. He was, for instance, a good friend of John Borland, a Scot who did not settle in Boston until 1685.[18] We must assume, therefore, that at some time after 1685, possibly in 1689 and 1690, he revisited Boston on business. Certainly he met up with Sir William Phips there at some stage, for we have evidence that he and Phips produced a plan for a chartered company to exploit the timber and copper resources of Nova Scotia for the benefit of the Royal Navy. The continued shortage of English oak made foreign supplies a necessity.[19] This was presented to the English government in the summer of 1691 and seems to have had its origins in the early months of 1690.[20]

What Paterson and Phips discussed over their meetings in Boston we cannot say for sure, but the story of the treasure hunt and the singular means by which it was financed must have been one of the topics of conversation. One lesson was pretty obvious. It was easy to raise a relatively small sum of money from a few rich men, and do this on a face-to-face basis. But it would be quite a different matter to raise very large sums of money, from very large numbers of people. How could they be convinced to risk their fortunes on great projects? It would require good research, a well-argued financial case, and a clearly written prospectus, such as gentlemen might read at their leisure and have time to consider the benefits arising from the investment. But, even then, in the age of the stock-jobber, people would be wary. The best way to still doubts and create enthusiasm for a new scheme was to persuade 'men of quality', men of some standing in the community, to be the first to put their names down for a large number of shares. Having these 'lead investors' could hold the key to success.

Certainly these were the conclusions Paterson had reached when he finally came to make his business base in London in 1691, an outsider with few friends in the city, a modest fortune of around £2,000[21] or so, and nothing to declare but his passionate commitment to Dutch business ideas and a belief that the joint-stock principle could be applied to banking, among other things.

The story of how this obscure man won over the greatest merchants in the city, and the most powerful politicians in the government, to his idea of a national bank for England has never been properly told. Indeed you will search hard in most history books for anything more than a cursory reference to Paterson and his part in the bank project. Outside the Bank of England itself, in London's Threadneedle Street, there stands a statue to William III, who granted the first royal charter to the bank in 1694 but there is no monument to the man who conceived the project and whose wisdom and persistence saw it through to a triumphant birth, not even a plaque on the outside wall of the bank, and certainly nothing so grand as a commissioned painting hanging anywhere inside. The mystery of England's historical amnesia about Paterson and his greatest achievement can now be unravelled.

As we have seen, Paterson's movements between 1688 and 1691 cannot easily be traced. He certainly did much travelling on business (both in Europe and in America). Asked about his past before the House of Lords in December 1695 he is recorded as saying: 'I have been conversant in foreign trade. I solicited abroad. In 1691 I returned to England...'.[22] His Dutch friend, James Smith, was more explicit, telling us that he arrived in London 'from transacting affairs of his own abroad' in May 1691.[23]

It was a propitious time for any man of ideas – the age of the 'projector' had well and truly come. To an extent, the seeds of this blossoming of ideas had been sown by Charles II. In 1660 he had founded the Royal Society to promote science in England. Such giants as Sir Edmund Halley, Robert Boyle and Sir Isaac Newton had subsequently emerged. But, until 1688, scientists were more concerned with establishing the great laws of nature rather than making the world a better place. The 'Glorious Revolution' had its effects on science too, putting it on a more practical course.

The rise of the joint-stock company combined with this new emphasis on useful science to produce a rash of new enterprises. Some of these were set up to provide for the needs of treasure hunters – companies manufacturing improved diving machines,[24] telescopes and sword blades. But most of the new entrepreneurs turned their talents to producing useful articles of everyday life, such as waterproof fabrics, fire-hoses, pumping-engines, large-brimmed hats, and the first mass-produced wall-papers.[25] In this budding age of improvement William Paterson was to take his place among the ranks of those projectors who wanted to make money by improving life in the capital.

His first joint-stock venture arose out of the sharp expansion of London that had followed the Great Fire and was designed to meet a fairly obvious consumer need – the provision of a fresh, clean, water supply. Although many people in the old city relied on drawing water from ancient wells or from the River Thames itself, the well-heeled residents of the city had had their water needs met by the 'New River Company' for over half a century. The 'New River' in question was in fact a man-made canal that brought spring water from Hertford – 20 miles north of the capital – to a reservoir in Stoke Newington, just to the north of the city. It had been a remarkable achievement for its time but it had been funded not by investors, but by the rate-payers of London, with some little help from King James I.

By 1691 London's new suburbs had spread out well beyond the old city boundaries, and were beyond the reach of the 'New River' water supplies. Paterson's first 'project' aimed to fill this hole in the market. Just three miles north-west of the city lay Hampstead:

> ...such an agreeable spot that many people ... have built handsome houses for themselves, where they remain for the whole summer, while many drive out from London on Mondays Thursdays and Saturdays and divert themselves there.[26]

Above the village was an impressive expanse of heathland where springs of fresh water came bubbling to the surface. Paterson put together a plan to tap these springs and bring their water into the suburbs, districts such as Kentish Town, Marylebone, Mayfair and Soho, through a network of underground wooden pipes. There would be no shortage of wealthy people willing to pay for the service.

The Hampstead Water Company was to be funded on the basis of a joint-stock – that is by the sale of shares. In many ways the Hampstead Water Company plan was to act as a dry run for his much larger scheme for a Bank of England. He began by thoroughly researching its feasibility – was there for example an adequate supply of spring water all the year round? Just what it would cost to build and maintain it? The projected costs were set against the likely revenues that could be raised from charging users for the service. He then produced a clearly written prospectus that gave anyone considering investing in the scheme all they wanted to know. He even made it clear that, as the 'projector', he would be awarded 'maiden shares' in the company to the value of £2,000, and would be entitled to any income flowing from these shares.[27]

Drawing perhaps on the experience of Phips, who had used Christopher Monck to give his treasure hunt credibility, Paterson then had the inspired idea of recruiting some 'big-name' shareholders whose names could be put at the top of the subscription list. Such 'endorsements' by so-called 'persons of quality' would be enough to convince many hesitant investors that the 'projector' was no fly-by-night fraudster.

Paterson in fact found two excellent names to head his list. The first, Sir Dalby Thomas, was one of London's greatest West Indian merchants and a man Paterson may have known through his West Indian trading ventures. The second was another 'knight of the realm' Sir John Trenchard. Like Papillon, Trenchard had fled to Holland for fear of his life during the time of Charles II. Perhaps Paterson had met him there, although their social backgrounds were so utterly different that it seems improbable. It is more likely that Trenchard represents the first fruits of Paterson's remarkable ability to recruit pillars of the community to his schemes, despite his own lowly social origins. How did he manage it? It seems by availing himself of the opportunity presented by the ever-increasing popularity of the London coffee house.

In the London of 1691 there was as yet no stock market and no organised means of bringing investors together to discuss new stock issues. There were no financial newspapers and indeed no real newspapers of any sort.[28] And there was a lingering suspicion of grand schemes, a result of the activities of the 'stock-jobber' so despised by Defoe. Life was difficult for entrepreneurs and investors alike. But the coming of the coffee house had begun to change all that.

In the past, Paterson would simply not have had the chance to meet and talk with his social superiors. The social hierarchy of London remained robustly rigid, with the landed gentry at the top, the great merchants of the city somewhere below them (though some like Josiah Child contrived to join the landed set[29]) and beneath them the minor merchants, the professions and the craftsmen. Below them, the lowest of the low were the serving classes, subjected (if we can judge by the account given by Samuel Pepys) to beating and abuse of all kinds.[30] The gulf that persisted between the top two classes and middle range of smaller merchants and professional people remained immense, as we can judge by the patrician irritation of the grand Sir Dudley North when he could not 'go through the 'Change without being followed around the piazza by goldsmiths, who with low bows, begged to have the honour of serving him.'[31] And goldsmiths, as we will see, were by no means people without some standing.

Paterson was in social terms no higher than a goldsmith – he had begun like Josiah Child at the bottom of his trade but could now qualify as a lesser merchant, well enough off, but not yet a truly wealthy man. On the other hand the years since 1681 had not made him any less of a distinct outsider, a man of Scottish descent when Scotsmen – as we have seen – were regarded as a race of disreputable pedlars by London society people.[32] He was certainly not the sort of man to be invited to sup at the high tables of the capital.

Fortunately for Paterson the conventions of the coffee house were far less formal. A small number of them, such as *White's*, were bastions of social snobbery, but most were refreshingly prepared to serve any 'gentleman' regardless of his wealth and place in society. While the coffee house would not open its door to a mere craftsman[33] the term 'gentleman' extended down to include the lesser merchant and the professional, such persons who might merit the title of 'esquire' on the letters they received. The great social historian of the period, G. M. Trevelyan, observed that: 'At the coffee house you could see blue ribbons and stars sitting familiarly with private gentlemen as if they had left their quality and degrees of distance at home.'[34] Paterson and others like him were able to take advantage of this degree of social condescension, although at the price of a certain obsequiousness in manner.[35]

It was in the relaxed 'classlessness' of the London coffee house that Paterson learnt how to project his ideas, and convince wealthy men of their soundness. We know he frequented them because it was through drinking coffee that he met the woman who was to be his second wife, Hannah Kemp: 'the red fac'd coffee woman, a widow in Burchin Lane',[36] as Herries unkindly described her. Coffee houses were male preserves apart from the woman in charge, the *Dame de Comptoir*, as Hannah Kemp must have been.

Although his link with Sir Dalby Thomas can be traced to his Jamaica days, his collaboration with Sir John Trenchard was probably sealed over a bowl of steaming coffee or chocolate. The partnership worked. Within a few weeks the share offer was fully taken up, a public meeting of shareholders convened, and Trenchard and Sir Dalby Thomas had duly taken their place on the board. But from the outset it was Paterson who was the acknowledged business brain, as the award of 'maiden shares' showed. Although Paterson was not to stay long with the company we know it survived many years and passed into healthy profit.[37]

For all its social purpose and the useful experience it gave him of London business, the Hampstead Water Company was no more than an interesting sideline for the 32-year-old Paterson. There was something in his character that attracted him to grand schemes and greater things. He had not for a moment cast aside his hopes that one day the whole world would be changed by the establishment of his great 'emporium' on the Isthmus of Darien. But, with England at war with France and under threat of invasion, he would have judged it hardly the most propitious time to launch the idea among his new-found business associates in London. On the other hand, the financial crisis brought about by the onset of 'King William's War' – a long-drawn-out affair that was to last until 1697 – presented him with precisely the opportunity he needed to bring forward his other great scheme, his plan for a Bank of England. The idea of a 'Bank of England' was not in itself new. On one estimate, there had been over 100 proposals for some sort of national bank in the years since 1600[38] but until 1691, not one of them had been taken seriously by parliament. Paterson was to change all that.

In that year the chief concern of the government at Whitehall was to find a way to fund the increasingly expensive war with France. Louis XIV had given shelter to James II after his flight from England, and had encouraged him in his invasion of Ireland in 1690, an invasion which temporarily threatened William III's hold on the throne of England. William, for his part, was determined to drive the French forces out of Flanders (roughly the territory occupied by modern Belgium) and so secure his own Dutch provinces from French attack. In the years after 1690 the war was to enter a phase of costly stalemate. Every spring King

William would set off to the continent to wage war and he would return to London every autumn to ask parliament to pay for it.

Taxes were increased, to the groans of the landed classes, but the costs of the war far outran the ability of the tax system to pay for them.[39] It was not surprising, therefore, that the Treasury ministers should consider the possibility of meeting the cost of war by borrowing from the wealthy. France had shown this could be done by borrowing the equivalent of £30 million during seven years of war between 1672 and 1679.[40] And the fact was that there were precious few outlets for the safe investment of the surplus cash held in the hands of wealthy families. The East India Company was the only large joint-stock company and Sir Josiah Child and his friends had effectively cornered the market in the shares. The result was that vast sums of money were lying idle. Macaulay tells us that the father of Alexander Pope, the poet, had a chest with £20,000 in coins under his bed.[41] Tapping into this wealth was very much on the minds of ministers, and in 1691 they openly canvassed for ideas on how to do it. They hardly expected it would all lead to the founding of the first and greatest of England's financial institutions.

Since King James' flight to France there was no longer any royal presence in the sprawling complex of buildings known as Whitehall Palace. King William III was an asthmatic. In autumn and winter, a miasma of smog rising up from the Thames could quickly engulf the whole complex and make the air all but unbreathable. The king had wisely taken the queen's advice and moved to live in Kensington House, about two miles west of the city, back from the river.

The old Palace had become more than ever the seat of government, with ministers and civil servants pacing the corridors and alleys or sitting together to tackle the pressing needs of the kingdom. At some time in 1691 the idea arose that a national loan could be raised if only a sufficient sum of money were set aside, year after year, to pay the interest on it. This was described in the language of the time as 'a fund of interest'. A 'fund for paying interest' would be a better way of putting it. It could be created by setting aside the proceeds of a specific tax – say a tax on tobacco or wine – to service the debt. And, indeed, a small 'fund of interest' could service a very large loan. Anyone who has purchased a house by the use of a mortgage will instantly grasp the idea. Today an annual commitment to pay £50,000 in interest can raise a capital sum of upwards of one million pounds. So, in theory, a country could raise huge sums by this method with comparative ease.

Could people with money under their beds – where it was always instantly available for emergencies – be persuaded to lock it away from use in a long-term loan to the government? They needed some assurance that they could have it back again quickly if ever the need arose. Paterson came up with the perfect solution. The responsibility for raising the loan should rest, not with the government, but with a new Bank of England. It would not even be called a loan. The Bank would be a joint-stock company and would raise the cash simply by selling shares in the business to investors. Once enough had been sold, the company would hand the money to the Treasury, and the interest received on the loan paid out as a dividend to the shareholders. The great advantage from the lender's point of view was that the loan could be redeemed at any time simply by selling his shares on the open market. When Paterson talked about 'a transferable fund of interest' this is exactly what he meant, transferable from one investor to another. He had seen this very system at work on the continent of Europe and had been convinced it made good business sense.[42]

Shareholders in the Bank of England could certainly expect their share price to rise, making it a very attractive new source of investment for the wealthy who hitherto either kept their money at home, or put it for safe keeping in the vaults of a Lombard Street goldsmith. Since the payment of interest was guaranteed by the state the shares would have 'blue-chip' status. But the company would make additional profits from commercial banking operations of the type undertaken by the Bank of Amsterdam. The credibility of the new bank would be ensured by the simple device of putting one-fifth of the money collected from the initial subscription into a reserve of gold and silver coins. As a result the bank could issue hand-signed paper notes[43] to depositors – 'promises to pay the bearer on demand' – knowing that the gold and silver was there to convert the paper into coin if it had to. Such 'paper money' would provide a shot in the arm to trade, hampered too long by an acute shortage of reliable metal coin, a shortage that had been getting steadily worse.[44]

Paterson was advised that the best way to advance his scheme for a bank was to gather together as many 'persons of quality' as he could to promote it. In the late summer or autumn of 1691 he founded a new organisation known simply as 'The Society', comprising men of means who were willing to invest in the new bank. The arrival of the colourful figure of Sir William Phips in London must have helped. He had come as part of a delegation from Massachusetts seeking a new charter for the colony.[45] Phips was quickly recruited to the cause.

By early October Paterson had brought in another 14 'persons of quality' including seven who listed themselves as 'merchants'. Phips had been at first the only titled person Paterson could boast as a supporter. But on 21 October he made a breakthrough. At a meeting held in the Sun Tavern close by the Royal Exchange, six new recruits were accepted into 'The Society'. Among them were another two knights of the realm, one of them Sir John Houblon, a mighty merchant of London, and one of five merchant brothers. Houblon was to go on to become the first Governor of the Bank of England less than three years later. Perhaps even more significant was the attendance at the meeting of two very senior civil servants from the Treasury – William Blathwayt and Henry Guy.[46] The proposal for a Bank of England was already being taken seriously.

We get some idea of the time, effort and ingenuity Paterson had put into the plan from the petition addressed to 'Their Majesties William and Mary' approved at the meeting that day:

> your Petitioners [for which we must read William Paterson] have with great study, labour, travail, expence, and charge, found out, invented, formed and designed a method whereby Your Majesties may ... be furnished with great and considerable sums of money for your present occasions with far greater expedition and with much more ease to the Nation than yet has ever been.[47]

For those, like the historian of the Bank of England, Sir John Clapham, who have discounted Paterson's role in devising the Bank of England, the letters written to Blathwayt after the meeting would make interesting reading. For Paterson shoulders all the responsibility of driving the scheme forward to the point where it was taken seriously in Whitehall.

His energy came not only from intellectual conviction, but also from a very personal commitment on his part. In a letter he wrote to Blathwayt on 23 October he most uncharacteristically let his emotions show. He was a man convinced that this was an idea whose time had come:

I must needs say that I have great hope of success – yet my zeal makes me dread a defeat … it seems that providence points out this as our time to [press ahead], and the English Proverb tells us it is good to strike while the iron is hot… we want neither reason nor demonstration to shew that our proposal is one of the best that ever any subject proposed to a prince and that ever any private persons presented to their native country.[48]

Blathwayt appears to have been impressed enough to push the idea forward at ministerial level. In the autumn the House of Commons met to consider what new taxes must be raised to pay for the ongoing war. While Paterson worked on his scheme, honing it to as near perfection as possible, some pressure was applied on MPs to open an inquiry into the issue of raising money for the war based on the principle of a 'fund of interest'. The inquiry was established on 12 January 1692, and heard proposals barely a week later, on 18 January. There were only two, and only Paterson's scheme was taken seriously. It was significant that it was Paterson, not any of the great merchants of London who were members of 'The Society', who was called upon to explain the proposal to the committee members.

The scheme offered a loan of £1 million to the government in return for a payment of £65,000 a year in interest (i.e. 6.5%). There would be a reserve fund of £200,000 to form the base of banking operations. All of this duly won approval. But the sticking point was the idea that the bank's paper receipts would be given legal status as currency. The idea that anyone might be forced to accept paper currency in payment was too much for the committee to swallow.[49] Unable to resolve the impasse, parliament settled for raising taxation sharply to pay for the war. This was a strategy, it is hardly worth saying, which could not be indefinitely adhered to.

It would be naïve to think that members of parliament were either well-informed on matters of finance, or strictly disinterested. Lobbying by opposing groups was to be expected and 'inducements' to MPs blindly to oppose this or that legislation was not at all uncommon. There were clearly interests within London who would use almost any means to stop the bank ever seeing the light of day.

First and foremost of these were the goldsmiths who had set up shop along the length of the City's Lombard Street. Many of these gentlemen had abandoned their metal-working craft to become bankers in all but name. They could offer a safe haven for the gold and silver the wealthy families of London had previously kept at home locked in their strong-boxes, a form of security no match for the determined thief or the dishonest servant. So, from about the middle of the century, the goldsmiths had offered to keep family fortunes safe in their specially built strong-rooms in the basements of Lombard Street.

In return they gave the owners receipts, or 'goldsmith notes', that had begun to serve as money in a capital where much of the old coinage was not only in short supply, but severely debased.[50] Goldsmiths could claim to be doing the public a service, but they were also making huge sums of money illicitly behind the backs of their customers. It had not taken them long to realise they could use the money lying idle in their vaults in more creative ways, lending it out, without the owners' permission, and charging interest on the loans, which were made chiefly to the government, at extortionately high real interest rates.

Governments had long borrowed money, on a short-term basis, to fund their everyday activities while they waited for taxes approved by parliament to be gathered in. This was done by the curious practice of accepting loans in ready cash and issuing receipts in the form of wooden sticks known as 'tallies' – small pieces of wood with notches carved on the edge to represent the sums involved and then split down the middle to allow the government to keep a copy for its records.

These tallies were 'sold' to the lenders at a considerable discount – reflecting the goldsmiths' near monopoly on the supply of credit. Typically for a tally worth £100, the lenders would hand over as little as £70. This blatant abuse of the tally system constituted one of the strongest arguments in favour of Paterson's scheme. It explains why, in the petition sent to Blathwayt, 'The Society' was adamant that their scheme would also create as we have seen:

> a method ... to supply Your Majesties for the future with such sums of money as may from time to time be given by Parliament with far more expedition and at abundant less expence than hitherto it could be done.[51]

In the circumstances, it is hardly surprising that the goldsmiths were among the most passionate opponents of the bank scheme, or that they chose to lobby against it in Whitehall.

Other opposition was less self-interested, but just as vehement. The Tory interest in parliament based their firm opposition to Paterson's plan on the belief that a national bank might be the first step on the slippery slope that led to a republic. In their wild imaginations they foresaw a day when the king and queen would be so beholden to the money-men of London that they would lose the power to rule. It was no coincidence, in their view, that banks flourished in Holland, Hamburg and Genoa – all republics.[52] Kingdoms such as Spain and France, had none.[53] Absurd as these arguments now seem, they were taken seriously enough at the time. England had been a republic for a short time under Cromwell. The memory sent shivers down the Tory spine.

When we add to this picture the widespread ignorance among MPs on such matters as banking and finance, the assumption made by many MPs from the shires that the interests of the City and the country were ineluctably opposed, and that all foreign ideas were suspect, then the decision of the House of Commons not to proceed with the bank scheme is hardly surprising. Paterson summed up the attitude of MPs as he saw it:

> Some said it was a new thing and they did not understand it, besides they expected an immediate peace and so there would be no occasion for it. Others said this project came from Holland and therefore they would not hear of it, since we had too many Dutch things already.[54]

As for the great merchants who had rallied to the cause of the bank, men such as Sir John Houblon, they quietly went about their own business and let the matter drop. 'The Society' was disbanded, leaving only shadowy traces of its existence in the archives of the bank.[55]

A lesser man than Paterson might have given up. But while he certainly turned his mind to developing his ideas on how to release the springs of world trade, becoming embroiled in the bitter battle that was once again building between Sir Josiah Child and his old corrupt East India Company on the one hand, and the new determined 'interloping' merchants who were emerging to challenge afresh the old trade monopoly, he doggedly persisted with his bank scheme. It was helpful, no doubt, that his Dutch business partner, James Smith had followed Paterson to London and was using his lobbying talents to promote Paterson to all who would listen. At some time in the following year, 1693, Smith was taken on by the City of London Corporation to act as a lobbyist, in parliament and elsewhere. It was the beginning of a career in the City that was to end with a whiff of scandal.

Smith has left one of the few accounts of how Paterson reacted to the setback of January 1692:

> The difficulties and disappointments, together with the slights of some, and the scoffs of others, instead of discouraging, seemed only to animate Mr. Paterson, who ceas'd not night or day, summer or winter, to do his utmost in promoting his proposal ... judging ... it was not impossible [that] even the weakest may be prevailed upon, by long cultivation and unwearied solicitations ...[56]

Persistence in the end was to pay off. In the summer of 1692 Paterson had found he had an unexpected friend at the heart of government, a rising politician called Charles Montagu. How they met up we do not know but Montagu had just been appointed a minister at the Treasury and was clearly much interested in finding ways to spread the crushing burden of the war over the peace that would eventually follow. Paterson's proposal was the most ingenious of any submitted to the government. The two men met up, and seem to have worked in tandem to bring the Bank of England to the nation, even if it meant introducing it in a cloak-and-dagger manner.

Montagu was of the same age as Paterson, but his early life history could scarcely have been more different. He was one of a well-known breed of politician, a man of impeccable manners and good breeding, but of very little wealth. He was a second son of a second son of a great landowning family (he was related by birth to the Earl of Manchester) and as such had inherited no great fortune.[57] He had to earn his way in the world but he had the advantage of a good brain, good enough to win a scholarship to Westminster School in London. From there he went on to Cambridge University, where he became a friend of the much older Isaac Newton. While at Cambridge he aspired to be a great poet (and succeeded to the extent of being so honoured in Dr Johnson's *Lives of the English Poets*). But from the evidence of his work he was no budding Byron. In 1685, he wrote an excruciating eulogy on the death of Charles II. It began:

> Farewel, great Charles, monarch of blest renown,
> The best good man that ever fill'd a throne:

And continued in like vein for 150 lines.

If this work smacks of youthful naïvety, he soon readjusted his political views, and placed himself firmly in the Whig camp. In 1689 he had been one of those who invited William III to rescue England from

James's misrule. In the heady days of rejoicing after James had fled the country he emerged as a leading light among the parliamentary Whigs. His reward in terms of ministerial office seemed long overdue when he was finally appointed a minister. He was determined to make his mark on history, chiefly by overhauling the creaking system of government finance. His main objective was to switch government borrowing away from the costly tally system. He obviously regarded William Paterson as a useful man to have on his side. And Paterson was glad at last to have someone to champion his idea inside the government itself.

Montagu judged that the mood of parliament was not ready for anything so radical and controversial as a bank. He also knew there were plenty of wealthy Londoners who could be inveigled into lending money if an element of gambling was involved. So he suggested, according to James Smith, that Paterson should draw up a plan for a 'Tontine', a bizarre 'winner-takes-all' scheme.[58] A loan of £1,000,000 would be raised by subscription (rather like the Bank of England plan). The interest payable on the million pounds was used to pay a small 'annuity' to each investor. The twist was that, when an investor died off, the interest due to him was then distributed to those who were still alive. This process went on until just seven investors were left. Each was then entitled to consider the income theirs to pass on to their heirs. The scheme passed through the House of Commons on 15 December 1692 with scarcely a voice raised in dissent. One man, William Duncombe, survived for 77 years and died a very rich man indeed.[59]

The episode may have confirmed Paterson in his view that most MPs were stupid, or immoral, or both. But it also demonstrated the benefit of ministerial backing. And the alliance with Montagu produced other benefits in the form of social connections. Through him, Paterson met Michael Godfrey, one of the leading merchants involved in the new struggle to topple Sir Josiah Child from his perch in the East India Company's Leadenhall Street offices. Through Godfrey, he would have met some of the greatest interloping merchants in the city. Thus Gilbert Heathcote and James Bateman (both to be future Lord Mayors of London) were drawn into the Paterson circle. About this time he called together the second version of his lobbying group, 'The New Society', this time 40 men strong, each prepared to invest £5,000 in the Bank of England. The proposition remained very much the same as the one put forward in early 1692 except that the idea of giving paper currency the status of legal tender was quietly dropped.

It made no difference. The scheme was rejected for a second time, Smith tells us, because the officers of the Revenue simply refused to believe that lenders would be prepared to lend their money on an 8 per cent interest rate, without the benefit of the sort of discounts already offered to tally holders:

> as they had been obliged to give twenty, thirty, and sometimes forty per cent, or more discount for tallies, they would perforce have to offer a similar discount on anyone lending [money to the bank].[60]

But in early 1694 events turned in Paterson's and 'The New Society's' favour, on the back of high farce. The year before, a rival banking scheme had been promoted by two naïve financial wizards, Hugh Chamberlen and John Briscoe. Their panacea for England's financial problems was to create a 'Land Bank', an incredible scheme to print enough money to make everyone rich overnight.

Lord Macaulay, whose great *History of England* covers this episode in detail, turned his coruscating pen upon these 'political projectors' and their miraculous scheme:

> A Land Bank would work for England miracles such as had never been wrought for Israel, miracles exceeding the heaps of quails and the daily shower of manna. There would be no taxes, and yet the Exchequer would be full to overflowing. There would be no poor rates because there would be no poor. The income of every landowner would be doubled. The profits of every merchant would be increased. In short, the island would, to use Briscoe's words, be the paradise of the world. The only loser would be the moneyed men, those worst enemies of the nation, who had done more injury to the gentry and yeomanry than an invading army from France would have the heart to do.[61]

Their hare-brained scheme had involved landowners lodging their deeds of property with the bank which was to issue paper money to the full value of that property, calculated on the basis of the supposed rent paid over a hundred years – an inflation of the true value of land by a factor of five. As the king was a mighty landowner, he would be rich. So would all the landed gentry. The bank would be in a position to lend the government 'on easy terms' whatever money it needed to conduct the war.[62]

It says something for the level of economic understanding on the part of MPs that they had swallowed this scheme so completely. Perhaps the fact they were mostly landowners themselves, facing heavy land tax because of the war, blinded them to the absurdity of the whole idea. When the proposal was passed to a special parliamentary committee for their consideration it astonishingly found in its favour in February 1694. The scheme would clearly have been unworkable and disastrous, flooding the country with paper money, jacking up inflation, and bringing about a ruinous devaluation of the currency. It was stopped in its tracks when William Paterson was called to give evidence to parliament (presumably on the initiative of Charles Montagu) later in the month and exposed its glaring flaws.[63] The collapse of the Chamberlen and Briscoe folly left the royal finances in total disarray at a time of great national peril. The war had been going badly and there was a real fear that the English and Dutch positions would be over-run when hostilities resumed in the spring of 1694.[64]

It was out of this peculiar set of circumstances that Paterson's Bank of England came to be born. Godfrey, Montagu and Paterson planned their new campaign with great care. Godfrey undertook to manage the London merchants, Montagu took on the job of managing parliament, and Paterson was charged with working on the detail of how the scheme would work. But even then they could not be certain of victory in the face of the opposition from the big landowners in the Lords and of the goldsmiths' supporters in the Commons. According to Macaulay, the goldsmiths and their allies the pawnbrokers 'set up a howl of rage' and 'fell like madmen' on anyone brave enough to advocate it.[65]

Rather than attempt a frontal assault, Montagu decided on subterfuge. Instead of putting the matter before the Commons as a bill to establish a 'Bank', he instead placed the proposal for a bank within the complicated piece of legislation setting up a new tax, the so-called 'Tunnage' Bill. The tax was, confusingly, to be levied both on the 'tonnage' of ships entering and leaving English harbours (the larger the ship the bigger the tax) and on each barrel (or tun) of wine, beer and spirits. This new tax was to form the dedicated 'fund of interest' that was to become the foundation stone of the bank. Tucked away within the Bill were sixteen sections devoted to a project that was described blandly as an arrangement for: 'the better raising and paying into the Receipt of the Exchequer the sum of Twelve hundred thousand pounds, Part of the sum of fifteen hundred thousand pounds'.[66]

Not a mention of a bank appeared in the preamble. Of course it was impossible to hide the detail from the prying eyes of interested MPs. Questions were raised and the plan amended in one crucial respect. The king was permitted to arrange loans with the bank only with the full consent of parliament. Thus was the Whig fear that the king might use the bank to undermine the power of the parliament quite simply removed. Once through the Commons, the brilliance of the tactics became clear. The Tunnage Bill was part of the Budget settlement, and traditionally the House of Lords were not allowed to alter any detail of it; it could only accept or reject the entire bill. When the proposal reached the Lords in early May 1694, many of peers, with the London 'season' over, had already set off for their country estates. No amount of argument on the part of the opponents of the bank scheme could persuade enough of them to come back to the capital to vote it down. The Tunnage Bill duly passed into law.

The new Act allowed the organisers less than two months to organise the promised loan to the government and to set up the bank. Strangely this proved to be an advantage. There would be a limited number of shareholders, accepted on a first-come, first-served basis. No doubt on Paterson's advice the prospectus was clear, and the list of prominent backers was there for all to see. On the day subscriptions opened in the Mercers' Hall, a royal servant arrived to place the name of the king and the queen as the first and second subscribers to the loan. Such was the allure of the joint stock, the confidence that this bank would endure and make profits to pay dividends on the shares, that a stampede to buy the stock soon got under way.

On the first day – 21 June – £300,000 was subscribed. By day three, the figure had reached £600,000, half-way there. At noon on 2 July, just ten working days later, the books were closed with the full £1,200,000 fully pledged. Lord Somers, keeper of the Great Seal, duly added the royal seal to the royal charter setting up the bank. In an incredibly short time, so it seemed, the new institution moved smoothly into gear and took up temporary accommodation in the Mercers' Hall.

William Paterson's grand plan was realised in every detail. But it had proved a bruising experience. During the last frantic months he had found himself eased out of his place as spokesman for the bank lobby, both in the halls of government and in the City. He did not possess, it seemed, the social standing considered essential for a city gentleman. Even in negotiations with the Treasury, 'The New Society' pressured him to step back to make way for a 'grander' person. James Smith perhaps expresses Paterson's own bitter feelings during those months when he writes:

> Mr Paterson was overtopt and brow-beaten by such as were strangers both to him and the Business; and that instead of being at the head thereof, as he had hitherto been, he was now obliged to promote his sentiments in the Treasury and elsewhere by others...[67]

Now, the very success of the subscription threatened to exclude him from any part in the running of his own creation. The charter setting up the bank provided for the election of a governor, a deputy governor, and 28 directors. Together they were to form the bank's governing council, the 'court of directors'.

There was no question of Paterson being elected as the first governor of the Bank of England – that honour was reserved for a 'person of quality' and Sir John Houblon, the head of London's richest merchant family, had quite possibly been groomed for the position by Paterson himself. To aspire to the post of deputy governor would have been scarcely more realistic. Michael Godfrey, to most City men, had been the public face of the bank campaign. He had made his name in his long struggle to create a new East India Company open to all investors. And he had impeccable Whig connections which appealed to City senti-ment.[68] So Paterson's only real chance was to seek election to the 'court of directors'. But here the very fact that he had been forced to take a back seat in the months before the bank was launched made his election doubtful. James Smith tells us:

> Tho' Mr Paterson was known to be the original contriver of the Bank by such as were acquainted with him, yet the common vogue and cry went for others, who at that time were more known and more popular than he was, [and] disdaining officiously to put himself forward, he had probably not had been chosen as a director, had not some of his Acquaintance, who were moved with a sense of justice and gratitude as well as zeal to the Bank, been apprehensive that he might be left out but a day or two before the Election.[69]

It is a fair guess that Smith was one of those who persuaded him he should stay to fight on, and in the end he proved to have sufficient sup-port among shareholders to win election to the boardroom table. But there was to be no happy ending. When the court first met in July 1694, he found the proceedings not to his liking. Many of his fellow directors were of the type that anyone who has ever sat around a committee table will be familiar with:

What they wanted in reason they made up in self-assurance, and tho' they
thought and did less of the essential business of the Bank than others, yet
to furnish their quota one way or another, they generally said more ...[70]

The evidence is that Paterson found himself uncomfortable in these surroundings. Although he was elected to a seven-man committee established to prepare the Company Bye-Laws in July, he failed to appear at
any board meeting for a period of almost three weeks in August. After
this he seems to have been increasingly sidelined. The final humiliation
came on 21 January 1695 when the board decided that all directors
must attend at the House of Commons on the following morning to
meet MPs. Only five directors were authorised to answer questions in
the House. Paterson, who knew more about banking than anyone else
on the board, was kept off the list.[71]

A showdown of sorts followed a week or so later at the beginning of
February. The issue this time concerned Paterson's claim that he should
be rewarded for the time and effort he had spent in developing the
scheme for the bank. As the bank was his idea – an idea that he had
spent years as a projector promoting and arguing for – he was surely
entitled to the now customary reward of 'maiden shares'? The majority
of his fellow directors gave the very notion of 'maiden shares' short
shrift. In his account, Smith tells us that they took a disdainful, down-
the-nose attitude, saying: 'They were not appraised of Mr Paterson's
services ... at other times, [and] that it was not the business of the directors ... but if it were they would not move a finger therein'.[72] These were
hurtful words. Paterson was after all the 'original contriver' of the bank
and deserved some respect. Smith reckoned that the man had spent
some £700 from his own pocket in promoting the bank. Add to this the
losses resulting from the neglect of his other business interests, and
Paterson's total losses, claimed Smith, came to around £5,000 – a small
fortune.[73] No-one else on the board, he observed, had put as much as
£50 into developing and promoting the bank.

Paterson's reaction was not to resign as a director – he perhaps hoped
that in time he could make his presence felt on the board – but to look
for the money he needed to maintain his London lifestyle elsewhere. In
fact he had been working with James Smith on an alternative and quite
different banking project for some two years and had somehow contrived to keep it secret to all but his closest business associates. It suggests
that even then there was something of the conspirator in his makeup,

a quality that was to show up later in his career, when he was camped out in the forests of Darien. Within a fortnight of the row over money this new bank project was ready to be launched.

Since 1693 James Smith had been employed as a lobbyist for the Corporation of the City of London in a long tussle to save the City from the embarrassment of its own bankruptcy. At the centre of the row had been the City's misappropriation of a pot of money known as the 'Orphans' Fund'. When the sons and daughters of City merchants lost their fathers before they had attained the age of 21, any money left to them in the parent's will was put in the hands of the City Corporation for safe keeping. Unfortunately, the existence of this money at a time of financial stringency had been too tempting for a succession of City treasurers who had raided it to balance the books elsewhere. In the early 1690s the City Corporation had been reluctantly forced to admit that the Orphans' Fund cupboard was bare.[74] The shortfall amounted to a staggering £700,000.

The disgrace was impossible to hide. James Whiston, a contemporary pamphleteer, reflected the growing public indignation when he published a stinging rebuke:

> Was it not scandalous, as well as abominably sinfule, and injurious, for the City to assume a right to force the estates of deceased citizens into their own hands, as Guardians to the poor orphans, and others: And when they have got about 700 000 pounds into their custody and clutches, unrighteously refused to pay the monies where they became due, to the utter ruin of great numbers of distressed children?[75]

Of course the 'orphans' were not children but adults intent on claiming their due inheritance. But propagandists like Whiston flogged the story for all it was worth. For the City it was a moment of great peril. Tory MPs saw their chance to humiliate their old enemy, suggesting virtually all power to handle money should be taken from it. It was out of this crisis that a new scheme to pay off the Orphans' Debt came to be born.

There is no direct evidence that Paterson devised the scheme, but it has his fingerprints all over it. And, in James Smith, he had a man at the very heart of the operation. The idea was to create a fund of £30,000 as a 'fund of interest', that would allow the City to issue 'bonds' to a total face value of £700,000, bearing interest at 4 per cent. These bonds would then be issued to the orphans and to other creditors owed money by the City Corporation. The fund of interest would be raised by taxing coal as it came into London, by taxing companies supplying street lighting and water, and by other new levies.

With the help of generous amounts of City Corporation cash to smooth the way, the scheme was rushed through parliament in the 1693–4 session, enthusiastically championed by Charles Montagu, who announced it was a proposal of the 'greatest importance'. By the spring of 1694 it was on the statute book. Only later was an enquiry set up into the use of bribes. Sir John Trevor, Speaker of the House, and John Hungerford, Chairman of the Committee considering the Bill, were both expelled from the House of Commons for having accepted them. James Smith, as one of the lobbyists for the City, was suspected of involvement and was hauled before the House, but no evidence was produced against him, and he walked free.[76] Paterson was probably above such political jiggery-pokery. But, as an expert on 'funds of interest', he may well have helped draft the scheme.

He was certainly involved in devising the scheme for the Orphans' Bank that arose directly out of the Act. It was always supposed that many of the needier 'orphans' would want to transform the interest-bearing bonds into instant cash. Paterson proposed creating a joint-stock bank for this purpose, along the lines of the Bank of England. The aim was to raise £400,000 in cash from investors and to use this money to buy up the Orphans' Fund bonds from anyone willing to sell them. For every £100 in bonds the bank would pay just £60 in cash, evidently a deal that many of the 'orphans' were happy to accept.[77]

All through 1694 Paterson and some close friends in the City – among them Paul D'Aranda, Paul Dominicque and William Sheppeard, one almost certainly Jewish, one a Huguenot, and the third a wily Londoner – worked out the details of just how the new bank was to operate.[78] Like the Bank of England the Orphans' Bank was to have shareholders and a reserve fund. It would issue notes and have a commercial purpose. But it was to deal not in trade but in land. This may well have attracted some interest from Tory supporters of the Land Bank, and it certainly would appear that some of the 12 'trustees' behind the Orphans' Bank were fierce opponents of the 'Whig' Bank of England.[79]

This was the scheme to which Paterson had been applying the finishing touches when the row over the question of his payment as the 'projector' of the Bank of England blew up. Barely ten days later, on 12 February 1695 the prospectus for the new bank was published under the heading: 'A Proposal for Consolidating the Perpetual Fund of Interest payable to the Orphans and other Creditors of the City of London.' The prospectus named 12 lead investors ('the trustees') who would be offered shares at a heavy discount. But, in the light of Paterson's dispute with the Bank of England about payment, one clause catches the eye:

> Clause 6. That the said William Paterson and such other persons as he shall name, shall have and receive Twelve Pence in the Pound of all clear profits [i.e. 5%] ... in regard of his or their Contrivance, Labour, and Experience, in and about the same.[80]

Paterson probably had always intended that such a clause should appear in the prospectus for the Orphans' Bank (as it had with the Hampstead Water Company). But, in the aftermath of the dust-up at the Bank of England, it would have been only human to raise the percentage of profits reserved for himself. In his account Smith hints that this was indeed the case, revealing that Paterson had asked for this figure and that the other trustees had 'generously conceded to Mr Paterson 5% of the profits'.

Paterson was clearly unprepared for what followed. On 16 February he turned up as usual to the Bank of England board meeting at the Mercers' Hall. The Minute Book of the Bank of England records:

> A printed proposal by Mr William Paterson dated 12 February Instant was read, upon which he withdrew and after some debate thereupon it was resolved that he should be called in and advised:

> 'That this Court take notice, that his proceeding in the business of the Orphans Estate, in Conjunction with those he told the Court were known enemies of the bank, is not becoming a Director of this Court, but a Breach of his Trust.'[81]

It was the beginning of the end. Not one of his supporters on the board – and Smith believed they numbered as many as nine[82] – spoke in his defence. Whatever the gloss Paterson put on the story of how he had become involved in the Orphans' Bank, even his friends on the Bank of England board apparently considered it an act of betrayal.

Four days later Paterson attempted to put his case. He explained that the Orphans' Bank was to deal in land, and was therefore not in direct competition with the Bank which had specifically avoided that kind of

business. He claimed he was a man of honour who would never know-
ingly betray the trust of the bank. And he protested that he had been
condemned without being given a chance to defend himself. But the
board refused to bend or withdraw its resolution. A week later, on 27
February 1695, he walked out of the next board meeting and never
came back.[83]

Smith sums up the bitter lesson Paterson drew from the Bank of
England affair:

> He now finds by experience, that had it been a miscarriage [i.e. a failure],
> it had been his, ... but now it is a success it belongs to other people, and
> they reap the fruits of it.[84]

That is not quite the end of the story. In the months that followed the
rupture between Paterson and his colleagues in the boardroom an
unseemly war broke out between the two banks. The Tories in
Parliament optimistically viewed the Orphans' Bank as an embryonic
Land Bank – a concept that still appealed to the landed classes. One
prominent Tory, Lord Godolphin, went so far as to sell his stock in the
Bank of England and invest the proceeds in the Orphans' Bank, boost-
ing its share price by 10 per cent. For its part the Bank of England
offered to lend money at 5 per cent on Orphan Bonds, making it more
attractive to hold on to them, and less attractive to sell them to the
Orphans' Bank.[85] It was a gentle sort of sabotage.

In May 1695 things turned nasty. The Bank of England stopped
accepting bank notes issued by the Orphans' Bank, and the Orphans'
Bank was involved in an attempt to dump counterfeit Orphans' Bonds
on to the Bank of England, a serious fraud. Of the two men who were
caught in the act, one was James Smith. He was arrested and held in jail,
but never charged.[86] Paterson was probably appalled by Smith's indiscretion. And he must already have known that Smith was lucky to have
escaped prosecution over the bribing of MPs. But for some reason it did
not shake his faith in a man who was possessed with great powers of persuasion, and who genuinely shared Paterson's dream of a new order for
world trade. He will figure in very controversial circumstances later in
this eventful story.

The two banks founded by William Paterson had very different fates.
The Orphans' Bank lasted for only two years, never able to convince
investors that a bank dependent for its income on the badly managed
'Chamber' (or treasury) of the City of London Corporation was ever

anything but a poor risk. On the other hand the Bank of England thrived. It raised further loans for the government throughout the war. It became the great foundation stone of the 'Financial Revolution' that transformed England, and later Great Britain, into the world's greatest financial power. Without it, King William III could scarcely have contained the military might of France or the imperial ambitions of Louis XIV. The world as we know it today would have been a very different place.

Chapter 4

The Go-Between

Villiam Paterson's decision to resign from the board of the Bank of England could not have been unexpected to those who knew him well. The bank had fast become the darling of the City mercantile classes and Paterson had found himself relegated to a minor role by the influx of men of great prestige and authority on to the board. It was no doubt particularly upsetting to find that his erstwhile ally, Michael Godfrey, deputy governor of the Bank, had not rallied to his support; rather the contrary. At some time in 1695 Godfrey published his own little pamphlet extolling the virtues of the Bank of England to investors. In it he stressed the high-minded disinterest shown by the board at the Bank of England:

> It is observable that the Promoters of the Bank have proposed no Advantage thereby to themselves above any of the other subscribers, all Profit being only pro rata, according to the Stock [they own]...[1]

This seems a well-aimed jibe directed against the rival bank, a reminder that William Paterson had been guaranteed 5 per cent of the profits, and that each of the 'trustees' were given the right to buy shares at a discount. The implication was that, in comparison, the Bank of England was squeaky clean.

William Paterson must have read the piece, and felt a stab of anger at the way men of ample means could so casually disparage the projector's role in developing the business. Shortly afterwards, Godfrey was sent to Flanders on behalf of the bank, to arrange for the payment of the troops engaged in King William's siege of the fortress of Namur. In his curiosity to see the reality of war he went to the front line. On 17 July 1695 he was killed by a cannonball fired from the ramparts as he stood by the king's side.[2]

By then William Paterson had taken his seat at the board table of the Orphans' Bank with a small group of close associates, men soon to join him in another new venture that was to rival the Bank of England in scale and ambition. This was the scheme known to history as 'The Company of Scotland Trading to Africa and the Indies', a great trading undertaking launched in Edinburgh only a few months after Paterson's resignation from the Bank of England board.

The short time that elapsed between his resignation from the Bank of England in February and the launch of the Company of Scotland in June allowed at least one of Paterson's critics, the ship's surgeon Walter Herries, to portray the scheme as a hurriedly concocted, and even wicked, attempt by Paterson to take revenge on England, by setting up a Scots base on the Isthmus of Darien with the specific purpose of siphoning off English American trade. According to Herries the poor Scots were fool enough to fall for it:

> The man [Paterson] thinking himself ill us'd by the Managers of the Bank Of England, study'd how to be up with them: and in opposition to it, he applies himself to the project of the Orphans Bank, where he was afterwards sometime a director; but ... he meeting with some disgrace there too,[3] was resolv'd at once to be even with the body of the [English] Nation. Thus discontented and uneasie in mind he roused up in his Darien Genius ... and marched bag and baggage to the Antient Kingdom [of Scotland] where it was met by such encouragement at first sight, that [it was] conceiv'd and born in a trice...[4]

Walter Herries, as we shall discover, held a post within the Company of Scotland that allowed him to observe Paterson at close quarters. But he was also a man with a decided axe to grind, believing he had been duped to join the Scottish adventure under false pretences. When he wrote his diatribe against Paterson in 1700 he was also in the pay of an English government trying its utmost to discredit the Company of Scotland and everyone connected with it.

His account is a travesty of the truth, and barely stands examination, yet for 300 years it has formed a distorting prism that has made it difficult to perceive the real William Paterson. Where Herries led, others followed. Thus, 160 years later, when Lord Macaulay wrote his history of the time, Paterson appears in it as: 'a foreign adventurer whose whole capital consisted in an inventive brain and a persuasive tongue'.[5] According to Macaulay, Paterson used his persuasive tongue to promote the greatest speculative bubble the world had ever seen, greater even than the more famous 'South Sea Bubble' of 1720:

> Of all the ten thousand bubbles of which history has preserved the memory, none was ever more skilfully puffed into existence; none ever soared higher, or glittered more brilliantly, and none ever burst with a more lamentable explosion.[6]

Somehow the story does not add up. How could the financial genius who masterminded the creation of the Bank of England with such patience and skill suddenly be transformed into the reckless confidence trickster described by Herries and Macaulay? Some degree of blame for the destruction of the Paterson reputation has to lie with his own refusal to answer the Herries charges at the time. But he had his reasons for keeping silent, as we will find out. Now it is time to set the record straight and restore Paterson to his rightful place as a man of great vision and determination, a man brought down, not by a foolish dream of empire, but by a combination of bad luck and the determined opposition of powerful vested interests in London.

By 1695 Paterson had in fact been working on the scheme for an ambitious Scottish Trading Company for a number of years. At that stage, the Isthmus of Darien nowhere featured in the plans. Instead he envisaged a great partnership between London and Edinburgh that would open up trade to the East, wresting the monopoly on such trade out of the clutches of Sir Josiah Child and his corrupt and wealthy circle of cronies in the East India Company's Leadenhall Street headquarters.

When we last met Josiah Child he had successfully seen off the threat posed by Thomas Papillon and his group in 1682, but only at the cost of aligning the East India Company ever more closely with the Duke of York, the man who took the throne as King James II in 1685.[7] With the downfall of James in 1688, few London merchants would have gambled on Child and the East India Company surviving for long. Thomas Papillon had come back from his Dutch exile and resumed a leading role in the House of Commons as the MP for Dover. Petitions were presented to the House demanding that the company should be wound up, and the trade to the East opened to all. Merchants who had been cowed by the fate of Thomas Sandys in 1685 no longer felt constrained. In

1690 a rash of new interlopers had popped up, willing to finance illicit trading with the East India Company factories in India and elsewhere.

The agitation against the old company had risen to new heights in 1691. A fierce pamphlet war waged on the streets of London with opponents likening Child to a Goliath soon to meet his doom, to the devil incarnate, and, worst of all perhaps, to King Louis XIV of France. In the House of Commons Child and his cronies were openly accused of running the Indian trade for: 'private Gain without any Regard to the publick Good'.[8] A large body of enraged London merchants had been granted the use of the Skinners Hall in Dowgate, close by where Cannon Street Station is today, and set themselves up as the Dowgate Association, a 'New East India Company' in waiting. At their head was Michael Godfrey, the future deputy governor of the Bank of England and a man soon to be drawn into a close working relationship with Paterson in the struggle to bring the bank into being. Under his leadership, Dowgate was always more than a mere pressure group. In the course of 1692 it organised a number interloping voyages, sending ships to India which successfully brought back lucrative cargoes of saltpetre to be sold on the London market.[9]

Early in 1693, just when the Leadenhall Street 'Temple' seemed about to fall, the wily Sir Josiah once more turned the tables on his enemies, using means similar to those he had employed in 1682. This time he attempted to stay out of the firing-line by first resigning as governor and passing the reins to his relative, the compliant Sir Thomas Cooke.[10] Mountains of East India Company cash were poured into bribing MPs and ministers and they proved as open to corruption as they had been under James II. Altogether some £80,000 was distributed secretly to buy support at Westminster. King William III himself may have drawn benefit from some of this cash.[11] At the same time the East India Company subtly turned the screw on government finances, finding excuses to delay paying the large amounts of customs duty it owed to the government. William III and his government capitulated. The Dowgate merchants found their ships were no longer cleared by the customs officers to undertake voyages to the East. Before the year was out the old East India Company had its Charter (and its monopoly) once again confirmed.[12]

This fierce battle was the talk of London all through 1693 and Paterson found time to involve himself in the thick of it.[13] He knew many of the Dowgate men, not just Michael Godfrey, but James Bateman (the great London wine merchant who was to join him in his 'Company of Scotland Trading to Africa and the Indies' enterprise in 1695) and very probably Gilbert Heathcote. It was quite in character that Paterson should come up with a secret and ingenious plan[14] to outflank Child and his cohorts through establishing a new type of trading company that would break the East India Company stranglehold on trade. He proposed a strange hybrid of a company. While it would be a chartered company armed with all the powers of the East India Company to open up trading posts and make treaties with foreign princes, its royal charter would be granted in Edinburgh. On the other hand it would be run from London, if only because that was where the business brains, and the great reservoir of capital lay.

The idea of a Scottish company based on the model of an East India Company was not new, and it may even have been suggested to Paterson by two Scottish merchants based in London.[15] But Paterson was the only one with the vision (or the cunning) to see that it could be used as a convenient front for those London merchants opposed to Child. It was a feasible proposition only because Scotland and England remained, in theory at least, quite separate countries – each with its own parliament and royal ministers – even if they shared the same king and queen. As a result, there was nothing to stop the Scots establishing such a company, and nothing to prevent it inviting London merchants and financiers to join it in a business partnership. Soon, Paterson hoped, ships sailing under the Scottish flag would be bringing East India spices, fine cottons and silks back to Scotland for re-export to growing markets in Europe. The Paterson plan would be the answer to Dowgate's prayers.

To trace the origins of Paterson's scheme for a 'Scotch East India Company' – as its English detractors were wont to call it – we must begin in the year of 1692. After his failure to persuade parliament to set up a national bank for England in January, Paterson was free to turn his mind back to matters of trade. The renewed hostilities between the East India Company and the 'Dowgaters' were rising to new heights with a committee of the House of Commons, stuffed with critics of the Josiah Child regime, set up to look into the future of the Company's monopoly. At this very time the paths of Paterson and a quixotic Scottish nobleman, Sir Andrew Fletcher of Saltoun, were to cross.

Fletcher, one of many Scottish political and religious refugees who had fled to Holland during the dark years of Charles II's reign in Scotland, had been among the first to follow William of Orange in his descent upon England. He had spent the early months of 1689 in London, before travelling north to Edinburgh to smooth the path of William to the Scottish throne.[16] Fletcher may have been a Scottish patriot to his fingertips, but he had soon become bored with the limitations of the Scottish social circle he moved in.[17] In early 1692 he ventured south again, to renew old acquaintances with the Scots merchants he knew there. Through them, it seems, he was introduced to William Paterson. According to Dalrymple of Cranstoun, a man who had access to documents bearing on the story, now apparently lost, they instantly struck up a remarkable rapport:

> Ingenious men draw to each other like and iron lodestone: Paterson formed a friendship with Mr Fletcher of Salton, whose mind was inflamed with the love of the public good.[18]

In many ways they complemented each other. Paterson was a man of business, much respected in the City of London; Fletcher had a reputation as a Scottish politician and philosopher (he was said to be the master of five languages – English, Latin, Greek, French and Italian). A man of the utmost probity, if unpredictable in behaviour, he was much respected in Edinburgh, where his irascible nature and his undisguised dislike of those who disagreed with him, were forgiven. It was, it seemed, the price to be paid for genius.

Fletcher had been born in 1653 (making him five years older than Paterson) and had succeeded to his father's estate of Saltoun, about ten miles east of Edinburgh, when he was only 12 years old. His education had been entrusted to Gilbert Burnet, a brilliant churchman and scholar, then the resident minister at Saltoun Church, where the library was uncommonly well stocked for its time with a remarkable 149 books,[19] many on classical history. Fletcher added something to the Paterson world view, giving him an interest in ancient forms of government, one of the Edinburgh gentleman's great passions.[20] In particular Fletcher was a fervent advocate of citizens' rights and of a citizens' militia that would act as a brake on tyranny, both practised, he argued, by the ancient Roman Republic. Some of his thinking duly found its way into Paterson's schemes.

For Fletcher, the immediate appeal of Paterson must have been his advocacy of trade as a panacea for a nation's ills. Scotland was mired in a cycle of poverty and had been searching for a means to break out of it for almost a hundred years. Paterson's vision of trade as the key that unlocked the door to economic growth seemed a perfect prescription for the Scottish disease. Fletcher forthwith invited Paterson to go back with him to his native land to advise those in Edinburgh how best this miracle could be achieved.[21]

Paterson was already showing an interest in his native Scotland as a possible home for profitable investment. One of his Scottish friends in London was a young merchant called James Chiesly, son of the then Lord Provost of Edinburgh. Some time later Paterson claimed that it was James Chiesly and another Scots Londoner, Thomas Coutts, who first suggested to him the idea of a great Scottish trading company.[22] Whether to please Fletcher or to seek new fields for his entrepreneurial talent Paterson agreed to make the trip to Edinburgh and travelled north with Fletcher at some time in 1692.[23]

We must imagine these two men, in their middling years, making the difficult journey on horseback to Scotland (there were no roads worthy of that term), a trip that would take around ten days.[24] There would have been plenty of time to talk and get to know each other. Fletcher had an interesting story to tell. He had spent much of his early life in London and Paris or on visits to the Low Countries and had fallen in love with city life,[25] especially it seems with hot chocolate and coffee houses.

In 1678, at the age of 25, he had come back to Scotland from just such a trip to find the country riven by religious conflict and fratricidal blood-letting.[26] Fletcher put the blame on a corrupt government in Edinburgh that meekly followed London's bidding. He wanted things to change, and stood for parliament in his own county of Haddington (modern East Lothian) on an anti-government platform soon after his return. He was duly elected by the gentry of the county.[27] In 1681 he made a speech in Parliament Hall in Edinburgh roundly condemning the ministers as tyrants. This was provocative to say the least and was enough to put his life at risk. He fled first to England and then to The Hague in Holland to join the gathering army of exiles.[28]

In 1685 he had jumped at the chance to take part in an armed rebellion that followed James II's accession to the throne of England.[29] This rebellion was mounted from Holland by James, Duke of Monmouth, the

illegitimate son of Charles II. As a protestant, the handsome and dashing Monmouth had hoped to be welcomed with open arms by a population deeply suspicious of James II's Catholicism. But the whole
adventure came to an inglorious end for Fletcher when he quarrelled
with a man over a horse, pulled out a pistol and shot him dead in a fit
of uncontrolled temper.[30] Bizarrely, this crime (for which he was never
tried) saved his life. Monmouth had him packed off in a ship bound for
Bilbao in northern Spain. Had he stayed he would almost certainly have
been killed in battle or, like Monmouth, have faced a traitor's death on
Tower Hill. He could not then have played the fateful role history
assigned him in bringing William Paterson and the Edinburgh merchants together.

Scottish affairs must have been a frequent topic of conversation
among exiled Scots in London. Paterson did not need Fletcher to tell
him that there were still pockets of resistance to King William's rule in
the mountainous highlands of the North and West where many of the
Gaelic-speaking clans remained loyal to the old line of Stuart kings, represented by the vanquished King James II, in Scotland King James VII.
This had led to a bloody outcome at Glencoe, on Scotland's beautiful but
bleak west coast, when a troop of government soldiers, billeted with the
Macdonalds in the glen, had fallen upon their hosts and brutally massa-
cred the chief and many of his tenants, for no more reason than he had
been a few days late in swearing an oath of loyalty to the new king. But
as they travelled north Fletcher could sketch in the gory details and discuss the political repercussions.

There was a rumour that the order had come from London and had
been signed by the king himself.[31] Voices had been raised in protest in
the Scots parliament, which for the first time in its history was now taking an important role in national life.[32] As a result King William and his
Scottish ministers were now deeply politically embarrassed by the whole
affair. Fletcher himself, a man who had staunchly supported William's
cause, was outraged. As they talked over the events, neither man could
have imagined the role to be played by the Glencoe affair in the creation
of the Company of Scotland in 1695.

At length the two men reached the old town of Berwick on the Tweed
and crossed the border. The contrast between Scotland and England
was the first thing to strike travellers who made the difficult journey
north. Scotland presented a bleak treeless landscape, the result of over-
grazing by tough wiry sheep, and a lack of foresight on the part of those

who had laid low the once abundant forests. A few years later, Joseph Taylor, an English traveller, kept a journal of his visit to Scotland. Even allowing for his prejudice against the Scots,[33] his description of crossing the border rings true: 'We now got into a very desolate country, and could see nothing about us but barren mountains and the black Northern Seas.'[34]

Where there were habitations they were often surprisingly primitive to English eyes:

> The houses of the commonality are very mean, mud-wall and thatch the best: but the poorer sort lives in such miserable huts as never eye beheld; men, women and children pig together in a poor mouse-hole of mud, heath, and some such matter; in some parts where turf is plentiful they build up little cabins thereof with arched roofs of turf without a stick of timber in it.[35]

But that was not true of all parts. Once over the moors of Berwickshire and on the descent towards Edinburgh the traveller entered the gentle lowlands of the Lothians with some of the finest agricultural land in Scotland, capable of great improvement. This was Fletcher country, and Fletcher had long been advocating the adoption of Dutch methods of agriculture, with the use of crop rotation and manure to keep the land wholesome. As yet he had had little success, but for all that the land sported some fine country houses.

One of these was Saltoun itself, a great castellated Jacobean house that had been the Fletcher family home for only a generation. Here the pair paused to rest and socialise. Fletcher was able to show off his new friend to his wealthy and powerful neighbour, John Hay, the Marquis of Tweeddale, then the Lord High Chancellor of Scotland. According to Dalrymple, Paterson fell into a discussion on trade with Tweeddale, and sold him the idea of a Scottish trading company there and then:

> with that power which a vehement spirit always possesses over a diffident one, [he] persuaded the Marquis by arguments of public good, and of the honour which would redound to his administration, to adopt the project.[36]

The tale helps capture the energy and power of argument Paterson so conspicuously possessed, but it can hardly be true, except in the most general terms. It would be nigh on three years before 'the project' was to emerge in detail and in the meantime Tweeddale had other more pressing matters on his hands, chiefly how to deal with the political fallout from the Glencoe affair, which was already being exploited by King William's enemies north of the border.

The same account tells us that Paterson took the political elite that ran King William's Scotland by storm. The two co-Secretaries of State, the elderly Lord Stair and the younger James Johnstone, Dalrymple tells us: 'patronised those abilities in Paterson which they possessed in themselves'.[37] Whether the account is accurate or not, these gentlemen certainly were all to play a role in smoothing the way for an Act of the Scottish Parliament establishing 'The Company of Scotland' some three years later. But the trip to Scotland was more significant for the chance it gave Paterson to meet the Scottish mercantile community.

The merchant barons of Scotland, largely based in Edinburgh, were no match for the great trade magnates of London. Daniel Defoe, who was admittedly writing as an English spy, mocked their pretensions: 'I do not believe there's ten in Scotland who deserve the name of merchant, that is, Men Universally known in Trade.'[38] But, deserving or not, these were men not short of ambition. They wanted to enrich themselves and in the process, they ardently believed, bring some measure of prosperity to their native land.

Despite being the capital of one of the poorest countries in Europe, Edinburgh was a striking town. At the west end, built on the 'plug' of an extinct volcano, stood the castle. At the other extremity, backing on to the bare hills of Arthur's Seat, was Holyrood Palace, a stern, grey, renaissance palace, the only serviceable royal residence in Scotland, but now deserted by kings who preferred to spend their time in London. Between the two ran the main street – one street but with many names the chief of which was the 'Hie Gate'[39] (or High Street) – stretching for a long 'Scotch Mile'. Behind the buildings facing on to the street the ground fell away sharply, the more so as the narrow neck of rising land approached the gates of the Castle. This restricted site had forced Edinburgh to become the most densely packed town in Europe. On this ridge of land were crammed the public buildings, notably St Giles Cathedral, the Tolbooth Prison, and Parliament House, and the homes of some 40,000 people. Joseph Taylor, who hated the stench of the city, advancing up the High Street with his fingers holding his nose, was nonetheless impressed by the architecture:

> The Parliament House is in a square ... where are perhaps the highest buildings in the world, for we counted one 14 story high; each staircase

may contain 28 familyes, for the Scotch houses are built after the manner
of the Inns of Court in England, and every appartment is called a
house...[40]

In this smell-ridden metropolis, where even the rich lived in these tall
tenement apartments, William Paterson came with Fletcher to meet the
leading merchants of the city, quite possibly in the Meeting House of the
Company of Merchants, situated on the cobbled alley of the Cowgate
that occupied a valley immediately south of the Hie Gate.[41]

Among those he would have met were two pivotal figures in our story,
James Balfour and Robert Blackwood. Balfour was an ancestor of the
Edinburgh novelist Robert Louis Stevenson and gave his surname to the
hero of *Kidnapped*. But he deserves to be better known as one of the
great entrepreneurs of his age, with shareholdings in a number of new
companies based in Leith, Edinburgh's port and industrial suburb, a
mile north on the shores of the broad Firth of Forth. Among them was
a ship-builders yard, a soap factory – for the better-off folk of Edinburgh
were taking an increasing interest in personal cleanliness – and a gunpowder factory.[42]

His investments were all part of a sudden flourishing of enterprise in
what was also in Scotland an 'Age of Projects'. Such enterprise was sorely needed because Scotland hitherto had had an economy of the most
basic kind, largely based on subsistence agriculture. It produced staples
such as oats and raw wool, coal (from mines near Edinburgh), salt, salt
beef, salt or dried fish, and precious little else.[43] It had a large surplus
population with no work, swept up by the royal army in times of war,
dumped back in Scotland in times of peace. Even when the country was
at war, as it was in 1692, there were beggars aplenty, and travelling pedlars, who were forced to leave Scotland and roam England scraping a
living through buying and selling what they could.

Since Charles II had come to the throne in 1660 there had been
attempts to ape the Dutch and create a manufacturing economy. This
had led to a flurry of new joint-stock companies. Some were set up to
produce articles that hitherto had had to be imported from England
and Europe. Huguenot silk weavers had been encouraged to settle in
what is now Picardy Place – on the road to Edinburgh's port of Leith on
the broad Firth of Forth – with guarantees of a local monopoly on the
sale of silk. A rope-making factory and a sail-making factory had been
set up in Leith on the same basis, in the hope of restoring Scotland's lost

reputation as a shipbuilding nation.[44] The most important of these projects was the 'manufactory' for woollen cloth established at New Mills
near Haddington by a colourful Englishman who had formerly fought
with Cromwell against the Scots, and who had stayed on. Colonel James
Stanfield had conceived the project with the help of two local Scottish
lairds and large flocks of sheep on the moors south of Edinburgh.[45]

But, well-meaning as it was, this industrial policy was teetering on the
verge of total collapse in 1692. Emerging industries, like silk-making,
were simply unable to compete with better-established firms in England.
And attempts to shut out English imports had simply backfired when
the English parliament banned imports of Scottish products in retaliation, a trade war that hit Scotland's textile imports hard.[46] By the time
Paterson found himself sitting in the Merchants Hall in the Cowgate, it
was pretty clear that Scots industry could never flourish without access
to new markets, and if English markets were to be closed to Scots goods
they would have to look beyond the seas to find them. The question was,
where?

Balfour was at one with Blackwood (a man soon to become Lord
Provost of Edinburgh) in looking to Africa and the associated trade to
the West Indies as offering the richest opportunities. Both men had
heard of the success the Royal African Company had enjoyed in finding
outlets for coarse English woollen cloth along the coast of West Africa,
where it could be bartered for slaves, and the slaves in turn (in the classic triangular trade of the North Atlantic) exchanged in the West Indies
for sugar and tobacco. These products in turn could then be sold all
over Europe, and particularly to the Dutch chocolate and tobacco houses. The fact that the RAC had fallen under a cloud since William III had
assumed the throne, damned for being too close to the vanquished King
James, may have made it seem an easy target. But there was one draw-
back. Trading with the West Indies meant invading the monopolies
exercised by England, France and Spain against foreign shipping.
There were risks of seizure and confiscation.

Some merchants therefore preferred a second option, that of com-
bining trade with the establishment of a Scots Colony somewhere in
America. They argued that colonies, or 'plantations' as they were commonly known, would by definition require people to go and settle them
as 'planters', mopping up Scotland's surplus labour more quickly than
any scheme based purely on trade could do. The crops grown on such
plantations, such as sugar and tobacco, could be exported to Scotland

and from there re-exported to Europe, while the needs of the planters for everyday necessities would create a demand for Scottish manufactured goods. But any colonial solution to Scotland's problems would depend crucially on finding some undisputed territory in the Americas where they could raise the Scottish flag and have some reasonable chance of making a go of it. And that was never going to be easy as the Scots had already found out to their cost. As long ago as 1629 they had made an attempt to settle in Nova Scotia in what is now Canada. During the first severe winter, 30 out of the 70 settlers were reported to have perished from disease. Soon afterwards Charles I as King of England handed the territory to France as part of a complicated diplomatic package. An order was made to remove 'all the people, goods, ordnance, ammunition, cattle and other things belonging to the colony, and to leave the bounds thereof altogether waste and unpeopled as it was'.[47]

Despite this first bitter taste of the colonial fruit, the dream of a 'New Scotland' somewhere in the new world had persisted, spurred on by the English attempts to exclude Scottish-owned ships from colonial ports in America and the West Indies. As recently as 1681 the Scots ministers of Charles II had summoned a conference of merchants in the august surroundings of Holyrood Palace to consider 'the cause of the decay of trade and what they would propose the remedie thereof'.[48]

The 41 merchants who attended had thought the answers self-evident. The cause of decay was the lack of markets, and the remedy was a Scots colony somewhere in the tropics, or near to them, to establish a toe-hold in the sugar and tobacco trade. In their 'Memorial' to the king they had concluded:

> It is aggried on by all who knows the tradeing of these places and have had occasions to navigate to most of these parts, both of the continent and iselands lyeing in the great spatious Gulf of Mexico, that there are several islands and continents wherein a Scottish plantatione might be erected and established.[49]

The driving force behind the notion of a Scottish colony in the sun were the merchants from the small city of Glasgow on the West Coast, led by the redoubtable Walter Gibson.[50] Gibson had for some years been sending his ships to trade with Virginia, bringing back cargoes of tobacco that could be processed and sent for sale in Europe. This brought new vigour to a sleepy university town, long handicapped by being on the wrong side of Scotland for trade with Europe. The development of

America had changed all this. By a quirk of geography Glasgow was closer to Virginia than either Liverpool or Bristol and this gave it some advantage over these towns.[51] And it was equally well-placed to trade with Jamaica and Barbados, allowing Glasgow to open two new 'sugaries'. In part based on the promise of the elusive boom, Scotland's first deep-water port had been opened at Port Glasgow, on the Clyde estuary, in 1668.

Like the other Glasgow Atlantic merchants, Gibson was doing well, but ran the risk of financial disaster since he was trading illegally with the English colonies. The full force of the Navigation Acts of 1660 and 1663 would fall upon him if he were caught. As a result he was only ever one voyage away from bankruptcy. Opening a Scots 'plantation' – where Scots ships would be welcome and English shipping banned – therefore had its attractions. And a certain appeal to the Scottish sense of justice. Sugar and tobacco would be the making of Scotland.[52] But where was this colony to be settled? The conference of 1681 had hankered after an island in the Caribbean, or even an un-colonised part of Central America, but in the end decided there was too great a danger of Spanish retaliation. They had settled instead for 'Cape Florida or some pairt of it … joining with Carolina on the North, which is already ane English plantation'.[53] And so Carolina had come to be chosen. It had all begun well enough with the Principal of Glasgow University, William Dunlop[54] acting as chief negotiator with the Lords Proprietor of Carolina. This took time, but three years later Walter Gibson, his close ally, was able to advertise for volunteers:

> To such as are willing to Transport themselves, with design to settle in Carolina, if they be able to pay for their Passage and Entertainment at Sea, … The said Walter Gibson is content to Transport them at the rate of five Pound sterling for each Man and Woman … and fifty shillings sterling for every child, from two to fourteen years of age, and those under two years of age for nothing.[55]

His brother, James Gibson, finally set sail in the *Carolina Merchant* with a complement of 121 colonists on 21 July 1684 to plant a Scots Colony in Stuart Town, some 50 miles south of Charlestown, South Carolina. The Scots discovered the land occupied by some native American tribesmen – whom they chose to regard as savages having no right to it. They then launched an ill-judged attack on a Spanish Roman Catholic mission. The settlement was duly destroyed by a

Spanish naval force, with Dunlop and James Gibson lucky to escape with their lives.[56]

News of this fiasco was carried by the survivors on their return in 1686. But it did not prevent the Glasgow merchants securing the backing of all the Scots merchants for another attempt at colonising America just five years later, in 1691, a year before Paterson arrived in Edinburgh. Nothing had come of it as yet. But the question in Scotland, it seemed, was not whether a colony should be founded, but where and when. We can safely guess how Paterson felt about this longing for a colony in the sun. A letter written in 1696 by someone who knew him well, mentions Paterson's distaste for 'the dull way of trading by planting'.[57] Paterson himself had put it more starkly in a letter written a year earlier:

> we may be sure, should we only settle some little colony or plantation, and send some ships, [the English and the Dutch] would looke upon them as Interlopers and ... crush us to pieces.[58]

But this was a lesson that many Scots merchants had quite clearly failed to grasp, despite the experiences in Carolina. As he heard the Scots merchants wax lyrical about the establishment of a 'New Scotland' overseas, Paterson very wisely refrained from mentioning his great hopes for a purely trading venture on the Isthmus. The word Darien never crossed his lips.[59]

There are no known records of Paterson's advice to the Scots merchants during that meeting in 1692. He was certainly against a colony or 'plantation' solution, although he may have been too diplomatic to say so in so many words. A 'trading' solution – with the Scots taking on the role of the Dutch in Curaçao – was much more in line with his thinking. But he must have doubted whether Scotland could ever make a stab at it alone. It was not just a question of acquiring and equipping the necessary ocean-going ships, for Scotland possessed none of her own and had no shipbuilding industry to build them. There was also the question of finding a compliant prince to allow the building of trading posts, and the posts then had to be fortified against possible attack. As the experience of the East India Company showed, all this required a great deal of money. Money was a commodity that Scotland was conspicuously short of.

Paterson, on the other hand, knew that London had merchants and financiers in plenty crying out for somewhere to invest their surplus cash.[60] In his fertile imagination the idea of a great Anglo-Scottish company that could exploit the potential of world trade must already have been taking shape. Before he left Edinburgh he seems to have drawn Balfour and Blackwood into his plan. He would scarcely have pursued it with such vigour when he returned to London later that year if they had not given him permission to sound out London opinion on their behalf.

In the summer of 1692 he bade farewell to Fletcher and took the high road south. When he reached the English capital he heard the surprising news from Jamaica. Port Royal had been almost totally destroyed by an earthquake. God, it seemed, had lost patience with the wicked.

Paterson now found himself in the role of a go-between, a role that allowed scope for his skills of persuasion and conciliation. He most probably enjoyed the experience, even if it brought in no income. Fortunately he had set aside some cash reserves from his years in business. He began sounding out his coffee-house acquaintances on the feasibility of raising capital for an Edinburgh-based company. It was encouraging that the Dowgate Association was awash with funds and had already successfully raised a subscription to fund an expansion of the interloping trade.[61] If Paterson could come up with the right kind of business proposition, there would certainly be no shortage of people ready to plough money into it.

From the beginning he was at pains to keep all details of his discussions secret. Certainly no record of the negotiations has ever been found and probably never will be. Most London business records of the time have been lost or mislaid. This makes it extremely difficult to trace the course of any negotiations between Paterson and the interested merchants in the Dowgate Association. However, the parliamentary records of the period provide some significant clues, especially when taken with recent research into the London business records of the period that have in fact survived.[62]

At Westminster those MPs opposed to Josiah Child had persuaded the House of Commons to appoint a Committee to enquire into the East India trade during the 1691–92 session of parliament. This Committee in turn invited some anti-Child merchants to join it in its deliberations. The best-known of these was Michael Godfrey. Another was Gilbert

Heathcote, a man who was to become famous in 1694 when he told MPs that the monopoly of the East India Company no longer had any legal basis. He formed part of a group of Dowgate merchants who later sat on the board at the Bank of England. Another was Robert Raworth.[63] But it is the presence on the Committee of no less than six London wine-merchants that is the most significant clue to who gave most support to Paterson's new project.[64]

The London wine-merchants were being hard hit by the war with France, both by the disruption of trade and the sharp increase in taxes on wine. They were in the vanguard of calls to open up the East India trade to all. The greatest of them was James Bateman who was also later to take a seat on the board at the Bank of England. He moved from being one of the most active interlopers of 1692, in partnership with Gilbert Heathcote, to becoming a leading light in the Scottish Company in November 1695, bringing with him two other leading wine-merchants, Abraham Wilmer and Anthony Merry. All three became leading shareholders and directors of the Company of Scotland in November 1695.[65] The wine-merchants were the first to send ships to India to exploit the powers given to the new Scottish Company in the autumn of that year.[66]

None of this would have happened had Paterson not laid the ground-work for the scheme in 1693 and 1694. Bateman, Wilmer and Merry were not ones to throw away a fortune in a reckless gamble. They would have made it clear to Paterson, from the very beginning, that the scheme would hold an attraction for them only if London merchants like them-selves were securely in the driving seat. There was no question of them giving any support to the idea of a colony in the Americas, or even on developing an African trade. Bateman, Wilmer and Merry had their eyes set on the riches of the east. They were sure that hundreds of London merchants would subscribe to the new chartered company pro-vided it set its sights on the East India trade.[67]

In 1693 Paterson duly travelled north to Edinburgh again, no doubt mulling over just how this news might be broken to the Scots. It would not be easy to persuade the Scottish merchants to play second fiddle in their own company, or to get them to surrender their own cherished ambitions. But he held all the trump cards. He had experience of rais-ing money and knowledge of the best Dutch business methods. He understood foreign trade, and had the reputation that could attract London investors to the cause. If the Scots chose to turn down his new proposition – and he returned to London with the news – there was simply no chance of Scotland going it alone.

The Dowgaters were vital to the success of the exercise. But they were not the only Londoners to be drawn into the top-secret scheme. In the two years since his arrival in London Paterson had become friendly with a number of Scots merchants who had come to live and work in the capital. None of them was a great merchant in his own right, but what they lacked in experience they made up for by their links with many reputable Scottish families. This group, which seems to have met regularly in London at the house of William Paterson in Denmark Street (where his wife Hannah made sure there were steaming bowls of coffee to hand) or at the home of James Chiesly in the London parish of Allhallows Staining,[68] were to assume a vital role in making Paterson's plan acceptable north of the border. As he foresaw it there would be 20 directors initially, ten from Edinburgh and ten from London. Eight out of the ten London directors were to come from this group of Scots exiles, which included Paterson himself. Thus, on paper, the Scots would appear to be firmly in command of the Company. In reality, this was not true. London would be first to raise subscriptions to the new joint-stock company. Every investor who had control over £20,000 worth of stock was entitled automatically to a place on the board. Within weeks, providing the launch was a success, the Edinburgh directors would soon be far outnumbered by new London directors.[69] Paterson was nothing if not a clever operator.

Until the time was ripe for launching the new Company – and much delicate negotiation lay ahead – Paterson seems to have mounted something of a confidence-building exercise north of the border. In the next few years a wave of new industrial projects were instigated in Scotland by many of his London Scottish friends. The details are mostly lost in the mists of time. But we have the testimony of an Edinburgh observer, writing in January 1696, about the differences these enterprising men had made to Scotland:

> We have at this time a set of most active and experienced countrymen in London, notably skilled in all the mysteries of trade... erecting and carry-

ing several companies and manufactories in this kingdom, where they
have met with considerable success, and thereby have benefited their
native country, as well as bettered their own fortunes.[70]

And there is one piece of hard evidence that helps us pin down just who
these men were.

In 1693 the Scots parliament passed an 'Act in favour of manufactory
of baises' giving legal force to a joint-stock company established to make
what the act describes as 'cloath commonly called Colchester Baise' – a
soft woven woollen fabric often used to make army uniforms. Attached
were the names of the eight London merchants who promoted it. All but
two of them were later to become involved with William Paterson in the
Company of Scotland. Interestingly enough, one of the two who kept
aloof was John Holland, an Englishman who had sat on the board of
Hampstead Water with Paterson. He was a man who had gained a formidable training in accountancy while working for Josiah Child's East
India Company. Two years later he was to found the Bank of Scotland,
by which time he and Paterson had certainly fallen out.[71]

Holland aside, all the promoters listed by the Act were London Scots.
As well as the enthusiastic and enterprising Chiesly – son of the then
Lord Provost of Edinburgh – the group contained such men as David
Nairne, banker to the Scots nobility living in London, Thomas Coutts,
possibly related to the Scot who was to give his name to Coutts Bank in
the next century, and Walter Stewart, an accountant soon to play an
important role as agent for the Company of Scotland in London.[72]

Paterson proved right in his assumption that the Scots would have to
take his advice and accept the scheme he had negotiated with the
London merchants. On his trip to Edinburgh in 1693 he had taken with
him one of the London Scots, David Nairne. These two met with the
Edinburgh merchants and took the first step towards establishing the
great trading company by drafting a carefully worded Act of Parliament
that was duly passed by the 'Estates' of Scotland – the Scottish parliament – in June of that year.

This Act, called simply an 'Act for Encouraging Forraigne Trade', was
a solid foundation stone. It authorised Scots merchants to join together
to form trading undertakings that could trade with any country or state
in the world, the sole proviso being that such countries or states must

not be 'at war with His Majesty'. Such a company was to be granted certain trading privileges 'in the usual manner, as such companies are set
up and in use in other parts, consistent with the laws of this Kingdom'.[73]

The meaning was unambiguous; any new company would have powers similar to the English or the Dutch East India Company. Paterson's
influence can be seen in the way the Act no longer talked of an African
Company or a colony in America but merely listed parts of the world
where such companies might operate.[74] He was already preparing the
ground for the emergence, two years later, of a 'Scottish East India
Company'.

Bringing the Edinburgh merchants on board proved a delicate business. Paterson knew that many of them remained wedded to their
African dream. So he first produced a formula that would satisfy both
camps. Before leaving Edinburgh Paterson and Nairne agreed a bond
with 46 other merchants that left the issue of where to begin the great
enterprise unresolved:

> We the underscryners merchants in Edinburgh, considering the great
> advantage that may redound to this nation by promoting a trade to the
> coast of Africa, America, and *other fouraign parts* and the Incouragement
> given therto by the late Act of Parliament:
>
> Doe Therfore [bind ourselves] to prosecute the said affair until a patent
> be obtained from their Majesties[75] for that effort.[76] (Author's emphasis.)

The use of the term *other fouraign parts* was deliberately vague. It served
a double purpose in that it disguised the true nature of the enterprise
from Sir Josiah Child and his friends in parliament, while it kept the
king's ministers both north and south of the border entirely in the
dark.

Paterson could return south, happy with progress. He brought back
agreement in principle that the London merchants should be closely
involved in the details of the scheme. James Balfour's papers include a
receipt for £24 he had been paid to arrange for 'writing several dubles
[i.e. copies] of the act of parliament and the patent, and charges in sending them to London'.[77] Even so, Balfour and Blackwood, and probably
others, still hankered after the idea of a profitable African trade.
Paterson seems to have humoured them. After all, it would not be
incompatible with an East Indian trade if the Company was well run and
had sufficient resources to commit to it. The next two years saw the

opposing factions north and south of the border engage in a subtle courting dance in which each side sought the advantage. Perhaps the image of a tug-of-war is more apt. In the summer of 1694 Balfour and Blackwood put their names to a paper headed 'Signatur for Ane African trade and Company'[78] and sent a copy to London. As well as suggesting that the new Company should be modelled on the 'Inglish African Company' it attempted to reassert Edinburgh's primacy in the proposed partnership by including a draft proclamation which ran: 'Their majesties[79] impowers them to meet at Edinburgh as the place appointed for their Generall Meetings in all tyme coming'.

This of course was completely unacceptable to Paterson's City backers who realised it was one sure way of scaring off London investors. Paterson somehow managed to make sure that this proclamation was quietly dropped. When a new Act establishing the Scottish Company was presented to the Scottish parliament in June 1695 there was no mention of any such limitation on meeting places and the Company was called 'The Company of Scotland Trading to Africa and the Indies', a formula that allowed the Edinburgh merchants to go on talking about the African Company, while in London it could be referred to purely as the 'Scotch East India Company'. The most respected of the historians of the company was surely right to conclude in 1921 that:

> As far as one could judge from the evidence ... available, the 'Act for a Company Tradeing to Africa and the Indies' was the outcome of a prolonged and persistent campaign carried on by a group of London merchants comprising both Englishmen and Scotsmen – a campaign which had for its objective the turning of the flank of the strongly entrenched monopoly of the English East India Company.[80]

In the months after Paterson's return from Edinburgh, while he was engaged in fleshing out the final plans for the company, London was seething with high drama. In the autumn of 1693 Gilbert Heathcote and a syndicate of merchants associated with Dowgate had fitted out a great ship, the *Redbridge*, for an interloping voyage to India and the East. Its papers announced it was bound for Alicante in Spain. (Since Alicante was a wine port this suggests that London wine-merchants provided some camouflage for the operation.) But before it could sail from the Thames it was seized on the orders of the Admiralty and its cargo impounded. This action produced an uproar in parliament, with MPs rightly suspecting that Child's bounteous handouts were somehow involved.[81]

In January Heathcote was called before the Commons to answer questions about the affair. Asked if he could deny that the *Redbridge* was fitted out for the Indian trade, he replied: 'It is no sin, that I know of, to trade with India, and I shall trade with India till I am restrained by Act of Parliament'.[82] Child's great foe, Thomas Papillon, as the MP for Dover, was in charge of the Committee looking into the East India Company. Two days later it reported in its findings to the full House of Commons that the detention of the *Redbridge* was illegal.

Five days later, on 11 January, the Commons declared that all subjects of England had equal right to trade to the East Indies unless forbidden to do so by parliament. At last, the end of the East India Company's monopoly seemed in sight. There remained the little matter of putting an alternative organisation in place that could make trade agreements with the emperors, princes and potentates of the East, and raise the capital to fund the expeditions. The new Anglo-Scottish company could not have been better placed to do both.

Paterson had more than a year to wait to see the project launched. In the early months of 1694 he was doubly preoccupied with the struggle to see his scheme for the Bank of England safely through parliament and with his secret discussions with the City of London Corporation to bring an end to the Orphans' Fund crisis. The delay in prosecuting his new plan for the Scottish company may have been frustrating but he could console himself that the Act setting up the company required the assent of the Scots parliament and that the Scottish MPs were presently kicking their heels at home. The running sore of the massacre at Glencoe had made the Scottish parliament of 1693 a noisy and fractious affair. An inquiry into Glencoe had been promised but never proceeded with. In the circumstances William and his ministers decided to forgo calling the parliament at all in 1694. Only in 1695, when the king's need for tax revenue from Scotland had become desperate, were the Scottish 'Estates' to be summoned once again.[83]

Indeed, the delay was not without some advantage to Paterson and the small team who helped him draft the details of the scheme, ready to have it dispatched north to Edinburgh when the time came. Meanwhile he could rely on James Smith to help whip up some discreet interest in the new Scottish company. Indeed it is interesting that among the 'Trustees' of the Orphans' Bank in 1695 were four of the men who were later to join the board of the Scottish Company, Paul D'Aranda, Paul Dominicque, Robert Lancashire and William Sheppeard. It is quite possible that Smith, while lobbying for the Orphans' Fund Act, took the opportunity to mention the proposed Scottish Company to those he felt could be entrusted with the secret. It is also notable that Paterson, as ever, looked to men with experience of foreign trade to form an inner circle of advisers. Paul Dominicque was a Huguenot merchant who had fled religious persecution in France to make his base in London. Paul D'Aranda[84] was probably of Sephardic Jewish extraction, and may have lived for a while in Amsterdam. Joseph Cohen D'Azevedo, another close adviser, was of a similar background, being referred to as *Monsieur* Cohen D'Azevedo in a letter written by Paterson himself, showing he was still seen as a foreigner in the capital. Later, when his new Scottish partners questioned his inclusion in the grand scheme, Paterson was prepared to fight to keep him, taking on the anti-Semitic views of the time with great resolve.[85] In return Cohen D'Azevedo was to stick with Paterson to the very end.

While such associates were helpful there can be no doubt that, without Paterson, the Company of Scotland scheme would never have seen the light of day. He was a meticulous organiser, a persuasive advocate, a man willing to devote hours of his time to composing and writing long letters in bold copperplate handwriting, a man possessed with extraordinary patience and restraint. This was a necessary virtue in an age when there were no telephones, no instant messaging, and it took a week for a letter to go from London to Edinburgh, if it got there at all. Despite the pressures on his time, and the difficulties of dealing with two groups of people of very different backgrounds and experience, he hardly put a foot wrong.

In early May 1695 the draft of the law to establish the new company was ready and Paterson handed it to James Chiesly to carry it to Edinburgh to have it laid before Lord Tweeddale, the newly appointed Lord High Commissioner, the king's 'regent' in Scotland. In the best traditions of spin-doctoring, Tweeddale had already 'leaked' its existence to parliament in the hope that it might distract the Scottish politicians from the issue of Glencoe. The draft, confusingly entitled at first 'An Act for Encourageing Trade' was then referred to the Parliament's

Committee of Trade. The members made but one major change – renaming it as 'An Act establishing the Company of Scotland Tradeing with Africa and the Indies'. This change had been suggested by the Scots merchant community, and, as we have seen, reflected their sensitivities. When the draft emerged from the scrutiny of the committee virtually unscathed, Fletcher of Saltoun was on hand to press the case for the Act to be allowed to pass without fuss through the single house of parliament.

To Tweeddale's discomfiture, after a long and angry debate, he was forced to concede a new enquiry into the events at Glencoe and promised it would report quickly. This meant there was now little time for discussing the new trade act. When it arrived before them, the MPs took the Act at its face value and passed it without a debate and without a division. Tweeddale then gave King William's formal assent to the new act by touching it with the royal sceptre, a procedure giving it the force of law. He may well have feared that any delay, to allow him to consult the king on how the Act might impact on England and on other powers, might provoke dissent, even disorder.

Some of the Londoners and the Glasgow merchants had been there to see the Act pass into law. That evening in St Michael's Tavern, Balfour and Blackwood, some Glasgow men, and a group of Londoners come to Edinburgh for the occasion raised their glasses to the new company.[86] The great catastrophe lying ahead was not for a moment contemplated.

Chapter 5

A Window of Opportunity

In London the year 1695 had begun with the 'Great Frost'. In January, a bitter chill fell across all of Britain and caused the Thames in London to freeze over for a month. This frost, the worst in living memory, brought misery to poor folk of the East End suburbs who lacked warm winter clothing. Even the respectable denizens of the West End suffered as the stocks of 'sea-coal' they used to keep the cold at bay began to run low. But it has been chiefly remembered as the occasion for the celebrated 'Frost Fair' held on the frozen river. Fiery braziers were lit on the ice and whole carcasses of ox roasted on a spit, with warm punch to wash it down. But the joy of those who could afford to indulge was not unalloyed. The city remained in the grip of an epidemic of smallpox that had carried off William III's adored Queen Mary just after Christmas 1694 at the age of 34.

John Evelyn, that inveterate diarist, recorded the big freeze in graphic detail:

January 13 1695 ... The Thames frozen over: the Infection of Smallpox &c. increased to 500 more this week than the former.

January 20 1695 The Frost and continual Snows have lasted here 5 weeks, with that Severity that hindred me yet from going to our distant parish Church to my no small sorrow: the Smallpox still raging.

February 3 1695 The Weather and Season has hitherto continued so severe and the Snow so deepe and now so slabby, slippery and cold.

Mar. 24 Easterday ... The latter Part of this Moneth sharp & severe cold, with much Snow & hard Frost. No appearance of Spring.[1]

This exceptionally severe winter was to be a harbinger of worse to come. The last five years of the 17th century witnessed some of the coldest and

103

wettest weather ever recorded in the British Isles, a veritable 'little ice-age' that was to hamper industry, ruin crops, and leave vast sections of the population on the verge of famine.

In the midst of the cold snap, provoked by it for certain, came the first spark that set off the debate on corruption and venality in high places. Officers in charge of one of the king's regiments, based in the small Hertfordshire town of Royston, 40 miles north of London, demanded a subvention from local people to feed the troops. How could this be tolerated when parliament had but recently provided ample funds to aid the war effort? The local MP complained to the House of Commons who summoned the extorting officers to appear before them to explain themselves. It emerged that their colonel had diverted funds meant to feed the troops into his own pocket.

The episode was but one small example of how those in authority feathered their own nests in this age of low standards in public life. William Paterson loathed the fraud and corruption that had spread equally to the business world, where good accounting practices were the exception rather than the rule. He once wrote that 'Bribery, cheating, … wilful bankruptcy and fraud… are the worst and most heinous of all [business practices]'. And added vehemently, on the subject of fraudsters: 'It is strange that those who invented the hanging of thieves did not begin with this sort first'.[2]

The Royston scandal may have ended there had it not been for the discovery that a minor government minister had a hand in the affair. John Guy was a Tory MP, and a leading member of the Church of England, adding the whiff of hypocrisy to the stench of corruption. The Whig faction in parliament, which could usually command a majority in the House of Commons on issues like this, had the minister despatched forthwith to the dark terror of the Tower of London.[3]

Emboldened by this success, the Whigs turned to corruption at the very top. There had been a simmering suspicion, a certainty almost, that the English East India Company would never have had its charter renewed in 1693 had there not been cash available to grease the palms of the ministers concerned. The chief suspect was Thomas Danby, Earl of Carmarthen, and the king's Chief Minister. Danby had just been created Duke of Leeds as a mark of favour by King William. This was a head worth collecting. So it was that in March 1695 a grand enquiry was established by a vote in the House of Commons, with unprecedented powers to inspect the company books kept in the head office in Leadenhall

Street. On examination of the accounts the company was found to have expended no less than £80,000 in bribes at the time of the charter renewal. But just who had received the money was harder to establish. Thanks to the adroit step he had taken in 1693, the man who was first in the firing line was not Sir Josiah Child, but his kinsman, Sir Thomas Cooke, the MP for Colchester. When Cooke refused to divulge the names of those who had taken the bribes, he too was despatched to the Tower.[4]

It took weeks of rifling through the company books and much enquiry before the evidence against Danby was strong enough to proceed against him. In May he found himself accused by parliament of 'high crimes and misdemeanours', in effect 'impeached', and sent for trial. He faced imprisonment if found guilty, but he escaped the ultimate humiliation of a full-blown trial before his fellow peers when a key witness fled the scene, an event not uncommon in such proceedings, as we will see. But, nevertheless, he found himself in disgrace and dismissed from office, his humiliation relieved only by the grant of a substantial royal pension.[5]

The fall of Danby took place just six weeks before the Scottish parliament was to make up its mind on whether or not the Company of Scotland should be given a royal charter. His fall and the imprisonment of Cooke in the Tower marked a new low for the East India Company in public esteem. And it could hardly have come at a better time for Paterson. It created a window of opportunity for Paterson and his new grand venture.

Paterson's plan all along had been to sell the new company in London as a more inclusive alternative to the English East India Company. It might carry the name of Company of Scotland, but in reality it would be controlled by London interests and would offer London merchants the sort of opportunities for profitable equity investment that Josiah Child had for so long withheld from them. Once London had sunk money into the project, Paterson reckoned the merchants of the City would have every reason to protect their investment. The disgrace of the East India Company was helpful because it made it far less easy for it to mount any effective counter-attack. But how long would the window remain open?

Child's performances in 1682 and 1693 had shown how quickly he could bounce back. England of 1695 was not a democracy and MPs had shown themselves too easily swayed by the well-directed bribe. The best chance for the Company of Scotland was to open its subscription books as soon as possible, and certainly before the Westminster parliament met again in November.

Paterson's greatest problem was his inability to control events, but he did what he could to leave as few hostages to fortune as possible. In the draft of the act that would set up the Scottish company despatched north to Edinburgh in May, he had done all he could to make the company attractive to London investors. Thus the draft Act laid out the company objectives in the grandest of terms. It was empowered:

> to plant Collonies, build Cities, Towns or Forts. ... to provide and furnish the foresaid Cities, Towns or Forts with ... Arms, Weapons, and Stores of War, and by Force of Arms to defend their Trade and Navigation. ... and to make and conclude Treaties of Peace and Commerce with Soveraigns, Princes, ... Rulers, Governours, or Proprietors of the foresaid Lands, Countreys, or Places ...[6]

But compromises were inevitable. Thus the places where the new company would set up such forts and make such treaties were defined as: 'in Asia, Africa, or America'.[7]

On the other hand, in private, Paterson would have reassured his City backers that their control of the company, cleverly assured by arranging for the subscription books to be opened first in London,[8] would mean that the focus of the company from the start would be on India and the territory generally thought of as the East Indies.[9] The Act also cleverly fudged the issue of how many shares were to be reserved for Scots. It gave the impression that half the shares would be reserved for Scottish residents. In fact, on closer reading, it made clear that this applied only if the Scots subscribed to all the shares offered to them. Should they fail to do so, the 'superplus' of shares (that is those left unallocated) could then be sold to 'Scots Men residing Abroad or to Forraigners'. Scotland was a poor country. The higher the target for the subscription to the new company, the less likely that the Scots would take up their full share. Paterson knew this, and, as we will see, the target figure to be raised from shareholders was soon raised far above the expectation of the Edinburgh promoters.

The act itself was broadly modelled on the charter granted to the Dutch East India Company in 1602 – recognition in itself of Paterson's debt to Holland. It granted the new Scottish company a monopoly for

31 years from the date of the act being passed (as against 21 years for the Dutch company) and broke new ground in Scotland by limiting the liability of the shareholders to no more than they had invested. But it went further than the Dutch precedent by granting the Scottish company a 21-year tax holiday: it was exempted from paying customs duties on the goods it brought back to Scotland during that time, with a few exceptions.[10] As we will see, for many London East India merchants this was a concession too far.

June 1695 had proved a tense month for Paterson. He had chosen not to go to Edinburgh since he was deeply involved with the Orphans' Bank and could not afford the time. He had therefore to rely on his Scottish partners, Sir Andrew Fletcher of Saltoun, James Balfour and Robert Blackwood to see the draft Act pass through the Scottish parliament. But that is not to say that his influence was negligible. In fact he had bombarded Balfour and Blackwood with letters of advice, dutifully read out to the assembled merchants in Edinburgh's Ship Tavern.[11] They were treated with the utmost seriousness. Paterson's progress towards achieving almost god-like status in Scotland had already begun.

On the whole Fletcher, Balfour and Blackwood managed rather well. Apart from the change in the title of the Act, a word was changed here and there, and the language of the Act given its own Scottish flavour. The only major change was to insert the names of the 20 'promoters'[12] of the Act. Otherwise, the Paterson scheme emerged as he had planned it.

The morning after the new Act was formally approved by Tweeddale, James Balfour and Robert Blackwood called a meeting of the ten Scottish promoters at the Lower Laigh Council House, close by Edinburgh's Parliament House. They had been chosen to reflect the balance of power and influence in Scotland. At the head of the table was John Hamilton, Lord Belhaven, a man who may have owed his place to the fact that he was chairman of the Scottish parliament's Committee of Trade. Without his co-operation the Act may never have navigated its way on to the statute book. John Macky, who acted as a French spy in Scotland, famously described Belhaven as 'a round, fat, black, noisy man, more a butcher than a lord'.[13] While this is a caricature, he was an undoubtedly fiery and somewhat coarse man. Most decidedly he was not a man to be meddled with. Unfortunately there is no evidence that he had any real understanding of business or trade.

Despite his lack of manners he was shown respect as the only man of noble blood among them. Apart from him, the Scottish board contained four lesser members of the Scottish country gentry, two civic dignitaries, and just three merchants – Balfour and Blackwood, and the Glasgow merchant, John Corse. It was hardly a group of people who could be trusted to run a brewery far less a great joint-stock trading enterprise.[14]

At the first meeting Sir Robert Chiesly, Lord Provost of Edinburgh, was appointed secretary of the group. He was instructed to write a letter to the London directors with the good news that the Act had received the royal assent. They then adjourned to await Paterson's advice on what first steps should be taken to constitute the new company.[15] It took four or five days for the post-horse to carry letters to London, meaning Paterson and the London promoters would not hear the good news until the beginning of July at the earliest. It would have been rather later if they chose to send it by way of James Chiesly,[16] who had been present in Edinburgh to see the Act through.

The London promoters who were to receive this good news were of a very different character. There had been ten of them, but one of their number – the Englishman Thomas Deans – had already gone north to Scotland and did not return. Instead he joined John Holland, who was putting the finishing touches to his scheme for a Bank of Scotland. Among the nine that remained Paterson was the dominant force, acting as Chairman and writing long letters to the Edinburgh men. Six of the others were Scots merchants in London, men very much in awe of Paterson as the founder of the Bank of England. The two remaining promoters were Paterson's close business associates, James Smith and Joseph Cohen D'Azevedo.

On behalf of the group, on 4 July, Paterson despatched his first letter to the Edinburgh group with a touch of well-aimed flattery. He also gave an early indication of the large sums of money that the Scots would be expected to raise:

> The Gentlemen here [i.e. in London] are satisfyed that they are joyned
> with so excellent persons, and doubt not, with their advice and assistance,
> to begin and carry on this undertaking to the honour and the profit of

themselves and the [Scottish] nation ... As to the quantity of stock, they think £360,000, wherof the half, being £180,000 will be for Scotland.[17]

Nobody in Scotland had ever tried to raise such a sum of money before.

Five days later, a second letter from Paterson gave the first indication of how he envisaged the great company should be set up. He took a surprisingly relaxed view of the timetable: 'the Gentlemen in London', he wrote, suggested late October or early November would be time enough for the first joint meeting of the two groups:

> It will be needfull that as great a Number as possible of the Gent[n]. named in the Act should meet, and sedately and maturely deliberate and settle the Constitutions of the Company, before any other steps be taken, ..., and its needfull the first Meeting should be in London, because without the advice and assistance of some Gentlemen here it will not be possible to lay the foundation as it ought, either as to Councel or money...[18]

As if to emphasise London's leadership, he suggested that any raising of subscriptions in Scotland should be postponed until the spring of 1696. It was best to allow time to publicise the scheme properly and maximise the chances of success.[19]

The news that the first joint meeting was to be in London evidently fell like a thunderbolt on most of the assembled Edinburgh group. On the nature of their discussions there is no direct record. But no reply was sent for a month and then only to indicate they had still not decided whether to send men to London or not.[20] That in itself suggests serious wrangling was taking place. Balfour and Blackwood, who must have known this was the plan all along, found themselves in an uncomfortable spot. They knew that the company had no chance of success without Paterson's guiding hand, and that London money was the bedrock on which the whole scheme was to be erected. But, argue as they might, Belhaven and the majority of the Edinburgh promoters still refused to see the need for it.

In the same letter Paterson gave the first hint that the Act had not gone unnoticed in high places in London. He stressed the need for keeping the business of the new Company away from outside prying eyes. There must be no careless talk:

> we ought to keep private and close for some months that no occasion may be given for the Parliam[t] of England directly or indirectly to take notice of it in the ensueing Session, which might be of ill consequence, and especially since a great many considerable persons are already allarm'd at it.[21]

But trying to keep the company under wraps was clearly not going to be easy. Meanwhile, tensions began to appear as the London men waited anxiously for the replies that never seemed to come. On 6 August Paterson despatched a new letter stressing politely that: 'The life of all depends on punctual correspondence'.[22]

He complained that they had not yet received an authentic copy of the Act as it had received the royal seal of approval. This was now urgently required if the business of recruiting shareholders was to get under way:

> If a Coppy of the Act as it past the Seal, as also some Coppies printed, be not dispatched before this comes to hand, we desire you to send them with all conveneient speed, because now they begin to be much wanted here among our Friends.[23]

But speed did not apparently have quite the same meaning in Scotland as it had in London. The Scots next letter did not arrive until 14 August and there was no copy of the Act in it. That did not arrive by post until 2 September.

In the meantime, Paterson's somewhat naïve notion that the precise contents of the Act could be kept a secret proved utterly unrealistic. Someone in Edinburgh – and probably no friend of the Company – had sent several printed copies of the Act south and they were to be found at the Royal Exchange and in the coffee houses of London, where Paterson himself would have come across them. But he hid his anger behind the polite understatement that men of civility embraced in this age of manners. He wrote on 15 August: 'We are much surprized to see some of the printed Acts of parliament in the hands of some who are no well-wishers to Us, before we who are concerned can have them'.[24]

At this point the whole enterprise seemed to be heading rapidly for the rocks. Yet Paterson remained remarkably sanguine. He had taken 'soundings' and could report to Edinburgh on 3 September:

> ... our Politicians here seem inclined rather to endeavour that England should follow our Example as much as may be in encourageing Forreign Trade, than to think of discourageing us, who if blest with prudent man- agement, have designed one of the least involved and freest fundations of Commerce that hath anywhere been proposed. And since the People here are already as much awaken'd as they are like to be, it becomes us to strike whilst the Iron is hott, and hasten our pace which will now be of advan- tage to our Proposal...[25]

The immediate effect of the scare surrounding the circulation of the Act was to awaken them to the urgent need for speed. The idea that 'the Gentlemen in London' could not conveniently meet before the beginning of November was quickly abandoned.[26] The precious weeks of September and October could now be used to prepare the ground for the subscription to be raised in London in early November, before parliament could meet. The Londoners would get on with the job, whether the Scottish directors came to London or not.

The nine London promoters met on 29 August, and appointed a young London Scot, Roderick Mackenzie, to act as secretary and immediately test the waters on the likely success of the subscription. They resolved that: 'All persons desirous to be incorporated into this Coy, do give their names, together with such respective sums for which they are willing to subscribe to Roderick Mackenzie, who is to keep a fair list thereof'.[27] This was purely a sounding-out exercise and confidentiality was to be guaranteed, Mackenzie being ordered to disclose to no-one the details of such persons and such sums: 'without special Directions of at least the majority of the members now assembled'.[28] To fund this exercise each of those present put up 25 pounds sterling out of his own pocket.

Even as Mackenzie set the wheels in motion, London was becoming increasingly awash with rumour. Insidious tales were being told and retold in the riverside taverns along the Thames and in the City coffee houses. These were a variation on the theme of the untrustworthy and rapacious Scot. They suggested there was a conspiracy on hand to defraud the English, a scheme hatched by Scots living in London, men who openly boasted of their grand design. Lord Macaulay, no friend to Paterson, took the view that 'there was undoubtedly a large mixture of evil' in this whipping up of feeling against the Scots.[29] It is not too speculative to imagine that Sir Josiah Child and his clique of directors at East India House may have had something to do with gently fanning the flames of ingrained English prejudice.

Towards the end of September the rumours had reached the ears of the nine London promoters. When they met formally again on 23 September, they hastily resolved to do what they could to combat this rising tide of prejudice against them:

... whereas it appears that some enemies to this Coy do industriously spread abroad surmises, as if some of the persons concerned in this Coy did openly speak reproachfully and contemptuously of the Power of the government and People of England in relation to this Company: Ordered: that the members of this Coy do, upon all occasions, speak with due respect... and that they endeavour, with all imaginable candour, to obviate and falsify the objections of any person or persons, without heat or reflection.[30]

The emphasis on the power of sweet reason is pure Paterson, but it was hardly likely to stem the increasing flow of anti-Scots propaganda.

London Scots were, of course, used to being the butt of jokes, and to being the victims of what would today be regarded as racist abuse. They could take it. What was more worrying was the beginning of the emergence of a coherent case against this strange new Anglo-Scottish company. Any close examination of the Act would reveal a clause that elevated it in rights and privileges above anything enjoyed by the East India Company, or any other of the English chartered companies.

Paterson had been anxious to reassure investors that their long-term investment in the company had every chance of producing a good return. So in the Act he had inserted an extra form of insurance against losses occasioned by the acts of third parties. Piracy was rife off the coasts of Madagascar, and the French were engaged in a long war in which any ships flying under the colours of King William were fair game. Nor were native princes always predictable in dealing with European traders. To guard against these real risks Paterson had inserted a cover-all clause in the Act:

If any of the Ships, Goods, Merchandise, Persons, or other Effects whatsoever, belonging to the said Company, shall be stopt, detained, damaged or away taken, ... His Majesty promises to Interpose His Authority, to have restitution, Reparation, and Satisfaction made for the Damage done, and that upon the publick Charge...[31]

In short, the full weight of royal power, if need be the full might of the British armed forces, was to be brought to bear on hostile third parties to extract compensation for the Company of Scotland.

Sir Josiah Child and his East India Company may have remained in the shadow of scandal and disgrace. But other monopoly companies, such as the Royal African Company, could now begin to tease out just what was implied by the 'insurance' clause. What would happen, for instance, if one of the English companies were to seize a ship of the Scottish Company found interloping in one of their ports? As the Act stood, it seemed that the Scots could ask for the king's help to exact revenge. But the same would not apply if an RAC ship were to be caught in a Scotch East India Company port. This, they could argue, was grossly unfair.[32]

Apart from the growing anti-Scottish sentiments in London, Paterson and his busy group of London promoters seemed blissfully unaware of the gathering threat, convinced that the window of opportunity still remained open. During these weeks of September Roderick Mackenzie was sounding out potential investors, while Paterson and his group considered such issues as just how much money the new company would need to set up its bases in the East, equip a fleet, and put the business on a solid foundation. It may have been that Mackenzie could report an unexpected high interest among those he approached, or simply that the earlier sum of £360,000 now seemed inadequate for the task, but in the middle of October when the figures were still being collated, Paterson and the London promoters decided the sights for investment could be hiked by two-thirds, to £600,000.[33] It meant that £300,000 would now be expected from the Scottish investors, a sum that may well have seemed beyond the capacity of the Scots to deliver.

This decision was made without reference to the Scottish promoters, who in early October had continued irritatingly to question the need to come to London.[34] At this point it seems all contact with the Edinburgh directors was effectively broken off. Paterson made it clear in his letter of 15 October that he considered it unsafe to continue any detailed correspondence, presumably because any mail was now likely to be intercepted. But he did make a final plea for the Scots to be in London by 1 November at the latest. Without their presence, none of the work of the London group had any legitimacy under the Act. It stated that a 'plurality' of the promoters, a bare majority, was required to make any decisions.[35]

The Londoners also chose the first headquarters of the company, a three-storied brick house belonging to the sympathetic Mr Nathaniel Carpenter in Clements Lane, just off Lombard Street in the heart of the City.[36] All future meetings of the promoters were to be held there, with the time measured out by the sonorous tick of his pendulum clock. It was there that the arrangements for the 'initial public offering' were finalised in every detail.

Pride of place went to the Preamble – equivalent to the modern day prospectus – a Patersonian masterpiece and once again far ahead of its time. It was everything such a document should be: clearly thought out, and beautifully written, defining the size of the 'Court of Directors' (the full company board) and laying out such details as the penalties to be imposed on those who subscribed the initial down-payment of 25 per cent of the sum to be invested but then failed to make good their promise to complete the subscriptions by stages.[37] To that eminent pioneer of economic history, W. R. Scott, it was 'a historic document', introducing terms such as 'subscription' and 'underwriting' into the vocabulary of business.[38]

In these heady weeks of October there came some good news. King William came back from his successful campaign in the Low Countries on 10 October, retired to his quarters in Kensington Palace and immediately announced he was to dismiss his present parliament and call new elections. This meant that parliament could not now meet until near the end of November. And even then it would have no immediate chance to consider the issue of the 'Scotch East India Company'. This is because Charles Montagu had persuaded the king that the shocking state of the English currency, debased by a century of 'coin-clipping', had to be put right, and had appointed his friend Sir Isaac Newton to mastermind the issue of new 'milled' coins with serrated edges. Montagu proposed there should be a withdrawal of the old coins. This was bound to cause an almighty row. The issue of the coinage would affect every pocket in the country, since the old currency would be valued by its weight in silver not its face value. Those who had hoarded the old silver coins stood to lose most. Parliament was bound to be preoccupied by this issue for the first few weeks at least. Paterson may have counted on this preoccupation with the coinage to have his new company fully subscribed and on its way before parliament had time to give any attention to the controversy surrounding the 'Scotch East India Company'.

The London promoters therefore decided to bring forward the issue of the prospectus to early November, with subscriptions to be closed by the end of the month.[39] In the middle of this frantic dash to bring in the subscriptions, three of the Scottish committee at last turned up to attend their first meeting in London at Nathaniel Carpenter's house on Saturday 9 November 1695, much to the relief of Paterson. Strictly speaking the gathering of subscriptions was unlawful without at least ten of the promoters voting for it, something that had not prevented the first subscriptions being taken on 6 November. Now the decision could be rubber-stamped and given proper authority.

At the head of this Edinburgh delegation was none other than Belhaven himself, a peer of the Scottish realm and as such accustomed to being kow-towed to in the manner of the time. He was hastily offered the chair, as a mark of respect and perhaps a well-judged peace offering. Even so, the atmosphere was tense, the boiling anger of Belhaven poorly concealed.[40]

He may have blustered and bored his audience with his highly metaphorical style of speaking but, like the other Edinburgh men, he went along with almost all that had so far been done in their name, with the significant exception of the decision to hoist the capital fund to £600,000. The Scots may have seen the obvious danger that this would mean control of the company slipping from their grasp, forever. The three demanded an explanation.

Paterson, as always in these situations, took the floor and gave a convincing answer. His arguments are lost to us but he must have pointed out that the English East India Company had a capital stock more than twice as large at £1.4 million,[41] and would have added that soundings among London investors showed there was a large appetite for investing in the new company. Indeed, the predicted rush to buy the shares was already underway, and may already have exceeded the original target of £180,000. Blackwood and Balfour were talked around by his arguments and merely asked Paterson to put them down in writing and to despatch them as soon as possible to Edinburgh, along with copies of the minutes and journals of the meetings held in London up to then.

Winning them over to accept the draft constitution produced by the London promoters took longer. There, for the first time, it was clearly spelt out that any man (or woman) controlling £20,000 worth of shares would have an automatic place on the new company board as a director. The Edinburgh men at first withheld their approval. But, a week later, at the second meeting of the new combined committee of promoters, they gave way. Paterson's prime aim of having a Company of Scotland run from London had been secured.

At this second meeting there was, however, another matter of fierce dispute. On Paterson's instructions, Roderick Mackenzie had appended a clause to the Preamble solemnly acknowledging that William Paterson, and 'others concerned with him' (chiefly it would appear James Smith and Joseph Cohen D'Azevedo) had been:

> at great pains and expence in making several considerable discoveries of trade and improvements in and to both the Indies, and likewise in procuring needful powers and privileges for a Company of Commerce from several foreign princes and states, and for which he and they have contrived, suited, and designed the said Company.[42]

As a reward William Paterson was to be granted 2 per cent of the Company shares and 3 per cent of any profits earned in the course of the first 21 years as the lead projector of the whole scheme. He was also able to transfer such shares and profits to others as he chose to see fit.

Paterson could argue that this was established practice, referring them to the precedents of the Hampstead Water Company and the Orphans' Bank. He was clearly anxious to have his reward as the lead entrepreneur specified in writing from the start, to avoid a repetition of the row at the Bank of England. But the Paterson bonus had been inserted without any reference to the Edinburgh promoters. Now it seemed they were asked meekly to rubber stamp the deal.

The clause may have been at the core of the resentment shown towards Paterson by some Scottish groups in the months to come. Balfour and Blackwood could see the sense in it but, all the same, it must have been hard not to see in Paterson a certain greed tinged with arrogance, as he sat there with his merchant's periwig and pipe, quietly lording it over the Edinburgh men. But, again, all three of them were talked into giving their approval.

It is perhaps significant that by this date subscriptions to the new company had been pouring in for ten days. The investors had signed up on the basis of the published Preamble, knowing that Paterson was to be given this payment. Indeed, had it not been for Paterson's name on the document as the lead projector they may not have signed at all. If the investors were happy with the clause, why should the Edinburgh three stand in the way? As for the London Scots, they supported it to a man.

With this show of support for Paterson, the stuffing seems to have been knocked out of the Edinburgh men. From now on they were decidedly in the back seat, with none of them being appointed to either of the key sub-groups – the Treasury Committee to look after the funds, and the Trade Committee to decide on where the first company ships should be sent.[43]

Just who the investors were remains something of a mystery. The original list of subscribers has been mislaid or destroyed, although a copy was lodged with the House of Commons and may turn up some day, if it escaped the terrible fire of 1834. But it is possible to sketch a general picture of the origins and interests of the leading investors from the evidence contained in the minutes of the company, and from the remaining mercantile records of the City of London.[44]

There were first of all the wine-merchants, James Bateman, Abraham Wilmer and Anthony Merry. This group had already celebrated the birth of the Company of Scotland by despatching several interloping vessels to India in the autumn of 1695. The new 'Scotch East India Company' offered them the opportunity to join in a properly organised challenge to Child's corrupt edifice. They were joined by Thomas Skinner, a leading petitioner against the East India Company in 1689, and by the London-Scottish merchant, Robert Douglas. We know little about his history, save to say he had met William Paterson in Amsterdam, and was well-versed in the details of the East India trade.[45] His later bitterness towards Paterson arose from the dramatic switch in the company's strategy in the following year, when the West Indies and the Isthmus of Darien suddenly loomed large in the company's ambitions.

Other investors came from the Orphans' Bank circle, people such as Robert Lancashire and William Sheppeard. Lancashire and Sheppeard have been identified as 'notorious stock-jobbers'[46] but it was by being in command of £20,000 of shares in the company that they rose to take a place on the board. They were, it seems, also interested investors in their own right.

Many of the lesser subscribers, it seems, were personal admirers of Paterson's prowess in business. Paterson himself told the House of Commons that many of the investors came from the Orphans' Bank and the Bank of England and from among the goldsmiths, who had found themselves pushed out of banking by the establishment of the Bank of England.[47]

Even before the formal closing of the London subscription book on 22 November, with some 200 investors signed up to pay £300,000 by instalments, the new company began to take shape with commendable speed. On the 18th the first of the new London directors – Robert Lancashire and William Sheppeard – took their place on what was now referred to as the board of the company. Each had produced 'deputations, in writing from Proprietors in the same joint-stock of this Company, amounting to 20,000 (pounds)'.[48] On the 20th a Committee of Treasury with William Paterson in charge was set up to make arrangements for calling in the funds. A week later an all important nine-man Committee of Trade was set up with such great merchants as James Bateman, Thomas Skinner, Anthony Merry and Abraham Wilmer joining Paterson on it. With people of this calibre the new company looked on course to become a truly formidable rival to the English East India Company.

With every meeting of the 'board' more turned up to take their place around the expanding table in Mr Carpenter's house. On 9 November there were 12 directors. By 4 December the number had risen to 20.[49] The debates must have been lively, the atmosphere invigorating. The contrast between the all-welcoming openness of the new Scotch East India Company and the narrow exclusivity displayed by Child's old company could scarcely have been greater. And on the board Paterson, a Scotsman of lowly origins, took his place among them as a *primus inter pares*, a man respected as the architect of the whole grand design.

But all was not plain sailing. Paterson was never at his best when surrounded by people he considered his social betters. And history has a strange habit of repeating itself. Soon after the new directors joined in mid-November Robert Lancashire and some others questioned the need for him to receive such a large reward for his services to the cause. Had he really worked for ten years on the idea as he claimed? On 29 November Paterson made a cringing withdrawal – or so it reads – of his claim for a 'golden handshake' in return for a vague promise of future reward.[50]

Despite this clearly unpleasant incident Paterson and the rest appeared determined to see the new company off to a swift and triumphant start. At the board meeting of 4 December, after some debate about feasibility, it was resolved: 'That one of several ship or ships be fitted out for the East Indies, from Scotland, with all convenient speed …'.[51] This decision was passed to the new Committee of Trade for action. It would be their job to decide which cargo to load, and what the destination of the voyage should be.[52]

Next they made the first steps to open the subscription book in Edinburgh, which was now agreed should be early in 1696. Blackwood and Balfour were instructed to prepare the prospectus, a gesture of confidence in their mastery of the niceties of Scottish financial practice. It was a job they completed in just two days. Everything now seemed set for take-off. Then the misty and muggy weather in London was replaced by the onset of winter for real. And the Scots Company found itself caught at the centre of a political storm.

The minutes of the company meetings bear no hint of a gathering crisis. The last meeting in December (held on Friday 6 December) was concerned more with punctuality than any threats from outside. The Scottish directors were lectured on the need to arrive on time for meetings, with any dispute settled by reference to Mr Carpenter's excellent clock. Then all the records come to a halt, a mystery of apparent *Marie Celeste* proportions.[53]

The window of opportunity – which Paterson must have believed would remain open until at least the middle of January – had been firmly shut. To explain why it closed so swiftly, and to such catastrophic effect, we need to go back to the late summer of that eventful year.

3 May 1695 merits a place in the history of the British newspaper. On that day, just two days before James Chiesly set out for Scotland, the law that placed the press under censorship expired. In the new spirit of the age there was no majority in parliament for its renewal. Within a month the first editorially independent newspaper appeared on the streets of the capital, the *Daily Courant*. It was followed in quick succession by eight others, including the *London Post*, the *London Newsletter*, and the *Postboy*.[54]

John Evelyn may not have noted the first editions of these papers in his diaries, but he was soon referring to stories reported in them as though they were the gospel truth, never an assumption to be safely made. Perhaps the weather had something to do with the curmudgeonly mood that settled over the land that autumn. On 11 August Evelyn recorded the extraordinary weather in his diary:

> Aug. 11 It is now so very cold, so that greater frosts were seldom seene sometimes in the midst of Winter. This succeeded much wet, and set harvest extremely backwards...[55]

September was, it seems, little better: 'Greate stormes began this mon-eth & unseasonable harvest weather'.[56]

But it was not the great storms but disasters at sea that dominated the newspapers. England and France were still at war and the English Channel a dangerous place for any ship sailing under English colours. Namur had finally fallen to King William on 26 August. As if to erase the memory of the French humiliation, French men-of-war and French pri-vateers unleashed themselves in the western approaches to the English Channel. Their first prize was a clutch of sugar vessels arriving from Barbados. Then in the middle of September John Evelyn read in the papers of the fall of a greater prize:

> September 15 My good & worthy friend Capt. Gifford ... adventured all he had in a voyage of two years to the East Indies, was with some other greate ship, taken by some French Man of Warr almost within sight of England, to the loss of neere seven hundred thousand pounds...[57]

Worse was to follow. In the course of a few weeks in September and October five large merchantmen belonging to the East India Company, returning from the East laden down with cargo, fell into the hands of the enemy.

John Evelyn's diary entries make gloomy reading:

> Sep 29 very cold weather ... the weather very sharp, winter approaching apace.

> Oct 13 King went on a Progresse into the North, and shewed himself to the people, ... against [i.e. in relation to] the calling of the next Parliament...

> We have now lost 3 most rich E. India Ships with about two million pounds.[58]

According to reports in the papers the East India Company had lost all but three million pounds worth of cargo in less than a month. Such fig-ures were wild exaggerations. Had there been any semblance of truth in the reports the company would have been bankrupt, which it most decidedly was not. When news of the 'losses' reached London the share price went into dramatic decline, and a share which had once changed hands at £500 fell below £100. On 22 October it fell from £78 to £54 in one day.[59] Such a fall had not yet the power to shake confidence in the whole economy, but it subtly changed the political agenda.

In September Montagu and his City supporters seem to have been arguing that the arrival of the Scots Company offered an opportunity to sweep away the corrupt old EIC and replace it with a new one.[60] By October the mood had changed, certainly in part a by-product of the reported East India Company losses. But there were other forces at work. On a closer reading of the Scots Act by civil servants, someone at the 'Commissioners of the Customs' had noted the clause in the Act that stated: 'That all ships, Vessels, Merchandise ... belonging to the said Company, shall be free of ... all Customs, Taxes and.. Duties... for and during the space of twenty one years'.[61] Paterson had more or less taken this clause straight from the Charter of the Dutch West India Company.[62] The idea was to avoid over-burdening the fledging company with tax until it was strong enough to stand on its own two feet. But what effect would such privileged treatment have on the import of goods into England and on the crown revenues?

The Commissioner for Customs knew of course that smuggling across the Scotland–England border was rife. In 1681 the Scottish parliament had slapped a total ban on the import of cloth from England, to which the English parliament had promptly replied in kind. The Scottish wool and linen merchants had shown their customary ingenuity in finding ways to send their goods south just the same.[63] And what was to become of His Majesty's customs revenue as a result?[64]

The commissioner despatched a pessimistic note to the Treasury warning that the diversion of trade from English ports to Scotland would mean a sharp fall in tax revenues.[65] Faced with evidence of this nature, Charles Montagu, Paterson's greatest admirer in the government and the incumbent Chancellor of the Exchequer, could hardly be seen to defend Paterson's scheme in public, and he took no further part in the debate.[66]

By now the scurrilous anti-Scottish propaganda noted by the London directors was also having its effect – enough to embolden the East India Company to climb out of its dark pool of shame and take a public stance against the Scots. Sir Josiah Child, scourge of the interlopers, master of bribery, struck back. On 11 November the East India Company summoned all its shareholders to a meeting. It was clearly concerned that some of its own shareholders had already taken shares in Paterson's new company. At the meeting a warning shot was fired across the bow of any others tempted to follow suit, in the form of a resolution:

> That, if any adventurer [i.e. investor] in the present Generall Joynt Stocke Shall Subscribe to ... the Stocke of the Scotch East India Company ... He

shall be accounted acting contrary to his Oath and to the Interest of this Company.[67]

And Child went further. A carefully orchestrated campaign was launched against the upstart 'Scotch East India Company'. By the time parliament met on 22 November, petitions were presented seeking action against the Scots, not just by the English East India Company, but by the Royal African Company and by other monopoly companies such as the Levant Company and the Hamburg Company. Merchants trading with the West Indies and America – presumably having read the details of the Scottish Act – added their voices to the protest. It was an impressive show of unanimity from bodies often at each other's throats.[68]

The first business before parliament was the question of the new coinage, and, as Paterson had assumed, the first two weeks of the new parliament were devoted to this most pressing, and controversial, matter. But on Tuesday 3 December time was allocated in the House of Lords for the urgent consideration of a petition from the English East India Company. A copy of the 'Scotch Act' had been circulated to all members of the House, causing enough of a stir for the House to ask the protesters to submit written papers on the issue. His Majesty's Commissioner of Customs, Sir Robert Southwell, was curtly summoned to give evidence on any possible loss of revenue to the English crown. All through those first two weeks of December representatives from the big trading monopolies and the merchants associations paraded their arguments against the iniquitous Scots company before the House. They painted a bleak, and surely an exaggerated, picture of the problems they faced. Losses by storm, hurricane and French action were all lumped together to depict a scene of unmitigated gloom. A total of 103 ships may have been lost to the forces of nature and hostile action in a single year, but how much worse this was than usual they did not choose to say.[69] But the hysteria had its desired effect. A trading empire apparently reduced to penury was now threatened by disaster. The Royal African Company summed it up in the apocalyptic terms: 'This Scotch Act is nationally so pernicious to us that once they have colonised themselves our commerce will be entirely lost'.[70] And Child's East India Company claimed that Paterson had simply taken every trade privilege ever granted by European crowned heads or states to a chartered company and given each and every one to the Scots Company, putting itself and other monopoly companies at a grave disadvantage.[71]

The reading of these reports was followed by a debate in which anti-Scottish passions ran high. One supporter of the English East India

Company, Sir Patrick Ward, put it simply. Scots people paid no taxes in England, and therefore had no right using London as a launch-pad for their new business.[72] Mr Doddington, who acted as spokesman for the East India Company on the threat posed by its Scots rival, went further, painting an alarming picture of a flood of 'Scotch Pedlars' bringing contraband East Indian goods south across the border to the ruin of his company's trade. He reminded parliament that the East India Company provided many jobs in London. Was it not shameful that 'a great many of our countrymen have subscribed large sum [in the Scots Company] ... against the interest of their own country?'[73]

Much of the information paraded before parliament seemed to be insider information. Outside on the streets of London a two-page 'flyer' appeared hinting darkly that:

a certain Scotch native of the tribe of Judas Iscariot, ... with his gaity of temper and affected humility, has stoop'd down to take up the honourable office of informer behind the curtain...[74]

Whether there was a traitor within the ranks of the London directors of the Scots Company we will never know. It is certainly odd that the House of Lords issued an order on Saturday 7 December requiring that seven of the Directors named in the Act (but not, strangely, William Paterson himself) should attend at the bar of the House the following Monday morning, 9 December. Somehow the House had obtained the home or business addresses of these men.

The action of the House of Lords in pursuing the directors of the Company of Scotland as though they were common criminals was enough to prevent any further meetings of the London 'Court of Directors'. After that rather uneventful discussion about time-keeping on Friday 6 December, the directors found themselves caught up in a remarkable process of inquisition that effectively decapitated the company and left the subscribers unable to fulfil their side of the bargain. By the time the storm subsided all prospects of the company retaining its base in London had effectively gone.

From the start the procedure was heavy handed. Those directors who turned up on Monday 9 December were forced to appear twice before the Lords committee, first as a group and then individually. The clipped answers that appear in the Lords' records are in themselves a form of shorthand, but the impression that the directors divulged as little detail as they could is probably right. But the unhelpful answers on that

Monday only convinced the Lords they would have to delve deeper into the whole affair, and they forthwith ordered Lord Belhaven, James Balfour and Robert Blackwood to appear on the following Thursday, bringing with them the full subscription book, with those 200 recorded names. The object, it seemed, was to smoke out the English backers of this 'foreign' company rather than punish the Scots for their impudence in setting up shop in the capital. Belhaven chose to ignore the summons and hastily beat a retreat northwards to the safety of Edinburgh. Blackwood took the precaution of despatching the subscription book to Scotland, in the hands of a trusted servant, so that he and Balfour appeared without this vital evidence on the Thursday.[75]

With Belhaven nowhere to be found[76] the Lords settled for interviewing William Paterson, followed by those subscribers whose names had been divulged under cross-examination on the Monday. But, try as they might, the Lords Committee could not see what action could be taken by them against the Scots Company. Technically, the king himself had assented to the Scots Act and granted the Company of Scotland his Letters Patent confirming its rights and privileges. Paterson's view that he had found a legal means to circumvent the English East India Company's monopoly of trade east of the Cape of Good Hope seemed vindicated.

When the Lords Committee reported back to the full house on the following Saturday they recommended only that: 'an humble address be made to His Majesty, to represent to him the great Prejudice, Inconveniences, and Mischiefs, the Act for establishing an East India company in Scotland may be to the trade of this Kingdom'.[77] The king himself was equally flummoxed. When a joint delegation arrived at Kensington Palace the following Tuesday he received the long petition listing the special privileges his Scottish parliament had heaped on the 'Scotch East India Company'. What could William say? There was no doubt that the Scots Act was legal. He contented himself with uttering the now famous words: 'I have been ill-served by Scotland'.[78] Then he retired into his palace. Later he was to show his displeasure by dismissing Tweeddale as Commissioner and sacking James Johnstone as co-Secretary of State in Scotland. But, for all that, the Scots Act remained law.

Despite the unsatisfactory response from the king, the House of Commons pursued the matter for another month.[79] In the process the directors of the Scots Company were once again humiliatingly hauled in front of their inquisitors, this time in the Commons, and forced to answer much the same questions about the origins and purpose of the Scots Company as were put to them by the Lords. William Paterson and James Bateman received a particularly rough ride. When Bateman was asked if he knew of the Company of Scotland plans to send ships to serve the 'East India trade' he denied there had been any. The minutes curtly recorded:

> Yet it appears by the minute-Book that Mr Bateman was present at a Committee, wherein it was resolved to send out a Ship from Scotland to the East Indies ... And being asked several other questions, gave contradictory answers, to the Dissatisfaction of the Committee.[80]

The hardliners in the Commons were bent on making an example of Paterson, Bateman and the other directors, but they could find no law that had been breached, no crime committed. To some the best solution was to give the East India Company the same rights as the new Scottish company, even if it was at some cost to the Revenue.[81]

Then someone looked further at the minutes of the company board meetings, handed over as good copies by Roderick Mackenzie. On 29 November the entry showed that all the Scots directors had taken an oath of loyalty to the company, a procedure laid down in the Scottish Act. A Scottish Act, not an English Act. Was this not the case of Scottish law being unlawfully applied in England? Was this not a usurpation of the powers of the English parliament?

This was a technical point, since all large and reputable companies engaged in trade recognised the need for business confidences to be kept. Paterson's greatest mistake, it turned out, was to suggest an oath of loyalty, rather than simply asking each director to sign a pledge not to divulge the secrets of the boardroom to third parties. But it was on this arcane argument alone the fate of the directors hung.

On 21 January 1696 the Commons resolved that the administering of such an oath amounted to a 'high crime and misdemeanour'. This meant that anyone so charged would be 'impeached' before the House of Lords and thrown into the Tower for as long as their Lordships judged appropriate – for life even. The weapon once turned upon

Thomas Danby was now to be turned on the hapless directors. In all 22 of them were found guilty by the Commons and the matter referred to the Lords for action.[82]

Whether Josiah Child and the East India Company had a hand in promoting this sorry end to the 'Scotch East India Company' has never been established. It certainly cannot be ruled out. It is also true that there was more support for Paterson's attempt to breach the old monopoly than the outcome suggests. Indeed, less than three years later a parliamentary majority deprived the old company of its exclusive rights and set up a 'New East India Company', a measure piloted through the English parliament by Paterson's admirer, Charles Montagu.[83]

As for the impeachment of the directors, nothing more was to come of it. The key witness was Roderick Mackenzie, a man who had co-operated with the inquiry to the extent of supplying names, the minute book, and, crucially, a copy of the subscription book, to the Commons.[84] He had been present at the oath-taking ceremony on 29 November[85] but now he fled north to chilly Edinburgh, nursing a deep hatred of all things English. The controversy over the new currency and the discovery of an assassination plot against King William soon occupied the centre of the political stage.[86] James Bateman could go on to become Lord Mayor of London,[87] the blemish of his association with the Company of Scotland glossed over, the shadow of the Tower no longer troubling his sleep.

William Paterson now made the most fateful decision of his life. He gave up all ambition for a 'Scotch East India Company' controlled from London and went north to Edinburgh. He was not, in the end, to prove any luckier in Scotland.

Chapter Six

The Lure of Darien

The resolutions passed by the House of Commons on 21 January 1696, arraigning some 22 directors of the Company of Scotland as treasonable criminals, effectively killed off the 'Scotch East India Company'. Of the 200 who promised their subscriptions in November only a handful, including Paterson and Smith, actually honoured their promise and made a down payment of 25 per cent in cash as required. The other shareholders, such as the wine-merchants Bateman and Wilmer – and even Robert Douglas – decided the risk was too great and withdrew.

Paterson now stood at a crossroads in his career. The Orphans' Bank was in its infancy and he had ambitions to build it into a rival to the Bank of England in terms of size and profitability. But he was also loath to give up the battle to launch his great challenge to the established monopoly companies. He had an undeniably stubborn streak to his nature. And Blackwood and Balfour stayed long enough in London to press him to continue. Perhaps they used similar arguments to those employed by Sir Andrew Fletcher of Saltoun in 1692, that Paterson: 'should trust the fate of his project to his own countrymen alone, and to let them have the sole benefit, glory and danger of it; for in its danger Fletcher deemed some of its glory to consist'.[1]

To the Edinburgh men the London débâcle had been a source of mixed feelings. Any perverse pleasure they may have felt at the discomfiture of the great merchants of London from the scheme was mixed with anger at the outrageous treatment meted out to them by both Houses of the Westminster parliament. Proud Scots as they were, they were determined to prove that they could make a success of the scheme, if only to show the arrogant English they could run a trading company without them. They were also canny enough to appreciate that there was little chance of achieving that goal without having Paterson at the helm. To persuade him to come and join them in Scotland, they could turn Paterson's own words to their cause. He had referred to the Company of Scotland as a 'great and noble undertaking'[2] and had raised the hopes of all Scotland. He surely could not abandon it now.

Paterson probably agonised over the decision. A move to Edinburgh, as Blackwood and Balfour urged, would mean turning his back on his London ambitions for many years to come. But, on the other hand, Paterson was never one to shirk a challenge. He also saw destiny (in the shape of God's will) at work in all things. He had a belief in an active God who had His own secret purposes for every man and women – the 'secret hand of God',[3] as Paterson once called it. And there could be no finer purpose than to rescue his fellow countrymen from poverty and despair. But it would not have been Paterson if the question of money had not also entered into it.

The collapse of the 'Scotch East India Company' meant that the 'understanding' he had reached at the board meeting of 29 November – that he would in time receive payment for his work in developing and setting up the enterprise – was now worthless. If the Edinburgh directors could renew the pledge that he should be properly rewarded he would be much more inclined to make the move north. Blackwood and Balfour undoubtedly gave him their promise that he would be amply compensated for his trouble, even suggesting that a payment of £15,000 would be a fair reward.[4]

Paterson made one other condition. He wanted his business partner, James Smith to join him in Edinburgh, indeed to be sent ahead to get the business of the company under way. Blackwood and Balfour had met Smith and had already seen him in action. They readily agreed.[5]

There was an additional factor at play in Paterson's decision to abandon London and come to live and work in Edinburgh. At some time during 1695 Paterson had been introduced to one of the world's great explorers. When we last heard of William Dampier he was taking part in the daring buccaneer raid across the Isthmus of Darien led by John Coxon. Now he was back in London, with an extraordinary story to tell. Herries for once may be right when he tells us that Paterson's interest in Darien was reawakened and revamped by 'some new light he had purchased by conversing with Dampier'.[6] But what exactly was this new revelation?

Dampier had spent nigh on six years with the buccaneers after he and the others had left Robert Allison guarding their ships at Golden Island.

When he had grown tired of chasing Spanish treasure ships and raiding Spanish ports he had turned explorer instead. In the company of Captain John Swan he had struck out west from Mexico across the still largely uncharted Pacific Ocean, found the coast of Australia, and then sailed by Java and the Cape of Good Hope to reach the English Channel in September 1691, one of the first Englishman since Drake, more than a century earlier, to complete a circumnavigation of the world.

During the long years of his Gulliver-like travels he had kept a detailed journal, a vivid account of the adventures he had enjoyed that reads today like a *Boys' Own* story. He had also exercised his talents as an artist and chart-maker in keeping a scientific record of the peoples and lands he had encountered, and the seas he had roamed. In the years after 1691 he spent long days assembling them into a manuscript that he hoped one day would be published as a book with the catching title of *A New Voyage Round the World*.

When Paterson met Dampier, the sea captain could show him his almost completed manuscript, and talk about the adventures he had had as he crossed the Pacific, the great South Sea. He had found it much easier to cross this vast ocean than he had imagined. This was a subject that became a favourite hobby-horse of Dampier's, as we know from an account of his having dinner with Samuel Pepys shortly after the book went on sale in 1697. The diarist John Evelyn tells us:

> I dined with Mr Pepys where was Capt Dampier, who had been a famous buccaneer ... [Dampier] seemed a more modest man than one would imagine by relation of the crew he had assorted with. He brought a map of his observations of the course of the winds of the South Sea, and assured us that the maps hitherto extant were all false as to the Pacific Sea.[7]

Dampier's voyage from Cape Corrientes in Mexico to the island of Guam, a distance of some 7,300 miles, had taken only 51 days with 'steady trade winds astern of them.'[8] Dampier reported that Spanish silver bullion ships were already sailing from Mexico to the Philippines on these winds, and then returning to America, courtesy of the equally dependable westerlies blowing across the Pacific at 40 degrees north.

Dampier's revelations immediately restored Paterson's interest in Darien as the natural crossroads of the world. If Dampier was right, then it was possible to reach the western Pacific rim by sailing west from Britain in as little as five months. A voyage from Britain to Darien,

taking advantage of the north-east trade wind could be accomplished in
three months. Once across the Isthmus, the onward voyage to, say,
China or Japan – on Dampier's evidence – could take at most a further
three months. Sailing by the established route by way of the Cape of
Good Hope, a ship could take up to a year to reach the same point on
the globe.

It throws light on Paterson's claim, made in 1701, that using Darien
as a bridge between the two oceans would mean that: 'The time and
expence of navigation [from Europe] to China, Japan, and the Spice
Islands, and the far greatest part of the East Indies, will be lessened
more than half'.[9] Expense would be cut, not only because of the saving
in the time taken to make the voyage but because ships travelling on a
steady course with a trade wind astern could manage with smaller crews
than ships that had to take the circuitous route around the southern
capes. Dalrymple of Cranstoun was certain on this point. He tells us
that:

> Paterson knew that ships which stretch[10] in a straight line from one point
> to another, and with one wind, run less risks, and require fewer hands
> than ships which pass through many latitudes, turn with many coasts, and
> require many winds.[11]

By the time Dalrymple wrote these words, 70 years after Paterson first
advanced the claim, this had become accepted fact.

Dampier's manuscript convinced Paterson that it would be feasible
and profitable to run a trade with lands and islands of the western
Pacific by sailing west. In Macaulay's words, his plan added up to 'the
original project of Christopher Columbus, extended and modified'.[12]
Sailing to east and south-east Asia by sailing west had another advantage
for a company based in Scotland. There would be no need to pass
through the English Channel, avoiding the unwelcome attentions of the
French privateers operating out of Brest. Instead the company could
send ships round the North of Ireland and from there to the Caribbean
by way of the open Atlantic Ocean. Freed from the restraints imposed by
the interests of his erstwhile London allies, Paterson allowed his dreams
of a new world trading order to come to the fore once again. And
Darien, it now seemed to him, had a major role to play in making it
happen.

Before leaving London his house in Soho and its effects had to be disposed of, his directorship at the Orphans' Bank brought to an end, and his other business affairs in London tidied up. Such details occupied January and February and delayed his departure until early March. In the meantime, James Smith, no longer employed by the City of London Corporation, had been sent ahead. He took up residence in Edinburgh around the end of January, and was quickly introduced by Balfour and Blackwood to the other 'nominees',[13] the Scottish promoters of the Company listed in the Act.

Smith found Edinburgh a city seething with dented Scots pride at the high-handed behaviour of the English parliament. To Scots eyes it showed the depth of English prejudice against her sister nation. The notion that the nascent Scots company would ruin the great East India Company was laughable. As one pamphleteer, describing himself as 'an unfeigned and hearty lover of England' put it:

> this Company which the Scots are establishing, is not to drive a traffic with some little island, or diminutive place … but is to carry on a Commerce between two vast continents, and all their adjacent islands, where besides what is … possess'd [by the English], there are many large Territories, for others to occupy and found a traffick in …[14]

It seemed to the Scots that the row over the privileges given by King William to the Company of Scotland was merely a fig-leaf to cover crude English prejudice against all things Scottish. Ensuring the survival of the Company of Scotland had become no less than a patriotic duty.

Smith was shrewd enough to see that the hurt national pride of the Scots could be turned to the advantage of the company. But only if the subscription books could be opened quickly while the mood lasted. Little or no preparation had been made for the Scottish launch of the company. Smith's chief priority would have been to put that right.

The very first meeting of the Scottish 'nominees' of which we have a record was held on Friday 14 February. Smith was on hand to advise just how the process of subscription should be organised. The first decision taken by the committee was to order an 'advertisement' for the opening of the subscription book to be urgently prepared and printed.[15] The next morning, Saturday 15th, they met again and agreed that the subscription book should open on Wednesday 19th, just two working days away. Even allowing for the fact that the preamble had been prepared by Belhaven, Balfour and Blackwood the previous December when they were in London, it seemed an impossibly tight timetable and so it proved. Paterson had stressed all along the importance of arranging for some big names to appear at the top of the list. That meant canvassing for support and cultivating the chosen few. Two working days was simply not enough time to do it.

In the end the subscription book was opened a week later than planned on 26 February in the unassuming surroundings of Mrs Purdie's Coffee House[16] in Edinburgh's High Street close by the old Mercat Cross, a snug enough place with sturdy doors that served in equal measure to keep in the heat and to keep out the stench of the street. James Smith had been appointed as one of a committee of five to receive the subscriptions. Any three had the authority to take the names and the pledges of shareholders. We can assume that the three most experienced in trade – James Balfour, Robert Blackwood and James Smith himself – did most of the work.

The subscription got off to a flying start. Some of the greatest grandees in the land came trundling up the High Street in their horse-drawn coaches to put their signature or their mark[17] on the page as underwriters to the scheme. First to add her signature was the Duchess of Hamilton, who held one of the great landed titles of Scotland in her own right. She picked up the freshly cut quill pen, dipped it in the company ink, and solemnly wrote in her curving decorated hand: 'We, Anne Dutches of Hamilton and Chastleherault, etc, doe Subscrive for Three Thousand Pounds Sterling'.[18] Close behind came another two noble wives, the Countess of Rothes and Lady Margaret Hope, each subscribing for themselves and for their sons. Only then was the first 'commoner' allowed to inscribe his name on the first page, and then no everyday commoner. The fourth signature belonged to the Lord Provost of Edinburgh, the city's chief magistrate and councillor. This was Sir Robert Chiesly who thus became the first of the nominees to have his name inscribed in the book.

There followed a string of Scottish 'lairds', country gentlemen who distinguished themselves by adding the name of their estates to their surnames as a status symbol of the time. All lived within a few hours travel on horseback from the capital and all were happy no doubt to find their names on the same sheet of paper as the Duchess. Such men, for example, as James Pringle of Torwoodlee, who subscribed for £1,000, and Sir William Hope of Kirkliston who put his name down for a more modest, if still substantial, £500. There were some distinguished lawyers, a smattering of merchants, and on that first day, one senior academic at Edinburgh University – Alexander Rule, a professor of oriental languages no less, perhaps anxious to serve the company as a translator and interpreter.

Late in the day the irascible Sir Andrew Fletcher of Saltoun, the man who had brought Paterson to Scotland and set the wheels in motion just four years before, bustled in and showed his continued enthusiasm for the company by subscribing for £1,000. For him, as for so many better-off Scotsmen, national pride had perhaps led him to subscribe more than prudence would have advised.[19] When the tellers totalled up the subscriptions on the end of that first day there was quiet satisfaction. £50,000 sterling had been pledged by 74 signatories, a sixth of the target for the whole subscription. But, thereafter, any hopes that Scotland might match the London subscription faded quickly.

A spell of severe winter weather blanketed Edinburgh in snow and ice for the two weeks that followed, cutting off country estates and making the cobbles of the High Street treacherous and unwelcome. Sheltered from the biting cold, Balfour, Blackwood and Smith kept an increasingly lonely vigil huddled around the fireplace in Mrs Purdie's. By 7 March, ten days after the books had opened, the number of subscribers coming to put their names in the book had slowed to a trickle, with just three investors calling to put their name on the list that day. It seemed that the doubters – those who argued that a poor country like Scotland could never raise a sum as large as £300,000 – were to be proved right after all.

It is a tribute to the reputation of William Paterson that the news of his arrival in Edinburgh was to transform sentiment overnight. On 14 March there had been just one solitary subscriber, even though the subscription book had now been moved to its own special room in Parliament Hall. Then news spread that the great Paterson himself had come to the Scottish capital to put himself at the head of the company. On 30 March, a week or so after Paterson's arrival, 135 investors came to Parliament House with their pledges of support. The figures peaked the following day when nearly 200 subscribers queued to put their name on the list.[20]

Of course the weather had its part to play in the upsurge. But nobody doubted at the time that the Paterson name had its own magic, leading many hitherto cautious and canny Scots to rush to pledge such savings as they had locked in their chests to this great new enterprise. Paterson for a while bestrode the narrow streets of Edinburgh like a colossus. He had given England its national bank after all. And his energy and eloquence won men to his cause as he raised Scots eyes up from the grinding hardships of daily life to the bright prospect of future riches. For a people that felt themselves oppressed and disadvantaged, a new champion had emerged, a new William Wallace, armed not with a sword but with a balance sheet and a pen.

Walter Herries captured well the mood of Edinburgh in the weeks following Paterson's arrival on its cold and windy streets:

> Paterson had more respect paid, than his Majesty's High Commissioner, and happy was he or she that had the favour of a quarter of an hour's conversation with this blessed man. When he appeared in public, he look'd with a head to be full of Bussiness and Care, as if he had Atlas his burthern on his back; and if [anyone] had a fancy to be reputed Wise the first step he was to make was to mimic Paterson's Fiz...[21]

Paterson's stature among the ordinary folk of Scotland was nowhere better captured that in an outburst of popular song, the Patersonian Ballads of 1696. The composers may have been lacking in sophistication, but they could still sing of 'wise Paterson', 'judicious Paterson', the prophet who came north to Edinburgh with a gospel of redemption and his own band of devoted disciples:

> They made it evident, that trade by sea
> Needs little support [other] than being free:
> Freedom's the polar star by which it steers
> Secure its freedom and it nothing fears;
> ...
> Trade has a secret nature none can see
> Tho' ne'er so wise, except they traders be.

These primitive versifiers glorified everything Paterson stood for, even the joint-stock principle:

> The want of money such joint stocks supply,
> Where many gain by few men's industry.[22]

Until now Scotland could boast of no great economic thinker, nobody who had a breadth of vision to see that prosperity depended on a mixture of enterprise and the creation of the financial institutions that gave enterprise the power to lever up wealth. There had certainly never been anyone with the ability to depict this process in a way that ordinary people could understand. As Herries describes it, with some element of malignant exaggeration, the Paterson effect flowed deep:

> They came in shoals from all corners of the nation, rich, poor, blind and lame, to lodge their subscriptions in the Company's house and to have a glimpse of the man Paterson.[23]

The vision of a great new trading company that would rival the Dutch and English East India Companies caught the public imagination. On 3 April, two weeks after Paterson arrived in Edinburgh, it was reported to the committee that the sum pledged had reached the target of £300,000 and that many landowners and town councils in the outlying districts, held back by a combination of the atrocious weather and natural caution, had missed out. The subscription target was therefore raised to £400,000, a staggering sum that has been estimated to equal just less than half of the entire wealth of Scotland at the time.[24] A quarter of this great sum was to be called up in June and the rest to be paid in instalments over ten years.[25] It was an encouraging start. But Paterson himself always appreciated that it was not enough, £400,000 being less than a third of the total capital of the East India Company. This would be one of the first issues the new elected directors would have to address.

The more immediate pressing issue was just who would sit on the 'Court of Directors' of Scotland's largest ever joint-stock enterprise. Paterson had naturally assumed that he would play the leading role, just as he had in London, and indeed he is hardly likely to have come to Scotland without some assurance on this point from Blackwood and Balfour. But now that the Company had a growing list of shareholders the decision was no longer theirs to make. The odd episode of the attempt to exclude Paterson from the board began on 24 March when the new subscribers elected a committee from their number to draft the company constitution. Seventeen out of the 20 of them were country gentlemen; among them there was but one solitary man of trade.[26] Paterson clearly expected little trouble. He and Smith had already produced a draft and they assumed the committee would act as a rubber stamp, rather than have a mind of its own. This had certainly been so in working with the ten nominees. It must have been something of a shock to find the new men were a distinctly unruly lot.

Under the Paterson and Smith plan, anyone named in the Act would automatically become a director, provided he held £1,000 or more of stock in the Company. Both he and Smith would therefore qualify through their subscription to the Company made in London. The other directors – bringing the total up to 25 – would be elected by all shareholders subscribing at least £100. There was no hint at first that the new constitutional committee was in a rebellious mood. Indeed by 8 April almost all the Paterson clauses had been accepted without serious opposition. But this was deceptive. Behind the scenes, a move was clearly afoot to block Paterson's path to executive power. On 13 April two surprise resolutions were placed before the committee. The first baldly declared: 'Those concerned are to take notice that none of the persons nam'd in the act of parliament are to be directors unless they be chosen'. The second, perhaps reflecting the resentment felt by some of Scotland's landowning elite at Paterson's celebrity on the streets of Edinburgh, sought to make his election impossible. It declared: 'that no persons can be chosen in this election who are not subscribers in Scotland'.[27]

Just which members of the committee were behind this move the records do not say. But Paterson must have been taken by surprise when the two resolutions were carried by a show of hands. It is safe to assume that the original promoters of the Act were just as shaken as Paterson, since they considered Paterson essential to the success of the whole enterprise. Still the situation was not irretrievable. They were aware that Paterson's draft constitution provided for another 25 directors to be co-opted on to the 'court of directors' by the elected directors. Paterson could still serve as a director provided his supporters commanded a majority of votes in the court.

For the next nail-biting four weeks, Paterson and Smith continued to guide the company as though nothing untoward had happened. It was agreed that £20,000 of the subscription money was to be assigned to Paterson to begin preparations for the first voyage,[28] while Smith was asked to seek out suitable trading cargoes in London. Neither knew if he would find employment in the company once the new board had been elected. The elections were to be held on Thursday 7 May, with the results to be announced at a general meeting of the subscribers in the High Council House, next to Parliament Hall, the following Tuesday, 12 May.

That morning of the 12th the shareholders packed into the Council House to hear Lord Belhaven read out the results. It was a tense moment, but it was almost immediately clear that the attempt to exclude

Paterson and Smith from the boardroom had failed. Of the original men named in the Act, men who had leant heavily on Paterson's expertise up to then, all but one were elected. The exception was Sir Robert Chiesly, who may have decided not to stand for election because of his duties as Lord Provost of Edinburgh. Some 16 new faces appeared on the new board, mainly landowners (reflecting their preponderance among the subscribers) but also a further three merchants from Glasgow (joining their fellow Glaswegian, John Corse), a clear indication of gathering interest on the West Coast of Scotland. By a rough reckoning all nine of the nominees might be expected to support Paterson, to which could be added the votes of the three new merchants. One or two votes from among the remaining thirteen would see him home and dry.

The issue was settled with a commendable display of urgency. No sooner had the body of subscribers left the building than an initial meeting of the new court of directors was convened in one of the smaller committee rooms. The first piece of business was to propose that Paterson be co-opted to the board and this was swiftly agreed to on a show of hands. Paterson was called in and gave a neat little speech thanking them for their support and pledging himself to work loyally and sincerely for the company. In the end his loyalty was to exceed even the highest expectations, and to go far beyond the call of duty.[29]

Two days later he was joined on the board by James Smith,[30] and a day later by another of his so-called 'acolytes',[31] a bright young man whose youthful looks concealed his depth of business experience. His name was Daniel Lodge. He had been born in Leith but put to the test as a businessman in the counting houses of Amsterdam. He had then come to London to work at the newly created Bank of England in the important position of 'cashier', an office that included guarding against fraud and counterfeiting.[32] We can only assume that he had quit the bank in disgust at the treatment meted out to Paterson and had in all likelihood followed him to work at the Orphans' Bank. Now in Edinburgh he was in at the birth of a third Patersonian project and could bask for the moment in his master's glory.

Indeed, the period from May to September saw the popularity of Paterson and his team at a peak, and his authority unchallenged. John Holland, busy launching the Bank of Scotland came back from a trip to London at this time and was able to report:

I found Mr Paterson very popular and in some measure Mr Smyth and Mr Lodge; and I found the whole nation universally in favour of the Indian and African Trade.[33]

Paterson was for the moment held in the highest respect. He had put the disappointments of London behind him and had bounced back to become the unchallenged leader of Scotland's greatest ever commercial enterprise.

Paterson in his life-time wrote hundreds of thousand of words on economics and business, but not one word about his own life and his family, except in his last will and testament. We can only suppose that he took the hardships of Edinburgh life in his stride. Whether his wife Hannah and his two stepdaughters found the change to their liking seems much more doubtful. In London they lived in one of the smartest little streets in the new West End, in a solid brick-built terrace house with its own front door. The sanitary arrangements – although primitive by modern standards – were among the best that could be found.

In Edinburgh things were very different. Unless the family dwelt in one of the larger detached house in the Canongate district close to Holyrood Palace – which seems unlikely – they would have had to reconcile themselves to life in one of the city's tenement buildings, many floors up, the only access by way of a steep narrow staircase that passed the doors of the poor on the lower floors. There was no running water. Bringing in supplies of water meant going to the nearest City well, hauling it up in a bucket from the dark depths, and then bearing it homeward, back bent, up those stairs. Of course the Patersons were now wealthy enough to have a serving girl to perform this daily task. But no amount of money could shelter the family from the squalor of the streets, watered every evening from above, as pails of waste of all description were thrown out with the cry of 'Gardyloo!' But this was an age where a wife in general obeyed her husband without question. And it was certainly not in Hannah Paterson's nature to question whether family life had to be sacrificed to the needs of business.

In that cool fresh May of 1696 William Paterson had other, more pressing matters, on his mind. The general hysteria then reigning in Scotland may have convinced many that Scotland was on the verge of commercial greatness. The reality was rather different. Scotland lacked the business brains, the men of experience needed to help organise and run the new trading concern. And the company was heavily under-capitalised. The first instalment of the subscription raised only £100,0000, a mere 6 per cent of the funds possessed by the English East India Company. What he had written in 1695 was no less true now: 'We must engage some of the best heads and purses for Trade in Europe [in our enter-prise], or we can never do it as it ought to be'.[34]

Smith and Lodge certainly provided some of that experienced brain power. When book-keepers and accountants were required it was to Smith the company turned. Perhaps he could recommend someone working in London with experience of this sort of enterprise and who might be prepared to come north. And when it came to deciding on which cargoes should be purchased for trading in the Indies they again sought his help, asking him to obtain suitable 'patterns' (by which was meant samples and prices), again from London. No-one seemed to believe, not even the most patriotic of Scots, that the backward Scottish economy could provide anything but a small portion of such goods.

As for the 'best purses for trade', Paterson had not abandoned hope that those in London might still be opened to them. Now that the storms of December and January had blown over, there was still a chance that many of the London investors could be brought back into the fold, if they could be approached discretely. So on 23 June Paterson and Smith presented a plan for reopening the books in London, a plan enthusias-tically endorsed by the board. It was agreed that Smith and James Campbell (a London Scot and partner of Walter Stewart, one of the original London promoters) should begin new soundings right under the nose of the East India Company.[35]

A week later, in a decision deliberately not entered into the minutes by a board anxious to keep its plans secret, it was agreed that a major effort should be made to raise finance in Holland and in Germany in return for a share of the capital and, of course, places on the board of the company. This was an idea that undoubtedly came from Paterson and Smith, a pair who had attempted to do just that once before in 1688. Secret plans were drawn up to send Paterson and Smith on a mis-sion to Europe in September, a decision confirmed on 3 August, when two of the Scots directors were chosen to accompany them. For the moment the record of the meeting merely hinted at the decision: 'no reasonable means or opportunities [are to be] omitted to make this the most diffusive and national joynt stock in the world'.[36]

Until the group was ready to leave for Europe, the company pressed ahead with other urgent business. One was a simple matter of what was to happen to the subscription money when it was gathered in. It could not all be spent at once, and it made no sense to leave it locked up in the company coffers earning no interest. Again Paterson had a plan, one which had already been discussed in London in late November of 1695, just before the parliamentary outcry against the company.[37] As early as 18 May, Paterson raised the issue at board level, pointing out that money should never lie idle where work could be found for it. The board therefore asked him to 'prepare a scheme of his thoughts concerning the improvement of the capital fund'.[38]

Paterson's thoughts were already well advanced. He envisaged that the Company of Scotland should establish its own bank, empowered to issue its own notes which could be used to finance business and create credit. But there was one formidable obstacle to this plan that he had chosen to gloss over. In July 1695 the Scottish Parliament had given a 21-year monopoly of all banking in Scotland to the new 'Bank of Scotland', the scheme projected by John Holland and Thomas Deans, among others.

Since 1693, Holland and Paterson had emerged as business rivals in Edinburgh. While Paterson was drawing up his scheme for the Company of Scotland, Holland had managed to sell the idea of a Bank of Scotland to the Scottish parliament, the first bank of its kind sanctioned by a special Act of Parliament anywhere in the world. Tweeddale had not wanted it, but he had been afraid to stand against the parliamentary will while the Glencoe controversy rumbled on.

Paterson had been furious, not only because Thomas Deans had jumped ship, but because he suspected the bank had insufficient reserves. He complained that the Act had been 'surreptiously gained and which may be of great prejudice, but it is never like to be of any matter of Good neither to us nor those that have it'.[39]

Holland was a formidable rival. He had learnt his trade as an accountant working as a junior with a great Dutch exponent of the art, Francis Beyer, a man who had looked after the accounts of the East India Company for 30 years and who certainly was no friend to Paterson. Despite Beyer's part in running Sir Josiah Child's corrupt empire, he and Holland have been credited with introducing the best Dutch accounting techniques to Britain, using a system based on 'checks and balances'. It was Beyer, himself a prominent shareholder in the bank, who backed Holland's election as first Governor in March 1696.[40]

Paterson could be headstrong, and his determination to go ahead with his scheme for recycling his company's money was probably driven in part by his dislike of Holland and Beyer. But he had an ingenious justification. He pointed to a clause in the Act setting up the Company of Scotland that expressly gave that Company power:

> by subscriptions *or otherways as they shall think fitt* to raise a Joynt-Stock or Capital fond ... to begin, carry on, & support their intended Trade of Navigation, and *whatever may contribute to the Advancement thereof*. [Author's emphases.]

This was a cover all clause that seemed to provide some element of legality – however scanty – for the banking project. Paterson certainly had no difficulty winning over the company's Treasury Committee, which gave the idea their blessing on 15 June. They were particularly impressed by the argument that, in an age of highwaymen and footpads, the work of their agents would be made safer since there would be no need to carry cash in the form of gold and silver coins. Rather like today's travellers cheques, endorsed bills were worthless except to the named person possessing them.

Within a fortnight, on 26 June, the first company 'notes' were issued. John Holland, who had himself come to live in Edinburgh in March, had his own intelligence sources on what was going on within Paterson's company, since four of its directors sat on his board. He was horrified at the whole idea. His own creation was as yet a fledgeling. Once word got around that the Bank no longer had a monopoly on business there was a risk of investor panic and a collapse in the value of the shares. Should this happen there was no way to restore confidence. Paterson's new scheme could have been calculated (and perhaps was) to bring the whole edifice of the Bank of Scotland crashing down.

Holland knew he could have put the matter in the hands of lawyers and have the issues hammered out in court (where Paterson must surely have lost on account of the specific monopoly rights given to the Bank of Scotland by an Act of the Scots Parliament) but he could scarcely do this without bringing the wrath of respectable Edinburgh down on his head. Some of the greatest families of Scotland had sunk their savings into Paterson's scheme, a project that now carried the hopes of the whole nation. The best Holland could do was to suggest that the two companies might meet and try to resolve the dispute amicably, but when the meeting finally took place in August Paterson was in no mood for compromise. The Company of Scotland was at the height of its prestige and he steadfastly refused to curtail its banking activities in any way.[41]

Paterson never found it easy to see the other man's point of view. He had a tendency to assume he held the moral high ground on most issues. It did not endear him to his enemies, and made even his friends feel uncomfortable. And it seemed to tempt fate unnecessarily. The fact that this particular display of hubris was to be followed within a year by public humiliation and disgrace must have given John Holland some grim satisfaction.

Unknown to John Holland, the Company of Scotland had just decided to take an enormous gamble on its future. Until July the directors had put off deciding just what the destination of the first voyage should be. Indeed they had agreed:

> That settlements or settlement be made with all convenient speed upon some island, river, or place in Africa or the Indies or both for establishing and promoting the traded and navigation of this company.

> [The] Committee came to several resolutions on ships, cargo's, stores and equipages needful for Africa and the East and West Indies but made no final decision on voyages and places of settlement until needful equipages have been prepared.[42]

But on the day these resolutions were passed Paterson had quite suddenly sprung on a few selected directors his new and startling proposal for a trading venture designed to open up the Pacific and create a new trade route to east Asia and to the islands and lands of the East Indies using the Isthmus of Darien as a staging post. He argued that establishing a base on the strategically sited Isthmus would give Scotland a chance to lead the world in demonstrating the benefits of free trade. They had enthusiastically embraced the idea.[43]

At the beginning of July when the first call was made on the subscribers for their initial 25 per cent, money had begun to pour into the company's coffers, almost £100,000 in the course of a week. This was a breath-taking vote of confidence by the shareholders, since 99 per cent of those who had subscribed to the company honoured their pledge to invest.

On 17 July, the company moved out of its temporary headquarters in the Town Council House, and into grand new offices in Mylne Square, then the most fashionable square in Edinburgh, just below the craggy heights of the castle, with a wonderful view over the rooftops of the Nor Loch (where Princes Street Gardens now lie) across broad acres of land enclosed with earth or stone walls, towards the Firth of Forth. There the small ships that used Leith harbour could sometimes be seen fighting their way in against the prevailing west wind. On a clear day you could catch sight of the distant mountains of the Scottish Highlands, wild country where Lowlanders seldom if ever ventured. It was one of the best views in Scotland. With the move into the brand new building, built by the king's own architect in Scotland, Robert Mylne, the company signalled to the world that it had to be taken seriously. The company directors got down to tackling the great issue of how the resources of the company could most judiciously be spent.

For this task they divided themselves up into committees. One committee considered just what industries should be promoted to supply cargoes for the great fleet of ocean-going sailing ships. Another sat considering the 'rules of employment' for seamen and clerks, accountants and ships' officers. But the most important committee was the Committee for Trade. It had been delegated the task of deciding the destination and cargoes for the first crucial voyage.[44]

The twenty-eighth of July was the day William Paterson had set aside to unveil his new project to the committee. He arrived at Mylne Square with Daniel Lodge carrying between them a great trunk full of maps and charts, journals and manuscripts, and other papers germane to the debate. The committee was small, just four Scottish directors plus Paterson and Lodge, meaning everyone had a chance to consider the materials it had taken Paterson years to collect. Some of the maps were stunningly beautiful, 'exact illuminated mapps' as the keeper of the minutes described them. As Paterson and Lodge passed them round the table they looked first at this option and then at that. There was much material on the East Indies and on Africa, but it was the exposition on finding a new route to East Asia via America that really caught the imagination. Paterson no doubt had a map of the known world to hand. On it he could point out how Darien lay at a natural cross-roads of the world, and was especially well placed to develop trade links with eastern

Asia and with the great new continent that everyone believed would one day be discovered in the South Pacific. Truly the country that established a base on the Isthmus would become, in a phrase he was to coin later: 'the arbitrators of the commercial world'.[45]

Prior to this meeting Paterson had never challenged the idea of a Scottish expedition to the East or the West Indies. And indeed as he outlined the choices round the table in Mylne Square, he was careful not to foreclose on those options. But it was the idea of Darien that captivated the committee. Now, all those dreams of a warm place in the sun, a million miles it seemed from dark and stormy windswept Edinburgh, were revived in the most vivid of colours. Paterson produced one piece of evidence that struck the Committee of Trade as conclusive. Among the maps and charts and papers lay the manuscript of a book unbound and in loose leaves that could be passed back and forward round the table. It had the matter-of-fact title of *A Description of the Isthmus of Darien*.[46] It was the work of Lionel Wafer.

This was the same Lionel Wafer who had raced across the Isthmus in 1680 in the company of Dampier, Coxon and Sharp, and who had then tried to make his way back with Dampier to the Caribbean in 1691. When Wafer had injured his leg, Dampier had been forced to leave him behind in the company of native Cuna Indians. Wafer was a clever man, and with the help of the little Spanish he knew, had taught himself to understand and speak Cuna in the six months he spent in their company. From them he learnt the secrets of the land.

He and Dampier had met up again soon enough and spent some years together on various buccaneering adventures, before Dampier set off across the Pacific and the younger man returned to London. When their paths crossed once more in London, possibly in 1692, Dampier had begun writing his great travel book on his global travels. As a result he had been quite happy to let Wafer describe their joint adventures in Darien. Wafer, after all, knew the place so much better than he did. Indeed he was happy to suggest to his readers they should acquire a copy of Wafer's book when it finally came to be published, which in the end was not until late 1699.

Just how Paterson had acquired the Wafer manuscript has never been explained. In all probability Wafer had given it to Dampier, who then handed it to Paterson, possibly in return for some payment.[47] This was the document that now lay before the Edinburgh directors in Mylne Square. Wafer had a way with words and a deep, if flawed, understanding of Indian culture. The picture he painted was of the noble savage, all but naked, capable of living at peace with the world, enjoying its god-given fruits. Here were seas teeming with fish, sandy palm-fringe shores where turtles could be easily caught, a land rich in wild pigs and wild cattle, and with a cornucopia of wonderful fruits and vegetables. It was a land in the Torrid Zone magically protected from the heat of the sun by tall tropical forests. Beneath the trees there was no dense jungle: there a man could ride a horse for days on end.[48]

There was something in the account for everyone around the table. For some it was the richness of the seas, for others the banana trees laden with fruit, for still others the forests rich in 'Nicaraguan Wood' the valuable dye-wood that Dampier himself had once cut in Honduras. One passage, in which Wafer described how the Spanish regularly gathered a ton of gold from the river beds in the course of a single year, may have made a particular impact. Some things were scarcely noticed. If this was a land unoccupied by the Spanish, what were the gold prospectors doing there? And no one seems to have picked up on the fact that the rainy season lasted for eight months of the year, or that rivers could become terrifying torrents in a matter of minutes. These were oversights they would live to regret. Paterson in his travels had experienced the wonder of the tropical downpour, and of the oppressive heat. He understood that tropical paradises could turn suddenly into tropical hells. The others around the table could see only the attractive side. Paterson never chose to disabuse them of their fantasies.

As far as Paterson was concerned Darien was no more than two great natural harbours, one on the north and the other on the south shore of the Isthmus, that one day would be linked by navigable rivers and a short road across the pass. But, try as he might to focus on his vision of Darien as the perfect trade hub, the four elected directors on the committee could not shake themselves free from the old Scottish yearning for a colony in the sun, a successful re-run of what had been attempted in Carolina back in 1684.[49] The clerks wrote down the agreed conclusions and read them back to what had become a highly excited body of men:

Upon viewing and perusing of several manuscripts books and journals and other papers of discovery in Africa and the East and West Indies produced by Mr Paterson and also hearing several designs and schemes of trade and discovery by him projected:

That it is the opinion of this committee that the said Mr. Paterson hath
with much pains & expence procured several Discoveries of Places of
Trade and Settlement which if duly prosecuted may prove exceeding benefi-
cial to this company.[50] [Author's emphasis.]

Paterson did what he could to get the project back on course. He
insisted he had not talked of 'places of trade and settlement', but merely
'places of trade'. The clerks duly amended the record, but clearly failed
to expunge the idea of 'settlement' from the minds of the Committee.
Indeed, for the moment, the meeting chose to fudge the issue. The people sitting round the table at Mylne Square agreed, it appears without
dissent, that the first expedition mounted by the company, to trade, to
settle, or do both, should sail to Darien.[51] In the best traditions of cloak-
and-dagger mysteries the committee then ordered that:

some particular discoveries of the greatest moment to the design of the
Company ought to be committed to writing and seal'd by Mr Paterson and
not open'd but by special order of the Court of Directors and that only
when the affairs of the Company shall necessarily require the same.[52]

They also asked Paterson to lodge all the manuscripts and papers
they had gazed on that morning with the company for its use. This was
asking a lot, since for centuries the possession of accurate maps and
charts, and reliable intelligence about trade in these faraway places, had
been the key to successful expeditions. The Portuguese had kept the
Dutch and English out of the East Indies for a century by keeping their
information to themselves. And the Spanish had gone so far as to ditch
their maps and charts in the sea rather than let them fall into the hands
of commercial rivals.[53]

Paterson knew this well enough, and he had not as yet seen a penny
of the £15,000 promised to him by Balfour and Blackwood. He took the
chance to suggest some financial reward was in order, a plea backed up
by that familiar litany – he had spent years of his life developing the
scheme, he had given up all to come here to Edinburgh, he alone had
the business expertise to mount a successful expedition. Some reward
was surely in order. So the committee did what it could, expressing the
opinion that

the said Mr Paterson hath ... been at a vaste charge of money in making
and procuring these discoveries of trade ... [and] that the pains expence
& dammage of the said Mr Paterson in promoting the said designs ...
ought to be taken into consideration by the Company.[54]

It was a delicate matter, since the £15,000 he had been promised by Balfour and Blackwood was a vast sum of money for the time and the company, as we have seen, was already short of capital. A week later the matter came before the full board. They made the right sort of noises, passing a resolution that acknowledged the enormous debt they owed to Paterson:

> considering the great experience that Wm Paterson, ... has been at for several years past in making valuable discoveries of commerce and navigation to the Indies And he having delivered in several curious manuscripts, books, Mapps, Journals, and other papers of commerce relating thereto henceforth to be appropriat to the company's use And having further evidenced his affection to his native countrey and The Company by relinquishing England and any profitable establishments he had or might present have in that Kingdom to his evident dammage and loss ...[55]

They suggested that Paterson should accept a payment of £7,500, payable in instalments, and as soon as the money was available. They assured him that more would be forthcoming if all went well. Paterson appears to have accepted the deal. In the end not a penny of this money came his way.

Still, from his point of view, another very positive decision arose out of this meeting. The plan to send him abroad to Europe to raise fresh capital was now to be implemented as soon as possible, with two of the elected directors in train. The choice fell on two of the most conscientious men on the board, Colonel John Erskine, a bluff military man and Governor of the second royal castle in Scotland at Stirling, and the well-meaning and honest landed gentleman, John Haldane of Gleneagles. James Smith who had yet to complete his work in London, where he had been sent to recruit sea captains and ship's surgeons as well as to attempt to bring the original London subscribers back into the company fold, was to join the party in Amsterdam.

Paterson now had to endure a frustrating two months before the chosen team got themselves ready to depart. Haldane and Erskine had to put their business in order, the one on his estate, the other in appointing a deputy to look after Stirling Castle. But you sense that they were never men in a hurry: that was simply not the way of doing things in Scotland.

Even when Paterson announced to the Board of Directors on 17 September that they were all ready to leave, it took another three weeks to get necessary arrangements completed. It was a bad augury for the future.

To be charitable, September was an extremely cold, wet month, and there had been a widespread failure of the Scottish harvest. Perhaps one in five Scots were facing starvation.[56] In rural districts, where these years of bad harvest had reduced many people to walking skeletons, it was said that the dying would crawl to the graveyard, for fear that otherwise they would never be given a proper funeral. Edinburgh became the home of thousands of beggars, squatting in rags at the narrow close entrances in the High Street, or begging on the steps of Parliament House. Both Haldane and Erskine, who had an estate at Carnock in Fife, may have found themselves caught up in arranging famine relief.

It was not until mid to late October that the three finally left on their mission, and agreed to meet up in Holland. Haldane made his way on horseback to London, where he was to pick up Smith. Paterson and Erskine were rowed out in a small boat, low in the water with the weight of their travelling bags, across the cold waters of the Firth of Forth to join a small man-of-war specially chartered for the purpose. As Paterson climbed aboard and settled himself into his cabin, he must have realised how much depended on this mission, and that his position within the Company was not as secure as he would have wished it. An unpleasant attack on his character had just made that abundantly clear.

In August, the London Scot and merchant, Robert Douglas, a man Paterson had not seen since the previous December, had arrived quite unexpectedly in the Scots capital, almost certainly at the invitation of one of the directors. Douglas was an East Indian man through and through and had signed for £1,000 worth of shares in London on the understanding that this was indeed a 'Scotch East India Company'. He had become a director the previous November, and had been called to give evidence before the House of Lords. He had of course never paid the money he had promised into the company.

The occasion of his visit is shrouded in secrecy. Certainly there had been some rumour round the board table in Edinburgh that the original plan of setting up a Company to exploit the trade with India and the East Indies had been quietly dropped. Douglas was just the man to

argue the benefits of such a trade to Scotland.[57] But once he had come
to Scotland Douglas somehow sensed – perhaps through discussing
trade matters with a member of the Committee of Trade, that the
Isthmus of Darien was now very much the favoured destination. When
he returned to London he sent back his thoughts in the form of an
extraordinarily prescient letter. He chose to assume that Paterson had
won the committee over to his plan, which he agreed was pure speculation. But, he argued, speculation made necessary by Paterson's obsession with secrecy. Paterson, he wrote, was:

> one who converses in Darkness and loves not to bring his deeds to the
> light that they may be made manifest Therefore all I can say at present
> against his projects must only be by way of supposing till tyme has brought
> his wonderful design to light.[58]

The 'wonderful design', he argued, was likely to be for a great trading emporium in Darien, a scheme he had first heard Paterson expound
to an entranced audience in an Amsterdam coffee-house as long ago as
1687. He warned that there was no 'Emperor of Darien' ruling in that
land, and therefore no-one to make a treaty with. Worse, he felt that
Paterson completely underestimated the Spanish presence there. They
would almost certainly fight tooth and nail to drive any Scots settlers out
of a site of such importance, overlooking as it did the sea-routes taken
by the ships of the Spanish treasure fleet. In the light of this he suggested the new Scottish project simply did not have the funds needed to
make a success of it. Paterson, he argued, should know this: 'He deceives
the Company [by] attempting so hazardous an undertaking with their
little stock... it may cost more millions than they have hundreds of thousands'.[59]

His diatribe was hardly fair. As far as we can tell, the secrecy over
Darien was insisted upon by the Committee of Trade itself and Douglas's
scheme for a conventional East India Company could scarcely have cost
less. But the fact that the Scots Colony in Darien faced exactly the sort
of problems predicted by Douglas has given him a reputation he scarcely deserves. We should remember that it was the same Douglas who was
the source of a particularly nasty smear that Paterson had been bribed
by the English East India Company to drive the Company of Scotland
to ruin.[60]

We do not know whether this letter was ever read out to the board,
but it appears in the archives of the company. It is safe to assume that

some of the points he raised would have been discussed privately among the directors. Paterson had certainly heard of it since he wrote a letter in his own defence to one of the grand and mighty directors, the Earl of Annandale:

> in all the course of my life my reputation was never called so much into question as about this matter, and it is no very easy matter to me, reputation being the only thing I am nicest in: and no doubt but malicious stories of me will fly like wildfire, in England at this time; since, I, in a special manner, lie under a national hatred. But patience, I must bear these as I have borne all the rest of my troubles.[61]

It displayed a certain Paterson weakness for self-pity. Heading out into the stormy North Sea, Paterson would need all the stoicism that was the other side of that particular character trait. One thing that Douglas wrote certainly rang true. This was a hazardous and dangerous undertaking, and the sums invested in it were not adequate to the task. Paterson knew, as the boat tossed and turned and the wind rose to a gale, that he was being put to his greatest test. The entire board were counting on his ability to extract large sums of money from the Dutch and Germans. He could not afford for his mission to Holland and Germany to fail.

Paterson left behind him in Edinburgh a company suddenly concerned about money. A quarter of the money paid in – £25,000 – had already been assigned for the purchase of ships on the continent. Now many of the subscribers found themselves in financial difficulty as Scotland entered yet another harsh winter and the famine intensified. The credit notes issued by the company under its banking arm alleviated the strain for some, but soon put the entire banking scheme into jeopardy. In October, within days of Paterson's departure for Holland, the company ceased the issue of notes and called a halt to any further banking operations. John Holland and the Bank of Scotland had survived their first great challenge.[62]

Paterson's dreadful ordeal as he crossed the stormy North Sea in a tiny ship got the mission to Holland off to a bad start. In typical understatement, he wrote of it as being 'a troublesome passage'. It had taken all of three weeks, and their ship had found it hard to keep course. As it approached the coast of Holland it encountered the 'Zeeland Convoy', a far-from-friendly Dutch fleet and had been forced to land at Campher, on the dunes north of Rotterdam. He and Erskine were forced to spend the night there to regain their 'land-legs' and return some colour to their cheeks.[63] In the early morning of 13 November they left for Rotterdam, where Erskine had been an exile during the grim years following the Monmouth Rebellion, and met some of the Scots community there to sow the seeds of interest before passing on swiftly to Amsterdam, where they arrived late in the afternoon of the same day.

The evening had already settled down to the sweet smells of fragrant smoke from a thousand pipes and the pungent aroma of exotic spices that rose from the warehouses of the Dutch East India Company close by the harbour.[64] Paterson knew the city well, and guided their horses to the great shipyard of Willem Direcksone, close by the Ij, where the hull of a great ship was to be seen slowly emerging from behind the lattice of the wooden scaffolding.

Alerted to their imminent arrival by that morning's post, Captain James Gibson would have been waiting to meet them. This was the same James Gibson who had carried the ill-fated Scots settlers to Carolina in 1684. One of Scotland's most experienced seamen, he had been selected on 23 June by the company to 'repair beyond the seas... where you shall inform yourselves of the most expeditious ways of purchasing or building five or six ships of about 600 tons each, well and sufficiently built'.[65] He was making good progress. He had purchased a fine ship, the *St Francis*, recently captured from the French and now being sold off as war booty, only four years old and fully fitted out with masts, sails, and 44 guns, and all for just under 50,000 guilders, about £1,500. This was generally considered a great 'pennyworth'.[66] And he had ordered a single new ship from Direcksone's Yard, the skeleton rising behind them. This was just a little smaller, but when finished would rival anything put to sea by the English East India Company, with its proud forecastle and its elegantly carved and gilded soaring stern.[67]

Gibson was undoubtedly a businesslike man of the sea and he had shown skill and initiative in his dealings with the Dutch shipmasters, although even he could not have foreseen that the forthcoming winter was to be one of the worst in Dutch history, bringing all shipbuilding to a halt. With such progress in hand, Paterson and Erskine could turn to the difficult job of raising capital. And they can hardly have thought their task was going to be otherwise. Amsterdam was home to the

United East India Company (the *Vereenigde Oostindische Compagnie* or the VOC), a company whose interests were threatened if the Scots had indeed found a new and more profitable route to the East Indies by way of the Pacific. And this was not London. There was no angry group of interlopers queuing up to put their names to the scheme. The VOC may have been a monopoly, but it was a popular monopoly with shares freely available to buy and sell. Why should Dutch investors rush to invest in a new Scottish Company when the Dutch company already had such an entrenched position? This would be a hard nut to crack. But Paterson and Erskine bent their backs to the task and seemed on the verge of a breakthrough when they reported in the icy dog days of January that they had found four men of sufficient stature willing to have their names placed at the top of the subscription list.

Jacob Larwood, Henry Wylenbrock, Isaac Cossart, and the Amsterdam Scot Alexander Henderson, were hardly names with the same rank as Anne, Duchess of Hamilton and Chatelherault, but Holland was a republic and men were valued more for their reputation than for any drop of 'noble blood' that might be said to be coursing through their veins. Certainly Paterson regarded their public support as a great coup, a view he somewhat naïvely felt was shared by all Amsterdam. He dashed off an upbeat letter to the anxious directors in Edinburgh:

> This fixing of these four men in our interests ... is looked on here as a great matter and a certain presage of success in our designs, their influence and example being considerable...[68]

In return for their subscriptions of £1,000 apiece, they were to be given a commission to act as factors for the Scottish Company in Amsterdam. They were to take charge of much of the planning needed for the first expedition – just how the ships should be fitted out, where the cannons and cannonballs should come from, even such details as what cargoes should be purchased.

Paterson regarded the deal he had struck with the four Amsterdam merchants as the first building block of his genuinely international company. And he was probably right in thinking these gentlemen would bring the benefits of Dutch business techniques to the new Scottish Company, where they were certainly needed. In a world where speedy communication over any great distance was impossible, he was also right to delegate such decision-making to the men on the spot. But he failed to anticipate the alarm that this decision caused to the conservative and cautious gentlemen in Edinburgh as the bills from Amsterdam began to flood in.

He assumed that the considerable number of Dutch merchants engaged as shareholders in the Company would act as encouragement to those wary burghers of Amsterdam who were holding back, just as had happened in London in the case of the Bank of England. But as a strategy it proved singularly unsuccessful. Admittedly the appalling freeze-up did not make things any easier, but the alternative homes for Dutch investment were just too many, and the risks inherent with the Scottish Company apparently too great. Indeed Paterson probably misjudged the Dutch attitude to risk. They had built their great companies one step at a time, organically. Paterson's scheme was simply too ambitious for Dutch taste.

When Paterson and Erskine quit Amsterdam for Hamburg in January not one subscription had come in to the four factors. But hope that a trickle of subscriptions would soon begin, a trickle that might grow into a flood when the warm weather returned, had not entirely been lost. Even so, the great mercantile cities of Germany now seemed a more likely source of the much-needed extra investment. In the North German ports of Hamburg, Bremen, Lübeck and Danzig, were to be found merchants who felt they had missed out on the boom in the trade to exotic lands. While Holland had been building up her presence in Africa, India and the East and West Indies in the first half of the 17th century, the German States were convulsed with religious and political conflict. The Dutch had rubbed salt into the wound by securing a stranglehold on much of the trade between the Baltic and Western Europe, a valuable trade in timber and furs, in iron ore and amber, that had once been dominated and controlled by the merchants of Hamburg and Lübeck.

Paterson would have known all this from his friendship with James Smith, whose father was even then employed as a factor for the Elector of Brandenburg.[69] He also knew that Hamburg had the capacity to be a new Amsterdam, strategically placed on the River Elbe 50 miles from where it joined the North Sea. The Elbe was the gateway to central Germany and beyond. It had been on Paterson's suggestion that the company had sent an agent to Hamburg in June 1696, to buy up ships or have them built in the city's very competitive shipyards. This man, the Scots sea captain, Alexander Stevenson, had made a good start, placing orders for four new Scottish ships to be built and fitted out. As early as October all four were well on their way to completion. But then a decision was made in Edinburgh that a London firm which also had an office in Hamburg should be appointed as factors to the Company, carrying out much the same job as the four Dutch factors in Amsterdam. This was the firm of Francis Stratford Snr and Jnr.

While in Amsterdam James Gibson seems to have come to a *modus vivendi* with Dutch factors, Stevenson in Hamburg chose to see the Stratfords as insufferable meddlers. On the other hand, as polite and well-mannered English gentleman they found the coarse Scottish sea captain hard to deal with. On 16 February the elder Stratford wrote to the Edinburgh directors describing the somewhat delicate stand-off that had arisen in Hamburg.

> When Messrs Erskine and Paterson have arrived … [we] shall obey their commands in everything relating to your affairs provided they do not enjoyn us to consult or have any business with Mr Stevenson, for he having shewn a great pique against us without the least reason.[70]

The fact that Stevenson was supervising the construction and fitting of four brand new ships in the most trying circumstances, the worst winter in living memory, cannot have made the job any easier. But the Stratfords reported that they were not alone in finding him difficult. He already had had more than one blazing row with the master shipbuilder.

Even as Stratford's letter made its slow way to Edinburgh Paterson and Erskine had taken to the road to make the 250-mile overland trip to Hamburg, an excruciatingly miserable journey since they sorely lacked the furs to keep out the cold. When they reached the Elbe they found it frozen over from bank to bank. Across the river the lights and the smoke of the city, beckoned – with the dim outline of the great cathedral of St Nicholas floating as a ghostly presence above the houses. They hastened across, entering the 'new city'[71] through its fortified gates, and hurried to the office of Francis Stratford, Snr and Jnr, to announce their arrival.

They brought close on their heels a change in the weather. When they arrived Paterson and Erskine were taken by the Stratfords to see the four ships ordered by Stevenson. They were fine vessels, which would weigh about 400 tons each when finished off. They had been ready to launch

for some time, but a thick layer of ice covering the harbour had prevented it. Then, around 1 March the thaw set in and spirits were raised.

On 5 March Peterson could write in his old, confident style, that
Hamburg could be the turning point. Where Hamburg led others would
follow. And the omens were favourable. The city already appeared
thrilled to be playing such a central role in this great new enterprise. He
declared that: 'This is the only place besides Scotland where both
Government and People favours us.'[72] Paterson added for good measure, with little sign of sympathy for the ship-builders, that:

> The four ships are like well to be the best that ever were built here and per-
> haps the cheapest that has been built in Europe and that everybody says that
> the builders will sustain great loss by them but that is no fault of ours.[73]

This air of bullish swagger was soon replaced by a more sober assessment of the difficulties that still lay ahead. When they were in
Amsterdam, Paterson and Erskine had been told that there were under-
cover moves by government officials there to discourage merchants
sinking their lot with the new Company of Scotland. But it had been
hard to prove. Here in Hamburg the chief conspirator against Paterson
and his subscription books was happy to come out in the open.

On 19 February, a few days before Paterson and Erskine reached the
city, Francis Stratford reported to the directors in Edinburgh that:

> ... three days ago [the British Resident here] sent for Deputees from the
> Senate demanding of them that they should not enter into any treaty with
> your directors but on the contrary should acquaint him ... with any
> Proposal that should be made on behalf of the Company.[74]

The 'Resident' of Hamburg had the status of King William III's official
representative in the free city of Hamburg, a sort of mini-Ambassador
for both England and Scotland. In 1697 the position was held by an elderly member of the Diplomatic Service, Sir Paul Rycaut. His formal
warning to the members of the Hamburg Senate that they should steer
clear of the Company of Scotland could hardly be kept a secret, certainly
not in a city as independently minded as Hamburg. There were many
English merchants here, members of the oldest of the English chartered
companies, the Hamburg Company. But they were outnumbered by the
Germans and the Dutch. To these European merchants, Rycaut was an
interfering old busybody who could be safely ignored. After all, the writ
of King William did not run there.

Stratford told Paterson and Erskine about Rycaut's interference soon after their arrival in Hamburg, provoking a bizarre meeting between the two somewhat bedraggled Scottish travellers and the well-dressed English 'Resident'. Two days after they arrived in the city, they turned up at the official residence and, against all protocol, asked for a meeting there and then. Rycaut had never expected that the wily Scotsmen would ever have the effrontery to come unannounced to confront him, but the rather frail old diplomat took the opportunity to sound them out on their mission. While they gave him evasive answers, they asked him, in a direct manner he was not accustomed to dealing with, why he had asked the Senators to become spies for him and the English government. He chose not to dissemble. He had orders from Whitehall to do all he could to oppose the Scots in their search for financial backers here in Germany.

It had been a year and more since Paterson and his fellow directors had been hauled before parliament. This was the first indication that the English government at Westminster was still determined to snuff out the upstart Scottish company. Characteristically Paterson made light of it. The meddling of Rycaut, he decided, had had the opposite effect to the one he intended. His intervention had:

> animated the People more and we find a great and general Inclination here to [invest] in the Company. [We] have now ordered the ... Preamble for [the] Subscription to be translated into High Dutch and hope speedily to make a beginning. The people here thinks it the most happy Proposal ever was made in Hamburgh.[75]

By 20 March the ice had melted enough to allow the launch of the first of the four Scottish ships: a second followed a day later. The shipyards rang to the celebrations and Rycaut feared that the sight of these fine new ships – fine advertisements for the sterling workmanship that went into Hamburg-built ships – might be enough to bring the Hamburg merchants in *en masse*. Rycaut's spies reported that Paterson was holding 'several conferences with the most rich and monied merchants of this city, at which several articles were agreed which were not as yet made public'.[76]

This sounded ominously like the makings of a real business partnership between Edinburgh and Hamburg – just the sort of shot in the arm Paterson and the Edinburgh directors needed. And not just Hamburg. Paterson announced at these conferences that they had the support of three prominent German noblemen, the Dukes of Cell, Brunswick and Wolfensmittel, and that subscription books were to be opened not just in Hamburg but in Bremen and Frankfurt, and even as far away as Leipzig and Dresden. He was on the point of calling into being a new economic alliance between Scotland and Central Europe.[77]

Yet, within a month, the well of sympathy was to suddenly run dry. The high hopes of March were swept away by a damaging scandal that seemed to come out of nowhere to engulf the little Scots delegation. The chief responsibility for this bizarre turn of events rested on the shoulders of one of Paterson's closest allies, the man who knew Germany best, James Smith. The disgrace of Smith and the fall of William Paterson were closely linked. Both were bound up with the great English financial crisis of 1696–7.

Chapter Seven

The Fall of Paterson

James Smith had made himself almost indispensable to the Company of Scotland by the middle of 1696. Nobody leafing through the minute books and other records of the Scottish Company for that year can fail to be impressed by the range of his work. Here he is engaged as a surveyor of coal-mines, there as the seasoned merchant expert in dealing with London manufacturers whose goods might be highly valued in the Indies. But most of all he is turned to for advice on all matters dealing with finance and book-keeping.

He is one of only five men, and the only one not a Scot, entrusted with gathering in from the sundry subscribers – from the highest Duke to the meanest of small merchants – the first quarter of their pledged investment in the company during June 1696. And it is to him that the directors turn on 23 June when they need a man of experience and influence to go to London in search of further investors. He is trusted to set up an office there and take care of the Company's good name. Then, on 3 August, in his absence, the whole board paid him the even greater honour of electing him as one of the four directors to be sent to Europe on a mission to raise the new funds and recruit the experienced business partners that Paterson maintained were vital if his dream of a new world order in trade was ever to be realised.

Smith (or Smyth – pronounced Smith – since the versions were interchangeable even in the course of a single correspondence) is clearly a man ranked second only to Paterson in terms of influence and authority within the Board of Directors. Of course Paterson had personally recommended him to the board, but he could scarcely have risen to such heights had his advice and business judgement not been valued. Yet there were some sitting at the boardroom table who never quite trusted the man, people who had heard the whispers about him behind his back, the wild rumours later to be published by Walter Herries in his scurrilous attack on Paterson and his circle. And indeed, there were events in his past that he must have wished to keep hidden from the Edinburgh directors. These concerned both his work as a lobbyist for the Corporation of the City of London when in 1693 and 1694 it was struggling to have the Act establishing the new Orphans' Fund pushed through Parliament, and his later involvement with what was seen at the time as an attempt to defraud the Bank of England by passing counterfeit bonds.[1]

His work for the City of London has already been touched on but it deserves closer examination. Smith was one of two lobbyists employed by the City Corporation to smooth the passage of the Orphans' Fund Act. The other was Charles Nowis. Both were paid handsomely, the City awarding each a payment of £3,500 for promoting the successful Act and for 'the greate charges and expenses they were at in soliciting the same, the promises and the encouragements given them by most of the Orphans and the great risk and hazard they ran therein'.[2]

The reference to 'great risk and hazard' quite clearly relates to their need to resort to bribery on a grand scale, especially in relation to Westminster politicians. Indeed, as mentioned previously, the case was so scandalous that the Speaker of the House, Sir John Trevor, was expelled from the House of Commons in disgrace because of it in 1695. Trevor was found to have taken a bribe of a thousand gold guineas (worth nearly £1,500 at the time) to make sure the Act had a smooth passage through the Commons. He was a notably corrupt man, rumoured to have received £10,000 a year in illicit payments from many different sources. The response of the Commons was to condemn him for a 'high crime and misdemeanour' with a thunderous shout of 'Aye'.

Macaulay did not spare him in his summing up: 'The indiscretion of Trevor had been equal to his baseness; and his guilt had been apparent on the first inspection of the accounts of the city'.[3] Smith was in all probability involved in this affair, along with Nowis. Nowis certainly seems to have been an unsavoury individual since he was later prosecuted for obtaining his payment from the City by deception.[4] If guilt were possible to establish by association alone, then Smith might stand condemned. But that, of course, would be unfair. The use of bribery was a regrettable but common practice at the time and Sir Josiah Child had showed how it could be done on a grand scale without ever facing prosecution. Without bribery the City could not have had its Act, since 'private bills', as they were termed, had no priority in parliament and would have become snarled up by the arcane rule that a draft Act could only be passed into law if approved by both Houses of Parliament in a single parliamentary session, which in the 1690s lasted barely six months.

Smith's work may have been unsavoury, but it hardly merits damning him as a rogue. He was merely trying to help the City grandees out of the hole they found themselves in.[5] However, the second incident, in which he attempted to off-load fake bonds in the name of the Orphans' Fund on to the Bank of England in the summer of 1695, looks more serious.[6] He was arrested with another man, Aubrey Price, and both were imprisoned on charges of fraud. They escaped prosecution only because the Bank of England did not press charges after they 'discovered their accomplices, and made satisfaction and restitution to the ... Governor and Company of the money they had defrauded them'.[7] This embarrassing business had yet to be fully resolved when Paterson and Smith launched the London subscription to the Company of Scotland: Smith's pardon was not authorised until 14 December 1695.[8]

This was a past that Smith was anxious to keep under wraps, lest it provide ammunition for any enemies he might have on the Edinburgh board. Of the directors in the Scottish capital, only Paterson knew the damning details, and that knowledge had not shaken his confidence in a man who seems to have been a friend as well as a business partner. Whether the board at Mylne Square would have been so forgiving is another matter, especially since Smith was assigned a central role in overseeing the company's finances in the critical months of 1696.

On 23 June Smith and James Campbell had been entrusted with the challenging task of raising new capital in London. They spent a fruitless few months calling on people like James Bateman, Anthony Merry, Abraham Wilmer, and many more, men who had so enthusiastically supported the cause of the company until parliament had stepped in. But not a penny was forthcoming. In the end only two subscribers paid what they had promised – Joseph Cohen D'Azevedo and Campbell himself.[9] This was effectively the end of any hopes that the London subscription might still supply the resources the company so desperately needed.

As a result, the most important function performed by Smith and Campbell was that of company's bankers in the City, a vital link in the chain that was to run from Hamburg and Amsterdam through London and on to Edinburgh. International trade depended on the issue of 'Bills of Exchange', bills issued in one country and settled in another in a different currency. London was second only to Amsterdam in having developed the necessary networks and the high degree of trust that was needed to make the system work. Edinburgh was simply not in the same league.[10]

Smith and Campbell might have been expected to work closely togeth-er on this task. But they did not. Campbell already had a business part-ner in Walter Stewart, one of the original group of London Scots Paterson had gathered around him. Smith, who enjoyed some standing as a London merchant before coming to Edinburgh, had his own premises in Bishopsgate Street, right in the heart of the City, some few hundred yards from Nathaniel Carpenter's house where presumably the pendulum clock still ticked away. It was hardly a satisfactory arrangement. Each party had their own systems of accounting, and no way of keeping an eye on each other's books. It was a division of labour that had significant con-sequences, especially for Smith, but ultimately for Paterson too.

It was not until September 1696 that the first whiff of a financial scan-dal reached Edinburgh. There was a board meeting on the 16th, for which Daniel Lodge, the bright young accountant Paterson had brought with him from the Bank of England, had prepared his monthly recon-ciliation of the accounts held in Edinburgh and those reported from London.[11] He reported his concern that his accounts and those submit-ted by James Smith did not seem to match.

There was no immediate panic. It was assumed to be no more than a simple book-keeping error, something a sub-committee could look into and easily sort out. Certainly, nobody at that point questioned Smith's competence or his honesty. In fact, on the following day, Edinburgh decided he should be asked to assume the demanding task of finding the experienced naval officers and deckhands needed for the first voyage, a job he was to share with Campbell, and with John Haldane, when he finally arrived from Edinburgh. The company looked to London to make up for the lack of seasoned sailors in Scotland. In the taverns along the Thames could be found many experienced Scottish sailors, some having risen to be in command of ships, others to be lesser ships' officers, and a few to become qualified ships' surgeons. These were men the company would need to mount its first expedition. It was a critical task that the board felt they could confidently put into the hands of Smith.

It was not until late October that Smith and his accounts were placed firmly back on the agenda round the Edinburgh boardroom table. Haldane had by then sorted out his affairs and was ready to leave for London, and from there go on later to Holland with Smith, where they were to meet up with Paterson and Erskine in Amsterdam.

For Haldane the journey to London was to be 'uneasy and troublesome',[12] buffeted by torrential rain and gale-force winds. But he rode grimly south, his three-cornered hat pulled down against the elements, two letters from the Committee of Trade, one for Smith, the other for Campbell, packed safely in his case. Each bore the company seal to protect them from prying eyes, but Haldane knew they contained a firm instruction that he, Haldane, should have full access to their account books.

At this stage nobody would have guessed that this investigation into an apparently mild accounting irregularity was to drag on for months, or that it would end with Smith humiliatingly shut up in an Amsterdam jail, an act that administered the *coup de grace* to the company's bid to bring in European purses and minds. Paterson was ultimately to take the blame in Edinburgh for this débâcle. He had been responsible, after all, for bringing Smith into the very heart of the company but, in fact, those who looked into the matter at the time exonerated him from all blame.[13] In the light of what we now know about the extraordinary currency crisis that gripped London over that miserable summer of 1696, it is perhaps time to look again at the events that led to Smith's disgrace. This was a crisis that turned England into a coinless society, the pound into the sick man of European currencies, and the Scots Company (which had no control over a situation not of its own making) into the hapless victim of the collapse of confidence in sterling, a collapse that was to add hugely to the company's costs.

Smith was a man caught in the centre of this economic maelstrom. Quite what he had to endure through these dark and stormy days of currency turmoil is easier to understand now. But at the time, the problems created for Smith were hardly appreciated, certainly not by the fair-minded but financially untutored Haldane. In its baldest version, the long-accepted Smith fraud story begins when £25,000 of the company's money is given in trust to William Paterson to finance the shipbuilding operations in Europe, with the hope there would be something to spare.[14] Most of the capital he transferred to Smith, in all some £17,000. Smith was able to produce receipts to prove he had spent

£9,000 of this on funding the London office and on the initial costs of buying, building and fitting out the ships. But the remaining £8,000 seemed to have vanished into thin air. This was a large sum certainly equal to hundreds of thousands of pounds in today's money.[15]

Smith should certainly have become a rich man if he had stolen such a sum. But no one has ever been able to show just what he might have done with this mountain of cash, if he had indeed embezzled it. Haldane, in his investigations, was forced to fall back on wild speculation: 'there is no great mysterie in this matter as people imagine he is a profligate person and had debt'.[16] How, when, and where he could have run up such debts in the first place was never explained. Nor did anybody seriously try to show just where he had ever shown signs of profligacy.

If the Haldane conclusions are unconvincing perhaps it is time to consider a second explanation for much, if not all, of the financial shortfall; that the time chosen to launch the Scottish enterprise in Europe was as bad a time to launch a Europe-wide trading business as could ever have been chosen. This was especially so because it was run, not out of London, but from Edinburgh, a small capital on the edge of Europe with as yet no significant foreign currency markets.

The financial crisis of the year 1696 was sudden and unforeseen, blundered into by statesmen who had no real understanding of how easily confidence in a currency could be undermined. The seeds of the disaster were sown a year earlier when William Paterson's old political ally, Charles Montagu, as we have seen, embarked on the radical reform of the English coinage. All the best thinkers of the time, including Paterson, cheered him on[17] and, indeed, the state of the English silver coins was quite scandalous. About 100 years previously Queen Elizabeth had issued a new set of coins in silver. They were made by the age-old method of cutting a pound's weight in silver into lumps of equal size and then hammering them into the shape of a disk and embossing them with the Monarch's head. No two coins were quite the same, nor of exactly the same weight.

After a century of use, this fine new currency had fallen prey to man's cupidity. The practice of coin-clipping was widespread. It involved clipping or shaving off a little silver from the edge of the coin – not so much as to make it obvious – and have the clippings melted down into bars of pure silver. By 1688 it was estimated that 15 per cent of the silver in English coins had vanished in this way.[18]

This was serious but not yet a crisis. The vast majority of coins still circulated without any great dispute between buyers and sellers (or between employers and workers) over whether a coin was really worth what it claimed to be. But this relatively benign situation was not to last. The practice of coin-clipping suddenly spread and expanded like a terrible plague across the length and breadth of England. Between 1688 and 1695 it is reckoned that the weight of silver in the average coin fell to below 50 per cent of its nominal value.[19]

We now know that the upsurge in coin-clipping was directly linked to the 'King William's War', fought so doggedly over nine years to drive Louis XIV's French armies out of the Netherlands. To pay his troops, William was in desperate need of supplies of silver that could be exported across the narrow sea to Amsterdam. It has now emerged that much of this silver came directly from coin-clipping. The king left it to London goldsmiths to conduct the transactions for him, and they had no scruples in buying up silver supplies from shady sources.[20]

Coin-clipping was, of course, a capital offence. William Paterson would have been well aware of that from his days in London, since there was a regular traffic of convicted offenders, poor wretches in open wagons, taking their last journey from the courthouse in Old Bailey to the public gallows at Tyburn, where Marble Arch stands today. The road to Tyburn passed not 100 yards from his front door in Denmark Street. But despite coin-clipping being an offence punishable with death, the goldsmiths do not seem to have lost much sleep over the fate of these little people. There were always plenty willing to take their place. It was the government's attempt to end coin-clipping that provoked the financial crisis of the summer of 1696.

The case for the replacement of the old currency with fresh new silver coins, milled at the edges to make clipping impossible, was overwhelming. In 1695 William Lowndes' *Essay on the State of the Currency* painted a dismal picture of a country perilously perched on the edge of economic chaos, with all trade 'smitten as with a palsy' by growing disputes over the acceptability of the old coins. Lowndes proposed a recoinage on the basis of his dictum: 'Take care of the pence and the pounds will take care of themselves'.[21]

The great question was not whether to replace the debased old currency with new shiny milled coins, but how it was to be done. Since the 1660s there had been a 'gradualist' approach. New milled coins had been turned out by their thousands on a new-fangled 'coin mill', based on a French design and installed in the Royal Mint. The new coins were then issued alongside the old coins, in the fond belief that people would rush to exchange their battered old coins for the shiny new ones where they could. The policy-makers had obviously never heard of a 'law' formulated by the 16th-century merchant and proto-economist, Sir Thomas Gresham, that 'bad money drives out good'.[22]

Gresham's Law had kicked in with a vengeance. The shiny new coins had the same face value as the old coins they were meant to replace, but of course contained much more silver. In an age when no man seemed more than a block away from a little metal furnace, the new coins were swiftly melted down and either reissued as counterfeited old coins or turned into bars of silver bullion, in each case delivering a tidy profit. Gradualism was clearly not working. But as to what a viable alternative might be – that had long baffled reformers. During the summer of 1695, with the currency fast becoming a source of conflict in every marketplace, great or small, Charles Montagu turned his mind to the problem. He came up with a radical plan – nothing less than the sudden withdrawal of the old coinage and its replacement within weeks by a brand new set of coins.

In an ideal world a complete set of replacement coins would have been produced and stockpiled in advance, and the change-over achieved within days.[23] But this was impractical, since it required a large reserve of silver that just was not there. So Montagu opted for a compromise. Each category of coin would be withdrawn – for instance all crowns on one day, all half-crowns on another, and the metal from them turned into a new set of coins of the same denomination. This would have to be done quickly, which meant the Royal Mint would have to gear up its production to turn out some 10,000 coins a day, ten times more than it had ever managed before.[24]

As we have seen, Montagu had the man in mind to run it, his own Cambridge colleague Isaac Newton. He first approached him in the summer of 1695 and wrote to offer him the job of Warden of the Royal Mint in October. He hinted that this was not really a full-time job: 'It is worth Five Hundred or Six Hundred Pounds per annum, and has not too much business to require more attendance than you can spare'.[25] This was disingenuous, since it would take all Newton's application and energy to transform the old Mint into a modern production facility, capable of producing the five million new coins that would be needed.[26] To his credit Newton recognised it was a full-time job from the start. He bent his back to the task, staying on site to keep an eye on the two shifts of workers, and on the 50 horses who drove the mills. He looked on the task with the eye of a 20th-century 'time-and-motion-study' man, timing key operations, imagining how the work could be co-ordinated, how each person could achieve maximum productivity. For instance, his observations suggested that a competent coiner could feed (and then remove) about 50 to 55 coins a minute into the press, if at the risk of losing the odd finger. It did not take him long to conclude that the Mint needed to be expanded and lots of little mints opened up and down the country.[27]

What Montagu and Newton did not foresee was the psychological impact of a sudden withdrawal of the old currency. Saturday 2 May was to be the last day that taxes could be paid using the old shillings and sixpences. The Treasury seems to have been taken completely by surprise by a last-minute rush to dispose of the old battered and debased stock. At sunrise, Whitehall was already packed by people desperate to pay the tax they owed, a scene of disorder that mounted steadily throughout the day, forcing the government to call in the guards. As the midnight bells rung over London, people were still angrily queuing, demanding that someone take in their money and hand them their due receipt.

The scenes of near-rioting marked the beginning of a long period of financial crisis. People now expected the new coins to flood the shops and taverns in the following week, but none appeared. Thus began the great coin famine of 1696. The Mint itself was partly to blame since the rate of production of new coins lagged far behind the target set (the peak of production was not reached until July 1697, more than a year later) but human psychology – and human greed – played the bigger role. Somehow a rumour started that the new coins would be given a higher value than the old ones, but only after all the old ones were safely gathered in. In these circumstances only a fool would pass on his new coins at face value; the wise man put them away in his strongbox. Those that were not hoarded in this way quickly vanished into the goldsmiths' vaults, ready to be melted down and despatched as bullion to Amsterdam, where the war had forced up silver prices to new highs.[28] As a result daily life in London became a strange ritual that mixed IOUs and barter in roughly equal proportions.

John Evelyn recorded on 13 May: 'Money exceeding scarce, so that none was paid or received: but all was on trust.' A month later he reported no sign of improvement: 'Want of current money to carry on the smallest concerns, even for daily provisions in the market.'[29] But if ordinary people were inconvenienced by the want of money, this was nothing to the sudden increase in costs imposed on business.

When James Smith came to London in early July 1696 he found a deepening crisis. The shortage of coins had put unexpected pressure on the Bank of England, which had guaranteed on its notes 'to pay the bearer on demand' if presented in person at head office. Not surprisingly, some cash-starved merchants thought the time had come to present themselves at the Bank to turn their paper receipts into good hard cash. This 'run on the Bank' was made much worse by an organised attempt by a number of London's goldsmiths – men who hated the bank for stealing their trade – to bring the bank down. One goldsmith alone asked for the colossal sum of £30,000 in cash to be paid to him over the counter.[30] The Court of Directors took the only decision they could to save the bank from bankruptcy. They ordered the doors to be closed.

It was a short-lived crisis,[31] but one with a long-term effect. It severely shook the confidence of the public in the security of the bank's 'paper money', which in turn undermined its value in the market-place. Macaulay remarked on the unsettling effect this had on everyday English life:

> The paper of the [bank] continued to circulate: but the value fluctuated violently from day to day, and indeed from hour to hour... One week the discount was only six per cent, in another week twenty-four per cent. A ten-pound 'note', which had been taken in the morning as worth more than nine pounds, was often worth less than eight pounds before night.[32]

For a new company that had chosen this very moment to order its first ships from shipbuilding yards in Holland and Germany the loss of confidence in such paper, the 'imaginary money' that William Paterson had conjured out of nowhere, was a serious blow.

Smith had come south with his £17,000 of company capital. But it was in the form of paper, bills of exchange bought with hard cash, rather than hard cash itself. Paterson has been criticised for having the 'ill-considered idea to pay for supplies and ships in Holland by [paper] bills drawn on London'.[33] But what was the alternative? It would have been madness to try to transport bullion and coin either by sea or land from Edinburgh to London. And the use of bills of exchange was standard business practice when trading with Europe.[34] Paterson's and Smith's misfortune was to find themselves holding these bills of exchange payable in London just as the crisis in credit reached a peak, and the value of the pound against the Dutch florin (or guilder) fell through the floor.[35] This meant, for instance, that a bill of exchange charging £1,000 in Dutch currency for, say, ships' cannon, would have been transformed into a bill for almost £1,400 in pounds sterling at the height of the crisis.[36]

The Edinburgh board followed the fluctuations on the exchanges during the late summer currency crisis – easy enough to do since merchants writing from one country to another usually took care to quote the latest exchange rates at the end of their letters – with something approaching panic. They saw the value of their already inadequate capital leaking away, day after day after day. Suddenly, in the middle of October their nerve seems to have snapped. They wrote to Smith in London ordering him to convert all the remaining paper money with all possible speed, into gold and silver coin. They recognised, however, that this would be impossible to do in coin-starved London. He was therefore instructed to negotiate to have his London paper bills turned into cash in Amsterdam, This was costly. Since Dutch confidence in London paper 'currency' had hit rock bottom, the Dutch dealers would only exchange English paper for gold or silver at a very heavy discount.[37] Smith would have been forced to scramble to find London merchants with the right contacts in Amsterdam, who were also willing to do a deal. He had very little option but to take whatever he could get. These transactions took place in October 1696 just before Haldane arrived in London to begin his inquiry. They cost the company dear.[38]

The inquiry began amicably enough. It was agreed that each of the London directors should examine the books of the other, with Haldane looking on as a sort of umpire to sort out disputed points. The three started with the Campbell accounts and found them in order. Haldane duly reported this in his first letter to the Edinburgh Committee for Foreign Trade:

> Mr Campbell did immediately show me his books wherein Mr Smyth and I saw the Company Accounts plainly and fairly stated ... we found them agreed with [your accounts] in every article... I wait further progress until I have seen Mr Smyth's accounts which are to be in consideration tomorrow after which you may expect to hear at more length.[39]

The next day Haldane and Campbell went to Smith's office in Bishopsgate Street. We can imagine that the neat and precise Campbell, a man who was a stickler for precision and accuracy, was appalled by the apparent chaos that reigned in Smith's office. Smith would have had an explanation. The rush to transform the company's paper into bankable coin reserves on the Amsterdam exchange had been so frantic that the struggling bookkeepers had not been able to keep pace with the work. Haldane certainly saw nothing amiss in this. Indeed, that very evening he went with Campbell and Smith on an amicable and seemingly successful tour of the sailors' haunts in search of officers and crews for the forthcoming voyage. Haldane could report to the Edinburgh directors that he had met a promising sea captain: 'His name is Pinkerton. He is very much talked of from this place and has spent the most of his time in the West Indies'.[40] All three seemed impressed by a man who was to play a central role in the history of the Darien colony.

That same evening they engaged three Scottish naval surgeons in conversation, sounding them out on whether they would consider joining the expedition. One of them was none other than the master of innuendo and rumour, the redoubtable Walter Herries, a ship's surgeon from Dumbarton in Scotland. Haldane, who was not yet privy to the decision to sail to Darien, appears to have given Herries the distinct impression that the voyage would be to the East Indies, and the surgeon embraced the idea enthusiastically.[41] Much bitterness was to flow from this early confusion. In the week that followed, Smith was so busy handling the flood of bills that poured in from Amsterdam and Hamburg that Haldane had no opportunity to examine Smith's accounts in detail. But he found himself sympathising with the Dutchman's predicament, the hard-pressed accountant obliged to meet demands for payment on every side, and watch the company's funds dwindle at an alarming rate. By the third week of November Haldane was satisfied that Smith was a man to be trusted and left it to him to put the details of all the money transactions in writing and send them off to Edinburgh.[42] This done, the two men happily embarked together on the voyage to Amsterdam where they were to meet up with Paterson and Erskine.

We have no way of knowing whether the Edinburgh directors grasped the import of Smith's letter when it finally arrived in the Scottish capital early in December. It read:

According to your [instructions] of the 10th and the 17th [October] to convert with all convenient speed [all your assets] in my hands from bank
notes into Specie [i.e. gold and silver coin] and remitt the same to
Amsterdam, I have in obedience thereunto contracted with some here to
deliver the bank notes at 15% discount and take the value to Amsterdam
at 38 [florins] in terms of Sterling.[43]

This was an accountant's delicate way of informing the board that 15 per
cent of the value of the assets still in his care and tied up in 'bills' had
been lost. He had been forced to conclude a deal at the worst possible
time.[44] As it happened the exchange rate of 38 Dutch florins he quoted
in the letter was already way out of line with the actual exchange rate
prevailing, a slump provoked by the lack of English ready cash. On 3
November the Hamburg correspondents – Francis Stratford Snr and
Jnr wrote that: 'The exchange is considerably fallen and may go yet
lower – for today no money was to be had'. They reported that the
exchange rate at Amsterdam stood at just 33 florins to the pound, a rate
that remained more or less constant over the next six months.[45] So some
£3,000 or so of the eventual shortfall in Smith's accounts could have
been accounted for simply by the monetary crisis of 1696.

It is also likely that some of the paper bills issued in Edinburgh to be
drawn or cashed in London had been, in the customary manner of the
time, lent out in the short-term to other needy London merchants. This
was one way of making 'dead' money earn some return and both Smith
and Paterson would have used such devices in the past in the course of
everyday trade. And there is evidence to support the view that Smith followed this practice when he first arrived in London in August. We have
Haldane's word that: '… [Smith] said he entered into a contract with
some persons of good credit in this place [i.e. London] who were to
answer money for these bills'.[46] As a result of the coinage crisis many of
these persons of good credit found difficulty in honouring their word.
In the files of the Company of Scotland is a whole series of letters from
Walter Stewart describing the difficulties he and Smith had encountered
trying to get at least some of them to honour their pledges. One was a
certain Scottish merchant in London by the name of Alexander Lang.
The tale gives some idea of the intricacies of a system of paper promises
that in the end rested on trust rather than legal sanctions.

Walter Stewart tells the story in a letter written in early January
1697.

Mr James Smyth came to me and desired that I would do him the favour
to present that bill to Mr Lang and procure acceptances and payment,
saying that Mr Lang being a Scotsman, it was not convenient that the company business should be too much nois'd abroad...[47]

But when Stewart approached Lang, the gentleman fobbed him off at
first with 'bank notes' drawn on other people who in turn owed money
to him. In the event not one of these debtors was prepared to settle the
bill in cash – as Lang had promised they would. Since Lang refused
point-blank to pay up, Stewart in the end was forced to fall back on the
only sanction he felt he had:

I told him that if he would not do me justice I would expose him publickly
upon the Exchange, and he persisting not to give me satisfaction, I told
publickly before his face in company of several merchants as how I was
tricked in this manner...[48]

Smith it seems was made of sterner stuff, instructing Stewart to pursue Mr Lang through the courts, although there is no record to show
that this was ever done. The case of Alexander Lang and his complicated web of debts and obligations was probably typical of the fragile business world of London at the time. Lang was at the end of a chain of
debtors, scarcely any of whom, it seemed, had access to hard cash. There
were even more complicated deals involved. One James Lamouche –
apparently a friend of Smith – had been used by Smith as a way to
spread the risks of sudden fluctuations in currencies and discounts. He
too claimed poverty and refused to pay up.

In January there were bad debts of some £1,600 entered against
Smith's name by Campbell and Stewart, presumably those represented
by Lang and Lamouche. Campbell was closely involved in both deals
and it is a pity that two letters from the office of Stewart and Campbell
that may have thrown light on the business have been torn from the
manuscript pages now held by the National Library of Scotland.

There may have been many more, since Smith and Campbell did not
always work so closely together. Without access to the Smith accounts it
is now impossible to say how much these liabilities amounted to. It is not
impossible, if added to the currency losses and the known bad debts,
that they could explain most of the hole in the Smith accounts. James
Smith always maintained his innocence as to involvement in any delib-
erate fraud.

The arguments over what should be done about the shortfall in Smith's accounts became a festering sore at the heart of the business for the next six months. It divided the directors into two feuding camps, and eventually destroyed any chance the company had of raising the capital it needed in Europe.

On the one hand there was the trio of Paterson, Erskine and Haldane. They continued to back Smith's version of events. Haldane's letter of 21 November gave no hint to the Edinburgh directors that any irregularities had taken place, although of course he was no accountant.[49] Early in December he travelled with Smith to Amsterdam, carrying copies for the Bills of Exchange Smith had drawn on Amsterdam for further checking. Once in the privacy of their Dutch lodgings Paterson and Erskine could talk the matter over with Haldane. They decided the best policy was to soldier on and hope that the Smith accounts could eventually be balanced. The one thing they wanted to avoid was any hint that the company could not be trusted with investors' money. On 22 January all three wrote to the Committee for Foreign Trade in Edinburgh to voice their fears that further discussion of Smith's accounts in London would dish the whole enterprise:

> This will, if once nois'd abroad, kindle a flame not easy to be quenched, some speaking whereof have already reached this place, but carefully smother'd. We earnestly request calm close proceedings in this juncture as you tender the honour of the nation and the good of the company.[50]

But Stewart and Campbell, who were bean-counters rather than risk-takers, sent a whole series of letters to Edinburgh harping on about the bad debt Smith had left behind in London.[51] Loose talk in Edinburgh picked up in London would easily carry to Amsterdam.

It is hard, on the other hand, not to sympathise with the difficulties Stewart and Campbell faced. On 23 February Walter Stewart posted a letter asking Edinburgh to remit more money to them as a matter of the greatest urgency to cover the bills now arriving from the Amsterdam shipbuilders, all in the midst of the continuing crisis in all forms of credit:

> Except you make your remittances at short sight [i.e. payable immediately] they cannot come in time to answer these demands and the scarcity of money here [in London] is so great that there is no such thing as credit

amongst us …. In short our circumstances here are such that except you were eye witnesses you will hardly believe it.[52]

In these trying circumstances Stewart and Campbell maintained that Smith should be held personally responsible for the huge losses his accounts showed and that he should dip into his own pockets to make them good. This was a point of view that appealed to an increasing number of the Edinburgh directors.

Through January 1697, Paterson, Erskine and Haldane had much on their plate. The collapse of the pound against the florin piled up costs; so too did the delays caused by the exceptionally severe weather. To make a bleak picture even bleaker the four factors in Amsterdam could report that the increasingly hostile attitude shown by the Dutch authorities towards any Scottish subscription made the likelihood of raising funds there increasingly remote.[53] In these circumstances if any whiff of scandal about the financial probity of this new Scottish company were to waft through the coffee houses of Amsterdam or Hamburg they might as well pack their bags and return to Scotland. Paterson was furious that Stewart and Campbell continued to complain about Smith's accounts. But his plea that the company refrain from washing its dirty linen in public seems to have fallen on deaf ears. Throughout February and March the debate about Smith's conduct raged on in Edinburgh. By then the Amsterdam subscription had fallen through and Haldane's attempt to raise a further subscription in Rotterdam had come to nothing. In March Paterson and Erskine had moved on to Hamburg in a last desperate attempt to find backers there.

As we have seen, Paterson was convinced that there was more than an even chance of raising subscriptions in several towns. The Scots Company had provided much work to Hamburg ship-builders and to the merchants of the city who brought in such essentials as ships' cannon from Sweden and pitch from Russia. And many German rulers and governments were genuinely interested in any plan that would give them a share of the lucrative foreign trade that had so enriched Holland and England. The thawing of the Elbe, as the spring of 1697 brought that grim winter to a close, raised the spirits. To Paterson, excited by the warm welcome he received from the merchant community in Hamburg, it seemed the tide of ill-fortune was at last about to turn.

Sir Paul Rycaut, the British 'Resident' in Hamburg was growing alarmed at Paterson's success in convincing the Merchants House of Hamburg, and others, that the Company of Scotland could act as a vehicle for the foreign trade they had missed out on. He had revealed these fears in a letter sent to Whitehall in early March:

> Mr. Paterson, who is a diligent Projector, lyes hard at them, and representing nothing but riches and a golden age... so people beginne to talk that the Subscriptions may become in a short time very considerable... in Case they should be successful in this city they will extend their Endeavours farther into the trading townes of Germany...[54]

He desperately needed ammunition to wage his war against Paterson more effectively. A small army of spies shadowed the Scots, searching for any snippet of information that could be of use. The breakthrough came with a letter Rycaut received from a contact in Amsterdam passing on a rumour then sweeping that city, to the effect that a Mr James Smith had been arrested for embezzlement. This Mr Smith was known to be a close business associate of the great Mr Paterson himself. Rycaut dashed off an exultant letter to London: 'Though there be nothing more to it than a report, yet it is sufficient to break the whole credit of the company in theses parts'.[55] Rycaut was determined to wring any advantage he could out of this unconfirmed report. He called in his Secretary, a certain Mr Orth, and instructed him to have the story circulated in an anonymous pamphlet, in German and in French, addressed to the merchants of Hamburg. Unfortunately, no copy of the pamphlet has ever come to light but we know that Orth added a touch of fascination to it by writing it as though he was in Holland.

A copy fell into the hands of Francis Stratford Snr, a fact he duly reported to Edinburgh in his letter of 30 March: '... yesterday a printed pamphlet appeared on streets of Hamburg in the form of a Letter from Amsterdam to a Friend in Hamburg'.[56] He added that the suspicion was that the Resident was behind it. Conveniently, it appeared on the streets of Hamburg just before the opening of the subscription book on 8 April.

Orth never owned up to authorship of the pamphlet but Rycaut privately conceded the point. In a letter to London, written to ward off any criticism from Scotland that a British civil servant had been involved in a scurrilous plot to sabotage the Scots' fund-raising in Hamburg, he wrote: 'They cannot prove him to be the author... yet, if they could, he and I are too well satisfied in having done this duty that we are both without fear of having gained His Majsty's displeasure thereby...'.[57] Undoubtedly it broadcast the rumour of Smith's arrest, to devastating effect. The origin of the rumour itself has never been established. In fact Smith had not been arrested and was to travel with Haldane to Hamburg[58] where he arrived much to the surprise of Rycaut. But we know there had been some talk within the company of seizing Smith to force him to make good the deficit on his account. A rumour picked up in Edinburgh or London could spread fast and grow in the retelling.

Rycaut, an elderly man in his 70s, followed up the propaganda war with an energetic political counter-stroke. On the day the pamphlet appeared, he summoned representatives of the Hamburg Senate to appear before them and warned that the Scots Company and its grand projects was an affront to the King of England and any favour shown on the part of the Senate would seriously damage relations between Hamburg and England. He begged them 'not to bestow on this new [Scots] Company any privileges of this City, [and] not so much to grant them licence to write over the door any motto for the house'.[59] But the Hamburg Senate had already agreed to let the Scots put their sign above the door of the room appointed for subscriptions the next morning. They refused to give way.

In normal circumstances the intervention of the British Resident would have only helped rally support to the Scottish cause. But these were no normal times. Rycaut's pamphlet had sown a poisonous seed of doubt in the minds of many of the Hamburg merchants who had earlier shown an interest in investing. After the meeting with Rycaut the doubts grew. Was it really worth making an enemy of the King of England when the whole enterprise seemed so inwardly rotten, so shaky that it could collapse at any time? The next morning, when the Subscription Book was formally opened in the Exchange not a single subscriber turned up. Paterson, Smith, Erskine and Haldane were forced to recognise that defeat was staring them in the face.[60]

The four passed the next fortnight in Hamburg, waiting long enough to see the last two of the fine Scots ships launched and work begun on fitting them out. Despite all the trauma of that year's fluctuating exchanges they could reflect on some good work done. Each of the Hamburg ships cost around £1,900 fully fitted with masts, sails and cables. The company had sent Stevenson to Hamburg because prices and workmanship there compared well to that of Amsterdam. Stratfords, the Hamburg 'Correspondents' could boast that: 'we shall leave it to your directors to give you an account not only of their cheapness but of their quality and goodness'.⁶¹ But of course they would have been cheaper still had it not been for the carnage exacted by the exchange rate and the delays caused by the weather.

Still, the Germans knew the Baltic trade well and had good trade connections with Russia, Poland, Lithuania and Sweden. This had paid off since excellent cannon and small arms were eventually brought from Sweden and carried overland from Lübeck to Hamburg. The whole package would be ready to sail to Scotland in October or November. In Amsterdam one ship – the captured ship *St Francis* – had already been fitted out and was ready to sail that summer. The other Dutch-built ship had fallen behind schedule, but it was a ship as good as any sailing across the oceans of the world.

If something positive had come out of that dreadful year there was much that left cause for concern about the future health of the Scottish Company. A series of bruising battles between the continental agents in Amsterdam and Hamburg and Stewart and Campbell in London had damaged the reputation of the Scots as reliable business partners, and lost goodwill that could have been of value later on.⁶²

Towards the end of April Paterson and the three others decided no further purpose was to be served by lingering in North Germany. The hoped-for subscriptions from Bremen and Lübeck, Leipzig and Dresden, Frankfurt and Danzig now showed no sign of materialising, the news from Hamburg had seen to that. Haldane, Erskine and Smith returned to Amsterdam, while the ever-persistent Paterson went to Bremen in search of those elusive subscriptions, doggedly trying to keep a dead horse alive. It was at this point that the Company in Edinburgh took its fateful decision that Smith must be made to pay.

How far Smith had anticipated trouble it is very hard to say. If he had really been guilty of a massive fraud he could easily have slipped away, but instead he travelled back amicably enough with Haldane and Erskine to Amsterdam. There, about the beginning of May, Haldane and Erskine received orders from Edinburgh to have Smith seized and interrogated. When he attempted to escape, the two had him seized and put in a private jail (kindly laid on by the four Amsterdam factors to the

Company's cause in December) until such time as he offered to make restitution to the company.[63] When Paterson journeyed back from Bremen empty-handed and joined them in Amsterdam, he was probably shocked by what he found.

Smith continued to maintain his innocence, claiming that he had at no time sought to cheat the company. But Haldane and Erskine, who had suddenly come round to the view that the missing money spoke for itself, now reached their rather silly conclusion that Smith had been indebted and needed the money to make himself solvent again. With Paterson now back in Amsterdam, Smith struck a bargain. If they let him return to England and refrained from ruining his reputation in the courts he promised to find the resources to make up as much of the shortfall as he could:

> He showed us all his papers [the three wrote] and gave us an obligation to give us a full and ample right to all he had in the world upon his arrival in England. The greatest part of his effects are in adventures to America. There is some of them in publick funds in this countrey and some in friends hands upon which he has given us bills which shall in due time be presented. In short one way and other we make up the whole sum and we are very hopefull that most of it will be made good.[64]

Paterson probably had much to do with this bargain. It minimised the risk of scandal and, to clinch it, he threw in his own guarantee. If James Smith could not raise the full £5,000 he had promised, then he, William Paterson, would make good any shortfall. As for the remaining £3,000, that burden he would also take on his shoulders.[65] He may have done this in part to protect his own back. He knew that some within the company judged him to be just as guilty as Smith. The scheme to fund the project by issuing bills in the company name, rather than using more established banking methods, had indeed been his.[66]

It was not the end of the story for James Smith. He was allowed to return to London to set himself up in business there and to realise some of his assets to repay the debt. A year later, he had repaid a portion of it, by selling off some shares he held in the Hampstead Water Company. But much remained outstanding. The company sent one of their servants to demand the rest. Smith did not have the money to pay, so he hired a coach and fled to Dover with his wife and his children. The company agent gave chase, accompanied by two constables armed with a warrant for his arrest. He was seized on the quay at Dover, brought back to London, and thrown into prison.

A year later he escaped and disappeared. No more is heard of him until he turns up some 15 years later as the leader of a colonists' revolt against their colonial masters – the Danish West India Company – on the tiny island of St Thomas in the Caribbean. This was the island where his father had been factor to the Elector of Brandenburg.[67] Strangely enough, St Thomas Island was to play a not unimportant part in the history of the Company of Scotland.

It was the unfortunate Paterson who was struck the more savage blows. Over the summer he too sold his shares in the Hampstead Water Company (depressing the share price for a time)[68] and those he still held in the failing Orphans' Bank,[69] raising some £3,000. This he paid to the Company as he had agreed. It ought to have been enough to make amends, especially since the Company, and the London bankers of the Company, Stewart and Campbell, were not entirely blameless in the affair. Despite this, or maybe because of it, there were those in the Mylne Square in search of someone to blame. In the autumn the company set up an internal inquiry to look into Paterson's conduct. The outcome was not perhaps what they expected.

The inquiry was conducted by two fair-minded men – Robert Blackwood and William Dunlop, Principal of Glasgow University. After close examination they found Paterson had done nothing wrong. On the contrary, they declared he had done much good for the Company and recommended he continued to be employed, since his knowledge and experience should not be lightly thrown away.[70] But the directors would hear nothing of it. Paterson's position on the board, since the attempted coup of May 1696, depended on his retaining the confidence of the 25 elected members. When the vote went against him that autumn, he was forced out. It was the Bank of England all over again. To add to his sense of injustice the manuscripts and papers he had placed in the hands of the Company were not to be returned to him. And the agreed payment of £15,000 for his services and his ideas was summarily withdrawn.[71] Paterson was reduced overnight to penury. The man who had been welcomed in Edinburgh as a philosopher and genius of the first order only eight months previously, now became its forgotten citizen.

Without him to act as mentor and guide, it was very doubtful if the grand enterprise which had so enthused the Scots stood anything but the slimmest of chances. He could have walked away, but he did not. There was something about Paterson that marked him out for martyrdom.

As the Company of Scotland decided Paterson's fate, the enemies of the company in Whitehall were mulling over new information that was suddenly to ignite their interest in the Isthmus of Darien. It came from the pen of Sir Paul Rycaut's Secretary in Hamburg, the same Mr Orth who had so inventively undermined confidence in the company in Hamburg. It had been his responsibility to employ spies to shadow Paterson and his Scots colleagues while they stayed in Hamburg. Some of these had attended meetings between Paterson and the merchants where the eloquent projector had spoken openly about the secret aims of the company, something he felt he had to do if there was to be any chance of raising the capital so desperately needed to fund the Darien enterprise properly. And after Paterson and his companions had left, Orth continued to be fed the stories being circulated in the city. All of this Orth duly relayed in a series of letters sent to King William's secretaries of state in London. One reported that:

> ... the Scots, after settling in South America, designed to trade with the East Indies in the gold and silver, and to make settlements there in places known to men.: ... I am further told that Paterson, who is well-known in London, is to go with the ships, as supreme director of the same, and of the conduct of affairs in these parts, where I hear they intend to enter into amity with the Indians, and to assist them against the Spaniards...[72]

A second added some further intriguing details:

> As to the Isthmus of Darien, they tell me that the River which doth discharge there into the North Sea is navigable to ships of 150 tons for six leagues from the North Coast; that from there to the isthmus or South Sea it was six leagues more, navigable for floats of planks... When well settled in America they will trade direct with the East Indies for goods.[73]

Together they represented a classic piece of jumbled intelligence, but good enough to make the civil servants in Whitehall take notice of a neglected part of the world, and act upon it.

In one respect, though, Orth was quite wrong. William Paterson was no longer to be 'the supreme director of the same'. If he were to go at all, it would be in a much more humble capacity.

Chapter Eight
Paterson Reborn

In February 1697 William Dampier had cause for celebration. His account of his life as buccaneer and explorer, *A New Voyage Round the World*, had come off the printing press and, bound in stout leather, went on sale in the shop of his bookseller at St Paul's Yard.[1] Here, in the shadow of the new cathedral – where mason's hammers still tapped away – a clutch of booksellers and printers had sprung up to cater for the printing boom that had followed the lifting of censorship in 1695. The *New Voyage* became an instant best seller and was to go to its third edition in a matter of weeks. It became the talk of London, lifting Dampier to the status of a celebrity overnight.

In a preface he warned that, since he dealt with parts of the world 'seldom … visited by English men, and others as rarely by any Europeans, I may encourage the reader to expect many things wholly new to him…'.[2] In this context he mentioned his excursion to Darien and added:

> I might have given a further Account of several things relating to this Country; the Inland Parts of which are so little known to the Europeans. But I shall leave this province to Mr. Wafer, who made a longer Abode in it than I, and is better able to do it than any Man that I know, and is now preparing a particular Description of this Country for the Press.[3]

A mile from St Paul's in the labyrinthine alleys and corridors of the Whitehall Palace, the publishing event of the year apparently went at first unnoticed, even by an expert body set up a year earlier to consider trade issues. This was the Board of Trade and the Plantations, a small group of two civil servants and three learned laymen, the most celebrated being the philosopher, John Locke. It sat regularly in one of the vacated royal chambers, taking evidence and issuing reports on the trade issues of the day. It was not until that summer that they took a close interest in Dampier and his friend Lionel Wafer. When they did, it was in direct response to the flow of intelligence received from Mr Orth in Hamburg. In May he had gone so far as to write directly to William Blathwayt, the Secretary for Trade, with the alarming news that William Paterson and his company were apparently planning to land an expedition on the Isthmus of Darien, in the heart of territory claimed by Spain. Blathwayt arranged for a copy of this letter to be passed urgently to the Board of Trade. He feared that the Scots were about 'to send to the Straits of Darien and to enter into a league with the Prince there in order to exercise hostilities and depredations upon the Spaniards'.[4]

At this point England and Spain were fighting on the same side in the war against Louis XIV and he did not want the Scots upsetting King William's allies. Blathwayt looked for advice on how the Scots might be forestalled. He was scarcely prepared for the answer that came back.

The Board of Trade first considered the question of Darien in June. None of them knew much if anything about the Isthmus save that few Englishmen had ever been there. But they had obviously heard of Dampier's book, and of reference to the new book being prepared by his companion, Mr Wafer. Accordingly, at their meeting of 28 June 1697, they 'ordered for Mr Dampier, who hath lately printed a book of his voyages, to attend Friday next, and give notice to Mr Wafer, that they may be examined as to the design of the Scotch East India Company to make a settlement on the Isthmus of Darién'.[5]

Dampier and Wafer had always intended that their separate works should be noticed, that they might be used as a practical guide to developing trade with distant, unknown lands.[6] Both were convinced that Darien was a territory that might bring enormous benefit to England. In his account of Darien, as yet unpublished, Wafer passionately embraced the notion that England should occupy this narrow neck of land to provide 'a free passage by land, from the Atlantic to the South Sea, ...which would be of the greatest consequence to the East India trade'.[7] The opportunity to appear before the Board of Trade gave them the chance to argue that there was but one response England could make to Paterson's scheme.

The route to Whitehall lay by the broad avenue of the Strand, a once fashionable street that had gone into rapid decline beneath a tide of brothels, theatres and gambling dens.[8] The two men may have found the means to take one of the new hackney-cabs to carry them from the City to the old palace, giving them a chance to discuss how best to present their case. They may have doubted that these stuffy gentlemen of Whitehall could ever grasp the true potential of Darien. To improve their chances of success they brought with them written testimony that could be left in the hands of the board.[9]

When they arrived they were led into the chamber to find only four of the five members of the Board awaiting them. The chairman was a nobleman, the Earl of Tankerville, a man who knew little or nothing about trade. He owed his elevation to his loyal support of King William a year earlier when a plot against the king's life had come to light.[10] But the loyal Earl was wise enough to lean heavily on the advice of his three fellow commissioners.

In their evidence Dampier and Wafer stressed how easy it would be to create a new route to the South Sea, across a neck of land less than 50 miles wide.[11] They also maintained that it would take far less than a thousand men to secure it, since the local Indians would welcome an English expedition. Here the dry-prose of the minute-taker has not quite expunged the excitement their answers produced:

The people have been so much abused by the Spaniards that they are jealous of strangers. If any Europeans settle there they must at first carry provisions. After that the Indians would probably grow more friendly and plant and sell them corn and make it easy for them to subsist. Then 500 men or even half that number might easy settle themselves ...

There are gold mines in the country. The Spaniards had some at Sancta Maria within 20 years. The Indians get gold that washes down from the mountains and the Spaniards get more of that by trade than from the mines.[12]

But surely, the commissioners enquired, this was Spanish-held territory, was it not? Not at all, replied the two former buccaneers:

It is possessed solely by the Indians who are enemies to the Spaniards and when Mr Wafer was there [they were] at war with them. Upon the North Sea ... the Spaniards have no settlement at all. All the inland country is in the hands of Indians.[13]

The message seemed clear enough. Here was a land rich with promise, a land easily won. The Committee concluded: 'It would be no difficult matter for any European Prince or State to make some secure settlement in Darien and engage [the natives] in defence against all enemies.'[14] The commissioners were torn. Any English settlement would throw down a challenge to Spain. But if no action was taken it could easily fall to the Scots, who might then turn this wondrous land to their advantage at the expense of English interests in the area. It was decided that John Locke should make further enquiries. He may have met privately with Dampier and Wafer to discuss the importance of Darien and to establish the exact location of the best harbours. He certainly went to St Paul's Yard in search of Dampier's book.[15]

Locke's research led to two simple conclusions: firstly, that this was indeed a site of immense strategic importance opening the way to the South Sea and secondly, that England must move quickly to acquire it. Hence the extraordinary recommendation rushed through by the commissioners in August:

> ... on further information of the circumstances of that country... having never been possessed by the Spaniards... we are of the opinion that a competent number of men should be sent thither ... from Jamaica, to take possession for the Crown of England of Golden Island and the port opposite to it on the Main, to the *exclusion of all other Europeans* [author's emphasis]...

> The work seems to us to require all possible despatch, lest the Scotch Company be there before us, which is of the utmost importance to the trade of England.[16]

For a moment it seemed a real possibility that England might forestall the Scottish plan, seizing the Isthmus as a base for exploiting the Pacific. But William and his ministers took a breath and for the moment chose to do nothing. It was not worth the risk of provoking Spain, still an ally – if a fractious ally – in the war against Louis XIV.

Such considerations were by nature short term. Peace talks between Louis XIV and William were at that very moment being held at Ryswick, a little Dutch village half-way between Delft and the Hague, and Spain was being increasingly regarded as the sick man of Europe.[17] The temptation to take advantage of Spanish weakness and seize Darien might yet prove too strong to resist.[18]

In Edinburgh the directors of the Company of Scotland knew nothing of this awakening interest in Darien within the shambling palace of Whitehall. This was the very time when the boardroom battles waged over James Smith's debt to the company were at their height. And indeed there was increasing doubt whether the Scottish fleet would ever sail – to Darien or anywhere else. The initial capital of £100,000 raised in Scotland (by the 'calling in' of the first 25 per cent of the promised subscription in June 1696) had drained away alarmingly as the bills from Amsterdam and Hamburg were presented for payment in London. In March the directors, in a panic, had ordered John Haldane in Amsterdam to cancel all orders he possibly could. A somewhat embarrassed Haldane wrote back:

> You are positive that without Foreign Subscriptions it is impossible for you to equip [the] already bought and contract'd for ships and therefore seem resolved to retrench your first equipage as to your subscriptions. I would willingly sell our ships or do anything it were possible for me to give you but … I saw ourselves so ingaged in them that I know no way for us to get off.[19]

Unable to cut back on these orders the company had no choice but to economise where they could, and hope for the best. By the summer it seemed that the bill for the five ships built to order and for the large second-hand ship secured by Gibson, when all were fitted out with sail and cannon, would come to about £50,000, half of all the capital so far raised.[20] Another £20,000 or so[21] had been put aside for cargoes and provisions. This left only £30,000 for all other expenses, and that only if the full £8,000 lost by Smith were to be recovered. Perhaps in the circumstances the company's decision to default on its promise to pay William Paterson a first instalment of the money it had promised him as the lead entrepreneur was understandable. But for him it was no less bitter a pill. For a third time he had been cheated out of his reward as projector.[22]

Paterson, living in comparative poverty in Edinburgh as he must have been, was approaching his fortieth birthday with little to show for a lifetime of dedicated work and yet he lived in hope. The precious maps, charts and papers that he had entrusted to the Committee of Trade he hoped some day to recover. In the meantime he entrusted his fate to God. There appears to have been something in his nature that refused to let him give up. He was the eternal optimist facing up to every test God chose to throw at him. This was not a metaphor but a deeply held belief. Thus he could write later to Captain Thomas Drummond, a fellow believer in Darien as a sort of promised land that 'I am nightly hoping that the Almighty will make us glad according to the days wherein He has afflicted us.'[23] And indeed, by the end of 1697, the dark clouds threatening the company with bankruptcy began to lift, and the future looked brighter. The possibility began to emerge that perhaps, just perhaps, Scotland might yet successfully establish herself in Darien before rival powers awoke to its unique potential.

The change in fortunes can be traced to the peace settlement between Louis XIV and King William, finally agreed at Ryswick in September 1697. It brought the 'Nine Year War' to an end.[24] Bonfires blazed the length and breadth of England in a wave of popular rejoicing. At the same time the new coinage had at last settled down and confidence in the Bank of England was restored. With that, 'paper money' became once again the accepted way of doing business. This, and some recovery in the value of the pound against the Dutch florin, began to lift the gloom in Mylne Square.

So too did the news from Hamburg where a late deal had been struck rescheduling some of the company debt by delaying the delivery of two of the four ships. Only the two ships launched in March were now to be completed that year. In early November, after the first winter storms had blown themselves out in the North Sea,[25] the contingent of Scottish sailors who had been kicking their heels on half-pay in Hamburg since February made the first two ships ready for their maiden voyage to Scotland. The arrival of the new ships in the Forth was to be the first hard evidence that the money put up by the shareholders 18 months before had been wisely spent, that Scotland was indeed to have a new merchant fleet that would excite the envy of other less enterprising nations.

In the last week of November the first of these new vessels, with the craggy menace of the Bass Rock kept well to port, sailed into the sheltered waters of the Firth of Forth and dropped anchor a safe distance out from the unreliable, shallow waters of Leith harbour. Not even the greyness of a late November day could disguise her grandeur, with her three tall masts, her array of gun ports, and her prow and stern a blaze of gold and red and blue. This was the *Caledonia*, and she announced her arrival with a cannon shot from one of her new Swedish cannon, the best that Nordkoping could produce.[26] A returning, welcoming round was fired from the heights of Edinburgh Castle. A few days later, on 29 November, she was joined by *Instauration*, the other Hamburg-built vessel, also a three-masted ship and equally a credit to her German builders. The directors toasted her arrival from the panelled boardroom in Mylne Square from where they could watch her drop anchor close to the *Caledonia*. They promptly resolved to rename her the *St Andrew*, a fitting name for the flagship of the Company of Scotland's fleet.[27]

A third ship arrived, this time from Amsterdam. She was the excellent 'pennyworth' purchased by James Gibson from the City of Amsterdam, the captured French vessel *St Francis*. She was to prove to be a fine seaworthy ship. In Amsterdam she had been given the name *Union*, possibly reflecting William Paterson's belief that Scotland and England must work together.[28] In the Forth she was promptly christened the *Unicorn*, in honour of the legendary animal that supported the Scottish coat of arms. By association it reminded people of the motto of Scotland – *nemo me impune lacessit* – or 'Wha daur meddle wi' me?'[29] The *Unicorn* was not so ornate or grand as the two made-to-order ships, but it was about the same size. All three weighed around 500 tonnes, large ships for their day, and each carried a complement of around 50 guns.[30] These were not ships to be lightly meddled with.

To this proud little armada were added two smaller cargo-carrying ships, the *Endeavour* and the *Dolphin*. The first had been purchased for £500 in Newcastle by an agent for the Company, Dr John Munro; the second came from Amsterdam, product of another bargain struck by the canny James Gibson. Sitting in the Forth, dwarfed against the snow-covered Lomond Hills of Fife, the five must have made a pretty sight, solid evidence to fanciful Edinburgh folk that Scotland was indeed about to take her place in the ranks of the great sailing nations.

The destination chosen for this small fleet remained a closely guarded secret. Some company employees, such as Walter Herries, were convinced the small armada would sail eastwards to India and the East Indies, others equally that it would sail west to America. But whatever destination was finally chosen, arrangements had been put in place to prepare these ships for a long voyage that would last months. A special task-force, the 'Committee for Equipping Ships', had already begun to order the provisions that would be required.

In charge of this complicated piece of planning was an ebullient Glasgow merchant, William Arbuckle, a man made famous by Sir Walter

Scott in his novel *Rob Roy*, where he is pictured laying out a bowling-green in his native city and being involved in developing Port Glasgow as a deep-water port on the Atlantic coast of Scotland. In real life he was a callous, ruthless man, a man who had established his fortune in the transportation of Scottish political and religious dissenters as indentured labourers to the English colonies in America and the Caribbean.[31] Hard-hearted he may have been, but no one knew better than he what was needed to sustain large numbers of people on long-transoceanic voyages.

Walter Herries, a man who worked with Arbuckle and who was actually sent to Hamburg to buy up supplies in Hamburg in October 1697, was later to mock the Committee for loading entirely the wrong sort of cargoes for tropical lands:

> Scotch hats, a great quantity
> English Bibles, 1,500
> Periwigs 4,000, some long some short... Spanish Bobs, and natural ones

His jibes provided barbs enough for later historians. Macaulay set the fashion:

> ... a cargo had been laid in which was afterwards the subject of much mirth to the enemies of the Company, slippers innumerable, periwigs of all kinds from plain bobs to those magnificent structures which, in that age, towered above the foreheads and descended to elbows of men of fashion, bales of Scotch woollen stuffs which nobody within the tropics would wear, and many hundreds of Bibles which neither Spaniard nor Indian could read...[32]

In fact the company made a reasonable stab in requisitioning and laying in the sort of cargoes that matched the changing vision of what the expedition could reasonably be expected to achieve. The process had begun as early as August 1695 when John Munro, a doctor from Aberdeen, was sent on a tour of Scotland to seek out the best and cheapest supplies of food for the voyage – salt beef, cured pork, salt cod and stockfish, prunes and raisins, cheeses, flour and oatmeal. The precise quantities could only be finally determined when a decision was taken on just how many men should be sent on the voyage. When that was fixed at 1,200 in March 1698, the supplies purchased earlier were topped up to take account of the final figure, enough to feed the expedition on the journey, with some left over to see them through the difficult first months.

Few luxuries, like chocolate and coffee, would survive the voyage and few were taken, but there were to be ample supplies of beer, red wine, brandy and rum, a cargo that Paterson – who was strictly teetotal[33] – must have feared would lead to no good. And many barrels of vinegar were ordered, since vinegar was thought to have cleansing properties when used to swab down the decks if fever should break out on board.

Some thought was also given to the inevitable wear and tear sustained by the ships on an ocean voyage. Nothing was forgotten. Spare ropes and sails were to be taken along, together with supplies of oakum[34] to seal the boards, and of course tar and pitch to keep the ship watertight. Then there were the articles that would be required to build the company's forts and warehouses – axes and saws, hammers and nails, spades and pickaxes. And everyday household items the settlers would need, such as pots and pans, needles and thread, candles and crockery. But the largest part of the cargo was to be tradable goods. Scottish wool cloth, yes, but also fine cottons, linens and silks, copperware and lanterns, mirrors and combs. To these were added the much-derided wigs. But wigs were in much demand in the English and Spanish colonies of America, as were English bibles in the colonies along the eastern seaboard of North America – always seen as part of the Darien trading hinterland.

Indeed, a study of the cargoes carried on the ships led the greatest historian of the 'Darien Scheme' to the inevitable conclusion that those who planned the cargoes had a vision of a Scots' colony somewhere in the Caribbean that would be used '... as a depot for trade with the English colonies of North America and the Caribbean'.[35] What Paterson made of this subtle transformation of his big idea into the much smaller, more limited, notion of an interloping colony we do not precisely know. But we remember his warning of 1695 that 'we may be sure, should we only settle some little Colony or Plantation, and send some Ships, [that the English and the Dutch] would look upon us as Interlopers, and all agree to discourage and crush us to pieces.[36] Would this prediction of doom prove accurate? Only time would tell.

Whatever he was, Paterson was no fool. Living in Edinburgh during the critical months of early 1698 he must have appreciated the immense pressures pushing the company away from the notion of a trading colony as such, and towards the idea of a colony whose prime purpose was to provide a place in the sun, a land where people could grow crops and nurture their families in a style impossible in the Scotland of the

1690s. The terrible famine had tightened its grip on the land in 1697. A depressingly wet summer was followed by a cold damp autumn, leaving crops rotting in the fields. Perhaps as many as one in ten of the population were to die of hunger in the course of the following year.[37] The prospect of building a new Scotland overseas, a land in tropical latitudes where fruitful harvests could be guaranteed, had captured the popular imagination. To the company directors, Darien seemed to promise a new beginning for the entire Scottish nation.[38]

Added to this longing for a better life in a tropical land came a sudden surfeit of young men in Scotland, a direct result of the peace agreed at Ryswick. As long as war raged King William had been allowed to keep a large army. Now peace had come, such an army was seen as unnecessary at best, at worse a serious threat to parliamentary government. William was reluctantly forced to disband his Dutch Regiment and lay off most of his veterans. The army was cut from 87,000 soldiers to just 10,000, and all in a matter of months.[39]

To ease the pain of what we would now call redundancy, the officer class were to receive half-pay 'until appropriate arrangements' could be made. Other ranks were sent packing with nothing more than the uniform they stood in. All over England banditry reached epidemic proportions. Indeed, as Macaulay memorably put it: 'robbery was organised on a scale unparalleled in the kingdom since the days of Robin Hood and Little John'.[40] Scotland was not immune. In fact, since about a quarter of the British army[41] was made up of Scottish regiments, Scotland had the heavier burden to carry. In the early months of 1698 the cobbled streets and narrow closes of Edinburgh were crowded by young men in red coats with no jobs and no immediate prospect of work. Robbery was common enough.

Yet there was good material here to man any colonial adventure. Scottish regiments were often organised on a clan basis with the men bound to the officers by blood and loyalty to the clan chief. This gave them a discipline that the redundant soldiery of England lacked and, since many of the redundant officers were the scions of Scots noble families, they had an enviable political clout in Edinburgh. The king's newly created joint Secretary of State in Scotland, James Ogilvy, Earl of Seafield – no friend to the company – was inundated by such younger sons of noble houses, convinced that he could secure them a position with the Company. He reported to London that 'I have multitudes of broken officers lying around my doors, and I know not what to say to them'.[42] Those who sat on the board of the Company, distinguished Scots noblemen and lairds, men such as the Duke of Queensberry, the young Marquess of Tweeddale[43] and Andrew Fletcher of Saltoun, were lobbied even more strenuously. The offices in Mylne Square were besieged by hopeful ex-soldiers of every rank and station.

On 12 March 1698 they found the following advertisement pinned up on the door:

> The Court of Directors of the Indian and African Company of Scotland having now in readiness Ships and Tenders in very good order ... to settle a Colony in the Indies; give Notice that for the general encouragement of all such as are willing to go upon the said Expedition:
>
> Everyone who goes on the first Equipage[44] shall receive and possess Fifty Acres of Plantable Land and 50 Foot Square of Ground at least in the Chief City or Town, and an ordinary House built thereupon by the Colonie at the end of 3 years...
>
> The family and blood relations shall be transported at the Expence of the Company.
>
> The Government shall bestow rewards for special service.
>
> By Order of the Court
>
> Rod. Mackenzie, Secy

One thousand, two hundred Scots were to go on this first expedition, almost ten times more than had gone on the ill-fated voyage to Stuart Town in 1684. Of these all but a handful were men. Wives and families were to follow later with the planned second expedition. Even so there were many more volunteers than there were places, allowing the Company to select what it considered the cream. Priority was given to recruiting ex-soldiers. Their plight was there for all to see, and they could form a useful defence force for the colony, capable – it was hoped – of beating off any likely attack. Despite the promise to transport relatives at the Company's expense there turned out to be little or no room for ordinary families.

A quarter of the expedition consisted of 'gentlemen volunteers', the sons or close relatives of nobles and lairds. The rest – with the exception of a few craftsmen, doctors, surgeons, apothecaries, clerks and church ministers – were drawn from the ranks of the rank-and-file soldiers, both from highland and lowland regiments. It has been reckoned that a third spoke not English but Gaelic, the language of the wild western highlands and islands.[45]

In all the planning that went into providing for the colony at Darien no-one seems to have given consideration to the importance of leadership. The Company envisaged a committee would make all decisions until a colonial parliament was set up. But there was to be nobody in command, nobody to lead by example from the front. This was the role Paterson had always seen for himself. He believed he had the right qualities. He knew the business of trade and he was utterly incorruptible. In addition, he combined utmost probity and high moral principle with a dash of charisma and a strong vision of how the colony ought to be developed.

There were others in Edinburgh who took rather the same view of his abilities. Among them was Robert Blackwood, a man who may have begun by resenting Paterson's demands that all should be run from London, but who had strongly advised against dispensing with his services in November.[46] Another was the Church of Scotland minister the Reverend Thomas James. James had met Paterson socially in Edinburgh and was impressed by his robust moral rectitude, and his ability to lead by example.

Around the time of the advertisement the Company approached James and asked if he would accept a post of chaplain with the expedition. James seems to have been an outstanding churchman of his day, a man the Company much desired to minister to the boisterous young men who were to settle the land and build the town of New Edinburgh. But he made it clear that he could be won over to the cause only if William Paterson was allowed to go along. He was convinced Paterson was essential to the moral health of the colony, a man who would serve as '… a propagator of virtue and a discourager of vice… [who] would be exemplary to others'.[47] But to reinstate the disgraced Paterson as one of the leaders of the first great voyage was too much for the directors to stomach. The matter of the appointment of the Rev James was politely put to one side, for the time being at least. But the issue was by no means settled, since James continued to be courted by the Company and he continued to press Paterson's claims.

Paterson's big chance came three months later and seems curiously bound up with the strange business of Lionel Wafer's secret visit to Edinburgh in June 1698. The directors were already familiar with Wafer's *Description of the Isthmus of Darien* since Paterson had brought it to them in manuscript form two years previously. Here was a young man whose knowledge of Darien exceeded that of Paterson himself. While Paterson may have had some knowledge of the coast,[48] Wafer had spent six months living among the Cuna Indians, knew their language, and had an intimate knowledge of the riches to be found there. Of course, the directors had no idea he had already been interviewed by the Board of Trade in London, or that he had urged the English government to seize this blessed land to forestall the Scots.

Earlier, in January 1698, instructions had been given to a company representative (quite possibly Andrew Fletcher himself) to go to London with a clear and specific objective: 'You would also engage Mr de la Wafer who was Chyrurgean to Capt. Dampier ... at £3 or £4 per month'.[49] Fletcher certainly met the young man at Pontack's Coffee House as winter gave way to a watery spring and sounded him out. Wafer was willing to discuss terms, and indeed he sent a letter in April offering his services, an offer that was turned down by the directors, presumably because he wanted to be paid rather more generously than the board could afford.[50] Then, at some time in June he was approached again, this time by Dr John Munro.[51] It was rumoured that Wafer's book was finally about to be published and the directors feared it would stir the English government to take action to claim the land before the Scots had a chance to get there. The publication of the book was to be delayed if at all possible.

Munro's presence in London had been occasioned by the renewed attempt on the part of the Company to squeeze money out of James Smith (it had been Dr Munro who had pursued the disgraced man to Dover and had him committed to prison). But with Wafer, Munro showed his gentler side, abandoning the nagging tone he had adopted with Smith, in favour of flattery and persuasion. And he took with him the company's London accountant, James Campbell, to be there to witness any deal.

This was a tough no-nonsense business meeting. Wafer had his agent with him, an Irish merchant by the name of Fitzgerald. In return for a payment of £1,000 (a considerable sum) Wafer offered his services to the Company for two years. Wafer struck a bargain, a payment of £700 for the two-year deal, plus an agreement not to publish the book until the colony was up and running. This was duly witnessed and handshakes exchanged.[52]

A week later, in late June, Wafer took the false name of Mr Brown and travelled north on horseback, being met in the little town of Haddington by a sea captain named Robert Pennicuik:

> ... who told me [Wafer wrote] that he was sent express from the secret committee of the Company to acquaint me it was not convenient I should be seen or known in Edinburgh for some private reasons, that he was to lodge me at a house about a mile wide of the road.[53]

The dark castellation of Andrew Fletcher of Saltoun's country house soon hove into view, with the venerable Scottish knight there to greet him and offer him hospitality for the night. Next morning, five of the men most intimately associated with the planned expedition (including Robert Blackwood and John Haldane) rode up to meet Wafer and discuss the terms of his employment. The fleet would be ready to sail in ten days or so. Asked if he was ready to go, Wafer replied: 'At a day's notice.'

Further meetings took place over the next three days in the spacious serenity of Saltoun Hall. Up to now they had known of Darien only through the filter of William Paterson's eyes, eyes narrowly focused on the potential of Darien as a centre for world trade. Now Paterson was not present and the Scots directors were for the first time free to explore their interest in Darien as a land where much gold and other riches could be found. They shared the belief of the time that gold was present in great quantities only in warm countries. And Mr Paterson's copy of Wafer's manuscript had done more than hint at many great treasures to be found there. Their pulses must have raced a little faster as Wafer confirmed that this was indeed a rich land, for there was much alluvial gold, and many seams to be dug out. And of course there were other treasures, such as the rich groves of dyewood that Wafer had discovered. According to Wafer's account of the discussion:

> having unbosomed myself of all the secrets of that country of Darien as likewise the treasure of Nicaragua wood unknown to any person in Europe but to myself, they insisted most on this treasure, where it grows, if it were near the sea, or easily shipped aboard. I satisfied them particularly of all and in every question they asked me.[54]

Wafer, 'not suspecting any design upon me by persons of such great honour' freely dispensed his knowledge, while the note-taker scribbled ever more furiously. Eventually the five great men rode back to Edinburgh. Soon after, Walter Herries arrived to conduct Wafer (under the cover of that eerie light that serves for darkness in a Scottish mid-summer) to be lodged in one of the capital's tall tenements. The gullible Wafer then found himself confined in this lofty chamber for several days, advised by Herries to stay indoors: '... lest their enterprise should take air in England, which they said must inevitably happen if I were known to be in Scotland.[55]

Wafer was first bemused and then angered. After a few days the pompous Pennicuik – the man he had first met at Haddington – returned as the bearer of ill tidings. The Company, after all, did not wish to employ Mr Wafer, but thanked him for his help and offered him 20 golden guineas for his trouble.[56] By the time Wafer's book came to be published the Scots had arrived in Darien.[57]

In time, the young man came to see the whole charade as an elaborate trick, designed to delay the publication of his book. But there could have been another perfectly simple explanation. The Company had finally been persuaded by the Reverend Thomas James that William Paterson should go on the voyage after all. Wafer's expertise was suddenly no longer required.[58]

The signs of an imminent departure were there for all to see. On 8 June the first of the volunteers were ferried out and lodged in their quarters aboard ship. By the standards of the day they were comfortable, with open decks about seven feet in height, hooks for hammocks fixed to the beams, and curtained areas to give a modicum of privacy. But even at the start there was a hint of indiscipline, a harbinger of trouble ahead. It took almost a month to bring the men on board, and then only after Roderick Mackenzie had circulated an ill-tempered proclamation round the coffee houses of the capital on Wednesday 29 June: '... that all officers and others who are resolved to proceed on the voyage be on board of the several ships allotted for them before or upon Monday next, at twelve o'clock in order to sail'.[59]

While Mackenzie worried about the lower ranks, it was with the leadership that the real problem lay. The question of how good government could be assured among seven 'councillors' appointed by the Company to lead the expedition has still not been fully considered. Three of these were naval officers and came to be known as the 'sea councillors', the other four became 'land councillors'. At sea the three sea councillors were to be in charge, but on arrival at the colony the land councillors had to share power with them. Nobody had ever worked out just how such a divided leadership was to function effectively once they reached Darien, and there was no time to work out some *modus vivendi* between them before they left. The selection of the seven was not finally completed until two days before the expedition set sail. The seven proved to be a strangely unimpressive body of men.[60]

Of the land councillors, two were soldiers shaken out of the army by the demobilisation following Ryswick. The first of these was James Montgomerie, a well-connected young man whose grandfather was an Earl, and whose uncle held the position of 'Lord of the Treasury' in Scotland. He had been a member of Sir John Hill's Regiment, based in Fort William at the southern end of the Great Glen, and may have been stationed at Glencoe immediately following the massacre of the Macdonald chief and his kinsfolk tenants. Officers in the Regiment had become enthusiastic shareholders in the Company of Scotland.[61] Once in Darien, Montgomerie was to be asked to take charge of military operations in Darien against the Spanish. While he was to lead his men into a jungle ambush, he could not be accused of lacking courage. However, he lacked the maturity and wisdom that a councillor needed.

Montgomerie's presence on the expedition may have been related to the fact that a fellow officer in Hill's Regiment, Major James Cunningham of Eickhart, had been keen to find office himself within the Company and had been himself invited to become a land councillor. The least said about Cunningham the better. He had never seen military action and in his entire life had never before left Scotland. Herries tells us he was 'a Pillar of the Kirk' and the influence of the Presbyterian Church of Scotland in the counsels of Mylne Square should not be underestimated. However, man of the church or not, the only impact he was to make on the colony was to be the first to leave it.

The third land councillor had been invalided out of the army after he sustained a serious wound fighting in the Low Countries six years previously. This man, William Vetch, had also sprung from a family of radical churchmen and might have ended up in the pulpit had not his father been forced to flee to Utrecht in Holland during the years of religious persecution that had marked the years of Charles II's reign in

Scotland. Vetch had opted to wear the fine uniform of an officer of the Royal Scots Greys, Scotland's fine cavalry regiment, rather than the sombre garb of a preacher. The war had left him with a nagging wound that still troubled him. In early July 1698, when he accepted the offer of councillor, it was impossible to say whether he would be fit enough to travel.

Daniel Mackay, completed the quartet. He was again a young man, in his early twenties, a man described by Walter Herries as: 'a scrivener's or writer's clerk, newly come out of his apprenticeship'.[62] In fact he was already practising as a lawyer in Edinburgh, although scarcely at the highest level. He was of highland extraction – the Mackays came from Sutherland in the North of Scotland – and of uneven temperament. He may have been chosen because the board of the Company of Scotland felt a lawyer would be needed to draft legal documents establishing land rights, and possibly to assist in drawing up peace treaties with the Indians of Darien. But he was a stirrer rather than a peace-maker, a man addicted to mischief making.

To these four 'land councillors' were added the three 'sea councillors'. The leading figure here was Robert Pennicuik, the man who had met Lionel Wafer at Haddington. Pennicuik had assumed the air of a man born to lead. Yet there was nothing about his past that merited such pretensions. He was now about 32 years of age – eight years younger than Paterson – and had risen up the ranks in the Royal Navy to become a captain. But his sole charge had been a 'bomb-ketch', a lowly sort of vessel. Perhaps his inner insecurity led him to display a streak of despotism that ran deep. He was to command the flagship, the *St Andrew*, and demanded, and was given, supreme command at sea. He liked to be called by his full title – the Commodore.

The second sea councillor was a sea captain who had in fact quit the life at sea some years before to become a merchant in Hamburg. It meant that Robert Jolly was the only one of the seven who could claim to have experience of trade. He was put in command of the second ship, the *Caledonia*, and saw her safely across the Atlantic. But he was decidedly no leader of men, although his real weakness was not to surface until he sat in sullen pique aboard the *Caledonia* as a great row between Pennicuik and Daniel Mackay threatened to wreck the whole project.

Only one of the seven chosen – the third sea councillor Robert Pinkerton – was to prove the sort of inspiring man the colony so desperately needed. He had no airs and graces, no inflated view of his own importance. And he knew something about building a team spirit among his men. He lived in great simplicity in his plain little cabin aboard the *Unicorn* – that 'good pennyworth' acquired by Gibson. Every member of his crew was given a velvet cap with a silver *Unicorn* embroidered on it. He showed a true Christian concern for the welfare of his men, no more so than when he and they were thrown into a Spanish dungeon in Cartagena and narrowly escaped with their lives. But even seven men in the same mould as Pinkerton would have been hard pressed to make the council work effectively. Without Paterson or Smith to draw up a working constitution, it was to fall apart under the weight of its inner contradictions.

Right up to the middle of July, William Paterson did not know whether he would go on the expedition or be part of the crowd who were to wave farewell to the fleet from the harbour walls of Leith. Unfortunately he has left us no account of how he felt, ostracised by his former fellows on board, his experience and wisdom totally ignored.

He had, for instance, determined that it was much better for the fleet to leave, not from the Forth – on the east coast of Scotland – but from the Clyde on the west. Not only was the water deeper there, but the Firth of Clyde gave easy access to the North Atlantic. In June 1696, at the height of his popularity, he had crossed to Glasgow on horseback and had inspected possible departure points, particularly the facilities at Port Glasgow and Greenock. But the board had quietly chosen to shelve those plans, which would have meant the fleet sailing directly to the Clyde from Hamburg and Amsterdam, depriving Edinburgh of the pageantry of both the arrival from Europe and of the departure for Darien.[63]

In the shallow Forth the great ships had been forced to anchor a mile or so out from Leith, meaning the stores and trading goods to be taken on the voyage had to be ferried by small vessels far out into the firth. Still, it must have been hard to avoid a sense of excitement as the day for sailing grew closer when the entire hopes of Scotland hung on a successful outcome to Paterson's 'noble undertaking'.

About the middle of July, fate – or the hand of God – intervened. It had become increasingly clear that William Vetch, the wounded councillor would not be fit to travel. At the same time the Rev Thomas James was once again engaged in negotiations over his part in the whole adventure. He still insisted he would go on the voyage only if William Paterson went too. Vetch's misfortune might yet become Paterson's opportunity. The strange events of July suggest the final decision to let Paterson go on the expedition was taken late in the day, with arguments going on behind the scenes up to the very last moment.

On Thursday 14 July, in fine sunny settled weather, and to the cheers of assembled crowds of relatives and well-wishers lining the harbour wall at Leith, the five ships raised anchor, ran up the company emblem and the Saltire flag of Scotland, let their sails billow out, and turned their prows to the north-east. But they had sailed only some three leagues – some nine miles – in a light breeze when they dropped anchor again off the coast at Kirkcaldy (the unassuming town that was to be the future birthplace of Adam Smith).

Here Robert Blackwood could make a last check of the ships' inventories, while they waited for Vetch to come on board. The check on the cargoes was to take four days. On the second day, the Saturday, a small vessel boat drew alongside the *Unicorn*, carrying a man and his wife. They were helped aboard and introduced to the Captain and Vice-Admiral, Robert Pinkerton. The pair turned out to be William Paterson and his wife Hannah.

✺

Whether Paterson had come to any informal arrangement with the directors it is hard to say. There are certainly hints of a deal of sorts. Paterson was offered a cabin at the stern of the ship and was not expected to rough it with the 'planters' on the decks amidships. He was also allowed to bring his wife, a privilege available to very few. There again, was it significant that he was allocated a place on Pinkerton's ship rather than on the Commodore's vessel the *St Andrew*? Robert Pennicuik was a notably prickly man who would brook no dissent. It seems hardly possible that he and Paterson could have shared the same deck. Pinkerton, on the other hand, made the Patersons and the Rev Thomas James welcome. Whatever the deal brokered by James, Paterson lost no time in reasserting a claim to leadership. He was rowed over to the *St Andrew* and suggested he might inspect the provisions to ensure they were ample for the voyage. Pennicuik gave him short shrift.

✺

Much ink has been expended describing the failings of the 'Committee for Equipping Ships' in terms of the cargoes they had selected, unfairly as we have seen. But this has been nothing to the harrowing tales about the failure to provide adequately for the voyage and the early days of the colony. These stories were probably exaggerated. Tales of food that rotted and water that turned sour were commonplace among sailors. And while many people died on the voyage, the casualty rate was low for the time. In 1771 John Dalrymple could write: 'Twelve hundred men sailed in five stout ships and arrived at Darien in two months, with the loss of only fifteen of their people'.[64] If he underestimated the length of the journey by a month, and the death rate by more than half, it still appears by the standards of the time to have been a healthy crossing. Some 35 people apparently were to die on the way, mostly of the 'bloody flux' – or dysentery. But a death rate of just three people in every hundred on a long voyage was surprisingly low for the time.

The first week of the voyage was in William Paterson's view the stormiest and most unpleasant. It was an ordeal the adventurers could have been spared if the expedition had left from the Firth of Clyde. On leaving the waters off Kirkcaldy on 18 July the commanders opened their first batch of sealed sailing orders and were instructed to sail to Madeira, the Portuguese island off the north-west coast of Africa. Because they had used the Forth as the point of departure, to sail south they first had to go north, hugging the East Coast of Scotland and braving the treacherous northern waters to round Cape Wrath (the most north-westerly point on the British mainland) to gain access to the Atlantic.

Many of the passengers suffered from sea-sickness. Paterson was later to write to the directors: 'For God's sake, be sure to send the next fleet from the Clyde, for the passage north about is worse than the whole voyage to the Indies'.[65] On 31 July, the five vessels found themselves scattered and adrift, still in Scottish waters somewhere off the Isle of Lewis. *The Unicorn*, perhaps because it was a faster ship, or simply because Pinkerton was the most seasoned of the captains, found itself ahead of the others. But a lookout spotted the sails of the small *Endeavour* and they headed together in convoy south for Madeira.

The crossing of the Bay of Biscay was rough and difficult but good progress was made. On 15 August, Cape St Vincent was spotted to the south-east and two white pigeons landed on the deck of the *Unicorn*, an event of almost biblical significance.[66] Ahead lay the coast of Africa. Only when the ships reached the known latitude of Madeira, at 33 degrees north, did they turn from the land and head west with the north-east trade wind filling their sails. On 20 August the mountains of Madeira were seen ahead, tantalisingly near. Then a storm blew them off course and they were unable to gain harbour at Funchal, the chief port, until the 22nd.

Here the fleet regrouped and Pennicuik convened the first meeting of the Council on board the *St Andrew*. William Vetch's last-minute withdrawal had left them a man short. A man of stature and experience was needed to fill the vacancy. Perhaps a deal had already been made. Perhaps it was obvious to the councillors that William Paterson was the person best-suited to share with them the burden of managing the expedition. He may not have been wholly surprised to be offered the job.

This was Paterson reborn, but not quite as before. He now had to share power with the six younger men, five of whom made a point of showing him scant respect.[67] But, for the moment that did not exhibit itself. At Madeira, the moment of truth was upon them. The instructions had been that the second set of sealed orders was only to be opened and read when they were ready to leave Madeira. The seven gathered round Pennicuik's table expectantly. Madeira was a staging post used both by ships bound for the Cape of Good Hope and for America. It was now that the true course of the voyage was to be revealed. The seal was delicately broken and the parchment gently unrolled on the table.

Below decks, Walter Herries, surgeon on the *St Andrew*, was also waiting to hear, still convinced that the destination was to be the East Indies by way of the tip of Africa. Paterson may have recognised his own handwriting on the orders, and felt a surge of excitement. Pennicuik read out the precise instructions: 'You are hereby ordered in pursuance of your voyage to make the Crab Island, and if you find it free, to take possession thereof on behalf of the Company'.

The Crab Island? Not everyone would have known where to find it, although Paterson did. It was a small island, now called Vieques and part of the US Virgin Isles. Paterson had written an assessment of this island for the Committee of Trade, and very revealing it was too:

> Your comm[ittee] have had under consideration an Island situate near the South east part of Porto Rico, called by the Spanyards Bioques, and by the English Crab Island, as having a good Road for Shiping, being fruitfull and well-watered, and Lying Convenient for the smugling or sloop trade from the Danish island of St Thomas, as also with the English and French Carribie plantations.[68]

Crab Island was clearly seen as a good base for an interloping trade with all the surrounding plantation islands and the description is vivid enough to suggest Paterson had some personal knowledge of the place. He could certainly point out its exact location on the charts of the West Indies. There at the point where the islands even then known as Lesser Antilles sweep in a great curve to point towards the larger islands of Puerto Rico, Hispaniola (the island shared by present-day Haiti and the Dominican Republic) and Cuba. Close by lay the little Danish island of St Thomas – a place which he may have known had connections with the father of James Smith. He certainly knew it remained the haunt of buccaneers.[69]

But tiny Crab Island did not in itself seem a destination worthy of a transatlantic voyage. Pennicuik read on:

> And from thence you are to proceed to the Bay of Darien and make the Isle called Golden Island, which lies close to the shore some few leagues to the leeward of the great river of Darien, in and about 8 degrees north of latitude; and there make a settlement on the mainland as well as the said island, if proper [and as we believe] unpossessed by a European state or nation in amity with his Majesty...[70]

The direction to sail to Darien could not have been completely unexpected – since rumours about Darien had been circulating at least since Robert Douglas had written his letter about Paterson's designs on Darien to one of the directors in September 1696. But none of the seven – not even Paterson – had ever set foot on Darien, and locating it exactly in these days of uncertain longitude could be tricky.[71] Paterson had an answer. When they reached the West Indies he would seek out some of his old buccaneering friends and recruit them to the cause. Golden Island, after all, had long been the haunt of pirates, a sheltered place to careen their bottoms or hide away from the Spanish Windward (or Barlovento) Fleet as it sailed past on its way from Cartagena to Portobello.[72]

From Madeira the course lay west-south-west until the latitude 18 degrees north was reached, with the steady north-east trade singing in the rigging. They would then turn the prows of their vessels to set a course along the 18th parallel until they reached Crab Island. On 10 September, at $23\frac{1}{2}$ degrees N, the Tropic of Cancer was crossed. They were about half way there – and the emigrants seemed to be almost enjoying themselves. Hugh Rose, the young man who kept the official journal of the voyage noted:

Sep. 10 This morning we passed the Tropick of Cancer with a fresh and fair gale, the ships performed the usual ceremony of ducking several of the Ships Crew, who had not passed before; they were hoisted to the main yard arm, and let down 3 several times with a soss into the sea out over heads and ears, there legs being tied somewhat closs, which was pretty good sport.[73]

Progress slowed as the wind moderated, but by 30 September the little fleet had passed through the Lesser Antilles and sailed along the line of the Leeward Islands – Antigua, Montserrat, Nevis and St Kitts.

On the first of October a new council was held with the fleet anchored off Santa Cruz (now St Croix). At Paterson's suggestion it was decided to break the fleet into two. *The Unicorn*, under Pinkerton with Paterson on board, was to make for St Thomas, where Paterson knew he would find the pilot they needed to guide them to Golden Island. The *St Andrew* and the *Caledonia* would head for Crab Island and lay claim to it in the name of the Company. This would then become the rendezvous for the onward journey to Darien.

Paterson's mission went well. On the morning of 1 October he was rowed ashore and was 'lively entertained by the Governor.'[74] The next day, Robert Pinkerton came ashore with the young and impressionable Colin Campbell, who recorded in his journal: '2d November: Our Captain and I went ashore to see the Island, where I saw all sorts of trees and fruits very pleasing to the eye'.[75] By then Paterson had encountered his old friend Robert Allison, the man who had anchored at Golden Island and stood guard over the pirate fleet all those years ago, in early 1680.[76] Now old and grey, and established as a considerable merchant,[77] he remembered Paterson well enough to agree to act as pilot. He packed his things and was taken aboard the *Unicorn*. But before they could raise anchor, the Governor of St Thomas, John Lorentz, who had so lavishly entertained Paterson the day before, approached Pinkerton in a very different mood. He had just heard of the Scots landing on Crab Island and their attempt to claim it for the Company. It was, he assured him, already Danish territory.[78]

While Paterson had put into St Thomas some watchful Danish lookouts had caught sight of the larger Scottish fleet sailing off towards Crab Island. A Danish landing party had been sent hastily to land on the island and raise the Danish flag. But they were too late to prevent Pennicuik from hoisting both the Scottish Saltire – the white cross of St Andrew on a blue background – and the Company flag high upon the island. There had been a real chance of conflict. Fortunately Pinkerton and the *Unicorn* arrived from St Thomas and wiser heads prevailed. Rather than risk a military stand-off over a land noted chiefly for its turtle fishing, the Scots fleet weighed anchor and, with the *St Andrew* in the lead and Allison at the helm, set off to make landfall at Darien.

The voyage to Golden Island proved far more difficult than the Atlantic crossing. This was the hurricane season and although the path of these tropical storms lay to the north, intense cyclones whipped up the wind and produced torrential rain-storms. About thirty of the party perished on this small part of the voyage alone, their bodies committed to the sea. Then, as the fleet approached the coast of Darien, the winds swung to the north-west and a strong current flowed against them, forcing them to tack painfully slowly along the coast. But finally on 30 October – some three months after sailing from the Forth – they dropped anchor off the deep sea inlet known as the Gulf of Darien and were greeted in a friendly fashion by native Indians. The next day a reconnoitring party established that Golden Island lay just a few miles to the north and west.

On 1 November while they explored the island 'with great exactnes' they came across another party of Indians, led by their chief 'Captain' Andreas. While his men were all but naked, he sported a Spanish red coat, white breeches and bare feet. The Scots attempted to do their first business with him.

> He inquired the reason for our coming hither and what we designed. Wee answered our design was to settle among them if they pleased to receive us as friends, our business was trade, and that we would supply them from time to time with such commodities as they wanted, at much more reasonable rates than the Spaniard or any other could do.[79]

Andreas turned out to have no love of Spaniards, and wondered if the Scots might be their enemies. Rose records:

> Wee made answer that wee had no warr with any nation; that if the Spaniard did offer us no affront nor injury, wee had nothing to say to them; but otherwayes we would make war with them. This they seem'd pleased with all, still beleeving us to be privateers and our design upon the South Sea.[80]

These Indians might perhaps be forgiven for thinking that the Scots were nothing more than pirates bent upon plundering Spanish treasure. Many such people had frequented these waters with exactly that purpose in mind. It would take time to demonstrate that these new-comers were intent on peaceful settlement and trade.

That afternoon a party of the Scots came back in great excitement after exploring the coast of the Isthmus that lay some three miles to the south east of Golden Island. They had come across a great natural harbour 'capable of containing a thousand of the best ships in the world, and with no great trouble wharfs may be run out to which ships of the greatest burthen may lay their sides and unload'.[81] The channel leading into it was marred by a rock over which the ocean waves broke in great spumes of foam. But on the landward side the water was deep and wide enough for any known ship. The entrance was narrow and easily defended. Once through the passage the natural harbour ran for a good two miles, with gently sloping sandy shores.

It was everything that Paterson had promised. On 3 November six of the councillors – with Paterson left aboard ship – landed on the peninsula and took possession of the colony in the name of the Company. The sun shone, its heat tempered by a stiff northerly breeze. The fine rivers running into the bay, the tall evergreen trees, the exotic birds that flew from their branches, all seemed like a dream come true. But for Paterson, the most unlucky of men, the moment when his great visionary project seemed at last to be taking off was no moment for rejoicing. His wife Hannah had suddenly died.

In later years her death was seen by his enemies as a curious, even scandalous, affair. A scurrilous ballad, produced in London in 1700, and entitled *Caledonia or the Pedlar Turn'd Merchant* repackaged the story:

> And Paterson's *maiden* was first brought to bed
> Of a *Bastard* and *afterwards* married
> As the *Fruit* of her *Womb*, more Luckily sped
> Than his *Fruitless attempt* which *miscarried*.[82]
> (original emphasis)

Of course this was a ridiculous slander. Hannah Paterson was a widow with two grown daughters and was possibly beyond child-bearing years. And the two were certainly married. The more mundane truth was that fever had broken out aboard the *Unicorn* in the fortnight before landfall. A number of passengers had died. One of the first had been Paterson's close friend, the Rev Thomas James, whose body had been committed to the waves to a salute of four muskets. A week or so later, Hannah had been struck down by the same disease. As the first work-parties laboured to clear the ground for the Company fort, Paterson sat vigil and prayed for her recovery. On 12 November Hannah slipped away and was among the first buried in the colony's new graveyard. Paterson's first public duty was not to proclaim the establishment of the new colony of Caledonia, but to enter a period of mourning for the loss of his wife.

Chapter Nine
Hope Rekindled

There were no secrets in the Caribbean, or precious few. When a large three-masted vessel, armed to the teeth and proudly displaying the Scottish flag, came sailing into the harbour of St Thomas on 1 October 1698 it had inevitably attracted the attention of prying eyes. Prying eyes too when Robert Pinkerton and William Paterson left the *Unicorn* to row ashore in search of a familiar face in the waterside taverns of the small town. And whispering tongues a-plenty.

Most were Danish tongues since it had been Danish territory since 1772. But there were German, English, Dutch, Portuguese and Spanish tongues too, since St Thomas was a 'free port' that had welcomed friendly ships from any European country for the past ten years.[1] The story soon spread about that this fine ship was part of a flotilla of Scottish vessels bound for the Isthmus of Darien to settle an island there, an island variously known as *Las Aves* or *Isla d'Oro*. And news of this sort was sure to travel. As a free port, St Thomas had excellent trading connections with the Spanish-held island of Cuba. Within a matter of weeks, one of the fast little trading vessels from St Thomas had swept past the chain guarding the entrance to the great fortified harbour of Havana, the cross-roads of Spanish trade in the Caribbean. Aboard were a crew of garrulous Spaniards whose amazing story was soon the talk of the quay-side taverns.

As with most sailors' stories it had already become more dramatic with the telling. They now spoke of a great fleet of Scottish ships, carrying 4,000 seasoned soldiers determined to set themselves up on *Isla d'Oro* with the help of the Darien Indians, and then exploit the crossing to the South Sea. The tale raised a stir – it seemed there was a new generation of buccaneers ready to repeat the exploits of Morgan and Sharp.[2] The Spanish sailors' stories were lurid enough to have them hauled before the local magistrates, who took their testimonies and sent the accounts with all due dispatch to Veracruz, the administrative centre of the great province of New Spain[3] on the east coast of Mexico.

The news, when it did arrive in January 1699, could hardly have been a surprise to the Viceroy of New Spain, a devout Catholic man of middling years bearing the name of Don José Sarmiento de Valladares, Conde de Moctezuma.[4] For one thing, news had arrived from Cartagena – in the province of New Granada (modern Colombia) – that the Scots were already well established in Darien. In addition, Sarmiento should have already received from Madrid a copy of a confidential letter sent by the Spanish Resident in the German city of Hamburg to the Spanish Government. It had been written more than a year previously and had warned them that the 'Company of Scotland' had plans to settle in Darien. This warning had been duly relayed to Spanish officials in America.[5]

The news of the arrival of a Scottish fleet in Darien only added to the trouble Sarmiento already had on his hands. French warships had been caught nosing around the coast of Western Florida and General Don Martín de Aranguren Zavala had been summoned from Spain to assist in securing the settlement of Pensacola from French encroachment. Zavala had only just arrived in Veracruz and was making ready to sail to that troubled land but the Scots threat seemed much more immediate.

The Havana intelligence was almost immediately confirmed by a dispatch from the Conde (or Count) de Canillas, *Presidente* of the Panama Province. Canillas was a nervous man, fearing a repeat of the terrible sacking of old Panama City, the remains of which could still be seen from the new city of Panama that had taken its place. His report, that 4,000 Scots had now installed themselves on Golden Island,[6] and that another 6,000 of them were already on their way to secure the settlement, was relayed with all possible speed to Veracruz.

Something close to panic was to seize Sarmiento. His first thought was that this was a serious threat to the Spanish settlements of South America, his second that urgent action was needed. Otherwise, he wrote:

> it may be impossible to prevent pernicious consequences, such as the Scots taking Portobello, Panama, and passing to the South Sea. The experiences of 1681 to 1688 when these coasts were robbed and devastated and the inhabitants ruined showed this to be possible. If this were done by 200 pirates, what may be feared from 4,000 veteran soldiers now supposed to be at Darien?[7]

Although Sarmiento doubted there could be as many as 4,000 of these potential pirates he regarded the danger as extreme. His sent orders to Zavala in January to abandon all plans to sail north to Pensacola. Instead he was to 'depart with the greatest speed ... with all the ships he could choose...'.[8] Zavala was commanded to sail east from Veracruz and gather further forces in Havana. From there he would sail south and west across the eastern Caribbean to descend upon Darien. His task was simple; 'to exterminate the Scottish pirates'.[9]

In early November in his quarters aboard the *Unicorn*, anchored in the safety of the great natural harbour of what was to be called Caledonia Bay, William Paterson would have known nothing of the gathering Spanish alarm over the arrival of a Scottish fleet in the waters of the Spanish Main. In his mind the Scottish Company had quite legitimately settled a land that, in the words of the 1695 Act was: 'not possest by any European Soveraign, Potentate, Prince or State...'.[10]

Paterson based his judgement on the evidence of Sharp, Dampier and Wafer. And, in their private deliberations, the Spanish more or less conceded that the land had not been settled by them.[11] But the word 'possessed' did not necessarily mean 'settled'. Even so, the Cuna Indians did not appear to be under Spanish rule. It is only now that we know for sure that a fledgeling form of Spanish administration was in place.[12] But Paterson remained convinced, in any case, that the Spaniards would welcome the setting-up of a free port along the lines of Curaçao and St Thomas in this undeveloped land.[13] They had already seen the benefits brought by Dutch trade. Once the Scots were properly settled in, he planned to send a letter to the Spanish authorities at Panama assuring them that they had come to trade, not to make war.

In the days preceding and following the death of his wife he seems to have played little part in the process of meeting the Indians and exploring the wondrous new land. This he left to the other councillors, and in particular to Robert Pennicuik. Now that the expedition had landed safely at Darien, the 'Commodore' was finding it difficult to adjust to being just one of seven councillors. In Paterson's absence he dominated the discussions and directed affairs much as though he were still on the high seas, supported by his two fellow sea councillors. As Paterson was later to rather dryly put it in his report to the directors of the company, during the voyage: 'Our Marine councillors ... browbeat and discouraged everybody else. [They] told us we knew nothing of the sea ... Yet we had expected things would mend when we came ashore, but we found ourselves mistaken.'[14]

On 5 November, while Paterson nursed his sick wife, Pennicuik and the other five had gone ashore at the tip of the peninsula guarding the great harbour to choose a site for the fort. The weather was dry and the ground may have looked deceptively well-drained. They took an ill-judged decision to build the fort on a low-lying site overlooking the narrow strait leading to the harbour. In good weather it was fine, but when any great rains fell – in the tropics a frequent and spectacular event – it soon became soggy and marshy. It would later take much effort by Paterson to right this error and have the site moved back from the shore to drier and better-drained ground.

The days that followed brought in a spell of settled weather of the sort to make the settlers believe that they had indeed come to a paradise on earth. Dawn came suddenly as the sun rose dramatically out of the Caribbean – a great orange ball. As the day progressed, gentle sea breezes rustled the fronds of the coconut palms that fringed the shores, and the canopy of the forests provided welcome shade. Brightly coloured parrots flitted among the trees, breaking the silence with their loud squawks. When night fell the canopy of the sky was filled with a dazzling display of stars. There could be no place on earth less like cold, bleak, Scotland.

The fine weather brought new visitors. First came a native canoe, spied by the look-outs coming in from the direction of Golden Island. As it approached they could see it contained a European, two men of mixed race, and four Indians. The Frenchman, who was something of a Robinson Crusoe figure, had lived in these parts for some time and could speak the native language. He rapidly dispelled any notion that the Scots would be able to negotiate a treaty with a single ruler, the 'Emperor of Darien'. Such a man, he assured Pennicuik, did not exist: 'the storyes of King Panco and Golden Cape were mere fables...'.[15]

In fact the Scots were to find that the Indians of Darien lived in many separate family groups, and not by any means always in harmony.[16] Each head man made such alliances as seemed best. Most of them, it seemed, despised the Spanish, although Andreas, the chief they had first encountered at Golden Island, had in fact been an ally of Spain until recently. While there was no single 'emperor' who could guarantee some order and peace – as Paterson had assumed – there was, in fact, one mighty chief who had bound most of the local tribes together in

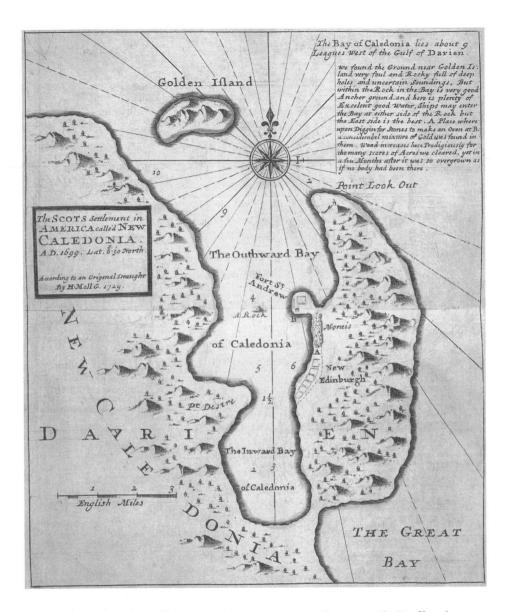

The Scots colony in 1699. To many it seemed a paradise on earth. It offered a safe haven on the north shore of the Isthmus for a thousand ships, or so the enthusiastic Scots believed. But the prevailing north-east wind made it difficult for ships to leave the harbour in the age of sail. The term New Caledonia is not strictly accurate. The leaders gave the colony the name of 'Caledonia'. The scale is misleading. It was just over two miles from Point Look Out to the southern end of the bay (Source: Glasgow University Library Department of Special Collections).

an alliance against Spain. He controlled the land to the north and west beyond Golden Island, in the direction of the San Blas Islands. His name was Ambrosio: 'a man about 60, but strong and vigorous, a mortal enemy to the Spaniard, with whom he has hadd a long warr: he is esteemed the bravest and most successful of their Commanders upon all occasions'.[17]

As the Frenchman extolled the virtues of this Ambrosio, a native *piragua*, a large dug-out canoe equipped with a sail, came into the bay, carrying the great chief himself. With him, he had brought his son-in-law Pedro: 'a brisk little fellow. He speaks good Spanish, having been kept as a slave to them at Panama for several years, and who can never forget their usage of him there'.[18] It transpired he could speak French too, having spent some time in Petit-Goave in French Hispaniola. He acted as translator. Accompanying them were half a dozen near-naked tribesmen.

Pennicuik welcomed them aboard his flagship. Ambrosio and Pedro wore white cloaks, gold nose-pieces, and many rows of beads around their neck and arms. They had come on a mission – to recruit the new arrivals as allies in their wars against the Spanish forces based at Portobello and Panama. The Spanish were their enemies, said Ambrosio, because several of his men had been forcibly abducted to work as slaves in the gold mines of Santa Maria on the other side of the Isthmus.

The mention of gold seems to have sent Pennicuik's pulse racing. How far away was the nearest gold to be found? Why, said Ambrosio, not more than five miles distant, opposite Golden Island, on the slopes of the high mountain. Ambrosio claimed that the Spanish knew of this gold, but had: 'taken great care... never to let them be opened, wel knowing that being so near the North Sea that they would have the least share of them'.[19] Indeed the Spanish fear that the discovery of gold on the Isthmus would act like a magnet to other European powers is well-documented.[20] Ambrosio's clear ambition was to recruit these newcomers to the cause of ridding their ancestral lands of such Spanish impositions.

Pennicuik tells us:

> They pressed us very hard to come and live by them, as also jointly to make war with the Spaniard ... if we would assist them with but a hundred men and as many arms, with 2,000 of their own people [they would] drive them out not only out of all the mines which are but 3 days journey from us, but even out of Panama itself.[21]

To give him his due, Pennicuik realised this would be madness. It would make a mockery of the Scottish claim to have come in peace. Pennicuik stuck to the Company line, that the Scots had come in peace to trade. But Ambrosio was persistent. He promised the Scots a warm welcome if they moved north-west along the coast to set up their base in his territory. Pennicuik decided it was worth a look: 'We ... promised to go westward with them to view the coast, and if there were any convenient harbours for our shipping wee would be their neighbours'.[22]

It was only later that the Scots discovered that Ambrosio and Andreas were bitter rivals. As to Ambrosio's warning that Andreas had not only been made a 'captain' by the Spanish but was: 'a very Spaniard in his heart',[23] the Scots refused to believe it.

Two weeks later, after the death of Hannah Paterson but before Paterson had been able to assert any authority over the council, Pennicuik embarked on his journey to cement the embryonic alliance he had secured with Ambrosio. The weather had been stormy with heavy rain, but now a calm spell allowed the Commodore and a small party to undertake a 20-mile journey along the mangrove-fringed shoals, bays, and sandbanks of Darien in the ship's ample pinnace.[24] As they travelled along the coast they had a chance to survey the grandeur of this new and apparently empty land, with its tall forests backed by the ridge of the divide. They did indeed find another great harbour, large enough, Pennicuik said with some hyperbole, to be home to 10,000 ships. He considered moving the settlement to this new site, but it lacked the security of the place they had already selected. It was open to attack from along the coast in both directions and there were numerous deep channels between the islands guarding it. Several forts would be needed to defend it and Pennicuik appreciated that this was out of the question. He took the matter no further.

As for Ambrosio's hope for an alliance against the Spaniards, nothing came of it. By the time Pennicuik returned to the comfort of his cabin on the *St Andrew*, William Paterson had emerged from his period of mourning to give absolutely no encouragement to the idea. It was dropped. But the trip did give the Scottish settlers their first chance to see for themselves the abundant promise of this new land. When they reached Ambrosio's village, a good three miles back from the coast on the banks of a river, they were welcomed by his entire extended family and invited to spend the night in the large communal hut with the sounds of the forest lulling them to sleep. In the morning they were treated to a sumptuous meal:

some plantans [bananas], potatoes, and wild hog dresst for breakfast after their fashion. Then Ambrosio and Pedro went out with their guns to kill some fowl for the strangers. Pedro returned with some partridges the largest and best [we] ever saw, being bigger than capons and exceedingly sweet.[25]

Later, on the return to the coast: 'Pedro did climb high coconut trees and threw down a great number most delicious for the juyce and kernel. They are very big'.[26] Such descriptions do something to counter the received wisdom, passed down from historian to historian, that the Scots settlers spent a wholly miserable time in this strange land, caught between death by starvation on the one hand, and death by fever on the other.

The trip had one unexpected and tragic sequel. About a month later Ambrosio made a return trip to the Scots base and found Andreas being entertained by Pennicuik aboard ship. The two chiefs quarrelled violently and had to be separated by the burly Scotsman. Pennicuik insisted they should be friends and joined them in a drinking session. That evening a drunken Ambrosio, Walter Herries tells us, 'fell or was rumbled down the main hatchway into the hold, where lighting on a spare anchor ... he was so bruised that he gave up the ghost soon afterwards'.[27] The death of Ambrosio, in the course of a drinking session, was a scandalous event, and all accounts of it were suppressed in the official reports. But there seems little doubt that Walter Herries told the truth. There is no further mention of Ambrosio in the records. In his place we find Pedro, his son-in-law.[28]

By the time the explorers returned from the journey along the coast, William Paterson was already focusing his mind on what was to be done to turn the dream of a great entrepôt in Darien into reality. Even the trauma of Ambrosio's death could not deflect him from that grand objective.

The first task was to make the council a more effective instrument of government. The choice of the site for the fort was symptomatic of the problem. Apart from Paterson, there seemed to be no-one among the seven councillors capable of standing up to Pennicuik. The first battleground was the question of the fort. One of the ex-army officers, a certain Captain Thomas Drummond, had been put in charge of the building work. Drummond was a military man to the core, a brave soldier who had fought in the Low Countries, but is better known to history as a member of the regiment that carried out the massacre at Glencoe. Whatever his reputation for heartless slaughter, he had the instincts of a good artillery officer.

Drummond had already made it clear that he thought the site chosen for the fort would be useless during the rainy season, which was due to start in April. But Drummond had no direct voice in the council's deliberations held round the Commodore's table on the *St Andrew*, and his pleas had gone unheeded. It did not help that Pennicuik had conceived an irrational hatred of Thomas Drummond and his brother Robert, who had captained one of the small ships, the *Dolphin*, on the outward voyage. Pennicuik was a proud man who had regarded the slightest display of criticism on the voyage as incipient mutiny. Now on *terra firma* his attitude appears to have been little different.

This was a tricky issue, but Paterson applied calm logic over the matter of the site of the major fortification. That, and a few tropical down pours, convinced a majority on the council that the fort would have to be moved, even if it meant bruising the ego of the Commodore. Pennicuik was not, unfortunately, the sort of man to forget such a slight.

Paterson was less successful in changing the strange rules that made good government of the new colony almost impossible. During his period of disgrace, the directors in Edinburgh had decreed that each of the seven men should take part in a bizarre game of musical chairs by taking turns as 'president' for a week at a time. Paterson complained that each new president spent most of his week undoing the work of his predecessor. He tried his best to persuade the councillors this had to change. As he later told board members at Mylne Square:

> ... it troubled me exceedingly to see our affairs thus turmoiled and disordered... To this disease I proposed as ... part of a remedy, that a President of the Council should be chosen for a month, and that the first should be a land Councillor, and that every land Councillor might take his turn before any of those of the sea should come in place. This I reckoned, would be four months; and in this time I was in high hopes that we might be able to make some laws, orders and rules of government, and... be better able to judge who might be most fit to preside for a longer time, not exceeding a year.[29]

Since there were four land councillors and only three sea councillors, Paterson must have been fairly confident of carrying the day. But the land councillors surprised Paterson by flatly turning down the idea. Paterson blamed it on the dreadful mediocrity of most of the councillors: 'mean spirits ... that had no virtue of their own.. ... which makes them so unwilling to believe [it] in other people'.[30] Perhaps they were brow-beaten by Pennicuik, perhaps they simply lacked the will to take on the responsibility implied in a monthly presidency but it meant the weekly merry-go-round continued.

Carving a colony out of the virgin forest of Darien was a daunting task. But here Paterson could take reasonable satisfaction with the progress achieved. On 5 November the first working parties went ashore to begin clearing some of the 'tall stately trees' that covered the peninsula. Applying some of the discipline learnt in the tough battles of Flanders, working parties under junior officers bent every sinew to levelling the ground and erecting the bamboo huts with palm leaf roofs, stretching out along the line of what was to be the main street of 'New Edinburgh'. Soon the first residents would move in.

With December came the onset of the dry season, somewhat later than expected, and Darien put on its most attractive face. Temperatures often soared into the 90s (32 degrees Celsius or more) but the great tropical canopy provided welcome shade, and sea breezes brought some relief from the oppressive humidity. Those settlers who could read and write penned descriptions to be despatched home by the first available ship. They wrote of the new colony with some genuine affection, describing the land in superlatives as 'one of the most fruitful and healthy on earth'.

Although some historians have seen the use of such phrases as part of an agreed strategy to talk up the success of the colony, there seems no reason to doubt that, in the dry season, this was a beguiling land. Some letters were certainly written for publication and may have contained an element of whistling to keep the spirits up, but even private letters, such as that written by young John Turnbull to John Erskine, spoke of Darien as a new Eden where fruit fell from the trees, the forest abounded with game, and the rivers poured with fish.[31]

As for the council, it boasted in its first report that the land abounded in: 'Cocoa-Nuts, whereof chocolate is made, Bonellos, Sugar-Canes, Maize, Oranges, Plantains, Mangoe, Yams, and several others... of the best of their kind found anywhere'.[32] William Paterson, writing in person to his friend, John Borland, in Boston, New England, was even more effusive:

> Our Sictuation is about Two Leagues to the Southward of Golden-Island ... in one of the best and most-defensible harbours perhaps in the World. The Country is Healthful to a Wonder; in so much that our own Sick, which were many when we Arrived, are now generally cured. The Country is exceedingly Fertile, and the Weather Temperate. The Country where we are Settled, is dry, and rising Ground, Hills but not High; and on the sides, and quite to the tops, three, four, five foot good fat mould, not a Rock or a Stone to be seen. We have but Eight or Nine Leagues to a River, where Boats may go into the South Sea...[33]

In short, this was as desirable a site for a colony and trading post as had ever yet been discovered, but only six months later, many were to learn that paradise had its darker side.

Despite the ups and downs, by the end of 1698, Paterson had managed to set his imprint on the new settlement. His persuasive rhetoric worked its magic on the council, convincing the majority that there was a higher purpose to this colony than merely the search for gold or for the elusive groves of dyewood.[34] The goal of building a great new emporium to serve the world was triumphantly reaffirmed.[35] On 28 December 1698 the Council approved a declaration announcing that the colony would henceforth be known as *Caledonia*,[36] and its citizens, of whatever race, as *Caledonians*. It also proclaimed that the site of the colony:

> ... hath the advantage of being a narrow Isthmus seated in the height of the World, between two vast Oceans, which renders it more convenient than any other for being the Common Storehouse of the... immense treasures of the spacious South Seas, the door of commerce to China and Japan, and the Emporium and staple [port] for the trade of both Indies.[37]

To turn this vision into reality the doors of the colony had to be thrown open to free trade. Following the lead of Amsterdam, religious and racial discrimination had to be cast aside.[38] The spirit of the later American Declaration seemed to be foreshadowed here in the humble little town of New Edinburgh:

... we declare a general and equal freedom of ... trade to those of all nations that shall hereafter be... concerned with us; but also a full and free liberty of Conscience in matters of Religion...[39]

Later, on Paterson's initiative, a friendly letter was despatched to the Spanish authorities in Panama, assuring them that the Scots had come in peace to open up trade and not to set up a pirate base to prey on passing Spanish treasure ships. But while they hoped the Spaniards would welcome the Scottish merchants to the mutual benefit of both, they also warned them that they would fight back if attacked.[40] With this combination of the carrot and the stick, Paterson hoped to open the eyes of the Spanish governors to the benefits that would flow from his great new entrepôt. But sound as Paterson's argument might me, the fates decreed that the Spanish were to be given an entirely different first impression of the Scots' purpose. The first ships to approach the harbour, and seek safe passage into its sheltered waters, were not the trading vessels Paterson had hoped for, but ships of a decidedly questionable kind.

The first visitor had put in an appearance a fortnight after they had first laid sight on the great natural harbour that now was to be called Caledonia Bay. On 13 November, a ship flying the English colours had been sighted to the west in the vicinity of Golden Island. It had vanished, lost in the bright shimmer of a now sunlit sea. Two days later a small ship's boat, propelled by sturdy oarsmen rounded the point guarding the bay, now named Forth Point, and came riding into the bay. At the back sat an English sea captain. He announced himself to be Richard Long, an English captain carrying a commission from King William to seek out sunken treasure along this coast. He was immediately suspected of being an English spy, but was shown great hospitality nevertheless, dining with Pennicuik and Pinkerton on consecutive days. The true nature of Richard Long's mission was never to be known to the Scots.[41] On this occasion he stayed two days and was gone.

Before that, on 11 December, two more ships put in an appearance, dropping anchor off Golden Island. One bore the French flag; the other was a Dutch vessel. Soon a long-boat was seen approaching, carrying a representative from each of the ships. The Frenchman bore the uniform of an officer of Louis XIV's navy, the Dutchman the air of a rough-and-

ready trading man. Pennicuik welcomed them aboard the *St Andrew*.
The Frenchman explained that he called on behalf of his captain, a man
of some repute in Petit-Goave (the French buccaneering base in
Hispaniola) by the name of Duvivier Thomas.[42]

Duvivier Thomas, too, was not exactly what he seemed. We know now
that he had been sent, on the pretext of putting a stop to French piracy
against Spanish shipping following the Treaty of Ryswick, to act as a
French spy along the Darien coast, and to carry off Indians as slaves to
serve in the French territories.[43] For their part, the Scots took him at his
word that he was operating under the commission of King Louis XIV
with the power to prey on any Spanish vessel he encountered. The fact
that his ship is referred to in the accounts by two quite different names,
the *San Antonio*[44] and the *Maurepas*, suggests it had itself only recently
been taken as a 'prize'. He was certainly later to boast, when drunk, that
he had a store of 60,000 Spanish pieces-of-eight in his roundhouse. Now
he sought a sheltered spot where he might beach his ship to repair its
leaking timbers.

The second man, who turned out to be the purser on the Dutch ship,
admitted that his was an interloping vessel, trading illicitly with
Cartagena, and that his captain was anxious to find a place to hide away
from the Spanish Windward Fleet that passed along this coast once a
year on its way from Cartagena to Portobello.[45] Without much thought
of the consequences, Pennicuik (who at this point was in more or less full
control of the colony) invited the ships to sail into the harbour. The
Dutch vessel came first, on the morning of 12 December, firing a seven-
gun salute, and allowing Pennicuik the pleasure of reciprocating with
five loud plumes of smoke from his fine Swedish-made cannons. That
afternoon Captain Duvivier Thomas himself paid a visit in a small boat
and brought news of how the Scots settlement had been received along
the coast.

His news was a strange mixture of gossip and hard fact. He was right
for example in believing that a fleet of four warships had just arrived
from Spain (under the command of Zavala) and that it was at this stage
(December 1698) preparing to sail to Pensacola but he was quite wrong
to believe that the Spaniards ever imagined the Scots' real objective was
the Mississippi. His view that the whole of Central America was on the
point of rebellion against Spain seems to have been pure fantasy. The
man enjoyed a good brandy and became more garrulous as the day
wore on. He talked of the French settlements already established along

the coast towards Portobello, and – looking round the broad expanse of Caledonia Bay – suggested that the French might take a leaf from the Scottish book and 'push fair for a great share of [Darien] upon the King of Spain's death'.[46]

Since the King of Spain was considered at this point to have not long to live, it must have given the Scots' leaders some satisfaction that they had landed and laid claim to this part of Darien first.[47] The next day, 13 December, the *Maurepas* made a grand entrance, firing a salute of no less than nine guns. Pennicuik replied in kind (a nine-gun salute was reserved for ships of the Royal Navy, but Pennicuik maintained the Scots fleet held the king's commission[48]) and then added a three-gun 'thank you'. The French replied, and then the Scots again. Quite a little ceremony. But the festive mood was not to last.

The following day Richard Long and his sloop, the *Rupert Prize*, came racing into harbour. Sailing south-east along the coast he had chanced upon four great ships of the Windward Fleet taking on water in a cove known as Burus. They would be upon the colony in but a day. The news set pulses racing. The gangs of men sweating to complete the new fortifications at Fort St Andrew, as the strongpoint had now been named, rushed to make them serviceable and the entire Scottish fleet was drawn up in line of battle across the entrance to the harbour. In his journal on the night of the 17th Hugh Rose recorded: 'The battery is going quickly on; our men are very hearty and seem to long for a visit from Jacque [the Spaniard].'[49]

There were a few days of high drama, with Ambrosio adding to the excitement and apprehension by reporting that a force of Spanish soldiers was on the way from Portobello to try to drive the Scots out. But in the end nothing happened. No fleet appeared, no soldiers. The Scots were free to turn back to the more mundane business of completing the simple little settlement of New Edinburgh and relax. Or perhaps not quite. There remained the matter of the armed French ship tied up in Caledonia Bay harbour.

☀

Two weeks after his arrival Captain Duvivier Thomas, apparently on an impulse, decided it was time to resume his cruise. All thought of repairing his ship seems to have been abandoned, suggesting the story of the leak in the hull had been only a convenient fiction. He was a drinking

man and, much to Paterson's distaste, he had spent little of his time
sober. The night before he had been drinking heavily – he enjoyed the
company and the brandy of the congenial Scots – and his seamanship
proved wanting. He fell foul of the tricky sea passage out of the harbour
in the face of a persistent north wind.[50]

On this occasion the wind had whipped the sea up into a heavy surg-
ing swell that threatened to push any vessel towards the rocky mainland
shore. The *Maurepas* hoisted enough sail to give it purchase to fight the
swell and make for the open sea. But the wind suddenly dropped just as
she entered the narrowest part of the channel. Beneath the flapping
sailcloth the captain and crew were helpless to prevent the ship drifting
steadily towards the menacing rocks on her port bow.

To his credit, Pennicuik and some of the crew from the *St Andrew* went
to the rescue in small boats, getting some lines aboard and towing the
Maurepas away from the shore into deeper water. The French ship
dropped anchor and the crisis seemed over for the moment at least.
Then everything went wrong. Hugh Rose in his Journal recorded what
happened.

> The ship did ride about 3 quarters of an hour after they anchored, and
> then her best bower cable broke, and in halfe and hour after the small
> bower gave way, so ashoare she went on the rocks, where in halfe and
> hour she was all to peeces, no boat daring to come near her.[51]

Captain Duvivier Thomas, who like most sailors of the time could not
swim, was personally rescued by Pennicuik, whose bravery cannot be
questioned. He stripped off all his clothes and plunged from the St
Andrew into the bay: 'Naked as I was born, without much ado, I swam
ashore. The seas broke over me, under each of which I was at least 20
seconds, and indeed two such more would have done my business'.[52]
Twenty-two out of a crew of fifty-six were drowned, some weighed
down, it was said, by the weight of treasure strung around their necks.

Sunken treasure had an irresistible lure for sailors of the period. The
news that a French treasure ship had gone to the bottom in shallow seas
spread quickly along the coast, attracting treasure hunters in the weeks
to come. Instead of building trade with the neighbouring islands and
along the coast of the Main, Paterson found his energies being engaged
in keeping out such undesirable traffic. But he could not keep the
thought of the wealth lying in the bay out of the minds of the toiling
Scottish settlers. That was beyond even his power.

Paterson was the first councillor to move from the comfort of his cabin aboard ship, to take up residence in the High Street of New Edinburgh, the newly named capital of Caledonia. Despite the sudden downpours of rain that could turn the 'street' quickly into a sea of mud, and despite the squabbles that marked the meetings of the Council aboard the *St Andrew*, Paterson retained his apparently irrepressible optimism. He was still able to write in February 1699:

> ... the Work here is the most Ripened Digested, and the Best Founded to the Priviledges, Place, Time, and other like Advantages, that ever was begun in any part of the Trading World ... If Merchants should once erect factories here, this place will soon become the best and surest Mart in all America, both for in-land and over-land trade.[53]

He certainly underestimated just how much time and effort would be needed to establish the fort and lay out the site. Clearing the land involved the felling of giant hardwoods, the cutting back of the snake-infested undergrowth, and the digging of deep defensive earthworks. For people from Northern Europe unused to the heat and humidity of the tropics it was exhausting work, all done without the benefits of anything more sophisticated than the hand-saw, the wheelbarrow and the spade. Many went down with fever, some died of it – although the death-rate still remained modest for trading posts of this type.[54]

Feeding a population of 1,000 young men, day after day, remained the biggest challenge. The convoy from Scotland had carried with it rations for six months or so. But only two or three days out from Edinburgh the calculations of just what was required were shown to be seriously at fault. Even the optimistic Paterson observed that the basic provisions fell 'exceedingly short of what was given out or expected; whereupon our people were reduced to a much shorter allowance'.[55]

The fact that the settlers arrived at Darien under-nourished as a result of the rationing helps explain the almost universal joy at the apparent fruitfulness of the colony. But no crops could be sown that year[56] and the feeding of over a thousand people on a daily basis made prodigious demands on the available supplies of yams, bananas, coconuts and yuccas. By March it was reported to the Spanish authorities that the Scots 'had devoured all the plantings which the Indians had in this ... region, such as maize and other plants called yuca'.[57]

Of course the seas abounded in giant turtle – one of them it was said could feed 100 men – but the Scots suffered from a sad lack of expertise when it came to catching them. And although fish were more easily caught, there was a shortage of the nets needed to provide anything like an adequate supply.

The result was that the colony had to rely on what was left of the provisions brought from Scotland, eking out the dried cod (known as stockfish), cured beef, and salt herrings as best they could, while making do with a ration of less than two pounds of flour per person per week. It did not help that much of the beef had become rotten, and the flour badly contaminated. One younger 'gentleman volunteer', Roger Oswald, confided in a letter sent to his cousin in Edinburgh that it was best not to examine too closely what was in his weekly ration of flour: 'if it had been well-sifted you would have got a quarter a pound of mouldy maggots, worms and other such beasts out of the same'.[58]

The problem of supplying the settlement with food during its first year had been anticipated by Robert Douglas, the London-based Scot who had warned the Edinburgh directors against attempting a settlement on a virgin site in Darien, as early as September 1696. He had written to one of the directors that: 'the uncertainty of finding provisions for so many men as the expedition will require on their arriving might prove fatal'.[59] But Paterson knew his West Indies, and fully expected supplies to be brought from Jamaica by enterprising merchants. And his expectation of trade was well based. Scarcely a year before, the Governor of Jamaica, William Beeston, had sent home to England a vivid description of the poor service the island was receiving from the mother country. He reported that: 'there came not from England necessaries enough to furnish the people's wants, nor ships enough to take away their produce'. He added, defensively: 'Their wants oblige them to countenance all importers'.[60]

This is the sort of information that would have been passed on to Paterson by Robert Allison, himself a trading man. As a result Paterson expected Jamaican vessels to come to New Edinburgh anxious to trade their produce for some of the Scots' cargo, so carefully selected by William Arbuckle. And ships not just from Jamaica, but from the English American colonies too. The Scots had already encountered just such a trading ship at Crab Island, under the command of Richard Moon. Moreover, Moon was, at that time, in business partnership with Robert Allison, and was presumably well-disposed to the whole Darien venture.[61] But the encounter had shown that the biggest obstacle to the development of this much-needed trade was the attitude of the Scots themselves.

At Crab Island they had insisted in offering their wares, mainly clothing and household items, at the prices assigned to them by the Company's agents in Edinburgh. But in the Caribbean, horse-trading was the norm and, since the colonists needed Moon's flour and herrings more than he needed their hats and saucepans, he had the upper hand. Paterson did his best to make his fellow councillors see they were hardly in a position to drive a hard bargain, that it was much better to cut their prices and strike a deal.[62] But such arguments were lost on them. They told him angrily (he later recorded) that: 'they were not obliedged to take notice of any particular man's assertions as to the over-valueing ... of the goods; but rather to believe that the prime cost was as in the Company's goods invoyce; and that they would not be so imposed on by Capt. Moon.'[63] So Captain Moon had sailed off from Crab Island with his cargo to Curaçao, where he knew both would have a ready sale, and where he would also have a chance to take on a cargo of Negro slaves. These he would then transport to the slave market in Cartagena and sell under the noses of the Spanish authorities.

Paterson had salvaged what he could from the encounter. He had taken Moon aside and quietly persuaded him not to write the Scots off but to call in at the new settlement at Darien before the year was out. By that time, he hoped, he would have taught the councillors a lesson or two. And indeed, on 20 December, just a week after the *Maurepas* had made her grand entrance, and just when the scare over an imminent Spanish attack was subsiding, Richard Moon's sloop did put in a fresh appearance and dropped anchor in the lee of the headland, close by the *St Andrew*. In command was a young sea captain by the name of Edward Sands.

Sands was to become a real friend to the colony. He had come with a new cargo of cured beef and flour, commodities now very much in short supply. This time the negotiations were handled with a little more subtlety. The Scots agreed to pay Jamaican prices plus 10 per cent for the provisions. No money changed hands, simply a credit note handed to Sands that listed the Scots goods to be given in return, and the price of each, when the sloop next visited the colony a month later.[64]

Paterson was all but alone in seeing that the future viability of the colony depended on building up such trade. There were dozens of interloping sloops just like this carrying on their illicit business with the English, French, and Spanish ports scattered around the Caribbean. If the Scots showed they had goods to trade at keen prices it would not take long for the word to spread to every corner of that sea. Merchants would be attracted in and would soon be conducting trade between themselves (just as they did at Curaçao), free of the heavy customs duties that were imposed as the norm elsewhere. This would be the small acorn from which the great trading emporium would grow.

Unfortunately, generally outvoted on the council, Paterson found himself a voice crying in the wilderness. His advice was ignored.

Sands stayed for nine days, time enough to get to know some of the Scots officers and to like them. He left on 29 December, carrying the Scottish goods he had chosen, a parcel of letters and papers from the colony to relatives and friends in Scotland, and a copy of Hugh Rose's engaging journal of the voyage and the landing. These would be forwarded from Jamaica by way of Bristol or London. Among the papers from the council to the Company in Edinburgh was an urgent request for the despatch of fresh supplies to the colony without delay. As Sands successfully reached the open sea and headed north on the voyage of some 600 miles to Jamaica, he also had on board three of the Scottish emigrants, the first to leave the colony. They stood on his poop deck, watching the coastline retreat to the south with mixed emotions.

The first was one of the chosen seven councillors, Major James Cunningham, a tiresome, conceited man, who had contributed little since he had first set foot on the *St Andrew* in the Forth. The second was Walter Herries, the Dumbarton surgeon who had been convinced he had been booked to sail to the East Indies. Herries marked his return to London by suing the company for unpaid wages and having John Haldane, then visiting London and still a director of the Company, committed to gaol.[65] Later he was to write his grossly misleading account of the whole enterprise, a copy of which was to fall into the hands of Lord Macaulay, allowing him to add the acid of ridicule to his critical prose. Paterson was not unhappy to see the back of both of these gentlemen. But, as to the third, it was quite a different story.

The council had decided to despatch the colony's Accountant-General, Alexander Hamilton, to make a full report to the directors in

Edinburgh on progress so far. Hamilton was honest and respectable and just the man to set at rest the concerns of the Scottish investors, who were naturally anxious to have news of the voyage and the colony. But Paterson argued he was also the very sort of man the colony most needed, a man with real experience of trade, a man who could not be easily replaced. His loss, he warned, 'would unavoidably reduce things to that disorder and confusion in which I am efrayd the Company will find them when they come to enquire into the management of their Cargoe'.[66]

This disorder and confusion was certainly in evidence when, in late January 1699, Richard Moon himself made his first call at Caledonia Bay. By this time the supplies brought by Sands had been distributed and largely consumed. The sight of the sloop riding into the harbour, low in the water with fresh provisions, must have heartened the hundreds of volunteers labouring to complete the great star-shaped fortification of Fort St Andrew. Watching the little ship drop anchor close by the Scottish flagship, they would have caught sight of two gentlemen in the broad-brimmed hats of the merchant class clambering down into the sloop's boat to be rowed across to the towering vessel nearby. Richard Moon, the sea captain, was one of the two. But the second was the real man of business, Thomas Wilmot, the owner of the sloop, merchant of Jamaica, and an old acquaintance of William Paterson.[67] Wilmot had come to the colony a very unhappy man.

Once in Pennicuik's quarters, with all six of the remaining councillors called to the meeting, Wilmot unburdened himself. He had supplied the cargo brought by Sands in December. Sands had been mistaken in accepting the terms offered by the Scots. According to his reckoning they had valued the Scottish goods a full 40 per cent above their real value. He went further, hinting at fraud. The invoice was not 'a true invoyce'. The accountant, who may have been able to clear the matter up, was no longer with them.

Against Paterson's advice the council chose to make only the smallest of concessions, not enough to smooth Wilmot's ruffled feathers.[68] We have only Paterson's terse account of the proceedings, but Wilmot certainly became very angry. He accepted the Scottish goods in payment for his first assignment, and beat a hasty retreat with Moon in train, without leaving behind as much as a bag of flour or a barrel of beef. Paterson knew that such trading men would retell their stories in the taverns of Port Morant[69] and elsewhere. It would do the Company and the greater project no good. The measured words he wrote later do not hide his anger and dismay: '[Wilmot] parted from us, complaining that he should be a loser. It vexed me not only to see us part with such a parcel of provisions, but also for the effect it might have to discourage others.'[70]

The story that the Scots colonists were given to cheating good honest English merchants like Wilmot was the very worst kind of publicity. It promised to make the provisioning crisis now facing the colony much worse than it ever should have been.

In these early weeks, other defects in planning the whole enterprise came to light and Paterson had further cause to rue his expulsion from the board. The Committee for Trade under William Arbuckle had not allowed for the fact that much of the trade in the Caribbean involved sailing into the prevailing north-east trade winds. Darien, situated at its south-western extremity, had a particular need for ships that could accomplish this. Otherwise, trade with the Windward Isles, or the north and east coasts of South America, would be all but impossible. It was because of just this ability to perform well against head winds that the sloop and the brigantine had become the workhorses of the Caribbean trade. The Scots owned neither. They owned the *Endeavour* and the *Dolphin*, one a 'pink', the other a 'snow', slow cumbersome shallow-keeled vessels, that were all but useless in the face of even a moderate breeze.

Paterson, with his years of experience of West Indian trade, appreciated this only too well. He was later to complain to the directors that:

When we arryved at first, we were, as it was, imprisoned for lack of sloop, brigateens, or other good, stiff, windwardly vessels: for the Snow and the Pink were utterly unfitt for that purpose.[71]

In January the council, once again against the advice of Paterson, came up with an ill-judged scheme to secure the necessary sloops. The *Dolphin* would be loaded with cargo and sent off to the islands of St Thomas and Curaçao – with the prevailing wind against them – to trade the stock of goods for one or two sloops. The council put its faith in the ability of their experienced seamen somehow to manage the impossible.

They compounded the error by putting not one but two sea captains on board, Robert Pinkerton and the younger Thomas Malloch. To Paterson this amounted to criminal folly, since 'either Pinkerton or Malloch could doe anything that was to be done as well as both, whom we could not well spare by reason of the scarcity of good sea officers'.[72]

If the ship was lost, these men might prove irreplaceable. He was equally concerned that important Scots trading goods, to the considerable value of £1,400 – a cargo that almost certainly included fine wool and linen cloth, pewterware and pottery, spices and silks, and maybe even periwigs[73] – might end up at the bottom of the sea. Paterson was to suffer many an indignity at the hands of his fellow councillors, but none more hurtful than on this occasion when his objections were contemptuously set aside: 'to all this I was answered in the usuall forme, that I did not understand it'.[74] The outcome was that Pinkerton and Malloch set off for Curaçao with a crew of 25 men in the last week of January 1699. It gave no pleasure to Paterson to find his judgement was soon vindicated.

The voyage started not too badly. On the first two days the *Dolphin* made slow but steady progress against a light north-easterly wind. Then a tropical storm struck. Pinkerton found himself forced to run with the wind behind him towards the Spanish Main. He chose to head for the great Spanish port of Cartagena, on the north coast of South America. With luck he would find shelter there until the gale blew itself out. But luck was not on his side. Attempting to negotiate the channel into Cartagena the *Dolphin* struck a submerged rock, holing the ship below the waterline. The crew desperately tried to stem the inflow but failed. There was nothing for it but to attempt to save the ship and her cargo by running her aground on a sandbank immediately below the white walls of the fortified town, within range of the city's cannon.

A great crowd of curious citizens gathered to watch the spectacle and the governor came riding out of town in a splendid coach of gold and polished wood to supervise the rescue of the crew. In his eyes, by the Grace of God, the Scots pirates from *Rancho Viejo* (the Spanish name for what the Scots called *Caledonia*) had fallen into his hands. Pinkerton and Malloch, and the entire crew were thrown into the town gaol, and the treasures of the *Dolphin* were carried off as lawful booty by the Spanish.[75] With that all hope of purchasing the much-needed sloop evaporated.

That was not the end of the story. The Spanish Governor had Pinkerton and his crew transported to Spain where they were found guilty of piracy in May 1700 and sentenced to be hanged. After spending an anxious summer in a dungeon in Seville, they were released only after King William III himself interceded on their behalf. They were to return to Scotland – as unsung heroes – in the autumn of 1700.[76]

The news of the loss of the *Dolphin*, and of the uncertain fate of her crew, did not reach Caledonia for nearly a month. In the meantime the Council had decided, with just a little hint of desperation, to despatch the other small ship, the *Endeavour*, on an equally uncertain voyage to Jamaica and New York carrying a more modest cargo, worth a hundred pounds, to be traded for the much needed provisions. The unwieldy vessel made predictably slow progress against the trade wind and, a month out from Darien, had travelled only 150 miles towards Jamaica. Around 500 miles of open seas lay ahead. The captain, John Anderson, quite wisely turned the *Endeavour* round and raced her back to port.

The lack of any progress in the task of turning the Scots settlement into the great entrepôt at the centre of world trade was a supreme disappointment to the visionary Paterson. At every turn he had been thwarted by inadequate resources, a quarrelsome and ignorant council, or both. In a rare moment of unguarded candour Paterson later compared his fellow councillors to: 'novices in the University, whose narrow understandings are compounded by their raw, rude, and mistaken conception of things'.[77] But there could be no reform of the council except by their consent. As February turned into March, he placed his hopes in somehow enlarging the council by bringing in new blood and in the imminent arrival of fresh supplies and fresh recruits from Scotland, an event expected daily, which could yet turn the project around.

All through the grim winter of 1698–99 Scotland had been much troubled by famine and its evil consequences. For those struggling to keep body and soul together the fate of the first expedition was a sideshow. But this was certainly not the case in Mylne Square. As the months passed the Directors of the Company of Scotland waited anxiously to hear of the progress of the five ships on that long passage to Darien. £100,000 of its capital – perhaps a tenth of the total accumulated wealth of Scotland – had already been spent.[78] Another £40,000 was due to be raised over the winter of 1698–99 by the second and third calls on subscribers. Some news of the expedition, some proof that the invested capital was being put to good use, was desperately needed. But news refused to come.

Letters had to be carried by such ships as would carry them, and by circuitous routes. As early as August of the previous year the council had sent word of their safe arrival in Madeira in a letter that stressed fresh supplies would be needed on arrival at Darien. This crucial letter was sent to Edinburgh 'by way of Lisbon and Holland', but for some reason did not reach its destination until the following April, eight long months after the expedition had set out.

In the absence of news, the directors in Edinburgh had pressed ahead with their own plans to send further supplies of food and men to the colony. Little progress on this front could be made in 1698. In truth the Company was teetering on the verge of bankruptcy and had only just managed to find the money to pay off the outstanding bills owed to Willem Direcksone's shipyard in Amsterdam in September.[79] But with the Direcksone's account settled, a start could be made in planning the second expedition. The ship ordered by James Gibson two years previously in Amsterdam could at last be released, and despatched to the Firth of Clyde. It was a grand and opulent vessel of over 500 tons given the name of *The Rising Sun* as the company flagship. The financial restraints were such that it would be nigh on a year before she would be ready to sail.

In the meantime, a cargo ship was chartered to carry supplies to the colony. The company described her as:

> a good vessel, of about one hundred and fifty tunns burden, very well equipt, with fourteen guns and good store of small armes, loadned with provisions only, viz brisket beef, flour, pork, stock-fish, oyl, brandy, etc, under the command of a very well experienc'd officer.[80]

The ship should have been ready to sail from Leith[81] in mid-February 1699 and might quite possibly have reached Darien at some time in April. But at the last minute there was a switch of plan. News had reached Edinburgh that the Spanish were assembling a fleet of warships at Cadiz in south-west Spain to mount an attack on the Scottish settlement. This had caused such alarm that it was decided the colonists should be informed of this new threat without delay. To do this, the cargo ship in the Forth was too slow, so a fast brigantine was chartered to sail from the Clyde under the command of Captain Andrew Gibson. She left for Darien around 25 February, expecting to reach the colony within a couple of months. Nothing was heard of her for six weeks; then news reached Edinburgh that she had not even left Scottish waters. She had been shipwrecked in a storm off the Atlantic coast of Scotland.

The irony was that the warning of Spanish preparations for war was hardly necessary. Five thousand miles away, in a colony which had yet to receive a single snippet of news from its directors in Edinburgh, the threat from Spain loomed only too large.

Some of the Scots settlers in Darien had been spoiling for a fight with the Spaniards from the early days of the settlement. Many of them were veterans of King William's war in Flanders, confident to a man that they would see off any Spanish attack. The rumours of the imminent arrival of the Spanish fleet, carried to the colony in December by Richard Long, had been enough to send an undeniable frisson of excitement coursing through their veins. But for those in pursuit of military glory, the threat of a Spanish attack, as we saw, annoyingly never materialised. The Spanish Windward Fleet sailed past the colony far out at sea, as though positively wishing to avoid a fight. The Spanish it seemed had no stomach for military conflict.

The truth was that the Spanish were not at all sure that they could dislodge the Scots or prevent them creating a new route across the Isthmus. Spanish power in America had long been on the wane, and even a comparatively small party of armed men stood a fair chance of establishing a foothold on the mainland, as Dampier and Wafer had suggested to the Committee on Trade and the Plantations in July 1697.[82]

For 60 years there had been a long history of rival European powers establishing colonies on what was nominally Spanish territory. The Spanish claim to the whole of Central America was based on the Papal decree of 1493 awarding all of North, Central and South America (save what was to become Brazil) to Spain. The northern European powers had shown their contempt for this notion by establishing colonies in North America. In the Caribbean itself, Spain had been forced to surrender its territorial claims, to the English in Barbados and Jamaica, to the French in Martinique, Guadeloupe and Hispaniola, to the Danes in St Thomas, and to the Dutch in Curaçao. Even parts of the 'Spanish Main' had been snatched from Spain. Surinam was a Dutch colony,[83] and Honduras, not so far north of Darien, had become a *de facto* English protectorate, a densely wooded and wet land producing some of the finest dyewoods in the world.

In the face of this encroachment by the emerging great powers of Europe the Spanish military commanders in the area were far from confident that the Scots could be winkled out of their fortress. It showed in their slowness to react to events, and in their use of almost any excuse to avoid a fight. The case of General Zavala, the man ordered by José Sarmiento to evict the Scots from *Rancho Viejo*, was typical. When the first order to that effect had reached him in January, before the Scots had completed their fortifications, Zavala had engaged in masterly inactivity. His excuse was that his fleet of ships, lying off shore at Veracruz, was not ready to undertake even the shortest voyage. The vessels had spent months at sea on their way from Spain and urgently needed to be repaired and 'careened'. Zavala maintained this process would take many weeks.

He insisted there were other pressing reasons for delay. The merchant ships lying at Veracruz, commandeered by him to take part in any attack against the Scots, were themselves using delaying tactics. He wrote to say that: 'the captains of the merchant ships were unwilling to join him in any, such expedition, nor could he get satisfactory information about crews'.[84] Faced with Zavala's reluctance to set sail, Sarmiento was forced to apologise to the king in Spain, making the lame excuse that he lacked the authority to force Zavala to take action. He had sent repeated orders to sail; Zavala had repeatedly chosen to ignore them. It was now up to the king to send a direct order.[85]

The performance of the much-feared Windward Fleet was scarcely any better. In fact it was in many ways a paper tiger, badly under-funded by the local Spanish provinces.[86] It sailed from Cartagena in December under the command of General Andres de Pez, who, as we have seen, took care to avoid the area around the Scots colony. He reached Portobello on 16 January. From there De Pez crossed the Isthmus by the *Camino Real* to Panama City to explain in person that his fleet was simply not up to the task of taking on the Scots. Canillas, the *Presidente* of Panama, tells us that De Pez:

> conferred ... with me concerning the small number of vessels of which his fleet consisted. They were only four and of unequal strength ... unseaworthy because they leaked badly and needed to be careened before they could be put to sea.[87]

It seemed that the full might of Spain in the Caribbean could not muster a naval force strong enough to evict the Scots. But De Pez had at least an alternative strategy. He suggested an overland march should be sent from Panama to attack the Scots in the rear as quickly as possible 'before the rainy season could set in among the mountains'.[88]

Canillas, equally keen to be seen to be doing something to assert Spain's right to Darien, embraced this plan, but with a marked lack of confidence in the outcome. At best, he suggested, it could deter the Scots from attempting to set up a base on the Pacific side of the Isthmus:

> it would let them know that in this kingdom there was force and inclina-
> tion to oppose them in the very province through which they must pass
> ... in order to fortify themselves on the Pacific coast or get beyond that
> coast to navigate these waters.[89]

This was the modest objective of what was to prove one of the most ill-conceived expeditions ever mounted by any major power.

On or around 4 February an Indian bearing a message from Captain Pedro, Ambrosio's successor as chief, arrived at Fort St Andrew, alerting the Scots to the presence of a Spanish force, poised in the hills above, ready to spring a surprise attack. The moment of truth had arrived. The Scots were to be given their chance to prove they were more than a match for the might of Spain.

A general alarm was raised, the cannons made ready in Fort St Andrew, the dust of the dry season wiped from the muskets. The council met in emergency session and appointed Councillor James Montgomerie to lead a battalion of 100 soldiers to investigate the nature of the threat. With buttons polished and packs on their back, the party left at dusk, guided through the forest by the Indians. When they reached Pedro's village they found a confused situation. A party of some 25 Spanish soldiers had briefly entered the settlement but had now retreated to a banana grove a few miles into the forest.

Montgomerie and his men advanced quietly, bayonets fixed, in the eerie light of a moonlit forest, intending to surprise the Spaniards as they slept. But nobody had informed the Indians who followed at a distance. Their loud cries echoed through the dense forest glades. Alerted to the danger the Spanish soldiers, outnumbered by four to one, left their campsite with the fires still burning, and prepared an ambush. The red-coated Scots made an easy target when they entered the clearing and they were struck by a fusillade of shots. The enemy then beat a hasty retreat. Two of the Scots lay dead, and fifteen injured, including Montgomerie himself with a slight musket wound to the thigh. But, even so, the commander was given a hero's welcome when he returned to New Edinburgh, claiming victory. But Montgomerie knew this had been simply a skirmish between a Spanish scouting party and a small Scottish force. The Spaniards had returned over the mountains to their base at Toubacanti, where they waited for the real Spanish offensive against Caledonia to begin.[90]

It was on 9 March, and more than a month after Montgomerie's 'victory', that the Conde de Canillas left Panama with a thousand veteran soldiers packed aboard a fleet of barges. At his side was General Andres de Pez and Don Francisco Buitron y Moxica, his deputy commander. Their objective was a landing place on the Pacific coast called *El Escuchadero*, six-days sail to the east. From there a river route would take them to Toubacanti, a native settlement from which they could mount an attack on Caledonia Bay. Here the Conde's forces would be joined by four companies of men under Major Don Luis Carrizoli, a man who bore the grand title of Field Marshal of the Province of Darien.

Carrizoli was a remarkable man who had formed a bridge between the Spanish and the Cuna Indians for more than a quarter of a century. His father, Juliàn, was a Spaniard who had been captured by the Cunas at the age of 13 and brought up in the Cuna ways. He had many Cuna wives, one of them the high-born woman who was Luis's mother. The Spanish had been using the Carrizoli family as the effective governors of Darien for some 50 years. Carrizoli was both Spanish and Cuna.

Such was the man waiting for Canillas when he arrived with his men at Toubacanti. The combined forces amounted to some 1,500 men, outnumbering the Scots by three to two. Canillas devoutly thanked God for the way things had gone, entering in his journal: 'We succeeded by Divine Favour, for the weather was favourable, without rains'.[91] He was anxious to press ahead while the dry season lasted. From now on the going was tough enough to test the fittest of men, for it involved finding some way through the dense, untamed, tropical forest to pass over the ridge that marked the divide between the North and the South Seas.[92] De Pez gives the most vivid account of the harrowing trek:

For two days we marched along a river bed, shut in between mountains where there were many boulders. There was no other way to cross the range. [Our soldiers] marched up the river with water to the thigh... laden with musket, subsistence, and munitions... there was not one but fell, and some three or four times, wetting everything they were carrying...[93]

Canillas, who was in his sixties and unused to walking any distance, had insisted on leading the expedition and on sharing the rigours of the journey with his men. This was a great mistake. After four days or so of this terrain, he fell victim to a seizure. De Pez tells us: 'It prostrated him speechless in such manner that I thought him dead. But God was pleased that he should recover.'[94]

Somehow the force got across the ridge and after five days of marching found themselves just six miles from Caledonia Bay. They decided to set up camp, and had just settled down for the night when a great crack of thunder heralded the onset of the rainy season. To be stranded on a mountain side in these circumstances was a truly terrifying experience. For three days and nights violent rains turned the river bed into a raging torrent. On its banks, the flimsy night shelters in which the rank-and-file soldiers had attempted some fitful sleep were swept away, leaving them exposed to the full fury of the weather. Only the more substantial huts for higher ranks seem to have survived the onslaught.[95] They were out of food, and the fresh supplies brought up from Toubacanti on the backs of African slaves (who had somehow clambered up the bed of the now swollen stream) proved soggy and unappetising. Even the ammunition was soaked through.

In his shelter constructed of palm fronds, with the rain outside beating down as though it would never stop, the Conde of Canillas called a council of war. General Andres de Pez, Don Franscisco Buitron y Moxica, and Don Luis Carrozoli were all of one mind. Retreat, retreat, and retreat, was the order of the day. After six days of forced marching, they regained the base at Toubacanti around the tenth of April, in their eyes lucky to have survived the whole dreadful experience.[96] Any further attack on the Scottish position would have to await the ending of the rains, leaving the Scots safe until November at least.

In the ramparts of Fort St Andrew and the length of the rain-soaked street of New Edinburgh, the Scots too were experiencing the tropical downpour, but from a position of relative comfort. Under the eye of Thomas Drummond, the gunners had spent some time testing the cannon in readiness to see off the Spanish. Every now and then a boom ran out, mimicking the thunder as it rolled in echo around the bay. Unknown to them the Spanish threat to exterminate the Scots had, for the moment at least, been largely washed away.

Chapter Ten
The Future Has to Wait

T wo months before the abortive Spanish attack on the Scots colony
of Caledonia a little fleet of ships could be found at anchor not far
from the White Cliffs of Dover, at a mustering point known to all of His
Majesty's naval officers as 'The Downs'. Pride of place in this little armada was reserved for His Majesty's ship, *HMS Roebuck*, under the command of Captain William Dampier, RN. The *Roebuck* was about to
embark on one of the most extraordinary voyages of the 17th century, a
journey in search of the undiscovered riches of the South Sea.
Dampier's journal of the voyage was to become an essential handbook
for all future explorers of this most mysterious part of the world. In style
it resembles *Robinson Crusoe* and *Gulliver's Travels*, for indeed Defoe and
Swift could find no better model for a tale of adventure. In began in typical matter-of-fact style:

> I sail'd from the Downs early on Saturday, Jan. 14, 1699 with a fair Wind,
> in his Majesty's Ship the Roebuck; carrying but 12 Guns in this Voyage,
> and 50 Men and Boys, with 20 Month's Provision. We had several of the
> King's Ships in Company, bound for Spithead and Plimouth ... We parted
> from them that Night, and stood down the Channel.[1]

Dampier's voyage was remarkable for another reason. The Admiralty
had taken something of risk in promoting England's then most famous
buccaneer to the rank of sea captain in the Royal Navy.

Dampier's account of his crossing of the Pacific had been published in
1697, dedicated to Charles Montagu, William Paterson's close ally in the
struggle to establish the Bank of England, then just elected President of
the Royal Society. Montagu had been impressed enough to secure for
Dampier a position in Customs House and an introduction to Edward
Russell, Earl of Orford and First Lord of the Admiralty. Dampier made
a simple plea. Give him a ship and a crew and he would return to the

South Sea to try to pin down the exact location and extent of the elusive
southern continent that he had searched for on his first voyage around
the world but could not find.

It says something about the growing English interest in exploiting the
fabled wealth of the South Sea[2] that Dampier was in the end fitted out
with a ship and placed in command of this new voyage of discovery, even
if the whole process took much longer than he had hoped. Dampier's
first thought was to sail south along the coast of South America to round
Cape Horn, and then cross the Southern Pacific to approach the undiscovered landmass from the east, in effect providing an alternative, if
much more risky route, to that proposed by William Paterson. But
because of the long delays in fitting out the expedition, there was now
no chance that he could reach the Cape before the storms of April and
May set in. He chose instead to take the eastern route by way of Africa
and the Cape of Good Hope.[3] As a result the mystery of the South Sea
was to remain unsolved for more than half a century.[4]

It was left to another English sailor to probe the alternative route to
the Pacific by way of the Isthmus of Darien. The Board of Trade had not
forgotten Dampier and Wafer's exposition of how easily a small force
might seize Darien and establish a land route to the Pacific. And it had
an unlikely instrument at hand in the person of an English Quaker and
adventurer. His name was Richard Long. This was the man who had
arrived unannounced at the Scottish colony in a small boat on 15
November 1698.[5]

Long had approached Whitehall as early as May 1697 with a plan to
mount an expedition along the coasts of central America in search of
gold. On the face of it, this was to be a hunt for sunken Spanish treasure in the tradition of William Phips.[6] But it was never what it seemed.
For his proposal suggested he should be given power to land on the
Spanish Main and search for gold in parts 'where no Europeans had yet
settled'.[7]

Whether Long knew Dampier and Wafer we cannot say, but the
phrase was uncannily like the one Dampier used to describe Darien
when he appeared with Wafer before the Board of Trade on 2 July
1697.[8] When in the autumn of that year, the Board of Trade recommended that Darien be seized by an English force as a matter of
urgency, Long's proposal was already on the table. Soon afterwards, he
was granted the use of a ship captured from the French, called the
Rupert Prize, and handed a 'commission' by the 'Lord Justices of

England' (the five elder statesmen who acted as regent when William III was on the continent fighting his wars). The document was cagey in its use of language, but Long certainly took it to mean that he had the power to claim territory on behalf of the king of England. It directed him to go to the Gulf of Darien, the point where the 'neck' of the Isthmus joins the 'body' of South America. There, Long was to survey the territory adjoining the gulf and ascertain whether it remained unoccupied (as Dampier and Wafer had claimed) by any European power. The written instructions then included this strange sentence:

> if the Gulf and great river Darién do lie vacant as it hath done since the Spaniards enjoyed America it may be well for England, but if it ... should be possessed by any other nation it would prove an unhappy thing to England.[9]

The Quaker captain certainly took this to mean that, in certain circumstances, he had the right to take possession of the land on behalf of the king of England. And it is hard to disagree.

Long was ready to depart in April 1698, a full nine months ahead of Dampier and nearly four months ahead of the Scots. If he had been able to sail to Darien there and then, the history of Darien could well have been different.[10] But he was held up by fierce storms in the English Channel. It was not until 6 June[11] that his little expedition left Portsmouth and headed out into the Atlantic. Unlike the Scots, there was no need for him to play games with secret orders. He set course for Jamaica.

In October 1698, when the Scots were involved in the stand-off with the Danes over the possession of Crab Island, Long was already to be found negotiating with Indian chiefs on the coast of Darien. They included the same Ambrosio who was to visit the Scots in their new harbour at Caledonia Bay a month later. The enthusiastic English captain reported that 'all along the coast of Darien the Indians came and invited me'.[12]

Long found the Indian leaders were happy to receive English settlers as friends, or so they told him.[13] He sailed south and east along the coast of Darien until he reached the southern end of the Gulf of Darien (the part called today the Gulf of Uraba) and sailed into it until he came across the great River Darien (now known as the River Atrato) pouring its waters into the Caribbean. There was no sign of Spanish, or indeed of any other European settlement in the area. And the Indian chief who ruled here was as friendly as any he had met along the coast. Pointing at the river, the chief (who was called Diego and spoke some Spanish) explained that from here the South Sea could be reached with great ease. The Quaker captain duly recorded, with some excitement, that: 'From one of the branches of that river it is but 12 hours travel to the South Sea'.[14] But at this time of the year, towards the end of the long rainy season, the river was impassable.

Long would have to wait to explore further. In the meantime he sailed back along the coast as it curved north and then west towards Golden Island. It was here that he encountered the Scots settling in at Caledonia Bay. As he related in his letter to the English admiralty, he was impressed by what he saw: 'About 1,200 men landed ashoar as proper as ever I saw. They are very healthy, and in such a crabbed hold that it will be difficult to beat them out of it'.[15]

He was a man who enjoyed a drink and he was royally entertained aboard both the *St Andrew* and the *Unicorn*, a compliment he was to return aboard the *Rupert Prize*. But he did not allow such junketings to sway his resolve. Now that the Scots were here, it was time to act:

> I was upon the coast of Darien and in the Gulph before *them*, and per- ceiving they would be upon the [most desirable[16]] of the vacant places in America...I thought it my dutie to his Majesty to take possession in his name for the use of the Crown of England. Accordingly I return'd to the Gulph from the Scots with all my might and ... took possession in his Majesty's name, leaving there the common flagg and four people to keep possession until his Majesty's pleasure be further known.[17]

Long stayed in Darien just long enough to return to Caledonia Bay and spread alarm among the Scots by warning them of the imminent arrival of the Spanish fleet.[18] He then set course for Jamaica where he despatched his report to London. He confidently expected that his

Opposite. **This map of the Isthmus was published in 1700 and admirably illustrates Long's adventures along the coast of Darien. In the west is the town of Portobello (or Portobel), linked by the 'Camino Real' to Panama City. This was the new city built to replace the old one destroyed by Morgan in 1681. Ambrosio ruled the land between the Conception River and the Isle of Pines. From there to New Edinburgh lay the territory controlled by Andreas. The Gulf of Darien is represented on the map by the deep inlet labelled the 'River of Darien'. This is where Long met the great chief Diego and raised the English flag (Source: Glasgow University Library Department of Special Collections).**

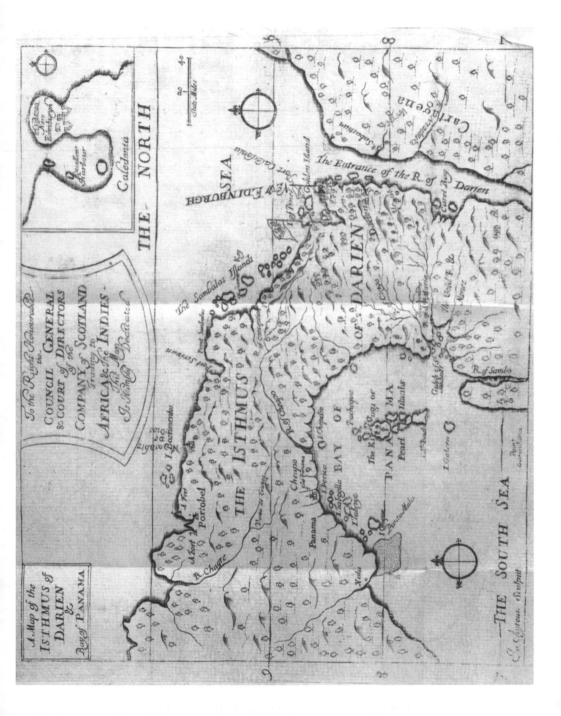

A Map of the ISTHMUS of DARIEN & Bay of PANAMA

To the Right Honorable the CUNCIL GENERAL & Court of Directors of the COMPANY of SCOTLAND Trading to AFRICA & the INDIES This Map is Dedicated by J. Hamilton

Galedonia

New Edinburgh

Caledonia Harbour

THE NORTH SEA

The Entrance of the R. of Darien

New EDINBURGH

The Sambalas Islands

DARIEN

THE ISTHMUS

BAY OF PANAMA

The Kings or Pearl Islands

R. of Sambo

R. Chagre

Portobel

Panama

THE SOUTH SEA

Co Chatelain Sculpsit

Sea Miles

claim to the land of Darien on behalf of the king of England would be confirmed. Was that not, indeed, what his expedition had been all about? Now he must wait and see.

Although Long had no way of knowing it, his masters in Whitehall had swung away from the very idea of occupying Darien since his departure from London. Interest in the scheme had evaporated almost as quickly as it had boiled up. In its place, a simple but overwhelming question had come to dominate the deliberations of England's rulers: who was to become the next king of Spain? It was a question that was only finally to be resolved on the battlefields of Europe, in that great military contest known to English historians as the War of the Spanish Succession.

The man whose failing health sparked off the crisis was King Carlos II of Spain. He was a member of the Habsburg family, one of the great ruling families of Europe, but a poor creature for all that. He is generally considered to have been a victim of Habsburg in-breeding. Mentally limited, with a misshapen lower jaw that jutted out beyond the reach of his upper teeth, he spoke haltingly, drooled, and found it difficult to eat. When he was born in 1661 he had not been expected to live long. But in 1665 he succeeded at the age of four to the throne of Spain and had proved the doctors wrong by surviving well into his thirties. He had even been married, twice, in the hope of producing an heir, but it had proved beyond his capacities. In 1697 his health had taken a turn for the worst. Death, it was thought, could not be far away.

The death of a king without a direct descendant as heir was not an unusual event. Charles II of England, had died without one in 1685. As we have seen, in England there were two competing contestants to the throne, a matter only settled by the capture and execution of Monmouth. But in the case of the Spanish king, two of the competing contestants belonged to the most powerful royal families in Europe, the French Bourbon family and the Habsburgs of Austria – families who were at each others throats, Capulets and Montagus on a European scale.

The inheritance at stake was vast. The King of Spain's dominions included not just Spain, but large parts of Italy, the Spanish Netherlands (what today we would call Belgium), the Philippine Islands, and most of Central and South America.[19] Should all these lands fall under the control of one or other of the rival families, the repercussions would be enormous, upsetting the military balance between the great powers of Europe.

William III, King of England and of the Scots, saw the danger, and decided to play the part of an honest broker, sending envoys in an attempt to strike a deal acceptable to both families. He could not pose as the honest broker and make a claim for land on Spain at the same time so all thought of acquiring Darien had therefore to be firmly ruled out. But one awkward truth could not denied. The Scots were already on the high seas aiming to set foot on Darien, placing him in an enormously delicate position in his relations with the court at Madrid.

The manner of his diplomacy only made matters worse. William decided that he must persuade Louis XIV of France – his long and bitter enemy – to accept a compromise on behalf of the Bourbon claim to the throne. In secret talks, Louis and William agreed to divide – or partition – the Spanish territories on the death of the Spanish king. The Italian lands ruled by the king of Spain, with the exception of the northern duchy of Milan were to go to Louis, Dauphin of France. The Habsburg claimant, the Archduke Charles, second son of the Emperor Leopold I, would be granted the great duchy of Milan in North Italy. All the rest of the Spanish king's dominions – Spain itself, the Spanish Netherlands (broadly speaking modern Belgium) and the Spanish empire in America and the Philippines – were to go to a third candidate, the boy prince of Bavaria, admittedly a member of the cadet house of Habsburg, but not in line ever to rule Austria. It was an ingenious solution with neither Louis XIV nor Leopold I gaining much from the King of Spain's death. But, in one detail, William badly miscalculated. He had not consulted Madrid.

The secret 'Partition Treaty' was signed on 24 September 1698, just as the Scots first sailed into Caribbean waters. The details were not long in leaking out.[20] When they did, the Spanish reaction was one of undisguised fury. How could William III – a staunch ally of Spain since 1689 – go behind their backs and make this cosy deal with Louis XIV, a deal which undoubtedly ignored Spanish interests? This was the act of an enemy, not a friend.

The row over the Partition Treaty of 1698 meant that King William, even had he wished to, could not give support of any kind to the Scots settlers in Darien, for fear of irreparably damaging his relations with the Spanish court. And at least one of his governors in the West Indies, Sir William Beeston, Governor of Jamaica, was aware of how sensitive the issue of Darien had now become in Madrid. In December he had received a complaint from Don Diego de Rios, Governor of Cartagena, that a Scottish expedition had settled 'among the Indians on the Gulf of Darien' a territory claimed by Spain. On 31 December 1698 he dashed off a diplomatic response:

> I am clearing a warship with this letter, to advise your lordship that although the Scottish nation recognizes the King of England as its lord, it is nevertheless a nation distinct from the English, and the English are in no wise accomplices in this design, or a party to the scheme of the Scots, or in correspondence with them; nor shall the Scots receive any aid from me.[21]

It was a washing of the hands. Spain, it seemed, had been given a free hand to do what they would as far as the Scots were concerned. News of this letter does not appear to have reached the Conde de Canillas before he set off on his overland march that aimed to drive out the Scots. But it must have certainly reached Panama City by the time of his return. From now on, it seemed, the Scots were on their own.

☀

At the end of March the first word of Canillas's retreat reached the new colony of Caledonia. It was brought by the Indians, who misleadingly claimed the credit for it.[22] In New Edinburgh there was some cause for celebration, and the colonists almost certainly paused to toast the defeat of the Spaniards with the assistance of their daily ration of brandy or rum. But the weather must have soon dampened their spirits.

They now faced a rainy season that would last until November. Tropical downpours were common, driving squalls of rain that soaked a man to the skin in seconds and imparted a northern chill to the air, despite the fact that the colony was only nine degrees north of the equator. The high humidity meant that nothing would dry, and even dry clothes became damp. In the huts along New Edinburgh's muddy high street, the roofing of palm thatch was severely tested. Persistent drips splashed into bowls and pots set out to catch them. There was simply no way to keep it out. And at times the winds came blasting in from the Caribbean, bending the palm trees, bringing great forest giants tumbling down.[23]

Now that the rains had come, the question of finding new supplies of food had become urgent. Hopes were more and more pinned on the arrival of the relief ships from Scotland. It was now a full seven months since the council had sent its letter from Madeira requesting the urgent despatch of provisions to the colony. On the worst days, when the rain lashed down all day and men had nothing to do but feel homesick and contemplate their present predicament, Jeremiahs among them predicted that these ships would never show up. On the days when the sun shone, and damp clothing quickly dried in the warmth of its rays, the duty watch on Forth Point, perched in their tall look-out tower, scanned the horizon hopefully for the promise of Scottish sails. But April was to pass, and May, and still no Scottish ships appeared.

As for William Paterson, the two months of April and May saw him climb out of a slough of despond to enjoy a brief intoxicating period of power. Then came a ghastly denouement. His subdued mood in early April was not a product of the weather (Paterson barely mentions it in any of his reports) but of a terrible two months in which his stock within the colony had fallen to an all-time low. By now he realised he had become a prisoner of the incompetent and worthless group of men raised up by the company to be councillors. And as long as the council remained unreformed, there was nothing that could set him free.

For months now he had busied himself at the table in his hut, writing letters, keeping his diary, drafting new laws, and working on his plans for opening trade across the Isthmus.[24] He even found time to devour some religious tracts sent by his friend, John Borland, from Boston that must have been brought to the colony aboard the sloop of Edward Sands in December.[25] But much of this activity was a matter of whistling to keep the spirits up. By the first week of April the dreadful truth of his predicament could no longer be ignored. He had been effectively sidelined and ignored, reduced to an object of ill-disguised contempt.

To understand how this came about we need to go back to mid-February, when he had made a new attempt to make the council see sense and reform itself. The game of weekly musical chairs had continued to hamstring policy making, the more so because the council had been reduced to just five people with the departure of Robert Pinkerton in January on his voyage to St Thomas and Curaçao aboard the *Dolphin*. The council now consisted of the two sea captains Robert Pennicuik and Robert Jolly, James Montgomerie the military man, Daniel Mackay the fiery young highland lawyer, and William Paterson himself. Paterson apart, they were as fractious and egotistical a group as any ever assembled, quite incapable of working together on any plan that might see the colony through to November, when the second expedition would for certain have arrived, bringing a fresh batch of settlers and some wives and children.

Luckily some of Paterson's private letters, written to trusted friends, have survived, giving us a rare insight into how he really felt about his fellow councillors. In a damning indictment he graphically described them as 'mean spirits, raw heads, jealous and presumptuous pates, that had no virtue of their own... involved and intreaging heads, that pretend one thing and intend another'.[26] It was Paterson's lot, it appears, to share the council table with a collection of self-centred and scheming men, masters of the art of self-deceit and hypocrisy on a grand scale. Yet he knew he could achieve nothing without their consent, unless of course, they would agree to expand the council and bring in fresh blood. But in February he had at least seen some progress.

His fellow councillors may have mocked his pretension but they at least accepted he had a fine way with words when it came to drafting treaties and other official documents. His high-sounding phrases gave them a sense of their own self-importance. Thus they were happy to put their names to the treaty he had drafted (with the help of the young archivist, Hugh Rose)[27] on the occasion of the visit by the great chief Diego of the Gulf on 24 February 1699. Both Diego and the Council put their names to it. It was headed:

TREATY OF FRIENDSHIP, UNION, AND PERPETUAL CONFEDERATION, AGREED AND ENTERED INTO BETWEEN THE RIGHT HON[BLE] THE COUNCIL OF CALEDONIA, AND THE EXCELLENT DIEGO TUCAPANTOS AND ESTRARA, Chief and Supreame Leader of the Indian Inhabitants of the lands and possessions in and about the River of Darieno and St. Matolome

In its articles it bound both parties to mutual defence by 'land and sea', and guaranteed 'the liberty of comerce, correspondence, and manuring, possessing, and enjoying lands in their respective countrys and places of their respective obedience in all time hereafter'. This was a treaty much in the Paterson mould. It decreed that the rule of law was to be established and that procedures were to be put in place to settle any dispute between their peoples in what was described grandly as a 'perpetual confederation'.

This was to be only a first step, since by the fourth article of the treaty it was agreed all the other local chiefs 'shall, upon application, be admitted into this treaty'.[28] It was a fine little document – although in drafting it Paterson was not to know that Diego had already welcomed the English captain, Richard Long, at the Darien River and had –

broadly speaking – given a similar commitment to him.[29] In time, he hoped, the five other named chiefs would sign the treaty, giving the company rights to their settlement in international law, insofar as it existed in the 17th century. But while the council looked to him to devise treaties and laws (which they of course would have to approve), in the day-to-day running of the colony his advice seems to have been treated with contempt.

To illustrate the point we need look no further than the manner in which the council had handled an unexpected offer of the services of two trading sloops at the beginning of February. The two vessels, one under the command of Edward Sands, the young sea captain who had traded with the Scots in December and who had ferried Cunningham, Herries and Haldane from the colony to Jamaica, the other skippered by a Jamaican-based Englishman, Ephraim Pilkington, arrived completely unexpectedly and announced they had come to put their ships at the disposal of the colony.[30] Such a development must have seemed the answer to Paterson's prayers. No longer need the colony be 'imprisoned for lack of sloop'. The two fast sloops were ideal vessels for the North American trade, capable of making the round trip to New York or Boston within a couple of months. Both ports had the ability to raise credit in the company's name. This would have allowed the beginnings of regular trade between the English colonies and the new Scots outpost. Fresh supplies could have been taken on and brought back.[31] But the council opted to use them as coastal trading vessels. Sands was sent to catch turtles, a task that he may not have been properly equipped to do,[32] while Pilkington was despatched in his ship, the *Maidstone*, on a hazardous trip along the Spanish Main in the general direction of Cartagena. Of course, no-one in the colony knew anything of the *Dolphin*, and her ill-fated attempt to shelter in Cartagena harbour. But the *Maidstone* set off just two days after Montgomerie's skirmish with the Spanish scouting party. The voyage seemed to be tempting fate.

The council did not only take pleasure in ignoring Paterson's advice. They seem to have gone out of their way to make life as unpleasant for him as they possibly could. Mid-way through February they had shown how vindictive they could be. Paterson had again brought up his plan to have the council enlarged by the addition of three new men. This perfectly sensible suggestion was met by a snub from Robert Jolly – who was president for the week. Jolly simply refused to accept his motion, and ruled that no discussion was to be allowed. This was an insulting way to

treat a man of Paterson's reputation. But worse was to follow. Paterson
tells us that afterwards 'This motion raised me much envy and trouble.'[33]
Envy and trouble was Paterson's euphemistic expression for what
amounted to a renewed campaign of humiliation and bullying.[34]

It was an extraordinary situation. Here was the man who had given
England its greatest financial institution, a man treated with the utmost
respect in Amsterdam and Hamburg when he had gone there to raise
money for the expedition. He was the originator of the entire Darien
project and the only council member who had any experience of the
Caribbean world. He was also a trader clearly respected in Jamaica and
across the West Indies. But in the eyes of his fellow-councillors his
record counted for nothing. A little respect would not have gone amiss.

Paterson was remarkably resilient, never raising his voice in anger,
praying that one day the council would see sense. But, as March drew
to a close, coercion was added to bullying. For the first time he was made
to do something he knew was both foolish and wrong – he signed a warrant for the arrest and imprisonment of innocent men.

The humiliating retreat of Canillas in the April rains had removed the
immediate threat of a Spanish attack. But one threat was replaced by
another. In early March, Pilkington had returned from his trading expedition along the Spanish Main, carrying the grim news of the loss of the
Dolphin and the imprisonment of her crew in Cartagena. The Council
had responded in a proud Scottish way. Pilkington and Sands were
instructed to carry a deputation with all the pomp and circumstance of a
sovereign power to seek an audience with the Spanish Governor of
Cartagena, Don Diego de Rios. The chosen ambassador was a young
highland officer, Alexander Maghie. When the two sloops had dropped
anchor in Cartagena harbour, he had come ashore in full military dress
under a flag of truce, supported by a drummer, and a guard of honour.[35]

There was an air of insolence about the young man. Brought before
the Governor he had wasted no time in diplomatic niceties. If the
Spaniards did not release Pinkerton and his men immediately then the
Scottish fleet would descend like wolves on any Spanish ship they could
find. De Rios replied in kind. He promised to 'gather such a force by
sea and land as would quickly, at one blow, root [the Scots] out of
Darien.[36]

Of course De Rios had no immediate means of carrying out the threat. But the Scots were not to know. When Maghie returned to New Edinburgh empty-handed, the Council took the threat seriously and wild rumours of an imminent Spanish invasion soon swept through the colony. It promoted a siege mentality. All visiting ships were now looked on with a suspicious eye. Might they be carrying Spanish spies coming to look over the colony and assess the strength of the defences? Powered by this paranoia, the council was now to sabotage, at a single stroke, the notion that underpinned Paterson's vision: that the Scots colony in Darien would provide a welcome and a safe haven for tradings ships of all nations.

It all began quietly enough, on 29 March, when a sloop, under the command of Richard Moon, with Thomas Wilmot in charge of a cargo of provisions, came sailing into Caledonia Bay. The pair had come back to the colony in good will, because they knew Paterson personally and genuinely wanted to see the trade centre on the Isthmus succeed. But the other councillors could not forget that they had sailed off with their cargoes still in the hold at the end of January. There was no warm welcome for Moon's sloop or for a second smaller vessel that came in its wake.[37] This vessel was captained by another Jamaican merchant, Mathias Maltman.

Somehow Paterson's fellow councillors had picked up an unlikely rumour that Maltman was carrying Spanish spies on board, men who might be carrying news from Cartagena to Panama City of the new Scottish threat to attack Spanish shipping. Paterson had clearly been kept in the dark for he invited Wilmot to pay his respects to Daniel Mackay, the councillor holding the office of president for the week. When they reached Mackay's hut, they found an unofficial council was already in progress. Leaving Wilmot outside, Paterson went in to find out just what was afoot.

His four fellow councillors sat huddled conspiratorially around the table. In front of them was a piece of paper, a warrant for the arrest of the sloop belonging to Mathias Maltman. Mackay looked up, and told Paterson he was just in time to put his signature to the document, alongside the other four. Paterson tells us:

> When I asked what the reasons they hade for it, Mr Mackay answered that they were informed that this sloop was a Spanish sloop, and was freighted by three Spanish merchants, now on boord her, and bound for Portubell.[38]

When the quill was offered to him, he hesitated. He knew that the charge was absurd. Maltman was Wilmot's man, and the ship had sailed into the bay with the Union Jack billowing at her stern. Mackay growled: 'I warrant you will not meddle, because your friend Mr. Wilmot is concerned'.[39]

The normally calm Paterson angrily protested there was not one solid piece of evidence to suggest this was a Spanish ship. But he clearly felt physically threatened by his fellow-councillors. He reluctantly signed, subject to an important proviso: 'I told them that if she was a Spanish sloop, I was ready as they: but if belonging to any other nation, I would [have no part in it].'[40] The sloop was then boarded by an armed platoon of men with orders to arrest any passengers found on board. It turned out that there were, after all, three Spaniards installed in a rear cabin. They had between them some £100 of money in pieces of eight, some Spanish pistols, and a bag of gold dust, all of which suggested they were peaceful, if prudent, Spanish merchants, going about their legitimate business. They were clapped in chains all the same, and the vessel seized. What made the act particularly ill-advised was the fact that the sloop in the end proved to be indeed a Jamaican vessel, flying under the English flag. Meanwhile, the Scots of Darien had technically carried out their first act of piracy.

Paterson was furious and, in his report of December 1699, could still not contain the anger he felt inside: 'God knows, my concerne was not upon my own account, or any humour of my own, but the true love of justice and good of the Collony.'[41] At the time, though, he had felt utterly powerless to stop this stupid, vindictive little act. The council had sent a clear message to the world that trading men were subject to arbitrary arrest if they ever dared to enter the harbour in Caledonia Bay.

This was a hammer blow to Paterson's plans for a free port, but the damage could still be limited if the men were released and an apology made. The present council would never countenance that. A new one might. It is a tribute to Paterson's political acumen that, within a fortnight, he had managed to arrange an unlikely *coup d'état*.

That February, Joseph Ferdinand, the young prince of Bavaria selected by William III and Louis XIV to become the next king of Spain had suddenly died at the age of six. This untimely death returned the issue of the Spanish succession to the melting pot. With their compromise candidate removed, both William and Louis could now only hope that the fading Spanish king could last out the rest of the year, giving them time to patch up a new deal. But, even then, there was no guarantee that Spain would accept it. William must have known there was a strong church party in Spain that favoured a more radical plan. To avoid the Spanish dominions being broken up the talk was now of inviting Louis' grandson, the young Philip of Anjou, to accept the crown. King William feared that Philip of Anjou would be putty in the hands of his grandfather. France and Louis XIV would emerge as the real winners.[42]

The situation was grave. William had more reason than ever to cultivate Spanish favour. In March, William's Principal Secretary of State, James Vernon, met the Spanish Ambassador in London and assured him that King William was as determined as Spain to see the Scots pack up and leave the colony at Caledonia Bay. The Spanish Ambassador duly reported to his masters in Madrid that William had: 'despatched royal orders to all the governors of the [English] plantations in these parts ... forbidding that any relief or assistance be afforded the [Scots].[43] But William could not convince the Spanish that he was on their side by words alone.[44] He had to be seen to act against the colony in Darien. For the Scots, grimly hanging on until relief arrived in the form of the relief expedition, this was a distinctly unwelcome development.

The pity was that Paterson's rise to a position of power in New Edinburgh came too late. That it came about at all is a tribute to his tenacity, and his shrewd judgement of character.

In the first week of April the council met to discuss what steps they should take to follow up Alexander Maghie's report that the Spanish governor in Cartagena had responded to the Scottish threat to seize Spanish shipping with a point blank refusal to discuss the release of Pinkerton and his crew, or to pay compensation for the loss of the *Dolphin* and her cargo. On the principle that once a threat is made it has to be carried out or all credibility will be lost, the council decided to send the two sloops west towards Portobello in search of Spanish merchants ships. They were to take any they came across by force of arms.

But this was not considered to be enough. The idea was already forming in the colony that a special appeal should be sent to King William. As we have already seen, when William Paterson had drafted the Act of

Parliament that granted the company its rights, he had been careful to include a guarantee of royal protection:

> If ... any of the [Company's] Ships, Goods, Merchandise, Persons, or other effects whatsoever, shall be stopt, detained, ... or away taken ... *His Majesty promises to Interpose His Authority to have Restitution, Reparation, and Satisfaction made for the Damnage done ...*[45] [author's emphasis].

The wording could not have been better drafted to cover the case of the *Dolphin*. The council agreed unanimously that it was time to call upon the king to honour his promise. A letter was to be sent forthwith, by special courier, to the king's ministers in Edinburgh. The hope was that, at the very least, the king could order the English fleet in the Caribbean (under the command of the celebrated Admiral Benbow) to lay siege to Cartagena until Pinkerton and the crew had been freed and the compensation paid.[46]

The council had the perfect ship on hand to carry the appeal quickly across the Atlantic. As Sands and Pilkington returned from Cartagena with Maghie and his soldiers, they had come across a fast brigantine out of New York called the *Three Sisters*. She had come looking for the Scottish colony and had sailed past it (easily done since the colony lay concealed in its sheltered bay). Interestingly, the ship had been chartered by some friends of the colony in New York, and brought a welcome cargo of flour, pickled beef and dried codfish. The brigantine was as fast as any ocean-going ship, and her captain was willing to sail her to the Clyde. There remained only the question of who was to carry the message.

Such an issue was bound to reopen the divisions among the councillors. Robert Jolly, James Montgomerie, and Daniel Mackay were all determined to be the one to carry the message home. Paterson cunningly realised that he could turn this situation to his advantage. Daniel Mackay, his chief tormentor on the council, became the unlikely instrument of Paterson's accession to power.

Mackay seemed particularly keen to go back; it was a chance to impress the company with his lawyer's gift for advocacy. It also happened to be the week in which he held the president's chair. In his best conspiratorial manner, Paterson put to one side his personal loathing of the young man and privately suggested a deal. Paterson would again propose enlarging the Council by co-opting new members, but this time by four rather than by three.[47] Mackay, in the presidential seat, would allow the motion to stand. Provided Pennicuik could be persuaded to support the move, the council would be deadlocked two against two, and Mackay, in the chair, could then use his casting vote in favour. Once the four new members (all hand-picked by Paterson) took their seats at the table, the reign of the old guard would be at an end. Mackay would receive the due reward of a swift return to Scotland.

Paterson somehow persuaded Pennicuik to back his plan, possibly playing on the commodore's well-known hatred of Montgomerie, the man who might otherwise win, since he was close to Jolly.[48] When the meeting began Paterson formally proposed the motion to enlarge the council, and Mackay let the motion stand. Montgomerie, who must have realised what was afoot, withdrew in a temper before any vote was taken. Jolly stayed on to vote and then – when the motion was carried – also walked out. Jolly and Montgomerie were never to sit at the council table again. Soon afterwards they decided they had had enough of Darien and took the first chance that came their way to leave the colony, arriving back in Edinburgh about the same time as Mackay.[49]

On the day following this delightfully engineered *coup d'état*, the new council sat and duly chose Mackay to be their envoy to Scotland. He set sail on 10 April aboard the *Three Sisters*, carrying in his valise a polite petition to King William, a report to the directors of the company, and many letters to relatives back home. Eventually he reached Edinburgh and made his report. On the voyage back to Darien he was to fall overboard in the Caribbean and was sadly lost: 'torn to pieces by those ravenous and devouring sharks'.[50] His enemies may have regarded it as a fitting end.

With Mackay's departure Paterson could now assume the role of leader, supported for the most part by councillors of a completely different calibre – young, purposeful, and practical in their approach. None of the new councillors were sea captains. Pennicuik, out-numbered five to one, knew that his days of power had come to an end.

Two of the four new men were to carve for themselves a place in history. The first of these was Thomas Drummond. He was a hard taskmaster, unpopular with the men under him, but a man who shared Paterson's enthusiasm for the site.[51] He was soon to carry off a considerable feat in New York harbour when he chartered a sloop to carry supplies and reinforcements back to the colony right under the nose of Governor Bellomont. The second, Samuel Vetch, was himself to become an important figure in New York history, a business associate of the de Lanceys, and a future Governor of Nova Scotia.

With men like these at his side Paterson quickly rediscovered his optimism. The new council he saw as a sort of renaissance, a rebirth of hope. The way ahead might be hard, but the colony in the end would surely pull through. He noted a new mood among the settlers themselves:

> It was no small ease and satisfaction to the Collony, to find ... their Councellers become so unanimous, patient, and prudent... and ... there was great contentment, and few or no grumblings among the people, as everyone [was] expecting with patience the arryveall of good newes, and the needful recruits from the mother countrey, to make way for happy dayes and glorious success to come...[52]

Of course Paterson wrote these words six months after the event, and in justification of his *coup d'état*. But he was also in a position to know how the average settler felt. Unlike any of the sea captains, he had lived among them in New Edinburgh and shared much of their lives.

Paterson may now have been in control, but he also knew the colony was near to collapse. Morale had fallen dangerously low. Paterson could look back wistfully at the chances that had been missed to build the colony into a successful trading entity.

> Had our young and mushroom politicians ... given any price for provisions rather than part with them, they need not have wanted at the last, nor wanted sloops to goe their errands, nor good seasoned men from the Indies to have helpt us in our need.[53]

Paterson's narrative provides an insight into what transpired in the council meetings. It is rather less effective in giving voice to the concerns of the common man. If someone had asked the hungry settlers of New Edinburgh quite how they had felt when they had seen ships laden with supplies sailing into the bay, only to depart with their cargoes undisturbed, they would have received a pretty answer. We know that the colonists suspected that the sea captains and their crews, quartered aboard the ships, secretly enjoyed a much better diet than they did. By April, the rations handed out to the volunteers had become more meagre as stocks had run low, reducing many of the settlers to pale shadows of the men who had left Edinburgh with such high hopes only seven months before. And as the belts were tightened so the anger grew.

It was a tricky situation for the new council to handle. With luck, the relief ships from Scotland would soon arrive. And when Pilkington and Sands returned from their hunt for Spanish ships along the Main, they could be sent to Jamaica where credit might be arranged for fresh supplies. But, for the moment, the best hope of reducing discontent was to look into the common complaint that the landsmen had not been given a fair deal in regards to the dwindling stocks of food.

And what better way of arranging this than by involving the settlers themselves in the process? Paterson was not exactly a democrat – he had once warned against importing people who held 'subordinate office' on to the council.[54] But a general parliament had its uses, and the constitution of the colony allowed for it. It was to be based on one-man-one-vote (an idea far ahead of its time) with one representative for each of the eight districts of New Edinburgh. Each member of parliament would serve a year.

The old council had dragged its feet on the question of when to call this parliament. Now, with new people in the driving seat, the parliament was summoned to meet. At its first meeting in mid-April, the popular representatives were told by Pennicuik that not a month's supply of food was left in the colony. The tiny assembly of eight men suspected that the bombastic Pennicuik was exaggerating the crisis to hasten the evacuation of the colony. And, indeed, when they ordered an audit of all available food stores, it was found that the situation was not quite as desperate as many feared. There was indeed three months supply left, although some of it was certainly rotten and 'damnified'.[55]

To conduct the audit the MPs had insisted on a thorough search of all remaining four ships – the St Andrew, the Caledonia, the Unicorn and the Endeavour. Pennicuik and Robert Drummond protested that the authority of the sea captain was being challenged aboard his own vessel. The more they insisted, the more suspicious the MPs became, voting in the end to overrule such objections. It surprised few when the audit found that secret supplies of food had been squirreled away for the use of the captains and their crews.

Could anything be done to rectify this scandalous state of affairs? The answer was, only so far as the captains will allow. When the ship captains were ordered to move the secreted supplies to be warehoused ashore, the captains of the *Unicorn* and the *Endeavour* agreed to bend to the will of the people. Pennicuik and Robert Drummond, captains of the larger ships, stood on their rights as captains to be in control of their own ships. It created an impasse, one that remained when the sudden events of May and June made the whole question academic.

It was Paterson's great misfortune to take over the colony just as the rains really came in earnest.[56] Many found them depressing and few relished the idea of lasting out to November. But not all saw it that way. Indeed one young settler, Lieutenant Robert Turnbull could write enthusiastically of Darien as a green paradise, even in April just as the rains came tumbling in torrents from the sky.[57] In the end what contributed most to the collapse of the colony was not the rain, but the disease that went with it. The rains produced ideal breeding conditions for the mosquito, whose bite carried strange and terrible tropical illnesses – chiefly Malaria and Yellow Fever. To European settlers they often proved deadly. Darien, it seemed, promised both heaven and hell.

One survivor of such extreme tropical fevers, Patrick MacDowall, left a vivid description of what he had gone through:

> It was a very severe spotted fever... I had, in the beginning a most extraordinary desire of vomiting. I continued very ill for four or five days. I took with it a great headache, soreness of my eyes, and weariness of all my joints and bones... I was very inclined to fainting all the while of my sickness, and it brought me so low that I am not yet able to walk alone...[58]

MacDowall was lucky to survive a severe attack of what seems to have been Yellow Fever. Malaria was not quite so deadly except to children and to under-nourished adults. Paterson's belief that hunger had made people less able to fight off such fevers has been proved to be substantially true by modern medical research.[59]

The wettest months from April to August were commonly referred to in the Caribbean as the 'sickly season' with fevers killing off many European settlers every year. And so it proved for the Scots.[60] During the months of April, May and June 1699 sickness was widespread, affecting, among others, Mackay and Paterson themselves. Of those who went down with fever as many as ten would die every day, an attrition rate

that the colony could certainly not sustain indefinitely without reinforcements and fresh food supplies.[61] But it was not the fever that dealt
the greatest blow to morale, nor hunger that dealt the killer punch.
That was delivered by King William and his English ministers.

On 7 April 1699 the keen-eyed sentries at Point Look Out caught sight
of three sails approaching from the north. Could this be at last the long-
awaited relief expedition from Scotland? As the ships drew closer the
telescope, disappointingly, revealed two familiar sets of rigging and hull,
the elegant little sloops of Pilkington and Sands. The third ship, also a
sloop, followed some distance behind, the sole result of their first
'reprisal' voyage against the Spanish. It was scarcely a week since they
had left.

As the three ships slid into the harbour there must have been wild
speculation as to just what treasure, or at very least goods of some value,
the captive ship had on board. But it soon emerged that this was not a
Spanish vessel, but an empty French ship that had been found lying
unattended in a cove only a few miles along the coast among the San
Blas Islands. When they first came across this ghost ship, the two captains had classed it as a buccaneering ship with a captain who had been
unwise enough to leave the vessel without a guard while the crew had
gone inland in search of booty. But, in the captain's cabin, Pilkington
and Sands had come across an empty bottle, employed as a primitive
filing-cabinet with a rolled-up letter popped inside. This they now presented to the council. Since it was written in Spanish the council called
on the services of the colony's translator, Benjamin Spense, to explain
what it said. Spense studied it for a while, then gave a rough and halt-
ing translation.[62]

It was a letter from the Governor of Portobello to a French captain,
presumably the commander of the abandoned ship. It instructed him to
sail upon the coast and carry this message to the Indian chiefs:

You may assure Ambrosio, Corbet, Pedro, and the rest of the Indians of
[Darien] that if they continue to help the Scots and keep correspond with
them, that not only the Spaniards but likewise the French, will revenge it
upon them. But if on the contrary, they will join us to destroy and sort out
these Scots, they shall be rewarded and gratified for their pains.[63]

It was a startling piece of news. The Scots knew that there was a settlement of French buccaneers living on the coast at the Rio Coco, in the
territory controlled by the great chief Corbet. Richard Long had visited
them in October of the previous year and thought them a great threat
to English interests. The Spanish had then been keen to drive them out,
since they were the subjects of Louis XIV, the mortal enemy of Spain
until the peace made at Ryswick in September 1697. Now, it seemed, the
Spanish and the French had been reconciled and were to join forces
against both the Indians and the Scots. For the Governor's letter also
revealed that the French governor in Hispaniola had promised to: 'send
four Friggots to assist us in rooting the Scots out of Darien'.[64]

This new and unexpected alliance was almost certainly a by-product
of the diplomatic courtship dance being played out between Louis XIV
and the court in Madrid. The new council reasoned that if William's
great rival, the king of France, was backing the Spanish claim to Darien
then their own king would rally to their support. But in this they were
profoundly mistaken. As we have seen, William simply could not afford
to side with the Scots if he was to exercise any influence at the Spanish
court.

The news of a new Hispano-French alliance against the Scots was of
course dispiriting, even if the Scots suspected there was an element of
bluff behind the threat. But what was more dispiriting was the abrupt
departure of Sands and Pilkington that followed. They must have
appeared unusually on edge, and this not because of the French and
Spanish threat, but because they had encountered an English sloop on
the coast sent from Jamaica to find them. The sloop carried letters
addressed separately to each of them from the governor of Jamaica, Sir
William Beeston. In the letters he threatened them with dire consequences if they continued to consort with the Scots colony, which in his
eyes now had pariah status.

The two sailing men did not elaborate on the nature of the threats
contained in the letters: they simply announced they must leave at once
and return to Jamaica. These were men who had stuck loyally by the
colony for three months now. They had become honorary citizens of the
colony. Their decision to leave so precipitately suggests that the threats
must have been severe indeed.

They were owed money of course, but in order to get away quickly
they accepted goods in return for payment, as far as there were cargoes
of the right type and quality remaining in the Scottish holds. The bal-

ance of £100 that remained to Pilkington, and the £20 owed to Sands would have to be paid at a later date. They left on 20 April anxious to be away, with the good wishes of the colony ringing in their ears. They had agreed to perform one last service. On their decks they carried the disaffected Jolly and Montgomerie on the first leg of their journey back to Scotland. When the Company in Edinburgh later learned that such 'deserters' had escaped so easily and pleasantly from the colony the wrath of the directors could scarcely be contained.

Pilkington and Sands left New Edinburgh for the last time on 18 April. They left behind a colony where men had little to do but sit and wait for the expected food supplies from Scotland, and to console themselves with alcohol. With the threat of a Spanish, and now a French, attack hanging in the air, the little settlement became a rumour mill, a place of Chinese whispers that could grow alarmingly into major alarms. A story swept through the colony, to the effect that Pennicuik was making his ship ready to sail, and would make off with his crew to begin the life of a pirate. Without the St Andrew some 250 settlers would be left stranded on the coast should ever a decision be made to evacuate the colony. This was indeed a damaging rumour.

Paterson and the new council acted quickly to uncover the facts regarding this much-repeated story. There was a systemic examination of those said to be involved in the plot. They discovered there was no truth in it: 'it was found to be the melancholy discourse of three or four fellows, who, among others, were miserably harassed by Pennicook's unequal government on boord.'[63] And there was new purpose around the council table. Paterson's analysis was that the threatened assaults on the colony were unlikely to materialise. It was the wrong time of the year. The colony should put such things to the back of their collective mind, and turn instead to planning for the future. The food shortage could be tackled in the short term by sending the captured French sloop to Port Royal in Jamaica for supplies, under the command of the seaman Henry Patton. Alexander Burnet, a man with experience of trade would travel with him to negotiate terms for the supplies, armed with the stock of money the colony still had, presumably recovered from the wreck of the Maurepas. There were volunteers enough to man it. It left on 3 May, carrying a copy of the letter found in the bottle, which, the

Scots hoped, would eventually reach King William, by way of a second ship bound for England.

Paterson surprised the council by revealing that he had arranged for additional supplies. He had taken the good Pilkington aside before he left on 20 April and quietly talked him into throwing his lot in with the Scots. He was promised full citizenship in the colony, and a place to live, if he returned with his wife and family. And of course he would get his £100 in due course. Pilkington agreed, perhaps surprisingly given the threats levelled at anyone having dealings with the Scots.[66] This, he believed, greatly increased the chances of the colony lasting out:

> Then we begane to expect these two sloops. Viz. that of Pilkington's and this from Jamaica; also, that other supplyes would be droping in till a reinforcement should come from our countrey.[67]

Had Paterson been in charge from the start the colony would have now been in a much better state to survive until the relief ships and the second expedition reached them. But the story of the threatened alliance between the Spanish and the French had leaked out, making people uneasy. This unease, when added to the increasing numbers going down with tropical fever, and the still persisting suspicion that the ships' crews planned to sail off, leaving them to starve in their watery little huts, created a gathering pool of defeatism that even Paterson could not dispel.

The great worry was that the store of food supplies would decline until they reached the point where there was not enough left in the larder to feed the crew and passengers on any return journey. It is the classic dilemma explorers have learned to face. When is it time to turn back? The difference in Darien was the sheer numbers involved, nearly 800 surviving pioneers who knew that every extra day they chose to stay in the colony would make death more likely on the return trip. Convinced that a general drunkenness (brandy kept better than the flour and beef) was adding to the wild talk and speculation, Paterson even devised a plan to wean men off drink. Anyone who took the pledge to abstain – and stuck to it – was offered a bonus in company shares. Only one settler enrolled in the scheme.[68]

Towards the end of April Paterson went down with fever, probably a mild attack of Malaria. He refused to give up, dragging himself out of his sickbed to attend council meetings, urging his fellow councillors to have faith in the future. Such trials, he said, were God's way of testing human resolve. As he lay ill in bed he wrote a letter to Roderick

Mackenzie, the Company Secretary in Edinburgh. It was a *cri-de-coeur* from a man whose judgement was clouded by fever:

> I hope ere this comes to hand that Scotland will be sufficiently concerned and busy to support us who are now at the head of the best and greatest undertaking that ever was to the Indies.

> I assure you that if you do supply us powerfully and speedily we shall in a few months be able to reimburse them all and make the company the best fund of any in Europe, but if through poorness of spirit [you let us down] ... then what we have sown, others will reap the fruit of, which I hope not to live to see.[69]

The day that sealed the fate of the colony was 18 May. Paterson was lying ill with fever in his hut. On that day one of the colony's piraguas, those shallow but fast native boats, was sailing east along the coast in the direction of Cartagena when it met a Jamaican sloop carrying news of a new proclamation published by Governor Beeston on behalf of King William. The sloop supplied a copy:

> IN HIS MAJESTY'S NAME, and by command, strictly to command His Majesty's subjects... that they do not presume, under any pretence whatsoever, to hold correspondence with the said Scots [in Darien], nor to give them any assistance of arms, ammunition, provisions, or any necessaries whatsoever, either by themselves... or by any of their vessels, or of the English nation, as they will answer the contempt of His Majesty's command, at their utmost peril...[70]

'At their utmost peril' had a chilling ring to it. It meant that any breach of this ruling would be considered a hanging offence. And the circumstances of its publication only emphasised the serious intent of the new edict. Apparently it had been printed most unusually on the Lord's Day – a Sunday – because Beeston had caught wind of a plan for two ships (whose captains had heard rumours of the new ban) to sail on that day for the colony.

The tone of the decree, the uncompromising hostility it displayed to fellow inhabitants of Great Britain, as though they were a totally alien and threatening people, must have been beyond the comprehension of someone like Paterson, who had always wanted the interests of England

and Scotland to be advanced together. And forty years later, the first historian of Jamaica still found it difficult to credit the inhumanity of the
English authorities: 'the poor Scots were treated like common pyrates,
were denied the necessities of life, wood and water and anything else
which the law of nations obliges one Part of Mankind to support another'.[71] And, indeed, news of the decree led some of the colonists to turn
their thoughts to piracy, on the grounds that they were regarded as
pirates in any case. The shattering blow to morale in the colony was
quickly followed by another, a wild rumour carried by the same sloop
suggested that the Scottish Parliament had abandoned the company,
and that the much-hoped-for relief ships would never arrive. There was
no point at all in scanning the horizon.

Something like a panic gripped the colony. Parliament met – the
voice of the settler. They had had enough of the hunger, the illness, and
the endless waiting for the relief expedition. The only sensible course of
action was to abandon the colony, while a little food was left, enough to
sustain them at least till they reached the established colonies on the east
coast of North America. People there, they supposed, would never have
heard of Beeston and his proclamation. The council was split, with only
Paterson and Drummond arguing that they must stick it out. The four
others plumped for immediate evacuation.

Paterson had dragged himself from his sickbed to attend, and he did
his best to talk the council round. He argued, with as much passion as
his health allowed, that:

> first rumours of this nature was always the most terrifying and that hap-
> pily our native country knew nothing of all this and if they did not, [and]
> remained true to the design, there was none of us but would afterwards
> be ashamed of our precipitant forwardness in going away.[72]

But he failed to carry the day. Both parliament and council seemed
resolved that the only sensible course was to pack up and leave.

Over the next few days Paterson used his fertile imagination to come
up with alternative schemes. He accepted that there was now so much
illness and malnutrition in the colony, that men had no longer the
strength to defend themselves. So instead they should embark on the
ships. Then, instead of sailing north for the English colonies, a course
should be set to meet up with the Scottish ships that he was sure were
already somewhere in the Caribbean. But no-one would countenance
the idea, sensibly, since it would have involved sailing into the wind. The

chances of meeting the fleet would have been slim indeed, given the lack of proper charts and the inability to fix a ship's position in relation to them.

The final blow came for Paterson personally when he was struck down by a severe recurrence of the fever on 5 June. While he lay sweating in his hut a French ship sailed into the harbour with news that the new Governor at Cartagena was about to sail with a strong fleet to attack the colony. There was no truth in the rumour. But it was enough to spur the settlers to gather such effects as they had and stand in lines at the water's edge, waiting to be ferried aboard the four ships anchored in the bay. In his hut, Paterson was all but forgotten, visited only by his friend and supporter, Thomas Drummond.

Paterson remembered little of what passed in these last hectic days. On 16 June he was carried by someone to a boat and taken aboard to his cabin in the *Unicorn*. Two days later the little fleet raised anchor and set sail. They left behind in the harbour two French ships, who had come to salvage the treasure from *Maurepas*. The Scots may have wondered if they would stay to claim for France what should have been Scottish.

Far out, at the edge of the Caribbean, were the first two ships of the Scottish relief fleet, laden with supplies and carrying some 300 fresh men. They arrived six weeks too late.

Chapter 11

'A Sad and Fatall Disaster'

❋

On 21 November 1699, five months almost to the day since the Scottish fleet had quit Caledonia, a sail was sighted in the Firth of Clyde. It rounded the low bluff of Cloch Point and steered a course for landfall at Greenock, then a little town on the southern shores of the river estuary with a magnificent view of the mountains of the Scottish Highlands to the north. The ship bore the noble lines of its Hamburg birth, but all the signs of a ship in poor repair, its rigging tangled, its sails patched and torn, its hull lying low in the water. As the shades of night closed in around four in the afternoon the ship dropped anchor a cable's length from the shore and a ship's boat carried the news ashore.

This was the *Caledonia*, under the command of Captain Robert Drummond. Aboard were some 250 sailors and volunteers, the pathetic remnants of the 1,200 colonists who had left Edinburgh in such high spirits some 17 months before. The sheer horror of the voyage home from Darien was written in the yellowed faces of the passengers and their emaciated bodies. And they were the lucky ones. About three-quarters of those who left Darien in June 1699 had died without ever seeing their native land again. Amazingly, considering that he had left Darien in another ship, the *Unicorn*, and in the grip of a terrible fever, one of the surviving passengers on board was William Paterson.

Moved by that extraordinary sense of duty, he came ashore and somehow struggled the 60 miles to Edinburgh to report to the Court of Directors. The journey took all of two weeks, and he spent days lying ill in bed on the way. His account of his harrowing homeward voyage, much of it spent in a delirium, was an understated, sanitised version of a horror that left its mark on all who had experienced it. And he could write only of half the expedition. The terrible fate of the other half had eventually to be pieced together from a number of different sources.

Looking back with the benefit of a 300-year hindsight it is easy now to see that the sudden decision to up sticks and leave the colony – a decision Paterson had resolutely opposed – invited disaster on a massive scale. The Scottish fleet had been lying inactive in Caledonia Bay for almost eight months. During that period of idleness the hulls would have grown a crust of barnacles and a thick coating of seaweed. Many of the timbers themselves would have been attacked by the notorious Caribbean wood-boring worm, *Teredo Navilis*.[1] Any sailor familiar with the conditions in the Caribbean would have known it was madness to attempt a transatlantic journey without first careening and repairing the hulls. But the decision to leave had been taken by the settlers, men with no understanding of the importance of careening. Of course, seasoned men of the sea such as Robert Pennicuik and Robert Drummond should have known better, and it is surprising that none of the sea captains seem to have thought there might be a problem. Perhaps they were caught up in the general hysteria that had, all of a sudden, convulsed

the colony.[2]

With the little fleet finally ready to set sail, a hurried council meeting had agreed a plan for the evacuation of the surviving 800 settlers and sailors. All four ships were to stay together and take a course back to Scotland by way of Boston or Salem in New England (where fresh supplies could be taken aboard) and from there across the North Atlantic with the benefit of the well-known and reliable south-west trade winds.3

But once at sea the sea captains found their authority restored and the authority of the council conveniently diminished. The impetuous Robert Drummond in the *Caledonia* had clearly no intention of waiting for anyone. Once clear of the harbour mouth on the day of departure, 18 June, he found a fair wind, and set off north-eastwards with his sails filled. The little pink, *Endeavour*, caught the same wind and followed behind. For twelve days the two kept visual contact. Then disaster struck the smaller ship. She sprang a leak in a heavy sea and went down bow-first into the deep. The survivors took to the boats and were picked up by Drummond, it seems with a certain degree of reluctance.[4]

Meanwhile the other two ships had made heavy weather of manoeu-vring their way through the tricky passage that ran between the sub-merged rocks, marked by a tell-tale plume of surf, and the dangerous shore where Duvivier Thomas had almost drowned seven months before. Pennicuik in the *St Andrew* had led the way, only to see the

Unicorn, captained by the inexperienced John Anderson, swept like the *Maurepas* towards disaster. She was saved by dropping anchor, but the mishap ate up precious time. It took two days for the *Unicorn* to reach safety in the lea of Golden Island, just five miles away.

On the 22nd the two ships at last set out and beat slowly northwards against an unfavourable wind. Before long, the look-outs spied a sloop bearing down upon them. This was the vessel sent off under the command of Henry Patton some seven weeks before to fetch supplies from Jamaica. In the rush to leave he had all but been forgotten, but now he was a welcome sight. However, the news he brought was depressing. He reported that, following the issue of Beeston's *Proclamation*, he could find no-one in Jamaica willing to risk trading with the Scots. He returned with the trading goods unsold and with no fresh supplies.

The news does not seem to have altered Pennicuik's determination to be a law unto himself. He had decided he should head first for Jamaica where he hoped to take on fresh supplies. He issued orders that Patton's sloop should turn about and follow in the wake of the *St Andrew*. Together they drew steadily away from the *Unicorn*, which was in obvious difficulty, like an injured whale unable to keep pace with its fellows.

By this time John Anderson must have realised that the *Unicorn* should never have taken to sea. She was dangerously under-manned with only six crewmen on duty at any one time. And her timbers were in a dreadful state. The constant influx of water could be kept at bay only by continuous manning of the pumps. Yet of the 200 planters aboard only 20 were fit and strong enough to bend their backs to the task.

The shortage of men to work on the rigging invited disaster, and disaster was only too happy to accept the invitation. When dawn came up on the 23rd a sudden squall of wind brought down the mainmast before the sails could be furled, leaving Anderson to watch helplessly as the *St Andrew* and her little sloop companion sailed steadily further away. Somehow the depleted crew managed to effect a repair of sorts. But, only the next day all this seemed to be for nothing, when a storm blew up, straining the timbers to the limit and bringing down much of the aft-rigging. Only superhuman effort on the part of the crew and the pumping team managed somehow to keep the vessel afloat.[5]

Next morning they caught sight of the *St Andrew* lying ahead, becalmed. Anderson made his last contact with Pennicuik, taking advantage of the calm seas to launch a boat and reach the Commodore's disease-ridden ship. He found Pennicuik himself down with fever, and quite unwilling to send any of his depleted crew to help Anderson rig a temporary mast. Instead Patton on the sloop was asked to chaperone the stricken *Unicorn* to a safe port for repair. With that, the *St Andrew* put on full-sail and, taking advantage of a freshening wind, made off in the direction of Jamaica.

Patton, an unpleasant, self-seeking man who was later to swindle the Company of Scotland by selling off his cargo and pocketing the proceeds, proved an unreliable escort. The very next night under the cover of darkness he slipped away and set off in pursuit of Pennicuik. The *Unicorn* was left in what seemed a boundless stretch of open water, more than 2,000 miles from landfall in New England. Paterson, the most distinguished passenger, lay too ill to care.

That the *Unicorn* somehow managed to make New York seems a feat and a half. Only partly rigged, her hull low in the water, she was forced to the west and rounded Cuba by way of Cabo San Antonio. She sailed across the front of Havana's great natural harbour to make landfall at Mantanzas, where she hoped to replenish her water and supplies. Instead she found a Spanish fort bristling with cannon. The landing party, led by Anderson himself, was sent on its way by a hostile volley of musket balls, forcing them to leave behind one Benjamin Spense, the Jewish Spanish-speaking interpreter, who was to spend the next eighteen months in a Spanish gaol, divulging much useful information about the Scots to his interrogators.[6]

Somehow the crippled ship put her head about and sought the open sea, heading towards the Florida Keys. Then she limped northwards for another four weeks, hugging the forested coast-line, avoiding the shoals, and resisting the temptation to turn into the wide reaches of Chesapeake Bay and the Delaware River, possibly for fear of being arrested as a pirate vessel, a real possibility since the English proclamations had pronounced that the Scots ships held no commission from King William to sail in these waters. Around the middle of August she finally reached Sandy Hook, off the coast of East New Jersey just south of Staten Island – as it happened, a favourite haunt of pirates. There her crew spent a restless night. The next day she sailed into the East River and dropped anchor off Manhattan Island. Anderson hoped that the community of Scots merchants who had made their home there might afford the help and succour that the English merchants in Jamaica had been forbidden to give them. The sight of a familiar vessel lying in those sheltered waters quickened their pulses. Robert Drummond and the

Caledonia had reached New York ten days before them.

On the voyage to New York nearly 150 out of the 250 on board the *Unicorn* had died, their bodies consigned to a watery grave, victims of malaria and yellow fever, and a new epidemic of dysentery. Many of these might have been saved had there had been people on hand to care for them, even if only to make sure they drank plenty of fluids. But those able-bodied people still on board had no time to attend to such matters as they had fought to keep the ship afloat and make it to the safety of New York.

Paterson had spent the voyage in his cabin, vomiting and sweating until he may have seen death as a welcome release. He descended into a sort of insanity. Three Scottish merchants in New York on business went aboard the *Unicorn* to see the great man. They were shocked to find a man who had clearly lost his mind. They reported that 'grief has

broken Mr Paterson's Heart and Brain, and now hee's a child'.[7]

The little city of New York had been founded by the Dutch as New Amsterdam and had passed under English control only recently.[8] With its red-tiled roofs, its multi-coloured brick façades and its stepped gables it still bore the look of a Dutch town. Quite overshadowed by Philadelphia and Boston, it had only just begun to make its name as a trading port.

In 1699, the natural harbour that lay between Brukelen and Manhattan would have had only a handful of ocean-going ships lying at anchor. But the chances were that at least one of them would be a Scottish ship, trading illegally with the English colonies. Certainly there was one prominent Scot in New York, one who had heard of the Scottish colony in Darien, and who wished it well. Robert Livingston was a man of about Paterson's age, born in the little village of Ancrum just north of the border with England. As a boy he had fled with his father, a radical minister in the Church of Scotland, to live in Holland and spoke perfect Dutch. By dint of a well-judged marriage to one of New York's richest Dutch families, he had become a great landowner and had acquired a vast estate on the east bank of the Hudson River.[9]

He had a family connection with Paterson's great project for Darien. His nephew, Andrew Livingston, had been the surgeon on the *Dolphin* when it fell into Spanish hands.[10] He had somehow escaped and returned to New Edinburgh with the help of friendly Indians. It is not impossible that he had survived and reached New York aboard the *Caledonia*. Certainly his uncle took a close interest in the tattered and sickly Scots who had survived the journey. He was quick to offer credit to allow them desperately needed provisions.

Other Scots who had set up in New York rallied round. Two of them, Adam Cleghorn and Patrick Crauford, had only just been appointed agents by the Company of Scotland and had arrived in late July from Edinburgh with orders to arrange for fresh supplies to be sent south to Darien with all possible despatch. The best they could do now was to help organise the feeding of the pathetic remnants of the colony still confined to the decks of the *Caledonia* and the *Unicorn* in New York harbour.

Some of the lucky few – gentlemen and councillors – were allowed to leave the ship and found quarters on Manhattan Island. There, Thomas Drummond and Samuel Vetch, both recovering from fever, were introduced to Livingston, and through him to two of the city's leading merchants, Stephen Delancey and Richard Wenham, men who were to figure in the later, dramatic events of September.

William Paterson himself was carried ashore, and slowly nursed back to health, almost certainly through the good agency of Cleghorn. The agent had spent a week or so sounding out the survivors on both ships about what had gone wrong. He found ready criticism of the quarrelsome younger councillors, but of Paterson none at all. He relayed his findings (by letter and a convenient ship) to Robert Blackwood in Edinburgh, one of the two men who had exonerated Paterson of any wrong-doing two years previously:

> I am informed... there was some divisions among the first elected Councellors, some of them being too hote headed, and others of them no wayes train'd up to soe great affaires, ... many young men being swell'd up with the expectationes of their futur and present preferments. [Only] Mr William Paterson ... was concerned in this affair to the uttermost of

diligence...[11]

The sight of the ill-fed wretches who inhabited the dilapidated vessels that had somehow made it to New York provoked widespread sympathy, the more so since much of their suffering had apparently been inflicted by the king's proclamations forbidding any resident or merchant in an English colony from going to their aid. These strictures now applied as much to New Yorkers as it did to those who lived in Jamaica. In May, the Governor of New York, the Honourable Richard Coote, Earl of Bellomont had issued his own version of the official 'fatwa' pronounced against the Scots by their own king:

> His Majesty has been pleased to signify his Royal Pleasure to me. That I should strictly forbid all His Majesties Subjects, or others, inhabiting within the Districts of my Government, that they forbear holding any Correspondence with, or giving any assistance to any of the said Persons while they are engaged in the aforesaid Enterprize, and that no Provisions, Armes, Ammunition, or other Necessaries whatsoever, be carried from hence for them.[12]

As early as 5 August, just two days after the arrival of the *Caledonia*, a request was made to the New York Colonial Council to allow well-wishers (a group that probably included Livingston himself) to undertake a mission of mercy and carry food, water and medicines aboard the stricken vessel. Their plight had so touched the hearts of the New York councillors that they risked the wrath of the governor by setting the official embargo aside. A nervous Lieutenant-Governor, John Nanfan – clearly aware that feelings about the treatment of the Scots were already running high along the shores of the East River – despatched a letter to the governor (who happened to be away up-country finalising peace terms with the Iroquois Indians) suggesting that some show of generosity would not go amiss.

Governor Bellomont had not witnessed the sorry state of the men aboard the *Caledonia*, and still harboured a fear that the Scots would take the provisions and sail straight back to Darien, especially since he had just been told that a new Scots expedition was already on its way to rebuild the settlement. But he gave his consent – with a certain reluctance and subject to strict conditions:

> you know how strict my orders are against furnishing the Caledonians with Provisions. Yet if you can be well assured that these ships will go direct for Scotland you may furnish them with just enough provisions for the voyage.[13]

That Nanfan took this command seriously we can tell from his paranoia when faced with a request by the still sickly Paterson that he might have some clothes and household linen to be brought to him from the *Unicorn*. Nanfan would allow it only in return for a promise that he would not leave New York, except to return to Scotland. Paterson, a mere shadow of his former self and barely able to walk, was hardly a candidate for some new adventure in the Caribbean.

In one respect Bellomont's suspicions proved right. In September the irrepressible Thomas Drummond – his energy and optimism miraculously restored by a few weeks ashore – mounted an attempt to seize a ship in New York harbour and sail back to Darien with a hand-picked crew, there to meet up with the second expedition which Drummond was sure would have finally arrived. Drummond was driven by a potent mix of family honour (he could not bear the thought that he would go down in history as a deserter, a man who had shirked his duty) and a genuine love of Darien, a sentiment shared by the young Robert Turnbull who wanted very much to be included in any scheme that would return him to the warmth and luxuriance of Caledonia Bay.

On the 9th the *Venture*, a small merchant ship out of Glasgow sailed into harbour. Drummond immediately saw that it might take his small party of volunteers back to Darien and expected the captain to hand over his ship for the good of Scotland. Unfortunately the master, Captain Powell, proved not to be amenable, claiming that Drummond and his crew were no more than pirates attempting to seize his ship. So the case landed on the desk of the Lieutenant-Governor, who brought Drummond, his brother Robert, and Samuel Vetch before the New York Council at Fort William Henry. Drummond and the two others escaped prosecution, thanks to the intervention of the New York colony's attorney who himself happened to be Scottish.[14]

Thomas Drummond was not to be deterred. A week after the arrests, he met with Delancey and Wenham to discuss how they might help him find an armed merchantman and the supplies he would need to make the voyage back to Darien. He could offer them a business proposition. In return for the ship and the supplies, the remaining trade goods held in the hold of the *Caledonia* would be taken ashore and placed in their warehouse until such time as the Edinburgh accountants recompensed them for their expense and allowed them a decent profit.

Drummond's plan to steal way under the nose of Nanfan may have appealed to Delancey who was an enterprising scoundrel of a man. Born in Caen in Normandy to a Huguenot family[15] he had fled to Britain in the 1680s and from there to New York where he had teamed up with

Wenham in the dubious business of financing the activities of pirate ships, preying on East Indiamen off the shores of Madagascar.[16] They had ample funds at their disposal, and perhaps developed a liking for the rough and ready military man who wore his courage on his sleeve. They agreed to supply the ship and the food and drink needed for the voyage. As for Bellomont's edict, they apparently gave not a tinker's curse. They knew that Bellomont had been compromised by his own involvement in the funding of an expedition of a different sort by a certain Captain William Kidd just three years previously.

Kidd, a Scottish merchant sailor from Greenock on the Clyde, had married a rich widow and had been living a respectable life on Manhattan Island for some time.[17] His ill-fated expedition had been set up as a business proposition with the backing of Bellomont (not yet Governor of New York) and some prominent English politicians. He had been given 'letters of marque' bearing King William's name and was authorised to seize French ships on the high seas. The king was to have 10 per cent of the takings, the rich shareholders 50 per cent, and the remaining 40 per cent was to be split between Kidd and his crew.

From the start it was at best a tacky enterprise,[18] but it soon became a very murky business indeed. Kidd had been away less than a year when the general peace made at Ryswick had removed his real chance of making money legitimately through helping himself to French cargoes. Off the east coast of Africa he had been persuaded by his rebellious crew to turn his sights instead on any merchant ships they encountered: one of them – the *Quedah Merchant* – scandalously turned out to be English. The legend of Captain Kidd the notorious pirate had been born, and already his exploits were the talk of the New York taverns.[19] Delancey and Wenham may have guessed that the last thing Bellomont wanted was a full-blown court case that would raise the whole question of the funding of pirate voyages. So Thomas Drummond was given command of the *Anna*, a fast armed sloop.

After sunset on Friday 20 September, suitably renamed the *Ann of Caledonia*, she raised anchor in the East River and was gone before the New York Customs House could stop her. Drummond carried a commission signed by himself, William Paterson and Samuel Vetch, in the name of the Council of Caledonia. (Paterson, as ever, wanted it to be done by the book.) With him he took his hand-picked crew of thirteen sailors, and a number of the original volunteers, itching to go back to reclaim Darien for Scotland. Significantly, in view of the problems encountered trading one cargo for another, Drummond carried with him bills of exchange provided by Wenham and Delancey. The failure to arrange such credit for the first expedition was by now seen as a serious error in planning, a mistake that Paterson himself had never been able to put right.[20]

Robert Turnbull, almost missed out on this adventure. He had been staying with some friends on Staten Island and he arrived to see the *Ann of Caledonia* already under sail. With commendable initiative he pursued

her in a small boat in the gathering darkness and was hauled aboard.[21] Just before the departure of the *Ann*, a letter sent by the company directors the previous April had been brought into New York by a friendly ship.[22] It was the first communication anyone had had with Edinburgh since the fleet had sailed from the Forth more than a year before. Some of the news it carried was already seven months old. It reported the loss of the *Dispatch* off the Island of Islay in February (it may be remembered that that news had taken a month to travel from the island of Islay to Edinburgh, barely a hundred miles as the crow flies) and spoke of the planned departure in April[23] of two fresh ships carrying provisions and 300 men to the colony. Thomas Drummond reckoned these ships should by now have reached and re-occupied the colony. There would be no question of taking on a whole Spanish fleet alone.

Drummond expected Samuel Vetch, who was as fit and well as he was, to join him on his triumphant return. But Vetch had by now other ideas. He had been introduced to Robert Livingston's daughter, Margaret, and perceived there could be a very prosperous future for him in New York. He had considerable charm and put it to good use in wooing the rather plain Miss Livingston. By the end of September, kitted out with fresh and fashionable clothes, he had become her habitual

escort.[24]

With Drummond and the *Ann* safely on their way, all that remained was to prepare the *Caledonia* for one last voyage back to Scotland. It had been accepted that the unseaworthy *Unicorn* was quite unfit for an Atlantic crossing in the autumn storms. She was abandoned. There was room enough for all those who survived to find accommodation in the patched-up timbers of the *Caledonia*, all the more so since not a few of the survivors from both the ships had quietly slipped ashore to make a new life in America.[25] William Paterson now was fit enough to take a cabin aboard the *Caledonia*, and Robert Drummond was at last ready to sail. He had fitted out the ship for the voyage it seems through a deal struck with Livingston, Delancey and Wenham, on credit arranged by Adam Cleghorn.[26] On 12 October the battered ship finally raised anchor at Sandy Hook and set sail for home. John Nanfan, and Lord Bellomont were relieved to see the troublesome Scots go.

It was late in the year and the weather was rough. But death was now a less frequent caller. On the last leg of the journey home it was time for people to gather their thoughts, and begin to worry how they might be received on arrival. One young gentleman, Roger Oswald, was troubled with the guilt of having given up too easily. His father, Sir James Oswald, a prosperous landowner just outside Glasgow, had packed him off with an admonition that he must do nothing to dishonour the name of his family. Oswald had arrived in New York so famished that he had drawn on his father's credit in the city to the sum of £21 sterling. So would his father see him as a miserable coward and a incurable spendthrift? The best thing to do was to put pen to paper and try to soften the blow. 'Dear Father' he wrote, 'I know that you have good reason to be angry with me, but Sir, if you knew what hardships I had endured since I parted with you, you would excuse me in some part ...'.[27] On making landfall, he chose not to go home, staying instead in an inn in Glasgow until Sir James had sent a reply. The answer, when it came back, was unforgiving. His father refused to see a son who had let down his country and sullied the family honour. Oswald wrote back to a mutual friend: 'I never intended, nor do intend, to trouble my father any more... Only I hope you will acquaint him that I wish him long life, health and happiness, and more comfort in the rest of his children than he ever had in me.'[28]

Paterson had no angry father to concern him, and no need to reproach himself for having given way to any sudden impulse to abandon the colony. He must have been a bitterly disappointed man but in his buttoned-up way he contrived to hide his disappointment. He could take consolation in the thought that the second expedition would by now have arrived in Darien and that the company flag once again would be flying over New Edinburgh and Fort St Andrew. As he slowly recovered his strength and the full faculties of his mind – despite himself perhaps – a glimmer of the old optimism returned.

About the middle of August, while Thomas Drummond was still in New York forming his plan to make a voyage back to the Darien colony, a pair of modest ships had sailed south from Golden Island and edged gingerly into the vast palm-fringed expanse of Caledonia Bay. These were Scottish ships, the *Olive Branch* and the *Hopeful Binning*, the advance party of the long-awaited second expedition. Their journey had taken longer than expected, largely because they had left from Leith and taken the circuitous route round the north of Scotland, a detour that added three weeks to the journey.[29]

In charge were the sea captains William Jameson and Alexander Stark, with a complement of men to reinforce the garrison, and three months' worth of supplies for the embattled colony. As they rounded the point they could see the fortifications of St Andrew, and further to the south and east some evidence of human habitation. But it was all strangely silent and deserted, with only the screeching of colourful parrots echoing in greeting across the bay. Once onshore they soon came upon the evidence of sudden abandonment. In the fort the guns had been removed from their embrasures, but there were large and small cannon balls still neatly piled and ready for use. And there were the empty huts, about a hundred in all, lining the solitary street of New Edinburgh. Most of them had been set on fire. There they stood, charred and roofless, sad intimations of some awful and tragic disaster.[30]

Jameson and Stark, to their credit, decided forthwith to reoccupy the colony and hold it until the main fleet arrived, which could only be a matter of weeks. They met the local Indians and told them that a much larger flotilla of ships would soon bring men and women to settle here. The Indians appeared friendly enough, and may well have produced the mirrors and hats given to them by the first settlers and showed them the treaty signed by Pennicuik and the rest of the council. But, for all that, the advance party found it an uneasy occupation. Three hundred men were not enough to rebuild the fort and make it secure, even if they had had sufficient cannon. And they could scarcely have failed to notice that there were armed Spanish ships in the area, bending their graceful silhouettes before the wind on the far horizon.

As the days passed there would have been much discussion about their vulnerability. Might it be better to put out to sea and wait for the main fleet to arrive? The debate was soon to be resolved in a way that no-one could have foreseen. One night, a crewmen on board the *Olive Branch* went with a burning torch to fetch some brandy from the barrels below decks. Perhaps he stumbled, perhaps he was already drunk: somehow he contrived to send the brandy up in flames. The ship was soon ablaze from bow to stern, destroying all the stores and provisions on board. This minor catastrophe took place at some time in November when, ironically, Drummond and the *Ann of Caledonia* were within striking distance of the harbour. Jameson and Stark, with 300 mouths to feed and much of the food gone, decided to abandon the colony for a second time, leaving a lieutenant and a troop of 12 soldiers behind to maintain a token occupation until the fleet arrived, which surely must be any day now.[31]

Indeed ships did show up. On 22 November – the day after his brother Robert and William Paterson were to make landfall in Scotland – Thomas Drummond arrived with a second sloop, the *Society*, following in his wake. He had come by way of the island of St Thomas (the route favoured by sailors at the time to take best advantage of the prevailing winds) where he had purchased fresh supplies on the credit drawn on Delancey and Wenham, and hired the sloop to help carry these to Darien.

Drummond had encountered a Spanish warship of twenty guns on the way. The Spaniard, following instructions from the Governor of Cartagena, had treated the ship flying the Scottish flag as a pirate, and opened fire. With only six guns at his disposal, Drummond had successfully fought the Spaniards off, escaping into the night, at the cost of a torn jacket, a holed sail, and some damage to the timbers.

The next morning Drummond found himself off the familiar coast of Darien, the volunteers aboard elated by their victory of sorts, only to find no sign of the expected Scottish fleet. But Drummond was never a man to give up. The *Ann* and the *Society* dropped anchor in the lea of Fort St Andrew, which Drummond himself had built. Once ashore, he would have come across the little platoon of defenders, who had been looking out for some grand ships, not these small trading sloops. Their arrival was a bonus of sorts, because everyone expected that the main flotilla out of Scotland would arrive within days. And indeed, for once, this proved to be more than mere wishful thinking. On 30 November 1699, St Andrew's Day, the second expedition sailed into the bay. Leading the way was *The Rising Sun*, the proud East Indiaman built by

William Direcksone in his Amsterdam shipyard.[32] There were three other ships in the fleet, the *Duke of Hamilton* and the *Hope o' Bo'ness*, both large ocean vessels chartered by the company, and the much smaller *Hope*, purchased outright with the new funds brought in by the second and third call on subscriptions. The fleet carried a complement of 1,300 men and women, keen to begin life in the New World. They were hard-

ly expecting to find a derelict and abandoned settlement.

Meanwhile, the survivors aboard the *Caledonia* had caught their first glimpse of the rugged Scottish coast. The voyage across the North Atlantic had taken a mere six weeks. Unlike the outward voyage, no-one kept a journal, but we are safe to assume it had been an uncomfortable passage, with the ship riding a huge ocean swell. Before they had sighted land the strong south-westerly wind that had sped them across the ocean had risen to a gale. Robert Drummond, anxious not to court disaster on the last leg, pulled the ship into the calm waters of the Sound of Islay and waited for the storm to blow itself out. Then he set course round the Mull of Kintyre, past the grim sentinel rock of Ailsa Craig, the mountains of Arran to the north-west etched against a wintry sky, and made safe harbour off Greenock, some twenty miles down-river from Glasgow.

As he was brought ashore the great Paterson must have evoked some sympathy. He was a shadow of the man who had left Edinburgh just 16 months before. He had lost his wife and his good health. Such clothes as he had were certainly ill-fitting, and very possibly dirty and tattered. He was totally destitute. How he made the journey to Edinburgh, and who gave him shelter on the way, we can only guess, but he was exact in his descriptions of time. The journey of 60 miles took 14 days to complete.[33]

He would have arrived from the west, passing through the Grassmarket underneath the shadow of the castle rock, and entered the old city up the steep cobbles of the West Port. From there it was but a short ride up the Lawnmarket to reach the company offices in Mylne Square. There is no record of how he was received. With his gaunt and thin body in those much-travelled clothes we must suppose he was an object of sympathy and concern. Somebody certainly offered him a roof over his head, a place to recover his health; it could well have been at the home of Sir Robert Blackwood himself. The emaciated traveller promised the company a full report on how the first expedition had fared and just why the grand plan had gone horribly wrong. It took him two weeks to write it out in his florid handwriting and deliver to the Court of Directors. In typical Paterson style it was cool and dispassionate – stating the facts as he saw them, leaving it to others to draw their own conclusions. But he was to be horrified at how his report was to be misused by those he came to see as his enemies.

As he sat at his table, perhaps looking out on the broad Firth of Forth where, just 18 months before, 1,200 pioneers had set out on a journey into the unknown with a sense of adventure and in high spirits, nobody would have blamed him for deciding that he had had enough of Scotland and of the Isthmus of Darien. He was exceptionally lucky to be alive and to have regained his sanity. Had all the expenditure of energy, all that battling against adversity, really been worth it? But Paterson was never a quitter. He believed mistakes had been made, but the Company, just like people, could learn from them and maybe yet put matters right. And somewhere deep inside his brain there was already the germ of a much grander idea. He would develop it in the course of the next year and startle London with the breadth and scope of his new plan. His best days as a projector, he told himself, could be yet to come.

Chapter 12

The Key of the Universe

I shall endeavour to make a proposal, so just, equal, secure, and advantageous in itself, as may render it fit for Scotland to make and for England to accept

William Paterson on his grand plan for a new Darien Scheme, 1700.

In January 1700 Scotland stood at the gateway to a new century, one that was to see it flourish mightily. But a visitor to Edinburgh would have found nothing to suggest a new dawn. This was a city bowed down under the weight of four years of crushing famine, and now driven to despair by the news of the terrible catastrophe that had befallen the first colony at Darien.

Despair and anger; and if the Scots chose to blame the English for the disaster, it was perhaps only to be expected. Although the two countries had shared a king – on and off – for almost a century, they had remained stubbornly suspicious of one another, a suspicion born out of centuries of conflict and an astonishing lack of mutual contact. It has been reckoned that not more than a dozen Englishmen might visit Scotland, other than for business, in any one year and that even letters between London and Edinburgh were rare.[1] As one social historian has commented on the relations between the two countries: 'ignorance was still the fruitful parent of hostility and contempt'.[2] The few Englishmen who did go north, such as Joseph Taylor quoted in Chapter 4, were shocked by the filth and poverty and bemused by the exaggerated pride and prickliness displayed by 'gentlemen' whose threadbare coats seemed to belie their pretensions.

As for the Scots, the English were the 'auld enemy', who had laid waste the Scottish borders on countless occasions, and who now ruled Scotland by stealth through the convenient fiction of 'Scots Ministers' who might meet in Edinburgh as the Scottish Privy Council but who were seen as little more than stooges appointed by the king and his advisors in London. Arguably these ministers, and indeed the whole of

Scotland, had less influence on King William than did the representatives of the single county of Cornwall, and certainly less than that enjoyed by merchants of the City of London.

It was against this background that the Act of 1695 setting up the Scottish Company had been seen in Scotland as such a momentous step forward. For once Scotland had taken her destiny into her own hands and struck out to found a trading empire of her own, albeit relying on English expertise in trade and on English capital. But such optimism proved misplaced and short lived. The die was cast from the moment the English parliament in Westminster had first caught wind of the Scottish plans to compete directly with the English merchants of the East India Company. Had it not been for the tenacity of Paterson and his decision to come north to Edinburgh, the Company may never have survived the experience. But it had. Now, after the Scots had succeeded in mounting their own expedition and setting up their colony in Darien, it seemed that the long arm of England had reached out across the Atlantic to strike at them once again, through the issue of the proclamations.

Such was the view of the many Scottish politicians who sat as major shareholders on the board of the Company, some of the greatest landowners in the country. It has been said that the board of the Scottish Company formed the true political opposition to King William and his Scottish ministers, rather than the Scottish parliament which sat in its fine hall in Parliament House only when the king decreed it should do so.[3] The Company board met as and when it pleased, and provided a platform for politicians like Sir Andrew Fletcher of Saltoun, Paterson's original patron in Scotland, and Lord Belhaven, a member of the Hamilton family whose leader, the Duke of Hamilton, had been excluded from the Scots ministry for being disrespectful of King William.

According to the likes of Belhaven and Fletcher the failure of the first expedition was sealed on the day in April when the Governor of Jamaica, Sir William Beeston, issued his hostile proclamation on the order of King William.[4] This inhuman edict had literally starved the Scots out of their colony by cutting off food supplies.[5] Was this not an act of unspeakable and unchristian inhumanity, perpetrated in cold blood by one brother country against another?

From October 1699 this had been the rallying call that stirred up national feeling against the English and brought the Edinburgh mobs on to the streets and wynds of the old city in pursuit of innocent Englishmen. Samuel Tuckey, a merchant who had come north on business, had been forced to flee for his life to escape their attentions,[6] and he can scarcely have been alone in putting the safety of the border between himself and the Scottish capital. In November, a move by Belhaven to petition the king to demand the recall of the Scottish parliament and to declare his backing for the embattled colony grew into something like a national protest. Word of the king's refusal to give way on either of these issues had reached Edinburgh just as a recovering William Paterson was putting the finishing touches to his report on what had gone wrong with first expedition. He chose not to pepper his account with anti-English rhetoric. He chose instead to stick to the facts.[7]

It was not that Paterson was afraid to speak out. It simply was not his style to indulge in polemics. In fact Paterson found the Belhaven and Fletcher arguments simplistic and misleading. And he had *nous* enough to perceive a fundamental truth – that the Company's rage against England provided a convenient distraction from the real issue of just how far the Company itself was the author of its own misfortunes.

In his report Paterson made it clear that the colony had been failing long before news of the proclamation had arrived. The reasons were plain enough. The Company had shown a deplorable lack of urgency in sending out supplies to the colony (for which there was some excuse[8]) and had failed to provide for the proper government in the colony (for which there was none). Paterson's was not the only voice to challenge the use of England as a convenient scapegoat to cover the Company's own failings. Adam Cleghorn, one of the New York agents of the Company, had canvassed the opinions of many of the survivors when he went aboard the *Caledonia* in New York harbour. He passed his findings to Robert Blackwood, still a prominent director of the Company:

> The cause of their leaving Darien was, as they say, for want of provisions and fresh supplies from Scotland. Besides, they add that they never had soe much as one letter or scratch of a penn from the Company all the time they were a standing Colony. Thus despairing of supplies, and a great sickness and mortality befalling their men, they thought fitt rather to commit themselves to the mercy of the seas with their remaining provisions than to dye upon the spott without hope.[9]

It was the lack of hope, particularly the failure of the second expedition to arrive on time, that had provided the chief trigger for the hasty departure. As for the proclamations, Cleghorn doubted if such edicts could be enforced. He believed that they could have been circumvented by the simple strategy of commissioning a good agent, with proper credit at his disposal, in New York or Jamaica: 'if that had been taken care of, supplies of men and provisions had been easily furnished [from] these places, and that notwithstanding all English Acts to the contrair'.[10] Cleghorn was no ivory-towered theorist but a practical man of trade. He knew what he was talking about. But, for the moment, no one listened.

The time and the energy of the directors was being consumed in denouncing those who had deserted the colony as cowardly traitors and in pressing the king for an audience to secure the recall of the Scottish parliament. And soon they had to contend with a wave of anti-Company propaganda that had suddenly engulfed the coffee houses of London. The propaganda built on the impertinent idea that the settlers who had abandoned the colony had never made a more sensible decision.

The pamphlet which occasioned most anguish in Mylne Square was a scurrilous, sardonic, and racy account of William Paterson's great project that appeared early in 1700. It was entitled *A Defence of the Scots Abdicating Darien* and is best remembered for its portrayal of William Paterson as a Scottish pedlar who:

> came from Scotland in his younger years with a pack upon his back whereof the [mark] may be seen if he be [still] alive: having travell'd this country some years [i.e. as a pedlar] he seated himself under the wing of a warm widow near Oxford...[11]

The account went on in the same vein, suggesting Paterson had gone to the West Indies and associated with pirates and brothel keepers,[12] before returning to Europe: 'with his head full of projects, having all the achievements of Sir Henry Morgan, Batt. Sharp, and the Buccaneers in his budget'.[13]

The implication of the story became clear as the tale unfolded: the gullible Scots directors had fallen for a confidence trickster who had engaged his own crooked friends to help defraud them of their cash. These foolish directors had nevertheless persisted in going ahead with the crazy scheme, sending an expedition into what was well-defended Spanish territory, an expedition that was under supplied with life's essentials, and under led, by a comedy troupe of complete incompetents. How wise were those settlers to give up.

The author of this mesmerising confection of lies and half-truths was none other than Walter Herries, the surgeon recruited by John Haldane and James Smith in London in 1696, a man with a murky past who had once almost killed his commanding officer aboard a Royal Navy ship.

Herries, as we have seen, had joined the Company believing that it was to sail to India and the East Indies (of which he had had some past experience) and had been amazed and angered, on reaching Madeira, to find the secret sailing orders were to go to Crab Island and from there to Darien. He had left the colony at the earliest opportunity and gone back to London, where he offered his services to James Vernon, the senior Whitehall Principal Secretary as a propagandist against both Scotland (his own native country) and the Company.

The pamphlet delighted those in London who liked making fun of the Scots, and in equal measure infuriated the directors of the Company and their political allies. The extraordinary step was taken to have the pamphlet condemned as a seditious libel and duly symbolically burned in Edinburgh by the public hangman.[14] The great libel was then answered point by point by a new Scots pamphlet with a long-winded title, which was in turn burnt in London on the order of the king.[15]

This war of paper, ink and fire only served to drive a further wedge between the Scots and the English. Adding to a darkening brew of national hatred was the news that reached Edinburgh that January of the sad fate of the *St Andrew*. Until then some hope had persisted that the flagship, last seen by Paterson sailing off in the direction of Jamaica the previous June, might one day return to the Forth with its surviving crew and passengers and its trading cargo intact. But such dreams were cruelly dissipated by the arrival at the Company's offices of a letter, carried by post-horse from London, from a well-educated young volunteer aboard the ship, a certain Colin Campbell.

The fever that had struck down Pennicuik in the Caribbean, Campbell now reported, had proved both virulent and deadly, killing Pennicuik, and one by one, all the naval officers aboard the ship. Left without any skilled navigator, Campbell himself had taken charge and, with some luck, reached Jamaica at a place called Blewfields, 100 miles west of Port Royal harbour. On the journey about 140 out of the total complement of some 250 had died. And even for the survivors there was no happy ending. They had been reduced to skeletal figures by sickness and starvation, and Campbell had known that death could not be far away. So he had borrowed a horse and ridden all the way to Governor Beeston's residence, to ask permission to trade the cargo aboard the *St Andrew* for urgently needed food.

Beeston had been hospitable, but absolutely firm. The proclamation was still in force and such trade was therefore illegal. Not to be outdone,

Campbell had then approached that renowned man of the people, Admiral John Benbow (whose fleet chanced to be anchored in Port Royal harbour) and pleaded for help to save the crew. But Benbow proved just as heartless and unyielding, refusing him supplies and equally dismissing Campbell's suggestion that the *St Andrew* might be towed as a prize to the safe waters of the harbour. Campbell's failure to raise any kind of help had proved to be a death sentence for most of the survivors. In his absence a pestilential fever then sweeping Jamaica was somehow carried aboard the ship and finished off all but the strongest. It seems that fewer than 20 in the end survived, of whom only a tiny number ever saw Scotland again.[16]

If anything were needed to add to the emotional power of the anti-English argument, the tale of the *St Andrew* now provided it. It admirably pointed up the argument that the wicked English proclamations were to blame for the sorry, sad, débâcle of the first expedition. If the second expedition was to have any chance of success then the king must be forced to rescind them, and send the same Benbow and his fleet to defend them from any threat of Spanish or French attack. For the revived colony was grimly facing its greatest challenge. The dry season was now well established. It created great cracks in the mud along the colony's only road. It also opened a window for a new Spanish attack.

The man who should have taken most offence at Herries slanderous onslaught apparently made no attempt to put the record straight. William Paterson, founder of the Bank of England, was no untrustworthy Scots pedlar. And the idea that he was a common criminal was ridiculous. He had been completely exonerated by the enquiry following the Smith affair. As for the scorn Herries had poured on his mistaken assumption about the existence of an all-powerful Emperor of Darien with whom a treaty could easily be made, we have seen that the concept of an Emperor reflected the wholly orthodox assumptions of the time, and was shared by many people who had spent some time in Darien, including William Dampier and Basil Ringrose (the chronicler of Bartholomew Sharp's historic voyage from west to east around the Horn). Above all, Paterson was a dedicated, moral man, about as far away from being a confidence trickster as anyone could imagine. Yet, as far as we know, he never issued a counterblast of any kind to Herries' wild claims. Because he let the claims stand unchallenged, his reputation has suffered ever since at the hands of historians, from Lord Macaulay through to John Prebble.[17]

Just why did Paterson take everything that Herries threw at him without hitting back? The most plausible explanation is that Paterson was dismayed at the way in which the Herries' broadside had contrived to ratchet up the level of ill-feeling between the Scots and the English. By any standard its author had played to the prejudices of London, stigmatising the Scots as dishonest pedlars,[18] religious bigots and general good-for-nothings. As you read the piece you can almost hear the loud guffaws and mocking laughter that shook the coffee houses of London as one cheap jibe succeeded another.

From Paterson's point of view, we know that one of his long-term objectives was to reconcile the Scots and the English. This was in part because he was by nature a tolerant, internationalist sort of man, and a man who loved the diversity of human nature – the exclusive nationalism he found both north and south of the border was alien to his worldview. But it was also because he was convinced that Scotland could never escape from the poverty trap she found herself entangled in except with the help of England, or more exactly with the help of the English markets – both at home and in the colonies. Indeed, when he had his private audience with Sir Paul Rycaut in Hamburg in April 1697 he had gone so far as to confess his belief that 'the Scots and English should be one nation under the name of Britain'.[19]

He clearly saw that a union between Scotland and England – with a single parliament and government for both countries – would not only remove the strange anomaly of Scottish government, the fact that Scotland was effectively ruled by a Westminster apparatus in which she had no representation, but would also open the English markets to the Scottish merchant. He argued that with such 'foreign' trade would come capital accumulation, capital accumulation would lead to investment in ports and harbours, in mining, fishing and manufacturing, and this in turn would create jobs and wealth.[20]

This conviction made Paterson loath to indulge in the sort of public abuse of the English and the king that had now become commonplace in the taverns, coffee houses and dinner tables of Edinburgh, and indeed across the whole country. That road would lead to complete separation from England, with each country having its own parliament and choosing its own king. It would be a reversion to the bad old days when

England and Scotland had squandered their wealth in a never-ending cycle of war.[21]

Paterson wanted to prevent such a regression almost at any price. Out of this came his idea for a bigger and better trading scheme that would require both Scottish and English capital, and would enrich both countries in the process. In the furnace of his mind, he had begun casting the 'Key of the Universe'. It was not to be thrown away by taking a few cheap shots at the likes of Walter Herries.

Before we turn to the fascinating story of how Paterson reinvented his idea in the course of 1700 and went on to project it in almost messianic terms, it may be as well to remind ourselves that Paterson was operating in a 17th-century cultural and moral environment, rather than in the world of today. Many of his ideas have a modern ring to them – his belief in free markets, his staunch embrace of religious toleration, and his distaste for a narrow nationalism that might dry up the wells of enterprise. But on the other hand, he deeply believed that God's hand was to be seen in everything, that the trials and tribulations inflicted on humanity were God's way of both punishing sinful humanity and testing resolve.

The only three letters of a personal nature written by Paterson that have survived have come down to us by a lucky accident from this very period of his life. They give us a rare insight into Paterson the man. His belief in the application of reason and logic to matters of business and trade goes hand in hand with a total conviction that it is God who decides whether any enterprise should flourish or fail. God might ultimately reward virtue, but even of that no-one could be sure.[22]

Early in February 1700 the Company directors chartered a fast vessel out of Leith – the *Margaret* – to carry fresh supplies to the second colony, incidentally suggesting that Paterson's strictures on the board's negligence in supplying the first expedition had not gone unnoticed. This gave Paterson a chance to send letters to people he knew, and counted as friends, people now assumed to have resettled New Edinburgh.

One of these letters, dated 6 February 1700, was addressed to Thomas Drummond, a man he had last seen through a haze of tropical fever in New York, before Drummond had captained the *Ann of Caledonia* back to Darien. After remarking that he was 'wonderfully recovered' though still suffering from fever attacks, he went on to describe a strange omen that had appeared in Edinburgh just three days before:

> There happened a dreadfull fire on Saturday… about 10 at night, which has burnt down a great many houses between the High Street and the Cowgate, and the whole Parliament Close, the Parliament House and some adjacent house only except[ed]. This is … a great blow, the secret hand of God…[23]

The 'Great Fire' of Edinburgh could not compare with that of London in terms of scale, but it left a gaping, charred hole of rubble on the south side of Edinburgh's High Street, and only narrowly avoided destroying St Giles Cathedral.

Paterson's view that the fire was a sign of God's displeasure was shared by the Edinburgh City Council, which gave notice that such destruction was 'a fearful rebuke of God' for the sinfulness of the city. And indeed the entire Presbyterian Church of Scotland would have echoed that verdict. Many in Scotland would still have believed that the worship of Satan, in the form of witchcraft, may also have been to blame. Paterson's belief in a harsh but merciful God places him in the centre of the religious spectrum, not at the extreme.

In the same letter to Drummond that spoke of the 'Secret Hand of God', Paterson showed that he combined a religious fatalism with a whole panoply of practical ideas. Almost as an afterthought, he added some advice about the day-to-day running of the colony:

> One thing I had forgot, which relates to the weekly precedency [sic]. I think it's ridiculous nonsense; [it] was the intention of mean spirits, raw heads, jealous and presumptuous pates, that had no virtue of their own … If my advice may therefore be taken, make it a monthly president… this will make your proceedings more certaine, stedy, and honorable.[24]

This letter and the two others left aboard the *Margaret* on 3 March 1700, but they were never to be delivered. The Captain sailed all the way to Darien, arriving there before the end of May only to find the colony deserted for a second time. Why we shall shortly find out. Had it sailed on the same day a year earlier and relieved the first colony, history may have been very different.

There is evidence elsewhere in these three letters that Paterson was now recovered enough to turn himself once more to securing the future of the colony. He still believed the second expedition could build on the experience of the first, and lay the foundations of the great international entrêpot that he considered the site demanded. But he was also acutely aware that Scotland lacked the resources to do the job properly, as he had always made clear. A way had to be found to break free of the strait-jacket imposed by Scotland's lack of capital. Already £100,000 of good Scottish cash had been lost with the first expedition, and most of the rest of the new cash, raised under the terms of the Company's prospectus, had been expended on equipping the second expedition. Although £400,000 had been pledged as working capital it was now clear that Scotland was unlikely to be able to supply it. In his letter to the Rev. Alexander Shields, one of the ministers sent off with the expedition, Paterson gave some idea of how his mind was already working: 'I am not without hope of returning to the Collony but shall endeavour, in the first place, to get the needfull reinforcements and supplies from Europe upon a better foot'.[25] If his intention was to resume his travels in Europe – where times had become more difficult in business terms because the late wars against France now needed to be paid for – there is no evidence to suggest that he ever managed to make the journey. But he may already have been thinking of a more radical plan.

At some time during the course of 1699, while he was struggling to impose some business discipline upon the struggling colony at Darien, Paterson had written out a detailed account of the money he claimed the Company owed him, and addressed it to the Court of Directors. There must be some doubt that this 'Petition' was ever delivered, but it provides a vital clue that Paterson's thoughts were already shifting towards launching a new proposal to exploit the potential of the Isthmus. In it he asked for some £9,500 to be advanced to him, £7,500 to his account in Scotland and £2,000 to his credit in Caledonia to allow him to 'follow trade for his owne and the Colony's advantage.'[26] This was presumably to give him a chance to conduct his own negotiations with the Jamaican merchants who called at Caledonia Bay and so establish the regular trade the entrepôt needed.

The careful, legible handwriting gives an insight into Paterson's character. He was, after all, working on this document in the shelter of his hut in New Edinburgh. We can picture it being written by candlelight in the warmth of the tropical evening, with the sounds of the forest and the breaking of the sea in the background being incongruously mixed, almost certainly, with the sounds of noisy disputes, provoked by the shortage of food and the relatively generous supply of brandy. Yet Paterson was able to shut all this out and quietly pen his complicated claim for the board's attention.

Part of the claim took the form of a rather ill-tempered request for the Company to return to him all of his books and maps, which he considered, as we have seen, had been 'forcibly extorted from him on the pretence of a sale'.[27] He offers to repay them the £150 he had been given as an inducement to hand them over. Why was Paterson so anxious for these books and maps to be returned to him? He could hardly have intended to sell them there in the forests of Darien. But if he was already contemplating reshaping his Darien scheme to make it attractive to new investors, books and maps would have been essential.

So, in his letter written a year later to the Rev. Alexander Shields, the term 'Europe' may have been a euphemism. Because other evidence strongly suggests that what he had in mind was a new business alliance, not between Scotland and Europe, but between Scotland and England, and this on a scale much more ambitious than anything attempted so far. Paterson was a patient man and he would have to wait for an opportune moment to launch the new plan. Edinburgh in February 1700, brimming over with anti-English passion, was not the place or the time to launch the idea.

In the faraway colony of Caledonia, December had been a month of bitter dispute. The abandonment of the first colony had, of course, taken all the new arrivals by surprise. They had come to buttress the original colonists, not to begin again virtually from scratch. The Rev. Francis Borland, the brother of Paterson's Boston friend, John Borland, later wrote an account of the dispiriting circumstances they now found themselves in:

> Expecting to meet with ours friends and countrymen, we found nothing but a vast howling wilderness, the Colony deserted and gone, their huts all burnt, their fort the most part ruined, the ground which they had cleared adjoining the fort all overgrown with weeds; and we looked for Peace... but beheld Trouble.[28]

There had been much grumbling, and a reluctance on the part of some of the new settlers to go ashore. And, once there, terrible arguments broke out about whether to stay put, and wait for the Spanish to attack, or abandon the colony for good.

Thomas Drummond was adamant. They must stay for the honour of their country, rebuild the fort and prepare to rebuff any Spanish attack. Opposed to him was one of the new councillors, the Edinburgh merchant James Byres. He suggested that two or three companies of soldiers should stay to guard the peninsula and the fort. The rest – the planters, and women and children – should be evacuated to Jamaica where they could find work.[29] After a bitter row it was agreed that 500 of the settlers should indeed re-embark and seek a new life in the English island colony. To smooth over the divisions, this decision was dressed up as common sense; it would leave the strongest men with sufficient rations and ammunition to last out until further help arrived, perhaps in the shape of Admiral Benbow and his fleet.[30]

Among those left behind morale was low, a dark mood not lifted by the arrest of a carpenter, Alexander Campbell, on a charge of planning mutiny. His arrest was ordered by James Byres, who was determined to rule the colony with an iron fist. Campbell was an unlikely conspirator, but was hanged on 18 December before the assembled garrison, on a scaffold erected outside Fort St Andrew.

Thomas Drummond argued that it was useless to lie waiting for a Spanish attack that might not come for months. Instead he wanted to lead an attack against Portobello, an attack in which Pedro's Indians could join – just as Ambrosio had once proposed. But he was voted down by the other councillors, and then, without warning, arrested and locked in a cabin in one of the company's ships, the *Duke of Hamilton*.[31] It was a fine way to treat a man who had done so much to keep the colony alive.

All through January 1700 the fear of a Spanish attack grew, with some justification. Indeed, it would have come earlier if the Conde de Canillas, the *Presidente* of Panama, had had his way. But once again the creaking Spanish military machine was not yet ready; an outbreak of fever along the coast became a sufficient excuse for the delay.

Meanwhile, the colonists kept a nervous watch on the ocean and sent look-outs into the hills, aware that a Spanish attack was bound to come sooner or later.[32] The tension proved too much for Byres. He suddenly announced that all war was immoral and that he must be allowed to leave the colony. He would withdraw to Jamaica, there to seek fresh provisions. His departure in the *Society*, the sloop chartered by Thomas Drummond at St Thomas, was precipitant, spurred on by the rumour brought by a Jamaican ship that a Spanish fleet was on its way. Byers had the temperament of a tin-pot dictator but the guts of a filleted fish. He slipped away on the morning of 4 February with his brother-in-law, his apprentice, and one of the few remaining women, a Mrs Dalgleish. The council sent with her a bald covering letter: 'She is big with Child. We are not in a position to treat her as her circumstances and good behaviour require'.[33]

James Gibson and William Vetch, left in charge, offered no hint of leadership. The colony drifted towards disaster. Then, when all seemed lost, a *deus ex machina* descended upon the colony in the shape of a dashing former infantry officer, Alexander Campbell of Fonab, a man the Company had sent out late to the colony with the highest recommendation. He was an associate of Thomas Drummond and, incidentally, a close friend of Robert Campbell, the man at the head of the troops who carried out the massacre of the MacDonalds at Glencoe. Lt Col. Campbell arrived from Barbados on Sunday 11 February in a sloop hired by the Company. It had taken four months to bring him to Darien, and he arrived safely only by out-sailing a patrolling Spanish warship, sent to keep an eye on the Scottish colony.

He found Thomas Drummond a changed man; after five weeks of solitary confinement he was ill and no longer interested in battle. But there were others willing to be inspired by his presence, including Robert Turnbull the young ex-officer who had pursued the *Ann of Caledonia* out of New York harbour. Campbell proposed launching a pre-emptive strike against the Spanish at their base in Toubacanti from where Don Luis Carrizoli – the man who could claim to be both Cuna and Spanish, and who sported the grand title of Field Marshal of the Province of Darien – was still striving to control the province. In the dry season it could be easily reached. Only four days after his arrival, Campbell took command of a force of 200 soldiers and was guided by Pedro and his warriors across the ridge, down to a 'river which flowed into the South Sea'.[34] From there it was an easy climb up to the plateau on the other side of the valley to the fort at Toubacanti. It was a palisaded fort, giving clear advantage to the defenders, but the Scots were undeterred. Many of them were highlanders, soldiers of legendary courage who believed a fierce charge might bring down the walls of Jericho itself. The fort duly fell but the heroics ended there.

Campbell had unfortunately taken a musket ball in his right shoulder and made his way painfully back to New Edinburgh. The colony could celebrate, but Campbell spent much of the next month in a fever and was never again to lead the colony forces. On 28 February, a sentry on Point Look Out spotted the first sails of a large Spanish flotilla on the horizon.[35] Six weeks later the colony was to be no more.

In Edinburgh, where no one could know of the drama unfolding in Darien, February and March were much occupied by the Company's new drive to persuade King William to bring the Scottish parliament back into session, and by this means to force him to revoke the proclamations and thus save the colony. All they were promised was a recall of parliament in May. Many feared, correctly as it turned out, that it would then be too late to save the colony.

On 23 May the Scottish parliament reassembled amid a pomp and ceremony that belied its powerlessness. The new commissioner, the Duke of Queensberry, was under strict instructions from King William to block any attempt to commit him as king to supporting the Scottish claim to Darien, not while the King of Spain was still clinging on to life and the question of who should succeed him had yet to be resolved. So, when the majority of the parliament pressed ahead with a resolution supporting the Company's position – that it had every right to settle in Darien and every right to expect the king to support it – Queensberry feigned a bad cold, and sent parliament meekly home on 30 May.

As the doors of Parliament House were closed on protesting MPs, now was perhaps the time for wiser counsels to prevail. Paterson certainly thought so. It was about this time that he made his first approaches to the Duke of Queensberry, sounding him out about the possibilities of winning King William's support for his new, more ambitious, plan. William had been increasingly alarmed about the deteriorating relations between Scotland and England. Indeed in February of the previous year he had told the English House of Lords that:

His Majesty does apprehend that difficulties may too often arise, with respect to the different interest of trade within his two kingdoms, unless some way be found to unite them more nearly and completely... His Majesty is of the opinion, that nothing more would contribute to the security and happiness of both kingdoms; and is inclined to hope that, after they have lived near an hundred years under the same head, some expedient may be found for making them one people.[36]

The Lords noted his proposal for a full union of Scotland and England, but did nothing. The union of the two countries had been proposed three times in the 17th century, and on each occasion it had been the English parliament that had stood in the way,[37] largely over fears that England would be swamped by poor Scots flooding south.[38]

Paterson's new plan was to offer the English some form of bonus to encourage them to drop their opposition to the Scottish colony in Darien and, eventually, to the union. He suggested a new company should be set up to exploit the potential of the Isthmus to become a focus for world trade. This company would have a capital fund of £2,000,000, making it twice the size of the fledgeling Bank of England and five times richer than the original Scottish Company. Four-fifths (or 80 per cent) of this capital would be offered to English shareholders, the remaining £400,000 being the capital Scotland had already raised or made a commitment to raise.

Of course, the whole scheme depended on King William accepting the original Scottish claim to ownership of Darien through treaty and possession, a claim that so far he had so adamantly resisted. But, if the City of London jumped at the chance of investing in this new 'British' scheme for the Isthmus, Paterson clearly felt he might yet change his mind, the more so if the King of Spain were to die, an event expected at any moment.

The Duke of Queensberry, now the King's Commissioner in Scotland, held the view that the Company of Scotland had never been up to the job of running a colony or developing a trading empire. He was perhaps now surprised to find that Paterson agreed with him on this, and on the need for Scotland and England to remain tied together by a common king. He was impressed with Paterson's efforts to cool the passions tearing Scotland and England apart.[39] But Paterson's move to create a new Anglo-Scottish Company in a new form may have come, even to him, as an unexpected twist.

In June, Paterson seems to have presented the Edinburgh directors with his elegant new model in the form of a 14-page prospectus. No original copy of this document has survived, but it was reproduced in full by Sir John Dalrymple of Cranstoun, an 18th-century admirer of

Paterson who had gathered together many of his papers. Dalrymple entitles it *Mr Paterson's last Proposal for the Darien Company* but he gives it no date. From internal evidence within the document it seems to have been presented to the company around the middle of June 1700, though this must remain an educated guess.[40] It is a truly astonishing document in its use of imagery and language. Take for example Paterson's description of Darien as a beautiful tropical paradise:

> The great number of easie hills and rysing grounds, with their interven-ing valleys, multitude of springs, brooks, and rivers of waters, render the prospect of this coast exceeding delightful, and the whole country pleas-ant and commodious... the coast is sensibly much cooler, and the heat more temperate and easy than any I have observed in any of the American Islands or other summer countries...[41]

Apart from the attraction of the fertile soil and the frequent occurrence of gold, the site commended itself by offering a swift passage to the South Sea by two easy routes across the Isthmus that are 'beyond com-parison' with any other.

It is worth quoting the document at some length since these descrip-tions have been used to discredit Paterson as a hopeless dreamer, a fash-ion begun with Macaulay who suggested such descriptions were written by a man who had never lived in Darien and were mostly the figment of an overactive imagination.[42] In fact they were written after he had lived in the colony for eight months. And we can now see that his views were by no means unique, corroborated as they are by a host of other accounts sent back to Scotland by the first Scottish settlers. It seems we need to abandon the accepted view of later historians that Darien was a sodden, swampy hell-hole. Instead we must now see it as a rather pleas-ant, if somewhat damp, tropical land.

The proposal of 1700 was the first time Paterson set out his vision of Darien in the form of a prospectus for interested investors, and he was intent on impressing them. The new scheme was principally to be aimed at the City of London, and at the king himself. (Had not William and his late wife Queen Mary been the very first investors in the Bank of England?) To this end Paterson dangled the prospects of the rich prizes that would come to England and to English business.

He was not beyond inserting rich purple prose of a type that would hardly be permitted by today's stock exchange rules. According to Paterson, through this door of the seas and the key of the universe will naturally circulate and flow all the treasures, wealth and rich commodities, of the spacious South Seas, such as gold, silver, cochanill, saltpeter ... pearl, saphires and other wealth, to the value of one hundred millions of crowns yearly...[43]

This was hyperbole on a grand scale, but it must be judged by the standards of the time. What set Paterson apart from the other entrepreneurs of his day, who also promised fabulous riches, was the fact that his was tied to a revolutionary concept; the harbours of the Isthmus must be open to ships of any nation, and trade encouraged by eliminating customs duties. Eventually 'all manner of impositions upon trade or shipping' were to be removed.[44] This would unleash the power of trade to generate wealth. That, after all, was the lesson Paterson had learned all those years before in Amsterdam. It is time to reveal that when Paterson memorably coined the dictum 'Trade will beget trade and money will beget money', he went on to add: 'the consumption and demand of English growth and manufactures, and consequently the employment of their people, will soon be more than doubled ...'.[45] This was a prediction that came true in the end, a glimpse of a future British prosperity in which trade and manufacture went hand in hand.[46] Paterson was, however, careful to avoid suggesting that this new Darien company might trade with India, or directly intrude on the East India Company monopoly in the India Ocean. Paterson remembered too well the power of that colossus to make mischief at Westminster, even if Sir Josiah Child and his tiny group of monopolists no longer held sway.[47]

It was a formidable restatement of his original idea, but this time with adequate resources and experienced management. But without the approval of the directors in Mylne Square it would be still-born. After all, they claimed to be the owners of Darien through 'discovery, possession, and the consent of the natives'.[48] He strongly hinted to the directors that the shareholders would receive compensation in return for transferring this right to the new company, and he appealed to their better judgement. Surely, he wrote:

> ... the respect which is due to His Majesty and the affection which we owe to our sister nation, will sufficiently incline this Company ... in using all endeavours for bringing the rest of our fellow subjects to be jointly concerned in this great, extensive, and advantageous undertaking.[49]

And he might just have won the day had it not been for the arrival of two pieces of news from Caledonia Bay. On Thursday 20 June despatches from Darien arrived, telling of Lt-Col. Campbell's rout of the Spanish forces at Toubacanti. It seemed that the colony, against the odds, had beaten off the Spanish threat. The news was greeted with joy in the streets of Edinburgh and, fast on its heels, by a wave of drunken anger, as mobs stoned the houses of government ministers. The rioting went on all night unchecked and was quelled only by the fatigue and drunkenness of the rioters. The Duke of Queensberry chose to pretend he had slept through the commotion, rather than to admit it would have been too unpopular to call out the troops.[50]

Those politicians and directors who blamed England for everything that had gone wrong in Darien enjoyed a week of popularity and fêting. Then on Friday 28th, a second despatch brought altogether more depressing news. The colony had surrendered to a Spanish force. Caledonia was no more.[51]

Don Juan Pimienta, the new Spanish Governor of Cartagena, was the man given the task of evicting the Scots from their 'crabbed hold' in Darien. He believed this would be no easy task if the Scots held fast in the site. In November 1699 word reached him of the departure of the *Hopeful Binning* following the brandy-inspired fire aboard the *Olive Branch*. This was a golden opportunity for the Spanish forces to move in and seize the near-deserted colony. But he could not act without authority from Spain. By the time it arrived, *The Rising Sun* and her three companion ships had reached Darien and reoccupied Fort St Andrew. An outbreak of fever in Cartagena, as we have seen, then delayed the departure of the Spanish forces. The Windward Fleet – hardly worthy of the name since it consisted of a flagship and a number of smaller attendant ships and barges – was not ready to sail until 11 February. Time now was of the essence, since the rainy season would arrive in April, just over six weeks away.

Before clearing Cartagena harbour the flagship, the *San Juan Bautista*, ran aground on a sandbank. It took a day to pull her off. It was a hesitant start and Pimienta, lodged in his quarters aboard the flagship, was himself a hesitant man. His soldiers, now dragooned into the barges, were hardly itching for a fight. But Pimienta expected help from elsewhere. From Panama City had come a promise from the Conde of Canillas that Pimienta's army of around 1,000 men would be supplemented by 500 soldiers from Portobello. While the combined force attempted a landing on the Caribbean shore, another three companies of infantrymen were to be brought across the Isthmus from Panama City. The colony of Caledonia was to be caught in a classic pincer movement.

This was the plan, but Pimienta was delayed by bad luck and his own cautious approach to the task. Two days out from Cartagena the ill-maintained *San Juan Bautista* lost her main mast when nothing stronger than 'a heavy wind' caused it to split at the base. The ship limped into the lee of an island and tied up until repairs could be carried out. The expedition then proceeded with the utmost caution, arriving off the Scottish colony on 28 February. There the *San Juan Bautista* was to be joined by two much smaller armed ships from Portobello, *El Florizante* and the *San Franscisco*. Because of the danger of coastal currents and off-shore rocks the warships stayed far out at sea, too far to bring the Scots within the range of their guns.

Then a messenger arrived on the *San Juan*, bringing news of Campbell of Fonab's heroic sacking of Toubacanti fort. It served to make Pimienta even more circumspect. The first Spanish troops were not put ashore until 13 March and then in a spot some ten miles from the Scottish base, and on a shore too precipitous to allow the landing of artillery. A force of 300 men started on the arduous journey towards the colony, through rough and hilly country. But a stroke of better fortune then came Pimienta's way. Some friendly Indians – possibly members of the Cuna people who looked to the chief Andreas[52] as their leader – told the Spanish that there was a much easier landing place just three miles from Fort St Andrew, and it was there on the 14th that the Spaniards were able to put a larger force ashore. It consisted of some 400 men, and several pieces of field artillery.

Even then the Scots held the higher ground above the landing place. Pimienta ordered his forces laboriously to dig themselves in. He then sent out a feeler to the enemy. A message, carried by a drummer under a flag of truce, to Fort St Andrew, politely asked the Scots to consider surrendering. In it Pimienta threatened them with assault by land and sea, rather blunting the menace of his words by admitting he was loath to bring his ships into Caledonia Bay, for fear that the north wind then blowing would trap them inside. These were decidedly not the words of a man with the stomach for a fight.

The Scots had so far put up firm resistance, stiffened by an appeal from the wounded Campbell of Fonab to fight for the honour of their country. At first they sent back a message of defiance. But then two weeks passed during which the Spanish forces slowly crept closer to Fort St Andrew, driven back occasionally by the wild charges of a platoon of highlanders, but nevertheless advancing day by day. Inside the fort, morale was now falling like a stone. Campbell of Fonab was too ill to offer any leadership, and an outbreak of dysentery was taking its toll. At a meeting of all the officers commanding the land forces it was decided they should swallow their pride and ask for terms. In their letter of 28 March they pretended not to have fully understood Pimienta's first note for want of an interpreter. They now wrote: 'later, when we came to understand it, we find that you bade us leave this neighbourhood... we have thought well to send these lines to inquire the conditions you offer us'.[53] Campbell of Fonab refused to put his name to the letter.

As the Spanish noose closed slowly around Fort St Andrew, negotiations continued. At first the Scots offered to leave if they could depart with all their ships, guns and ammunition. Pimienta rejected this out of hand. They could leave, but without their arms or their ships. The Scots suggested a compromise and Pimienta offered to go some way towards meeting their terms. Eventually on 31 March the terms of capitulation were agreed.[54] The Scots were to keep their great warship, *The Rising Sun* and all their other vessels. They were allowed to take with them such arms as were sufficient to defend themselves on the homeward journey, including cannon, shot and gunpowder. They were not required to renounce their claim to Darien.

Pimienta was more relieved than he could say. His troops were on the point of exhaustion as he confided to his diary:

> most of my men were ill because of the continuous marching through mountains never trodden by human foot before, over which they had to [physically carry] all the subsistence and munitions, and in many places water as well... the rains threatened and the wet season was now beginning...[55]

Under the agreement the Scots had two weeks to evacuate the site. Ten days later, on 10 April, they were ready to leave for home.

The voyage home now undertaken by the second expedition proved even more disastrous than the homeward voyage of the first. Almost before they had left harbour the *Hope o' Bo'ness* sprung a leak and threatened to sink. Her passengers and most of her crew were transferred to *The Rising Sun*. The smaller vessel then raced for survival towards Cartagena, where the captain, Richard Dalling surrendered her to the Spanish in return for his liberty and that of his men. They were lucky to escape the fate of Robert Pinkerton and the crew of the *Dolphin*.

Meanwhile, *The Rising Sun*, the *Duke of Hamilton*, and the *Hope* had set course for Jamaica and all safely made landfall there. But, thereafter, they each faced catastrophe. First the *Hope*, heading north for America, ran on to rocks just south of Cuba on the island of Camanos. Those who survived were put to work in the Spanish plantations. William Vetch, the councillor, had, perhaps mercifully, died before the mishap and had been buried at sea. The *Duke of Hamilton* made it safely to Charleston in what was now called Carolina and tied up in the river. They found a town blighted by a fever epidemic; God, it seemed, did not spare the English any more than He did the Scots and the Spanish.[56] Meanwhile *The Rising Sun* had been caught in a gale off Florida and had lost her three masts. Somehow, the captain James Gibson – the man who had commissioned her building in Amsterdam – managed to organise a temporary sail and brought her into the shelter of the sand bar outside Charleston harbour. She was shipping water fast and her crew were exhausted through the continual manning of the pumps. When the ship struck the sandy floor of the bay, they could rest at last. James Byres, the man who had cravenly fled to Jamaica – was one of those aboard. He had not lost his talent for self-preservation. He took himself ashore in a longboat with fourteen others, including one of the chaplains, the Rev. Alexander Stobo[57] – a man of little charity but who went on to found one of America's great political dynasties.

It was the hurricane season, and the remaining crew of *The Rising Sun* may have slept uneasily aboard their listing ship as they waited for the hull to be patched up. Three nights later a great tropical storm ripped up the eastern seaboard of America and struck Carolina. *The Rising Sun* was swept out to sea and went down with the loss of all hands. It was a sad ending for a magnificent ship.

The *Duke of Hamilton* fared little better. She sank at her moorings in Charleston harbour. The survivors went ashore and disappeared into the history of early America. Only three little ships successfully made the trip back home – the *Margaret of Leith*, the *Content* and the *Speedy Return*. The last two were to become the most infamous ships in Scottish history.

As for the *Ann of Caledonia* – the ship chartered out of New York – she successfully made the return journey in good time arriving in New York in less than a month, with Alexander Campbell of Fonab on board. He returned to a warm welcome in Edinburgh in July 1700.[58] Of the 1,300 who had set sail from the Clyde in July 1699 less than a hundred returned to Scotland. Of the others, many hundreds had died.[59] But one man in particular had very much survived.

Thomas Drummond, whom we last encountered being released from his locked cabin in February, had since sailed with the *Speedy Return* to Jamaica to fetch provisions back to the Scots. There he had met James Byres and returned with him to the colony, arriving on the day after the terms of capitulation had been signed. While Byers took what he thought would be a safer passage aboard *The Rising Sun*, Drummond took his chances in the much smaller *Speedy Return* and successfully reached Edinburgh. With his brother Robert, he was to continue working for the Company, until their mysterious disappearance brought a terrible retribution upon innocent Englishmen.

The news of the failure of the second expedition proved a hammer blow to Paterson's new plans to involve England in a new Darien company. He met with the directors in August to suggest that England could be persuaded to come in. But it was hopeless. In Edinburgh, those who led the Company, together with most of Scotland's opposition MPs, had hitched their star to the popular cause of separation from England rather than to the unpopular one of a closer union of the two countries. But before he left Edinburgh to go back to London Paterson gave his native country a farewell present. If Scotland must go her own way, and pick up the pieces left behind by the collapse of the Darien affair, then he suggested it would be best done by placing the affairs of the country in the hands of a 'Council of Trade', a sort of economic development board.

His detailed proposals for such a council have been described as 'breathtaking'.[60] But nothing came of them: Paterson had estimated the budget for such a body, entrusted to develop Scotland's manufacturing, fishing and financial economy, as being as much as £3,000,000.[61] This was simply beyond the resources of Scotland.

By the end of the year Paterson would seem to have set himself up once again in London. In November the long-awaited death of the

Spanish king came at last. Before he died – encouraged by the French – he had left all his possessions, including the Spanish colonies to Philip of Anjou, Louis XIV's grandson, paving the way for renewed war between England and France. And this time Spain was to be on the French side. Darien seemed certain to fall under French influence if not control. News of the king's death, and of the enormous growth of French influence in Spain, gave Paterson one last chance to get the Darien project off the ground, suitably modified to the new political reality. Now he argued that England must seize the Isthmus from the Spanish and open up trade in the Pacific at the expense of both Spain and France. Spain – with its opposition to free trade – should not be trusted with ownership of the world's future most important trade route.[62]

Back in London, it took him time to find his way back into political favour. His old admirer, Charles Montagu, now ennobled as the Earl of Halifax, had temporarily fallen from power, himself 'impeached' by his political enemies. Montagu was to fight his way back. But it took Paterson a year before he was granted what he had long wanted, a private audience with King William III. It took place at Kensington Palace in late 1701. The king listened attentively to Paterson's suggestion that a bold move was in order if England was to lead the world in trade. He seemed interested. But, early in 1702 he fell from his horse while hunting in Richmond Park, outside London, and broke his collar-bone. Within a month he was dead.

His successor, Queen Anne, lacked William's Dutch concern with trade. When war came, the seizing of the Isthmus was never an English objective. In the treaty that brought the war to an end in 1713, a victorious Britain gained only one small piece of land in the Caribbean. She already owned most of the tiny island of St Kitts. Now the French handed her the remainder. The Isthmus and its potential were ignored.

William Paterson was never able to resume his business career in London. Instead he took a job teaching mathematics, working from his house in Soho. But he maintained his contacts with the political world in Westminster. His old supporter, Charles Montagu, came back into the limelight, at the centre of a group of powerful Whig politicians much feared in the predominantly Tory early years of Queen Anne's reign. It was nicknamed the 'Junto' by its enemies. Paterson could be found operating on its fringe, rather as he had done in the years of lobbying for the Bank of England. The man was by no means a spent force.

As for the Company of Scotland, surprisingly perhaps, it kept itself going until the full union between Scotland and England in 1707. The focus of the business shifted to less ambitious, and more profitable, schemes. A few ships were chartered and sent off on successful voyages to Africa. But even so, the Company could never hope to make enough money ever to repay the shareholders the capital they had invested in the heady years that began in 1696 and ended in 1700.

Even then, this modicum of progress was to be cut short by a shocking tragedy in 1705. It had its origins in 1701 when the Company despatched from the Clyde two of the ships that had returned from Darien the previous year, the *Content* and the *Speedy Return*. They were sent on a voyage to the Indian Ocean in the care of the Drummond brothers. A year later, in 1702, the two ships were to be found on the island of Madagascar, a notorious pirates' nest, carrying a cargo of Negro slaves that the Drummonds hoped to trade for ivory, gold and spices. Neither of the ships was ever to return to Scotland. The Drummonds proved unreliable trustees of the Company's property and allowed the ships to be borrowed by a pirate, John Bowen, in return for a share of any cargoes or ships he might seize. The *Content* caught fire off the coast of India, and the *Speedy Return* was sent to the bottom of the sea when the pirates replaced it with a better ship they had taken as a 'prize'. No-one knows what happened to the Drummonds.

Two more years passed and an English vessel called the *Worcester* sailed into Leith harbour under the command of Captain Thomas Green. That night their crew went ashore and had rather too much strong Scottish ale to drink. They boasted of their days as pirates, and of the ships they had seized. Somehow, someone who overheard them got the idea that the ships they were talking about were the *Content* and the *Speedy Return*, vessels not heard of now for three years. The Edinburgh rumour mill soon took this tenuous reasoning and converted it into absolute certainty. One who heard the story was a certain Roderick Mackenzie, Secretary of the Company of Scotland, a man who had nursed a grudge against Englishmen for almost ten years. It was he who took the story and embellished it in a ballad, more doggerel than poetry. According to Mackenzie, Green and his officers had captured the Drummond brothers, brutally beheaded them, and thrown their bodies into the sea. Before the week was out, Green, his ship's mate, and his gunner had been arrested and thrown into the Tolbooth prison.

Their trial for murder and piracy was as shocking a miscarriage of justice as ever disgraced a Scottish court, since Green and his colleagues had documentary proof that they could not have been involved in the disappearance of the Drummonds and the *Speedy Return*. Edinburgh was once again gripped by a wave of anti-English hysteria. A jury pronounced them guilty, and they were sentenced to be hanged in public on the Leith links. The reigning Scottish Secretary – James Ogilvy, the Earl of Seafield – had not the courage to face the wrath of the mobs who thronged the route from the Tolbooth to Leith, despite having the order of Queen Anne herself to grant the men a reprieve. He locked himself in his house and left them to their fate. They were executed in April 1705 before a baying mob.[63] One who had witnessed the travesty of the trial, and the ugliness of mob wrote:

> The tragedy was completed and from many points of hilly Edinburgh the bodies of the victims might be seen swinging on the sands of Leith. The national vengeance was more than satiated, and many of those who had been foremost in the strife were afraid to think of what they had done.[64]

Thus by 1705 relations between Scotland and England had reached their nadir, and the Company of Scotland had played a large part in the souring of Anglo-Scottish relations.

Union was now seen in London as the only solution to the mounting risk of a deep and lasting rift between the two countries. In the following year, Queen Anne appointed two groups of commissioners, both chosen by herself – one to represent Scotland and the other England – with instructions to negotiate a treaty of union between the two countries.[65] This time the opposition to union was subdued from England; the Scottish parliament had threatened to choose its own king to succeed Anne on the throne of Scotland. This could scarcely be anyone other than the pro-French and Roman Catholic candidate, James Stuart, the son of James VII of Scotland, James II of England. In Scotland, on the other hand, passions were running high against any closer association with England, still fuelled by the failure of the Darien project and the perceived hand of England in bringing it down.

Not all Scotsman felt this way. Many of the better informed could see the advantages that could accrue to Scotland if she were to hitch her wagon to a rapidly expanding commercial power, while avoiding the problems that would arise from any complete separation from their southern neighbour.

In London, Paterson was one of those Scotsman, and he offered his services to the cause of the union. He had the gall to write to Robert Harley, the Queen's chief minister, threatening him with the wrath of 'The Junto' if his offer was not taken up.[66] He was duly sent as an 'observer' to report on events in Edinburgh and to persuade all he met of the merits of such a union.

He was soon involved in one of the greatest accounting exercises in British history. If Scotland were to join England the countries would be united in a customs and tax union. This meant that Scotland would have to pay interest on England's growing national debt. But if Scots were now to pay interest on the English debt how were they to be compensated? In discussions, in which Paterson may have played a part, the idea of the 'Equivalent' emerged, a capital sum equal to the calculated extra costs imposed on Scotland through assuming part of the English debt.

The calculation of the Equivalent was certainly left to Paterson, the one man recognised to have the skills to do it. He calculated it to come to £398,085 and 10 shillings precisely.[67] The Equivalent could be used to pay the Scots for the expense of the new coinage they would need. But it could also be used to provide compensation for the shareholders of the Company of Scotland, who had ploughed their wealth into the venture and had seen not a penny in return. Thus the Darien company would be formally wound up, and a sum equal to the total money invested – £170,000 – plus interest at 5 per cent per annum up to the date of the union of the two countries, would be made available out of exchequer funds.

The terms of the deal were duly written into the Treaty of Union drawn up and submitted to both the Scottish and English parliaments in 1707. Article 15 of the Treaty defined the amount of the Equivalent exactly as Paterson had calculated it, and decreed that a due portion of it should be paid as compensation to the company shareholders. There was no compensation for the loss of life incurred in the Darien adventure. But since it gave the shareholders a return on their investment it undoubtedly smoothed the passage of the Act of Union through parliament.

It says something for Paterson's increasing interest in the machinery of government, and for his commitment to making the Union work, that he put himself forward for election to the new British parliament in early 1708, standing for the constituency of Dumfries Burghs. He put himself forward through the good offices of one of the great noble landowners of the district, the Earl of Annandale, to whom he had written:

> Being advised by some of my friends to offer my service to the [constituency of] Dumfries as their representative in parliament, and well knowing your Lordships interest and influence ther, I hereby apply myself to you ... If my friends think fit to choose me there, it will naturally bring me to lay myself out as much as possible for procuring the good for that part of the country... towards which the justice favour and regard I have lately had from the parliament of Great Britain will very much contribute...[68]

With the support of the noble Earl he might expect to sail into the new parliament.[69] Perhaps a glittering career now lay ahead of him as a politician, representing his native district, helping to cement the two countries more firmly together. But it was not to be.

The constituency consisted of no fewer than five separate towns. On 26 May the 'commissioners' from each borough met in Dumfries to judge who had won the election. Paterson clearly expected to receive a rubber-stamped approval. To his surprise one of the commissioners, William Johnston from Annan, announced his own candidature, voted for himself and gathered the support of two of the other towns. Paterson was outvoted three to two.

It was a highly dubious manoeuvre since the election had already been held, and Johnston had not apparently had his name on the list. Paterson petitioned the new parliament confident of being declared the winner. But the bad luck that dogged his every step kicked in. The new parliament was dominated by the Whigs, and Johnston was known to be a solid Whig supporter. Paterson, on the hand, was apparently the Earl of Annandale's man. He paid the price when the first British parliament, dominated by the Whigs, handed the result to Johnston. Paterson's promising political career had crashed to the ground before it had begun.[70]

As for the Equivalent, the matter of transferring the funds agreed under the Act of Union proved to be a long and difficult process. Scandalously, much of the money laid aside to compensate the shareholders was misapplied, to the benefit of the 25 'commissioners' appointed to distribute it. They were accused of lining their own pockets and favouring the wealthiest creditors. In the end, it was not until 1719 that the whole mess was finally sorted out in true Patersonian style. An annual fund of transferable interest of £10,000 a year was created to support the issue of new bonds to the value of £248,550, a figure Paterson had also calculated.

The long wait had proved too much for many of the needy shareholders. They had sold their entitlement to compensation, mainly to London investors, for any price they could get. After the deal of 1719 had been agreed, and the bonds issued, some two-thirds of them were now held by London merchants. The bondholders included such figures from the past as Paul D'Aranda, James Campbell, Lord Belhaven, and – intriguingly – even James Smith, who was credited with ninety-one pounds, nineteen shillings and eight pence, precisely.[71]

In a curious coda to the story, the debenture holders wanted to use the fund as the basis of banking operations, along the lines established by William Paterson when he founded the Bank of England in 1694. Just as had happened in the case of the Orphans' Bank, they found themselves opposed by a Bank of England that feared the Debenture Fund plan would create a strong commercial rival in the field of banking. Next, the debenture holders approached the Bank of Scotland to sound out the possibility of a merger. They were rebuffed. There is some irony in the fact that when the Bank of Scotland's monopoly (granted amid such controversy in 1695) came to an end in 1727, the bondholders in the Equivalent Fund (who had been granted their own Royal Charter in 1724) became the founding shareholders in a new bank, The Royal Bank of Scotland. So both the Bank of England and The Royal Bank of Scotland, now one of the world's great financial institutions, have a Paterson connection.[72]

As for Paterson, throughout the early part of the 18th century, he continued to battle on for his ideas. In 1708 he wrote the *Philopatris*[73] essay on transforming Scotland from an economic backwater to economic powerhouse. It was to be done by developing foreign trade. He showed he had lost none of his passionate belief in its power:

> Foreign Trade is of such a chemical nature and virtue, that it can extract the finest metals out of the basest, convert the worst commodities into the best, turn a barren land into fruitfulness, and make a contemned and sleighted people, a formidable and aweful nation.[74]

And his appetite for denouncing false prophets was undiminished. In 1705 John Law, the Scotsman who was to found the Bank of France, had visited Scotland, advocating the issue of unsecured paper money, a project that was to ruin the French economy and set it on a course that led to the French Revolution.[75] Paterson argued that such money, not being convertible into gold or silver on demand, would never win the trust of the public. It would end in: 'considerable loss for the possessor of these notes, who will be obliged to allow great discount for them in all their transactions'.[76] Do we find a painful memory here of the financial crisis of 1696?

When it came to money, Paterson continued to display an almost mystical ability to fail to get his proper share. He had lost out with the Bank of England and the Orphans' Bank, and he had ended up repaying the debts that stood to the name of James Smith. With the granting of the Equivalent he had fully expected to receive the compensation agreed for shareholders in the company. But the directors of the Company ruled that the compensation should go only to Scottish shareholders, a group to which Paterson did not belong by virtue of having paid his sub scription in London.[77] As the man who had calculated the Equivalent down to the last penny, Paterson knew this was an absurd ruling. There was nothing for it but to begin the long and tedious process of petitioning parliament. In the end, it was not until 1714 that the new parliament of Great Britain voted him a sum of £18,241 as thanks for service to his country. But, even then, there were a further four years of delays and calculations while his various debts were deducted and the interest owed to him were added on. In the end he received a final payment of £16,754 in 1718. He may well have reflected that getting money out of the treasury was almost as difficult as extracting it from the treasurer's box in the Company. Less than a year later he died in London in the parish of St Margaret in Westminster.

Both his wives were dead and he had no direct heirs. But, careful man that he was, he had prepared a will which he and a witness signed 'At the Ship Tavern without Temple Bar, July 1718 about 4 in the afternoon' – lawyers, it seemed even then, enjoyed a drink. He distributed his new-found fortune in an even-handed manner to his step children and their spouses, to his step grandchildren, to his surviving sister, and to both his sisters' children and their dependants.

Within the year he was dead. In January 1719, we must suppose with his faithful friend Paul D'Aranda at his bedside, he passed away at his house in Westminster after a short illness. As to where he was buried, that remained and still remains an issue of some controversy. The likelihood is that he was interred in some long-lost grave, possibly in St Anne's churchyard in Soho. But there is a persistent folk-memory that maintains that his body was carried back to Scotland and buried in the grounds of the ruined Sweetheart Abbey, in the village of New Abbey, where his younger sister, Elizabeth, had married John Paterson of Kinharvey. There have even been claims that a tombstone marked the grave until it was broken up 'and used by the masons for paving'.[78] It seems unlikely, given the time it would have taken to bring the body north from London. But, in death, as in life, Paterson continues to stir controversy.

Whatever the truth, the little plaque erected at Sweetheart Abbey in 1974 to his memory, remains the only memorial to William Paterson to be found in Scotland. That seems a decided shame.

Epilogue

istory has been unkind to William Paterson. He has been depicted as a mad dreamer when in fact he was a man of business with a strong practical bent. It was hardly his fault that he found himself on the wrong side of the East India Company at one of the most corrupt periods of its history, or that the English government chose to try to block its Scottish rival at every turn. Nor could he be blamed for the re-coinage crisis or the financial disaster that overtook James Smith. It was also an extreme misfortune that his ambitious scheme was launched just as Scotland and Northern Europe was struck by 'the little ice-age' which made shipbuilding impossible, brought starvation to so many, and made it extremely difficult for the Company to find the food supplies needed to keep the colony afloat.

Then there was the strange business of King Carlos II of Spain. Had he died sooner and released William III from his dilemma over the Spanish succession, William may well then have seen the point of joining with the Scots in their great Darien enterprise. King William himself was not totally unsympathetic to the Scots. In October 1700, when the Scots had abandoned all hope of ever re-establishing the colony in Darien, he wrote to the Scottish parliament expressing his profound sadness that he could not have done more to help:

> It is truly our regret that we could not agree to the asserting of the right of the companies [sic] colony in Darien... if it had not been for invincible reasons, the pressing desires of all our [Scottish] ministers with the inclination of our good [Scottish] subjects... had undoubtedly prevailed. But since we were ... satisfied that our yielding in that matter had infallibly disturbed the general peace of Christendom...We doubt not that you will rest satisfied with these plain reasons.[1]

Yet the 'general peace of Christendom' was to be disturbed nonetheless. Just two months after the message was conveyed to the Scottish parliament, Louis XIV triumphed in the question of the Spanish succession, and by the summer of 1701 William found himself once again trying to patch together a grand alliance of European powers, to counter the threat of Franco-Hispanic domination in America as much as in Europe.[2] Had the death of the King of Spain come as expected in 1699, William may have found it made sense to back the Scottish claim to Darien, if only because it offered a base for the ships of the Royal Navy in the coming naval war against the French.

As it was, just as the Darien project foundered, the great powers of Europe plunged into a period of prolonged war that distracted all attention from the great South Sea and the supposed treasures that it held. Although the South Sea Company was formed in 1711, it was essentially interested in exploiting the African slave trade, not in opening up the Pacific. For much of the 18th century the real contest between Britain and France was for supremacy in India, North America and the Caribbean. The race to be first to discover the great Southern Continent simply never started. There was a lull of more than 60 years between Dampier's last voyage and the voyages of Captain James Cook that finally determined the extent of Australia and established that New Zealand was not a part of a much larger continent. And as for the Isthmus of Panama and Darien, it was only in the 19th century, 150 years after Paterson's expedition, that the possibility of opening up a trade route that would avoid the difficult passage round Cape Horn was seriously considered.

In 1847 a group of New York financiers floated the Panama Railroad Company and began work on a railway to cater for a growing trade between Europe, North America and Asia, very much as Paterson had envisaged. At the same time America and Britain reached an agreement to co-operate in building a canal across the Isthmus. But there was no agreement about which route it should take.

In 1853 the English engineer, Dr Edward Cullen, published his survey of five possible routes across the Isthmus, one in Mexico, one in Nicaragua, and three on the narrowest part of the Isthmus in present-day Panama. Only the route from Punte Escoces (the abandoned colony of Caledonia) offered the prospect of a canal without locks. Cullen envisaged using the tides to drive the ships through the grand channel – in a cutting that nowhere had to be more than 150 feet deep:

> The canal, to be on a scale of grandeur commensurate with its important uses, should be cut sufficiently deep to allow the tide of the Pacific to flow

right through it, across to the Atlantic, so that ships bound for the Pacific to the Atlantic would pass with the flood, and those from the Atlantic to the Pacific with the ebb tide of the latter. Such was the plan recommended in my Report to Lord Palmerston [the British Foreign Secretary].[3]

It was another sixty years before the present canal running from Panama City to Colon, was opened, and then only after long arguments in the United States as to which route was best.[4] It requires a system of twelve locks to carry vessels from ocean to ocean and had never quite developed the potential Paterson foresaw for this great natural crossroads of the world.

Paterson saw the future in so many ways. He envisaged a world in which trade would be facilitated by the use of financial instruments, not hamstrung by a shortage of gold and silver coinage, and helped bring such a world about by founding the Bank of England. He preached the virtues of free and open global trade, where one country would not discriminate against another and anticipated Adam Smith by almost a century. He saw the huge importance of the Isthmus as the key to opening up world trade, two hundred years before the Panama Canal made it at least feasible. His belief that European countries should compete through trade, not war, makes him an early advocate of the principle that led to the emergence of the European Economic Community over 250 years after his death.

Yet this man has been virtually written out of the history books. He simply did not promote himself sufficiently, kept no diaries, left no memoirs, and allowed himself to be reduced to little more than a historical footnote. Almost 300 years after his death it is surely time to rescue him from obscurity.

Notes

Introduction

1 Sir John Dalrymple of Cranstoun, *Memoirs of Great Britain and Ireland*, London, 1771. Part III, Book VI p. 128.
2 Walter Herries, *A Defence of the Scots Abdicating Darien*, Edinburgh, 1700 p. 1.
3 Sir John Clapham, *The Bank of England, a History*, Cambridge, 1944. vol. 1 p. 14.
4 William Pagan, *The Birthplace and Parentage of William Paterson*, Edinburgh, 1865. p. 72.

Chapter 1

1 William Paterson's *Last Plan for the Darien Company* reproduced in Sir John Dalrymple of Cranstoun, *Memoirs of Great Britain and Ireland*, London, 1771. Part III, Book VI p. 162.
2 The barque was the favoured vessel of the pirate fraternity. They were small three-masted ships, square rigged on the forward two masts, with triangular sails fore and aft of the third. The sloop had a single mast, fore and aft rigged, with a bowsprit. It was generally smaller and slower than the barque.
3 Edward Ward, *A Trip to Jamaica, etc.*, London, 1698.
4 Port Royal was reckoned to have one tavern for every seven inhabitants.
5 John Esquemeling, *The Buccaneers of America*, London 1684 quoted by Angus Calder in *Revolutionary Empire*, London, 1998 (Pimlico Paperback) p. 212.
6 Walter Herries, *A Defence of the Scots Abdicating Darien*, 1700 p. 1.
7 Ibid. p. 1.
8 William Paterson's *Last Plan for the Darien Company*, reproduced in Sir John Dalrymple of Cranstoun, *Memoirs of Great Britain and Ireland*, London, 1771, Part III, Book VI p. 161.
9 According to later evidence Paterson appears to have chosen his spot well. In 1853 Dr Edward Cullen published his assessment of five possible routes for a canal across the Isthmus. Only the one projected by Paterson offered safe natural harbours on each coast. He concluded 'none of the above routes, except the last, (i.e. Paterson's route) have good harbours, without which it would be a fruitless waste of money to cut a canal.' It was also the only route that could be cut without the need for locks. The projected canal – never built – was to be 39 miles long. *The Isthmus of Darien Canal*, Dr Edward Cullen, London, 1853, p. 13.
10 There would be a small charge for using the harbours.
11 Pirates preferred to call themselves by this term. The original 'buccaneers' had

315

been cow farmers on the islands of the Caribbean, given to smoking their beef over an open fire using a metal grill called in French a 'boucan'. Many of these 'boucaniers' took to piracy, and the name came to mean pirate. Pirates were also known as freebooters.

12 The buccaneers were actually invited to make their base in Port Royal in 1657 by an early Governor of Jamaica, Edward D'Oyley. See Angus Calder, *Revolutionary Empire*, p. 211.

13 The correspondence between London and the governors of Jamaica make it clear that Governors often made personal gains from any 'pyrated' goods that fell into their hands. See Journal of William Blathwayt, 1680-1688 PRO.

14 The term was applied to all the mainland coasts of Spanish Central and South America, from Mexico south.

15 Modyford Commission to Morgan July 1670. Reproduced on the web at www.blindkat.hegewisch.net/pirates/lommorgan.html

16 For a good account of Morgan's story see Raynald Laprise, *Histoire Generale de la Flibuste* at www.geocities.com/trebutor/Livre/L1/L108.html. English accounts to be found on the Internet are generally unreliable.

17 The 'piece of eight' was a silver coin about the size and weight of an American silver dollar and worth 8 reales, hence the term. The first American 'dollars' were simply 'pieces of eight' used as an unofficial currency in the American colonies.

18 Others on the trip wrote their memoirs too, notably Basil Ringrose. But Dampier and Wafer's accounts were almost scientific in their detail of the land and people.

19 Walter Herries, *A Defence of the Scots Abdicating Darien*, 1700 p. 3.

20 See Arthur Percival Newton, *The Colonising Activities of the English Puritans on Providence Island*, London, 1914. Translated as *Providencia: Las actividades colonizadoras de los puritanos ingleses en la isla de Providencia* Bogota 1985.

21 Raynald Laprise, *Un Dictionnaire Biographique de la Flibuste (1648-1688) presenté par le Diable Volant* at www.oricom/ca/yarl/05p.html. See Under James Modyford.

22 Raynald Laprise, *Un Dictionnaire Biographique de la Flibuste*, op. cit. Under Coxon.

23 Byndlass also sat on the Island Council. Ibid.

24 Allison and Paterson certainly knew each other well, since the pirate acted as guide to Paterson in his voyage of 1698.

25 See Angus Calder, *Revolutionary Empire*, p. 115.

26 See *Le Diable Volant* website for details. Indigo is one of the oldest dyes known to man, and was used to dye the original Levi Jeans. It can be extracted from a variety of plants by a process of fermentation. In the 17th century a barrel of indigo was worth a small fortune, one reason for the development of indigo plantations across the Caribbean region. Coxon had transferred the indigo to small coastal ships to evade detection.

27 It was also known as 'Nicaraguan Wood' and was allegedly to be found in Darien.

28 Many buccaneers were woodcutters before they took to buccaneering.

29 Two of the captains left later than the rest, and sailed to meet them at a prearranged spot, nowhere near Honduras. See Lionel Wafer, *A New Voyage and Description of the Isthmus of Darien*, London, 1699. In addition Carlisle gave a free pardon to a notorious pirate, Cornelius Essex, and allowed him out of prison in Port Royal to join the others. See *Le Diable Volant* website.

30 Over 700 men eventually assembled at Bocas del Toro near Portobello but only 330 continued on the great adventure across the Isthmus. See Le Diable Volant website and the article found there on John Coxon by Raynald Laprise.

31 Modyford had been disgraced along with Morgan in 1671 but had since re-established himself in Jamaican society. The fact that he should crop up here in this story is more proof that Jamaican society of the 1670s and 1680s was a very small world.

32 Lionel Wafer, *A New Voyage and Description of the Isthmus of Darien*, London, 1699.

33 *Teredo navalis* is not in fact a worm but a mollusc.

34 See Introduction by Sir Allbert Gray to Dampier's *A New Voyage Round the World*, London, 1927, p. xxvi.

35 Quoted in W. Clark Russell, *William Dampier*, London and New York, 1899.

36 William Paterson's *Last Plan for the Darien Company* reproduced, in Sir John Dalrymple of Cranstoun, *Memoirs of Great Britain and Ireland*, London 1771. Part III, Book VI, p. 161.

37 Dampier and Coxon did not re-cross the Isthmus until the following year and apparently did not return to Jamaica. Ten years later Dampier returned from his voyage around the world and became the talk of London.

38 Although Charles was King of both England and Scotland they remained separate countries with their own laws and parliaments.

39 Richard Steele, *The Tradesman's Calling*, pp. 1, 4, London, 1684. Quoted in R. H. Tawney, *Religion and the Rise of Capitalism*, p. 239, London, 1937 (Pelican Edition).

40 Ibid. p. 244.

41 William Paterson, *An Historical Account of the Rise and Growth of the West Indian Colonies*, London, 1090. Attributed in part to Paterson by Saxe Bannister in *William Paterson: His Life and Trials*, Edinburgh, 1858, p. 58.

42 The bold copperplate handwriting is certainly a fact. See the Letters of William Paterson to the Lord Provost of Edinburgh, Robert Chiesly, in the National Library of Scotland 'Darien Papers'.

43 William Paterson, *An Historical Account of the Rise and Growth of the West Indian Colonies* in Bannister, *William Paterson: His Life and Trials*, Edinburgh, 1858, chapter 3.

44 Ibid.

45 For the historical background refer to John Keay, *The Honourable Company*, London, 1991.

46 Many of the early immigrants to Jamaica were convicts and others judged to be social misfits, such as dissenting Scots. They came as 'indentured servants', paid no wages but fed and watered. They were slaves in all but name, but only for a fixed period of time.

47 See Calgary University Specialist Website.

48 There were three Dutch Wars in a period of 20 years, the last ending in 1672.

49 See Hugh Thomas, *The Slave Trade*, London, 1997, p. 202.

50 See Calder, *Revolutionary Empire*, p. 180.

51 Quoted in *Consolidating Capitalism*, chapter 7 – M. Rosen North Illinois University (published on the web).

52 The Merchant Adventurers of Bristol tried to exclude non-members from their trade. See Patrick McGrath, *The Merchant Venturers of Bristol: A History of the Society of Merchant Venturers of the City of Bristol from its Origin to the Present Day*, Bristol, Society of Merchant Venturers, 1975.

53 Despite English efforts to exclude the Dutch from the sugar market there were still 30 sugar refineries in Amsterdam in 1700. Jonathan Israel, *Dutch Primacy in World Trade 1585–1740*, London, 1989, p. 265.

54 In today's values about $10,000 a ton – $2 a pound.
55 The Journals of William Blathwayt in the PRO are full of hints of wrong-doing by officials. See the letter of Charles Molesworth to the Treasury 12 March 1684 PRO manuscript T64/88.
56 See Website for Scottish Electric. The source is Bank of England Archivist.
57 See Calder, *Revolutionary Empire*, p. 198.
58 See *A Proposal for a Council of Trade* 1700 where he uses Curaçao as an example of the virtuous effect of free trade. Saxe Bannister, *The Writings of William Paterson*, London, 1858, vol. 1, p. 65.
59 The Dutch had acquired the region of Surinam, modern Guiana, from the English in 1667, swapped for the settlement of New Amsterdam on the island of Manhattan, but Surinam was as yet relatively undeveloped.
60 See Jonathan Israel, op. cit. p. 324.
61 If there was a model for Curaçao, it was Amsterdam itself. See J. Israel and Simon Schama, *The Embarrassment of Riches*, New York, 1987, for Amsterdam as Entrepôt.
62 See Jonathan Israel op. cit. for examples of Dutch self-confidence.
63 Words from 'Patersonian' Ballad, reprinted in Saxe Bannister, *William Paterson, His Life and Trials*, Edinburgh, 1858, p. 47.
64 Jonathan Israel, op. cit. p. 324.
65 Simon Schama, *Rembrandt's Eyes*, London, 1999, p. 321.

Chapter 2

1   Theses are rough and ready estimates based on the best research available. See for example *Population* on the web at www.ined.fr. There are many more similar pages.
2   The East India Company had a dock at Blackwall, reserved for its own use. The first real dock, the Howland Dock at Rotherhithe, was not commissioned until 1696. It impressed by its system of locks and by the speed with which ships could be loaded and unloaded. For the queues of ships, see Maureen Waller, *1700 – Scenes from London Life*, London, 2000, p. 240.
3   See Chapter 1 above.
4   G. M. Trevelyan, *English Social History*, London, 1944, p. 333.
5   Claire Tomalin, *Pepys – the Unequalled Self*, London, 2002, pp. 318–19. Pepys had fallen under suspicion during the hysteria over the 'Popish Plot' in 1679 and been sent to the Tower by parliament.
6   See Maureen Waller, *1700 – Scenes from London Life*, London, 2000 p. 9.
7   See Chapter 3.
8   Herries would surely have mentioned her in his account had she ever come to London. As to Paterson's motives in marrying Elizabeth Turner, it was not uncommon at the time for men of modest means to marry rich widows as a means of establishing themselves as men of property. The fact that Paterson's second wife was also a widow may be significant.
9   The fact that he lived in Denmark Street was revealed to the House of Lords in December 1695. See House of Lords MSS New Series 1903 Vol. 2. Paper C3. p. 15.
10 It had been rebuilt since the Great Fire, on the corner of Cornhill and Threadneedle Street. With its high spire, it had more the look of a Wren church than a merchants' meeting hall. The present Royal Exchange Building – in the classical style – was built much later.

11 Daniel Defoe, *An Essay Upon Projects*, London, 1797, p. 20. See under heading *History of Projects*. According to Defoe the fashion of 'projecting' began in London in 1680, about the time Paterson took up residence.

12 Ibid, pp. 32–3.

13 The prejudice of Londoners against the 'Scotch Pedlar' is well-documented. For an example see *The Diary of Samuel Pepys*, entry for 20 October 1660. See also House of Lords MSS. New Series Vol 2. p. 3 Section 955 where the remarks of a member of the Lords on the subject of 'Scotch Pedlars' who might flood into London on the coat tails of the Paterson scheme of 1695 are recorded.

14 Saxe Bannister, *William Paterson, His Life and Trials*, Edinburgh, 1858, p. 31.

15 The 'East India Trade' was a term that included trade with the Indian sub-continent, Indo-China, and China, as well as with the East Indies proper.

16 The line that divided one hemisphere from another ran south through the North Atlantic, 100 leagues (about 300 miles) west of the Azores. As a result a small corner of South America was judged to belong to Portugal – a territory that became today's Brazil.

17 The word 'factory' has changed its meaning over the years. Then it meant the post where a 'factor' or agent carried out business.

18 From *A Treatise Concerning the East India Trade*, in Josiah Child, *Selected Works*, London and Farnborough 1968.

19 Asia was the main source for this chemical, an essential ingredient in gunpowder.

20 See W. R. Scott, *The Constitution and Finance of English, Scottish and Irish Joint Stock-Companies to 1720*, Cambridge 1910–12 vol. 2 pp. 128–130.

21 In 1661 Cromwell's body had been dug up and hung on display at Tyburn gallows (modern Marble Arch in London). His head was cut off and put on public display at Westminster Hall for nearly 20 years. Thirteen of the hundred or so men implicated in the death of Charles I were hanged, cut down before they were dead, their heads cut off and their bodies quartered.

22 Figures are from K. N. Chaudhuri, *The Trading World of Asia and the English East India Company, 1660–1760*, Cambridge, 1978.

23 Macaulay's *History of England*, vol. 4 p. 244, Sully and Kleinteich, New York, 1899, University Edition.

24 Diary of Samuel Pepys 16 November 1665. Quoted in Claire Tomalin, *Samuel Pepys – the Unequalled Self*, London, 2002, p. 183.

25 The description comes from Macaulay's *History of England*, vol. 4, p. 242, Sully and Kleinteich, New York, 1899 University Edition. An engraving of the building is to be found in the *Gentleman's Magazine* December 1784, London.

26 The Child story is told in William Letwin, *Sir Josiah Child, Merchant Economist*, with a reprint of *Brief Observations Concerning Trade, and Interest in Money*, London, 1959.

27 The supply of oak for shipbuilding was a major problem of the time, since the wood for just one warship of the line required the felling of a small forest of oak. Hence the 1691 scheme of William Phips and William Paterson for a company to exploit the timber of Nova Scotia. See Chapter 3.

28 D.W. Jones, *London Merchants and the Crisis of the 1690s*, in Clark and Slack (eds), *Crisis and Order in the English Towns 1500–1700*, London, 1972, p. 344.

29 Daniel Defoe, *The Anatomy of Exchange Alley*, London, 1719.

30 It was doubly galling that they were allowed to buy the low-interest bonds used to fund the Company's capital expenditure. The ordinary shareholders had their profits 'levered' up at the expense of the bondholders. See John Keay, *The Honourable Company*, London, 1991, p. 173.

31 An estimate based on that fact that of the 47 merchants who can be identified, 30 were London based. See D. W. Jones, *London Merchants and the Crisis of the 1690s*, in Clark and Slack (eds), *Crisis and Order in the English Towns 1500–1700*, London, 1972, p. 342.

32 The story is to be found in John Keay, *The Honourable Company*, London, 1991, p. 173.

33 Papillon was chosen as Chairman of a House of Commons inquiry into the East India Company monopoly in late 1693. The Committee found the retention of interlopers illegal. See Macaulay, op. cit. vol. 5 pp. 579–580.

34 Charles had many illegitimate children by his many mistresses. One of them was James, Duke of Monmouth.

35 Both names were coined as terms of abuse. The original 'Whigamores' – shortened to 'Whigs' – were Scottish Presbyterian outlaws. The 'Tories' were Irish Roman Catholics deprived of their land and homes by Cromwell.

36 Child owned 14% of the shares, his relative, Sir John Cooke, owned a further 11%. Between the two of them they controlled something over a quarter of the shares. Cf. John Keay, *The Honourable Company*, p. 176. See also D. W. Jones, *War and Economy*, p. 248 for a listing of the share ownership of the top ten shareholders in 1691. Between them they owned more than half of all the shares.

37 £10,000 was a huge sum of money in these days, expressed in 2003 prices certainly more than £1 million.

38 Jeffreys famously placed interloping on a par with regicide.

39 John Keay, *The Honourable Company*, London, 1991, p. 179. See also Macaulay, op. cit. vol. 4 pp. 247–248.

40 She married the Duke of Beaufort, and Child handed over a dowry of £50,000, a staggering sum.

41 See Chapter 4.

42 The correct name for the country in 1683 was the 'United Provinces' but Englishmen then as now tended to put all the provinces together under the single name of Holland, which was in fact just one, if the most important of the provinces. I follow this convention here, with apologies to the Dutch.

43 See Chapters 4, 5 and 6.

44 See Minutes of a Committee on the Decay of Trade 28 Oct. 1669, in the House of Lords Westminster MSS.

45 The links between London and Amsterdam are well established. See, for example, Stephen Quinn, Gold, Silver, and the Glorious Revolution: Arbitrage between Bills of Exchange and Bullion, *Economic History Review* XLIX, 1996, pp. 473–90, and Chapter 6.

46 A feat not achieved until the 20th century.

47 '*Geld, geld, en nog eens geld,*' Jan and Annie Romein, *Erflaters van Onze Beschaving*, Amsterdam, 1979, p. 168.

48 J. de Vries and A. Van der Woude, *The First Modern Economy*, Cambridge, 1997.

49 The lack of central authority was underlined by the fact that the Dutch lived in what was officially a republic, electing the Prince of Orange to preside over the weak central government.

50 Simon Schama, *Rembrandt's Eyes*, London, 1999, p. 431.

51 Louis XIV revoked the Edict of Nantes in 1685, ending official toleration, but the Huguenots had been leaving in droves before this final act.

52 See Jonathan Israel, *Dutch Primacy in World Trade 1585–1740*, London, 1989.

53 He took wine with the ship-builder Willem Direcksone in the cabin of the uncompleted Scottish flagship in 1697. See John Prebble, *Darien, The Scottish Dream of Empire*, Edinburgh 2000, p. 96.

54 Prebble, *Darien*, op. cit. p. 78.

55 A summary of the books in Paterson's personal collection appears in the Introduction to Saxe Bannister, *The Writings of William Paterson*, London, 1858.

56 Sir John Dalrymple of Cranstoun, *Memoirs of Great Britain and Ireland*, London, 1771 Part III, Book VI, p. 128. The names of the four appear in the Brandenburg Archives in Berlin. For details see Waldemar Westegaard, *The Danish West Indies Under Company Rule*, New York, 1917, p. 69. Available on the internet at www.mapesmonde.com/books/danish-west-indies/danish_book.pdf.

57 Of course, he had a blind spot when it came to the 'negroes' he encountered in the Caribbean. See Chapter 1.

58 His library contained no fewer than 33 books in the Dutch language.

59 The chief evidence for this lies in the Berlin archive. The project proposed by Paterson is for 'An American Company'. His notion of Darien as offering a fast and sure route to China and Japan may have come only after he met William Dampier and discussed with him the new route the buccaneering explorer had discovered across the Pacific.

60 Now Kaliningrad in the Russian enclave between Poland and Lithuania.

61 Danske Saml., II R. 5 B, p. 145 in Westergaard, op. cit. p. 43.

62 The fact that the Spaniards laid claim to the territory – a claim hotly denied by Paterson – may have been no deterrent. Brandenburg was still seeking compensation from Spain for the money it was owed.

63 Waldemar Westergaard, *The Danish West Indies Under Company Rule*, New York, 1917, pp. 65, 66, 68, 71.

64 Grand projects were referred to by this French term. *Octroi* is literally a 'granting'. The reference to the audience is to be found in Westergaard, op. cit. p. 69.

65 The Stadhouder was an anomalous position, a hereditary prince in what was a republic.

66 From Josiah Child, *A Discourse on Trade*, 1694. Quoted in William Letwin, op. cit.

67 See Saxe Bannister, *The Writings of William Paterson*, London, 1858, Introduction.

68 See for example the recent essay by Steven Pincus, *Whigs, Political Economy and the Revolution of 1688–89* to be found at www.src.uchicago.edu/politicaltheory/Pincus02.pdf. p. 11 'The notion that trade was finite and that international competition was necessarily fierce, led Child and his ideological fellow travellers to insist that foreign trade be conducted in a monopolistic fashion...'

69 William Paterson (penname Philopatris), *An Essay concerning Inland, Publick and Private Trade* etc., Edinburgh, 1708. Reproduced in Saxe Bannister, *The Writings of William Paterson*, London, 1858, vol. 1, pp. liii–lix.

70 See for example Simon Schama, *The Embarrassment of Riches: An Interpretation of Dutch Culture in the Golden Age*, New York, 1987, p. 42.

71 Niall Ferguson, *The Cash Nexus*, paperback edition, London, 2001, p. 113.

72 Simon Schama, *An Embarrassment of Riches*, op. cit. p. 345.

73 William Letwin, *Sir Josiah Child*, op. cit.

74 P. G. M. Dickson, *The Financial Revolution in England: A Study in the Development of Public Credit, 1688–1756*. London, 1967.

Chapter 3

1 The Phips story is told in Emerson E. Baker and John G. Reid, *The New England Knight*, Boston, 1999. He was originally from Arrowsic in the territory of Maine.

2 Carolana later became North and South Carolina. It included territory that Virginians thought was theirs.

3 Whitehall Palace had grown up in an unplanned way since the time of Henry VII. But it had one fine building, Inigo Jones's Banqueting Hall, scene of Charles I execution in 1649. The meadows below Piccadilly became the modern Green Park and St James's Park.

4 The house stood where Albemarle Street is to be found today.

5 Its full name was rather grander – *Nuestra Senora de la Limpia y Pura Concepcion* (Our Lady of the Pristine and Pure Conception).

6 James was married to Mary of Modena.

7 James II was so concerned that what remained of the hoard might fall into the hands of treasure hunters that he wrote to the Governors of Jamaica, Barbados, and Bermuda telling them that he was entitled as king to 50 per cent of anything recovered from the wreck. See Journals of William Blathwayt 1681–1688 PRO. pp. 244–247.

8 Pepys had brought his diary to a close in 1669 because of his failing eyesight.

9 *The Diary of John Evelyn*, Oxford, 1955, vol. 4. Entry for 12 June 1687. Luttrell recorded the same rumours in his diary, published as Narcissus Luttrell, *A Brief Historical Relation of State Affairs*, etc, Oxford 1857. See vol. 2.

10 Evelyn reported that King James received £10,000, the Duke of Albemarle £50,000 and each of the other investors £18,000 but this was gossip. Phips claimed to have received £11,043 and a gold chain worth £5,000. See W. R. Scott, op. cit. vol. 2, pp 485–6 for details.

11 He died the next year after drinking too much to celebrate the birth of a male heir to James II. He was only 35 years old. See Emily F. Ward, *Christopher Monck, Second Duke of Albemarle*, London, 1933, p. 319.

12 The scientist, Sir Edmund Halley, produced his own design for an improved diving bell, with a system to replenish the air inside it. See note 24 below.

13 Quoted in Emerson and Baker, *New England Knight*, Boston, 1999, p. 252.

14 See W. R. Scott, *The Constitution and Finance of English, Scottish and Irish Joint Stock Companies to 1720*, London, 1910–12, vol. 1, p. 326.

15 Phips appears as a member of Paterson's bank lobby group, 'The Society' in 1691. See manuscript in the Bank of England Archive Location 969, Box 20.

16 Phips became the first native-born American to be honoured in this way.

17 Herries, who knew of Paterson's domestic arrangements, never mentions this first wife. She cannot therefore have come to London with him in 1681.

18 See *Diary of Samuel Sewell*, published by Massachusetts Historical Society, Boston, 1878. Entry for 27 April 1699. It is on the net at http://www.gordon.edu/bible/Hildebrandt/BiblicalStudiesTAH/NEReligiousHistory/Sewall-Diary1674-1729/Sewall-Vol-1-1674-1700.pdf It is interesting to note that the Society used the Latin motto adopted by William Paterson as his own: *Sic vos sed non vobis* – 'Thus you strive but not for yourself'.

19 See the example of Josiah Child's timber company as early as the late 1660s in Chapter 2.

20 *New England Knight*, op. cit. pp. 120–3. In the summer of 1690 Phips led a military expedition against French Canada and would not have been around to

discuss the plan any later than the spring of that year.

21 He had the funds to invest £2,000 in the Bank of England in 1694. He had not by that time sold his maiden shares in the Hampstead Water Company.

22 Evidence of William Paterson to the House of Lords in House of Lords MSS, vol. 2 New Series, London, reprinted 1965, p. 7.

23 Guildhall Folio Pamphlet 896 London 1695.

24 In 1690 Sir Edmund Halley himself produced a new design for his diving machine complete with a system to bring fresh air from the surface by means of barrels filled with air. See website www.adventuredive and snorkel.com/id59.htm.

25 Sir John Clapham, *A Concise Economic History of Britain*, Cambridge, 1949, p. 267. See also the chapter on 'The Projecting Age of the 1690s' in Edward Chancellor's more recent study *Devil Take the Hindmost*, New York, 1999.

26 Zacharius C. Von Uffenbach, *London in 1710*. Translated from the German by W. H. Quarrell and Margaret Mare, London, 1934. Quoted in Maureen Waller *1700, Scenes from London Life*, London, 2000, p. 229.

27 For Hampstead Water Company, see W. R. Scott, *The Constitution and Finance of English, Scottish and Irish Joint-Stock Companies to 1720*, London, 1910–12, vol. 3, pp. 5–6.

28 The *London Gazette* was not a newspaper but a meagre organ of official announcement. See G. M. Trevelyan, *English Social History*, London, 1944, p. 239.

29 He purchased a large estate at Wanstead, some seven miles north and east of the city. There he built a great mansion and laid out an ornamental park in the style of the time. It still exists as Wanstead Park.

30 See Claire Tomalin, *Samuel Pepys, the Unequalled Self*, London, 2002, p. 243 for an example of 'maid-beating'. Richard Ollard, in *Pepys: a Biography*, London, 1974, gives many more examples of the ill treatment of servants. See in particular pp. 94–5.

31 Lord Macaulay, *History of England*, op. cit. vol. 4, p. 596.

32 See Chapter 2.

33 In any case the price of a bowl of coffee could be more than a craftsman earned in a day.

34 G. M. Trevelyan, op. cit. p. 324.

35 See the example of the goldsmith and Sir Dudley North above. This is a factor worth bearing in mind when considering the obsequious courtesy of Paterson, even to his enemies. See, for example, his letters to the tiresome Edinburgh directors of the Company of Scotland, and his deference to his fellow directors over his fee in Chapter 4.

36 Herries, *A Defence of the Scots Abdicating Darien*, Edinburgh, 1700, p. 4.

37 Details are given by W. R. Scott, *The Constitution and Finance of English, Scottish and Irish Joint-Stock Companies to 1720*, London, 1910–12, vol. 3, p. 7.

38 Sir John Clapham, *The Bank of England: a History*, Cambridge, 1944.

39 In 1684 the Government budget for the year ran to £1,400,000. By 1692 it had risen to £6,000,000. Macaulay, op. cit. vol. 4, p. 426.

40 Macaulay, op. cit. vol. 4, p. 432.

41 Ibid. vol. 4, p. 427.

42 J(ames) S(mith), *Some Accounts of the Transactions of Mr William Paterson, etc.*, London, 1695.

43 The original banknotes were individually signed by the bank's cashiers. Printed banknotes as we know them came much later.

44 The coinage issue is discussed in Chapter 6.

45 It was also there to lobby for the Nova Scotia Company plan. See *New England Knight*, pp. 120–3.

46 The Bank of England Archive holds the original of the attendance list at the meeting of 21 September 1691.

47 Bank of England Archives Accession No. 969/2.

48 Letter of 23 October from Paterson to Blathwayt, Bank of England Archives, Accession No. 969/3.

49 *House of Commons Journal* Vol. X January 1691/2, p. 632.

50 Some goldsmiths were themselves involved in paring or filing silver or gold from the edges of coins; often they merely encouraged it by acting as 'fences' for those who did. See Chapter 6 (page 165).

51 Petition from the Society to William and Mary. Bank of England Archive Accession No. 969/4.

52 Holland (or the United Provinces) had the Prince of Orange at its head as *Stadhouder*, but he was elected by parliament. The state was technically a republic.

53 See Macaulay, op. cit. vol. 4, p. 604.

54 Saxe Bannister, *The Writings of William Paterson*, London, 1859, vol. 2, p. 64.

55 Guildhall Folio Pamphlet 896 London 1695. Smith tells us 'The Society' was 'broken to pieces', suggesting some acrimony.

56 J(ames) S(mith), *Some Account of the Transactions of Mr William Paterson, etc.*, London, 1695, p. 3.

57 Land descended by the law of primogeniture to the eldest son. Younger sons went into the army, or the church, or might try politics as Montague did to great effect.

58 The idea of a Tontine is said to have originated with Lorenzo Tonti, an Italian financial advisor to Cardinal Mazarin in France. See P. G. M. Dickson, *The Financial Revolution in England*, London, 1993, p. 52.

59 Macaulay, *History of England*, op. cit. vol. 4, p. 433.

60 Guildhall Folio Pamphlet 896 London 1695.

61 Macaulay, *History of England*, vol. 4, p. 59, 1898 edition.

62 John Briscoe, *Proposals for Supplying their Majesties with Money on Easy Terms*. Third edition London 1696. Referred to in Lord Macaulay, *History of England*, op. cit, vol. 4, p. 599.

63 Saxe Bannister, *William Paterson, His Life and Trials*, Edinburgh, 1858, p. 28. See also *Journal of the House of Commons*, vol. X, 18 January 1692.

64 It was the custom to call a truce that lasted throughout the wet and cold winter months, allowing the king to come back to London for the season.

65 Macaulay, *History of England*, vol. 4, p. 604, 1898 edition.

66 J. Giuseppi, *The Bank of England: A History from its Foundation in 1694*, Chicago, 1966, p. 29.

67 J(ames) S(mith), *Some Account of the Transactions of Mr William Paterson*, 1695 London.

68 Right from the start the Bank of England was seen as a Whig institution. It guaranteed the 'Glorious Revolution' of 1688, secured William on the throne, and gave parliament new power over the raising of royal revenue. See Maurice Ashley, *17th Century England*, London, 1961, p. 185.

69 J(ames) S(mith), *Some Account of the Transactions of Mr William Paterson*, London, 1695.

70 Ibid.

71 Bank of England Minute Book. 21 January 1695.
72 J(ames) S(mith), *Some Account of the Transactions of Mr William Paterson*, London, 1695. The board did offer to send a letter to the King recommending he be paid a grant of £1,000. But this does seem to have been acted upon.
73 The figure of £700 comes from Guildhall Folio Pamphlet no. 893. The larger sum of £5,000 from J(ames) S(mith), *Some Account of the Transactions of Mr William Paterson*, London, 1695.
74 The best account of the Orphans' Fund is that of I. G. Doolittle, 'Origins and History of the Orphans' Fund', *British Institutional History Research*, vol. LVI No. 133, May 1983.
75 James Whiston, *England's Calamities Discovered* published in *Harleian Miscellany*, London, 1745, vol. 6, p. 339.
76 The best account of the Orphans' Fund scandal is I. G. Doolittle, 'Origins and History of the Orphans' Fund', *British Institutional History Research*, vol. LVI No. 133, May 1983. W. M. Ayres, *The Bank of England from Within*, London, 1931, 2 vols in 1 p. 18, gives details of the charges against Smith.
77 The figure of £60 comes from Doolittle, op. cit. James Smith says it was only £50.
78 All three were to become shareholders in Paterson's next big project, his 'Company of Scotland'.
79 We have their names but not their political affiliations. See Accession No. 930 Bank of England Museum, a copy of the document printed in February 1695.
80 Accession No. 930 Bank of England Museum.
81 Bank of England Minute Book, 18 February 1695.
82 Guildhall Folio Pamphlet 896 James Smith, London, 1695, pp. 11–12.
83 Bank of England Minute Book, entries for February 1695.
84 J(ames) S(mith), *Some Account of the Transactions of Mr William Paterson*, London, 1695.
85 I. G. Doolittle, 'Origins and History of the Orphans' Fund', *British Institutional History Research*, vol. LVI No. 133, May 1983.
86 W. M. Ayres, *The Bank of England from Within*, London, 1931, p. 59.

Chapter 4

1 Michael Godfrey, *A Short Account of the Bank of England*, London, 1695 p. 1.
2 Macaulay, *History of England*, op. cit. vol. 5, p. 52.
3 A reference perhaps to the controversy over Paterson's 5 per cent of any profits earned.
4 Walter Herries, *A Defence of the Scots Abdicating Darien*, Edinburgh, 1700.
5 See Lord Macaulay, *History of England* op. cit., vol. V, 1899, p. 453.
6 See Lord Macaulay, *History of England* op. cit., vol. V, 1899, pp. 455–6.
7 See Chapter 2.
8 *Journal of the House of Commons* Vol. X p. 541.
9 D. W. Jones, *War and Economy in the Age of William III and Marlborough*, London, 1988, p. 297.
10 Child was commonly considered to be still the real governor of the company.
11 William III was desperate for cash to fight his wars. In the subsequent official inquiry the question of whether the King had received any of the EIC largesse was not looked into.
12 Macaulay, op. cit. vol. 4, pp. 533–534. Child did not have his own way entirely since the new Charter decreed that no new shareholder was allowed to buy more

than £5,000 worth of shares. But since he held onto his shares – valued at over £50,000 – his position remained secure.

13 The 'Tontine' occupied his time early in the year. The 'Bank of England' project was not resurrected until late in the year. This gave Paterson time both to go to Scotland and to dream up his scheme for his new trading company.

14 Paterson was not alone in developing the concept of the revolutionary Company of Scotland but no-one reading the company minute book for the latter half of 1695, and Paterson's correspondence with the Edinburgh directors, could doubt that it was mainly his idea. For details of both see Chapter 5.

15 Paterson told the House of Lords that the idea of a company was suggested to him by James Chiesly and Thomas Coutts. House of Lord MSS 1695–1697. op. cit. Vol. 2 Section 955, p. 7.

16 At this stage of his career he favoured a union between Scotland and England. Later he became the apostle of a fully independent Scotland. See W. Ferguson, *Scotland – 1689 to the Present*, Edinburgh, 1968, pp. 5, 48–9.

17 See John Robertson, *Selected Writings of Andrew Fletcher of Saltoun*, Cambridge, 1997, Introduction, p. xiii.

18 Sir John Dalrymple of Cranstoun, *Memoirs of Great Britain and Ireland*, London, 1771. Part III, Book VI, p. 128.

19 Books were still very expensive. To have over 50 books in a personal library was most unusual. Fletcher's collection is now kept in the National Library of Scotland as the Saltoun Manse Collection. Andrew Fletcher was to add many more rare books to the collection in the course of his life.

20 Fletcher admired the Roman Republic and its perceived liberties. The backbone of its constitution, he believed, was the dependence on a people's militia rather than a standing army. See John Robertson, *Selected Writings of Andrew Fletcher of Saltoun*, Cambridge 1997, Introduction.

21 The earliest source for this story is *Memoirs of Great Britain and Ireland*, Sir John Dalrymple of Cranstoun, London, 1771. Dalrymple picked this up as an oral tradition in Scotland. We can certainly prove Paterson was in Edinburgh in 1693 and Fletcher was one of the stoutest supporters of his scheme, sitting on the court (or board) of the Company of Scotland.

22 See his evidence to the House of Lords in House of Lords MSS 9 December 1695.

23 The timing is something of a guess, but it could not have been before 1692, since Fletcher did not travel to London until then. Reaching Scotland in that year would have allowed Paterson good time to consult his London backers on the details of the trading scheme that emerged in June 1693.

24 A post boy could carry a message from London to Edinburgh in six days, but ten days made for a more comfortable journey.

25 See John Robertson, *Selected Writings of Andrew Fletcher of Saltoun*, Cambridge, 1997, Introduction.

26 There was broadly a three-way split. Charles II had restored royally appointed bishops to the Church of Scotland – creating the Episcopalian Church. The Presbyterians could continue to exist only illegally. Many were willing to die, and did, rather than accept bishops. The third group were the Roman Catholics, confined mainly to the remote highland regions. In the 1660s Charles attempted to crack down on the militant protestants, ushering in a period of civil war that lasted until 1679.

27 The Scottish parliament (or the Estates of Scotland) at this time was made up of

peers of the realm, leading churchmen, and representatives of both the land-owning class and respectable townsmen. They all sat together in a single chamber.

28 Gilbert Burnet apparently advised the move and soon joined him in Holland. Burnet became the confidant of William of Orange and returned to England in triumph in 1689, rewarded by being appointed Bishop of Salisbury. Burnet went on to write *A History of His Own Times*, an early classic of narrative history. There is no evidence to suggest Paterson and Fletcher met each other at this time. One was in Amsterdam, the other in The Hague.

29 James was James II in England, James VII in Scotland. Since Fletcher went with Monmouth to fight in south-west England, the king is given the English version of his name.

30 The French had a saying at this time about Scotsmen: 'They have pepper in their noses'. Fletcher was apparently a Scotsman of this type.

31 William's guilt in this matter was glossed over by the subsequent enquiry, a point worth bearing in mind when we deal with his later claims to have known nothing of the Act that set up the Company of Scotland.

32 The verdict, at any rate of G. P. Insh. See *The Darien Scheme*, Historical Association, 1947, p. 3.

33 Like most Englishmen he exaggerated Scottish poverty retelling the story that the Scots had only 8 Commandments instead of 10, 'because they have nothing to covet and nothing to steal'. Better-off Scots, especially the landed gentry, were covetous enough, bringing in fine furniture from Europe and consuming much claret and brandy.

34 Joseph Taylor, *A Journey to Edenborough in Scotland in 1705*, p. 94.

35 Thomas Kirke, *A Traveller in Scotland*, 1679, quoted in P. Hume Brown, *Early Travellers in Scotland*, Edinburgh, 1891, p. 260.

36 Dalrymple of Cranstoun, op. cit. Part III, Book VI, p. 129.

37 Ibid. p. 129, Dalrymple of Cranstoun, the main source for Paterson's visit to Scotland, was related to Lord Stair – he may have had access to family papers and reminiscences, now lost.

38 Daniel Defoe, *The Advantages of Scotland in a Corporate Union with England*, Edinburgh, 1706. Quoted by T. C. Smout in *Scottish Trade on the Eve of the Union, 1660–1707*, Edinburgh and London, 1963, p. 80.

39 Or High Street – the Scots used the Scandinavian word for street – the Gait – a relic of the Norse settlements in Scotland.

40 Joseph Taylor, op. cit. p. 107.

41 See Chambers, *Edinburgh Merchants and Marchandise in Old Times*, Edinburgh, 1859.

42 Details from *The Story of Leith*, Chapter 28, John Russell, Thomas Nelson and Sons, Edinburgh, 1922.

43 Macaulay remarks that there was more wealth within a five-mile radius of Amsterdam than in the whole of Scotland, op. cit. vol. V, p. 457.

44 In 1513 Scotland had built the *'Great' Michael*, one of the largest ships of its day as a royal flag-ship. But in the years since then the skills had been lost. Scotland's only shipbuilding yard in Leith produced only boats weighing less than 50 tons. See T. C. Smout, *Scotland Trade on the Eve of the Union*, Oliver and Boyd, Edinburgh, 1963, p. 47.

45 Stanfield's story is vividly told in a historical novel by the late Nigel Tranter, *Triple Alliance*, 2001, Hodder and Stoughton. By the time of Paterson's visit he was already dead, and his son unfairly executed for his murder.

46 T. C. Smout, *Scottish Trade on the Eve of the Union*, Edinburgh, 1963, pp. 234–5.

47 Quoted by Peter Landry on www.blupete.com/Hist/NovaScotia/Bk1/TOC.htm.

48 Quoted in G. P. Insh, *Scottish Colonial Schemes*, Maclehose Jackson, Glasgow, 1922, p. 21.

49 G. P. Insh, *Scottish Colonial Schemes*, Maclehose Jackson, Glasgow, 1922, p. 21.

50 For a summary of his career see George Eyre-Todd, *History of Glasgow*, vol. 3 pp. 56–8, Jackson Wylie and Co, Glasgow, 1934.

51 The 'great circle' route from Britain to America curves north over the Atlantic, as any modern air traveller will know.

52 They were not alone in thinking sugar and tropical crops guaranteed a nation's prosperity. The Danes had established their plantation on the Caribbean island of St Thomas in 1671. Ominously the Danish Company was to end up in debt. See *The Danish West Indies Under Company Rule (1671–1754)*, Waldemar Westergaard, New York, 1917.

53 From *Memorial Concerning the Scottish plantation to be erected in some part of America* 1681, quoted in G. P. Insh, *Scottish Colonial Schemes*, Maclehose Jackson, Glasgow, 1922, p. 21.

54 Dunlop was to play a crucial role in the drama that unfolded in 1685. See Chapter 5.

55 G. P. Insh, *Scottish Colonial Schemes*, Glasgow, 1922, p. 278.

56 G. P. Insh, *Scottish Colonial Schemes*, op. cit. pp. 201–10.

57 Letter of Robert Douglas to a Member of the Company Board, September 1696.

58 Letter dated 9 July 1695, Paterson to Edinburgh 'directors' of Company of Scotland, Darien Papers, Bannatyne Society.

59 We know this for the simple reason that when Paterson unveiled his ideas on Darien in July 1696, the Scottish directors were taken completely by surprise. See Darien Papers, No 34 NLS Minute of Committee of Trade, July 1696.

60 See D. W. Jones, 'London Merchants and the Crisis of the 1690s', in Clark and Slack, *Crisis and Order in the English Towns 1500–1700*, London, 1972, p. 344.

61 D. W. Jones, *War and Economy in the Age of William III and Marlborough*, Oxford, 1988, p. 295.

62 Especially the work of D. W. Jones in his *War and Economy in the Age of William III and Marlborough*, op. cit. and in his essay on 'London Merchants and the Crisis of the 1690s', in Clark and Slack, *Crisis and Order in the English Towns 1500–1700*, London, 1972.

63 Heathcote and Raworth were associated with several interloping voyages in 1691–94. See D. W. Jones, *War and Economy*, op. cit. p. 294.

64 D. W. Jones, *War and Economy in the Age of William III and Marlborough*, Oxford, 1988, p. 296.

65 D. W. Jones, *War and Economy in the Age of William III and Marlborough*, Oxford, 1988, p. 299. See also the Minutes of the Company of Scotland, in *Journal of the House of Commons* Vol. XI, pp. 400–4.

66 Ibid., p. 299. See also Chapter 5.

67 Bateman and his group would scarcely have encouraged Paterson in his new enterprise had they not believed this. They were proved right when London merchants queued up to subscribe to the Scots Company in 1695.

68 Prebble, *Darien*, op. cit p. 20.

69 The formula was to grant a directorship to any shareholder who had the support of other shareholders and their total share-holding reached £20,000 sterling. See Chapter 5, p. 115.

70 Quoted in Saxe Bannister, *William Paterson, His Life and Trials*, 1858, p. 94.
71 See Chapter 5 for the row between Holland and Paterson.
72 See the tribute paid to them in *A Letter from a Gentleman in the Country to His Friend in Edinburgh*, 1695, reproduced by Saxe Bannister in *William Paterson, His Life and Trials*, 1858, p. 94.
73 Act of Parliament of Scotland – *An Act for Encouraging Forraigne Trade* 1693.
74 The Act defined the areas to be considered as Europe, the East and West Indies, the Straits (i.e. the Danish straits leading to the Baltic), the Mediterranean, the coast of Africa and even 'northern parts' – there was no mention of America. A. P. S. 1693 *An Act for Encouraging of Forraigne Trade*.
75 William and his wife Queen Mary.
76 Quoted in G. P. Insh, *Historian's Odyssey*, Edinburgh and London, 1938, Chapter 5.
77 Insh, ibid.
78 Broadly translated as 'Subscription for an African Trading Company'. See G. P. Insh, *Historian's Odyssey*, Chapter 5.
79 William and Mary.
80 G. P. Insh, *Historian's Odyssey*, Edinburgh and London, 1938, Chapter 5.
81 The parliamentary inquiry into the use of bribes by the East India Company reported in March 1695 that bribes amounting to over £80,000 had been spent by the East India Company in 1693. See Macaulay, op. cit. vol. 5, p. 15.
82 *Journal of the House of Commons* Vol. X. 6 Jan 1694. Quoted in Macaulay, op. cit. vol. 4, p. 580.
83 William Ferguson, *Scotland 1689 to the Present*, Edinburgh & London, 1968, pp. 25–6.
84 He later dropped the apostrophe and became Paul Daranda. Saxe Bannister in *William Paterson, His life and Trials* refers to him as Paterson's 'dearest friend'. He was the executor of Paterson's will.
85 See Letter of Paterson to Lord Provost Chiesly, 9 July 1695, Darien Papers National Library of Scotland. Paterson is obviously addressing some objection to a man on religious grounds. This could only have been Cohen D'Azevedo.
86 Prebble, op. cit. p. 26.

Chapter 5

1 E. S. de Beer (ed.) *The Diary of John Evelyn*, London, 1959, vol. 4, pp. 202 and 207.
2 'Paterson's Proposals for a Council of Trade 1700' in Saxe Bannister, *The Writings of William Paterson*, London, 1858. vol. 1, p. 85.
3 Macaulay, op. cit., vol. 5, pp. 10–11.
4 Macaulay, op. cit., vol. 5, pp. 16–18.
5 Macaulay, vol. V, pp. 20–6. See also Harleian Miscellany, vol. 6 p. 284, London, 1745.
6 *Act of Parliament Constituting The Company of Scotland Trading to Africa and the Indies*, 1695. A. P. S. King William III, Parl I, Session 5.
7 Ibid.
8 See Chapter 4, p. 96.
9 As we have seen the term 'East Indies' loosely included the lands of Indo-China, and even China itself.
10 The idea of a tax holiday may also have come from Holland. The Dutch West

India Company had been granted fredom from customs duties for 21 years by its charter of 1621. For details of the Charter of the Dutch East India Company see G. Masselman, *The Cradle of Colonialism*, London and New Haven, 1963, pp. 146–51. The Charter of the Dutch West India Company will be found in F. Newton Thorpe, *The Federal and State Constitutions Colonial Charters, and other Organic Laws, Etc.*, Washington D.C. 1909. Duties on sugar and tobacco imports had to be paid.

11 Prebble, *Darien*, op. cit. p. 29.

12 Until the subscription was raised they could not be formally called 'directors'. In Scotland they were referred to as 'patentees', the men named in the 'Letters Patent' that accompanied the Act.

13 *Memoirs of the Secret Services of John Macky, Esq.* London 1733, p. 236. For a more sympathetic portrait, see *The Peerage of Scotland*, Edinburgh and London, 1813, vol. 1, pp. 204–5.

14 Although Fletcher of Saltoun had spoken in favour of the Act he was not at this time a member of the Scottish parliament. Possibly for this reason he was not included in the named 'promoters'. When the subscription books opened in Edinburgh in 1696 he became one of the first to subscribe.

15 No records of the Edinburgh meetings have come to light. But much of what happened can be deduced from Paterson's letters to them, which have. See Darien Papers I, National Library of Scotland.

16 Paterson tells us he gave Chiesly and Thomas Coutts the draft Act to take north in May. Chiesly almost certainly would stay to see the Act through parliament.

17 *Letter from William Paterson to Robert Chiesly*, 4 July 1695, Darien Papers I, no. 19, NLS.

18 *Letter from William Paterson to Robert Chiesly*, 9 July 1695, Darien Papers I, no. 20 NLS.

19 Ibid.

20 No copies of Sir Robert Chiesly's letters to Paterson have survived. But the content can in part be deduced by reading Paterson's replies.

21 *Letter from William Paterson to Robert Chiesly*, 6 August 1695, Darien Papers I, no. 21 NLS.

22 Ibid.

23 Ibid.

24 *Letter from William Paterson to Robert Chiesly*, 15 August 1695, Darien Papers I, no. 22 NLS.

25 *Letter from William Paterson to Robert Chiesly*, 3 September 1695, Darien Papers I, no. 23 NLS.

26 *Letter from William Paterson to Robert Chiesly*, 9 July 1695, Darien Papers I, no. 20 NLS.

27 *Minutes of the Company of Scotland*, 19 August 1695, reproduced in *Journal of the House of Commons* vol. XI, p. 401.

28 Ibid.

29 Macaulay, vol. 5, p. 467.

30 *Minutes of Company of Scotland*, 23 September 1695, *Journal of the House of Commons* vol. XI, p. 401.

31 *Act Constituting the Company of Scotland Trading with Africa and the Indies*, op. cit.

32 A summary of the arguments used by the RAC and others can be found in *Manuscripts of the House of Lords* vol. 2, pp. 3ff.

33 *Minutes of Company of Scotland – London Directors* 22 October 1695. Reproduced in *Journal of the House Commons* vol. XV, pp. 401–2.

34 *Letter from William Paterson to Robert Chiesly*, 15 October 1695, Darien Papers I, no. 25 NLS.

35 Ibid.

36 Prebble, *Darien*, op. cit. p. 35.

37 As with the Bank of England the shareholders were to pay their subscription by instalments.

38 W. R. Scott, *The Constitution and Finance of English, Scottish and Irish Joint-Stock Companies to 1720*, London, 1910–12, vol. 2, p. 211.

39 In fact the shares were fully subscribed by 15 November. Evidence of Roderick Mackenzie to House of Commons. *Journal of the House of Commons* vol. XI, p. 400.

40 An inference from the tone of the minutes and the known character of the gentleman.

41 W. R. Scott, op. cit. vol. 2, p. 214.

42 The full preamble is reproduced in *Journal of the House of Lords* vol. XV. Paper C1 p. 15.

43 Minutes of the 'Court of Directors' of the Company of Scotland, 20 November and 29 November 1695, *Journal of the House of Commons* vol. XI, pp. 400–1.

44 D. W. Jones, *War and Economy in the Age of William III and Marlborough*, op. cit.

45 A long letter from Douglas to a member of the Edinburgh board is preserved in the Darien Papers at the NLS. He produces powerful arguments for the East India Trade to be made the first priority of the Company, a line of argument that marks him out as an informed East India man. There was some speculation that one of the London Scots was a shareholder in the EIC in December 1695. See Darien Papers Letter of 6 September 1696 and *Caveto Cavetote*, Broadside of 14 December 1695 BL.

46 The phrase is quoted in D. W. Jones, 'London Merchants and the Crisis of the 1690s', p. 344, in Clark and Slack, *Crisis and Order in the English Towns*, RKP, 1969.

47 Evidence of Paterson to the House of Commons January 1696, *Journal of the House of Commons* vol. XI, p. 401.

48 Minutes of the Company of Scotland, 18 November 1695 in *Journal of the House of Commons* vol. X, p. 403.

49 The attendance figures come from the Minutes of the Company of Scotland, Darien Papers NLS and *Journal of the House of Commons* vol. XI pp. 400–4.

50 Minutes of the Company of Scotland, 29 November 1695. Reproduced in *Journal of the House of Commons* vol. XI, p. 404.

51 Ibid. 4 December 1695.

52 Minutes of the Company of Scotland, 4 December 1695. Reproduced in *Journal of the House of Commons* vol. XI, p. 404.

53 Minutes of Company of Scotland, 6 December 1695. Reproduced in *Journal of the House of Commons* vol. XI, p. 404.

54 Macaulay, op. cit. vol. 5, p. 65.

55 E. S. de Beer (ed.) *The Diary of John Evelyn*, London, 1959, vol. 4.

56 E. S. de Beer (ed.) *The Diary of John Evelyn*, ibid.

57 E. S. de Beer (ed.) *The Diary of John Evelyn*, ibid.

58 Ibid. 29 September, 13 October.

59 Macaulay, op. cit. vol. 4, p. 460. Prebble, *Darien*, op. cit. p. 35.

60 W. R. Scott, *The Constitutions and Finances of English, Scottish and Irish Joint-Stock Companies to 1720*, London, 1910–12, vol. 2, p. 208.

61 Act Constituting the Company of Scotland, op. cit.

62 See F. Newton Thorpe, *The Federal and State Constitutions Colonial Charters etc.*, Washington DC, 1906.

63 See T. C. Smout, *Scottish Trade on the Eve of the Union*, op. cit., p. 235 for one merchant's account of this smuggling.

64 This was an argument deployed in the East India Company Petition to Parliament in November 1695. See *Journal of the House of Lords* vol. XV, p. 611. They also pointed out that more revenue would be lost if European markets were served from Scotland rather than England.

65 See S. P. Col. Col. Entry Book, c, pp. 348–52 Public Record Office. Quoted in F. Russell Hart, *The Disaster of Darien*, New York, 1929, p. 31.

66 It is noticeable that Montague keeps his head down on the EIC issue in December 1696 but is a leading critic of the EIC in the debates of 1698. See *Journal of the House of Lords* vol. XV, p. 608. While Montague was not a member of the committee drawing up the House's recommendations regarding the Company of Scotland the notoriously corrupt Earl of Leeds (Danby) was. So also was the Marquess of Normanby, a man who was corruptly gifted valuable land by the City of London in 1693. See I. G. Doolittle, op. cit. p. 51. See also Macaulay, vol. V, pp. 234–5.

67 East India Company's Court Book, Library of the India Office. MS No 37. Quoted in F. Russell Hart, op. cit. p. 32. By this date Robert Lancashire, an avowed EIC man, had already put £3,000 into the Scots Company.

68 Details from Prebble, op. cit. p. 43. The Levant Company and the East India Company were traditional enemies.

69 Prebble, *Darien*, op. cit. p. 47.

70 Lords MSS vol. 2 New Series Reprinted by HMSO 1965, p. 13.

71 Ibid. vol. 2 New Series pp. 14–15.

72 Ibid. vol. 2 New Series pp. 14–15.

73 Ibid. vol. 2 New Series p. 15. The records are somewhat confusing. On Monday 9th Paterson and the others were ordered to appear on the 16th but this was then changed to 12 December.

74 Prebble, *Darien*, op. cit. p. 42.

75 But Roderick Mackenzie had a copy which he handed to the Commons in January 1696. See *Journal of the House of Commons* vol. XI 21 January 1696, p. 400.

76 Some accounts have suggested Belhaven was excused from appearing before the House of Lords, but there seems no doubt that he was summoned to appear. *MSS of the House of Lords*, op. cit. p. 15.

77 *Journal of the House of Lords* vol. XV, 12 December 1695, pp. 610ff.

78 Prebble, *Darien*, op. cit. p. 48.

79 The final report appears under 21 January 1696. See *Journal of the House of Commons* vol. XI, p. 405.

80 *Journal of the House of Commons* vol. XI, pp. 400–4.

81 A House of Lords inquiry into the affair reported on 20 December 1695. It recommended that the English company should be given 'such powers and privileges as shall … obviate the inconveniences that otherwise be caused by the Scottish Act', *Journal of the House of Lords* vol. XV, pp. 618–19.

82 *Journal of House of Commons* vol. XI, p. 405. Prebble, *Darien*, op. cit. p. 51.

83 Macaulay, *History of England*, op. cit. vol. 5, pp. 322–9.

84 Perhaps knowledge that the Commons now had a copy of the subscribers list was enough to persuade all but the most ardent subscribers that their promised

investment should not be paid. In the end only five of the 200 subscribers honoured their word. See Chapter 6.

85 Minutes of the Court of Directors of Company of Scotland, 29 November 1695, *Journal of House of Commons* vol. XI, p. 404.

86 It came to light in February 1696. See Macaulay, op. cit. vol. 5, pp. 110–18.

87 In 1716.

Chapter 6

1 Sir John Dalrymple of Cranstoun, *Memoirs of Great Britain and Ireland*, op. cit. Part III, Book VI, p. 129.

2 *Letter from William Paterson to Robert Chiesly*, 9 July 1695, Darien Papers 1, no. 20 NLS.

3 For instance see letter to Thomas Drummond, 11 January 1700, in J. Hill Burton, *Darien Papers*, op. cit. Section XXIX, p. 257.

4 This can be deduced from the minute books of the Company of Scotland for 1696, held in The Royal Bank of Scotland Group Archives. See Minute Book 1, Entry for 21 July 1696. On 6 October the company recommended a payment of £15,000 to be paid in instalments. It seems inconceivable that Paterson would move north to Edinburgh without some promise of reward.

5 It is hard to see how otherwise Smith would have gone ahead of Paterson to Edinburgh, or be trusted with so much responsibility.

6 Walter Herries, *A Defence of the Scots Abdicating Darien*, Edinburgh, 1700, p. 1.

7 John Evelyn, *Diary*, op. cit. Entry for 16 August 1698.

8 Christopher Lloyd, *Dampier*, p. 54. Compare the time for this voyage with the year or so it took to sail from London to Madras by way of the southern tip of Africa.

9 Dalrymple of Cranstoun, *Memoirs*, London, 1771, Part III, Book VI, p. 141.

10 'Stretching' meant sailing with the wind directly or almost directly behind the ship.

11 Dalrymple of Cranstoun, *Memoirs*, London, 1771, Part III, Book VI, p. 124.

12 Macaulay, op. cit. vol. 5, p. 457.

13 In Scotland the men named in the Act setting up the company were generally referred to as 'the nominees'. They became directors only after the company was properly constituted.

14 See *Some seasonable and modest thoughts partly occasion'd by and partly concerning the Scots East India Company*, Edinburgh, 1696, p. 26.

15 Minute Book, The Company of Scotland, 14 February 1696. The Royal Bank of Scotland Group Archives, Edinburgh.

16 Prebble, *Darien*, op. cit. p. 56.

17 The records show that many investors, even from great families, could not write their own names. See the original subscription book in The Royal Bank of Scotland Group Archives.

18 Company of Scotland Subscription List, The Royal Bank of Scotland Group Archives.

19 Ibid.

20 Subscription lists The Royal Bank of Scotland Group Archives, Edinburgh. The figure for 31 March was 185.

21 Walter Herries, *A Defence of the Scots Abdicating Darien*, 1700, p. 1.

22 The Ballads are reproduced in Saxe Bannister, *William Paterson, His Life and Trials*, Edinburgh, 1858, Chapter 2, pp. 46ff.

23 Herries, op. cit. Quoted in Prebble, *Darien*, op. cit. p. 57.

24 In *The Wealth of Nations* Adam Smith states that the total wealth of Scotland around 1700 could 'not be estimated at less than a million sterling'. See *The Wealth of Nations*, Everyman Edition, 1957, vol. 1, p. 262.

25 The company books indicate that around 50 per cent of the promised capital was to be called in during the first five years. Ten years is therefore an estimate. See F. Russell Hart, *The Disaster of Darien*, New York and Boston, 1929, p. 40 for the calculation. The original records are reproduced in J. Hill Burton, *The Darien Papers*, Edinburgh, 1849, p. xxvi.

26 See entry for 3 April 1696 in Minutes of the Company of Scotland, The Royal Bank of Scotland Group Archives.

27 To follow the story see Minute Book, no. 1 'The Company of Scotland Trading to Africa and the Indies' held in The Royal Bank of Scotland Group Archives, Edinburgh. The details are not entirely clear from the cryptic form of the minutes. The entry for 13 April 1696 is the most important.

28 This was later increased to £25,000. See Chapter 7.

29 Minutes of the Company of Scotland. The Royal Bank of Scotland Group Archives, 12 May 1696.

30 Minutes of the Company of Scotland. The Royal Bank of Scotland Group Archives, 14 May 1696.

31 Walter Herries is the first recorded to have used this expression to describe Paterson's inner circle.

32 Minutes of the Court of Directors of the Bank of England. Bank Of England Archive. See entries for 19 December 1694, 22 December 1694, 26 December 1694, 12 January 1695, and 19 January 1695.

33 Quoted in G. P. Insh, *The Darien Scheme*, op. cit. 1947, p. 12.

34 *Letter from William Paterson to Robert Chiesly*, 9 July 1695, Darien Papers I. 83.7.4. No. 20 NLS.

35 The question of the London subscription is dealt with in Chapter 7.

36 The Royal Bank of Scotland Group Archives contain a copy of Roderick Mackenzie's submission to the parliamentary enquiry of 1714 into Paterson's rights to a share in the compensation money paid to Scotland, the so-called 'Equivalent'. His description of what the meetings decided, and what they actually put down on the record, illustrate one of the many pitfalls that lie in the path of the business history researcher.

37 See Minute for 27 November 1695, *Journal of the House of Commons* vol. XI, p. 404.

38 Minutes of the Court of Directors of the Company of Scotland, 18 May 1696, The Royal Bank of Scotland Group Archives, Edinburgh.

39 *Letter from William Patterson to Robert Chiesly*, 15 August 1695, Darien Papers I. 83.7.4 Letter 22 NLS.

40 See Richard Saville, *The Bank of Scotland, a History*, Edinburgh, 1997, pp. 23–4.

41 Among the beneficiaries of the company bank was the City of Glasgow, which borrowed £500 in October to pay off some of its debts. See George Eyre-Todd, *History of Glasgow*, vol. 3 p. 30, Jackson Wylie and Co., 1934.

42 *Minutes of the Committee of Trade*, 28 July, Darien Papers I. 83.7.4 No. 34 NLS.

43 Ibid.

44 See Darien Papers I. 83.7.4. Document numbers 35, 36 and others.

45 The phrase is taken from Paterson's proposal for a greater Darien scheme presented to the Company of Scotland in 1700. But Paterson is likely to have had a

phrase of this kind ready for use in 1696. Dalrymple of Cranstoun, *Memoirs*, op. cit. Part III, Book VI, p. 161.

46 Lionel Wafer, *A New Voyage and Description of the Isthmus of Darien*, London, 1699.

47 Paterson always harped on about the great expense he had gone to acquiring his materials. He may well have paid Dampier for the copy.

48 Lionel Wafer, *A New Voyage and Description of the Isthmus of Darien*, London, 1699.

49 In 1701 he adapted his plan to suit the wishes of the English and the Scots for 'collonies'. See *A Proposal for a Collony in Darien*, presented to William III, 1701, reproduced in Saxe Bannister, *The Writings of William Paterson*, London, 1858 (2nd edition).

50 Minutes of the Committee of Trade of the Company of Scotland, in Darien Papers I. 83.7.4 No. 34, 28 July 1696 NLS.

51 The best evidence that they had already decided on Darien is the fact that the English Resident in Hamburg would report that Paterson had set his sights on Darien. When negotiating for subscriptions in Holland and Germany, the Scots had to give some idea of what they had in mind.

52 Minutes of the Committee of Trade of the Company of Scotland, in Darien Papers I. 83.7.4 No. 34, 28 July 1696 NLS.

53 The possession of maps and charts was the key to commercial success, as the Portuguese had established in the 15th and 16th centuries. The Dutch had used spies in Lisbon to obtain copies. The Spanish ordered their sea captains not to allow their precious maps and charts to fall into enemy hands. Rather than do that they were to be destroyed. See David Landes, *The Wealth and Poverty of Nations*, Abacus Edition, London, 1999, p. 40, and the British Library Website for details of the William Hack atlas, copied from a captured Spanish atlas.

Bartholomew Sharp, the buccaneer, captured a large batch of Spanish charts after they had been thrown overboard by a Spanish ship he was about to capture. He handed them to King Charles II and they became the basis of a great atlas prepared in manuscript form by William Hack. The maps are now to be found in the British Library.

54 Minutes of the Committee of Trade of the Company of Scotland, in Darien Papers I. 83.7.4 No. 34, 28 July 1696 NLS.

55 Ibid, 3 August 1696.

56 Fletcher of Saltoun estimated 200,000 people, about 20 per cent of the population actually died of starvation during these terrible years of crop failure. See Michael Lynch, *Scotland a New History*, London, 1992, p. 309. Fletcher's estimate is considered to have been an exaggeration. Perhaps 1 in 20 died, but in some areas it was as high as Fletcher claimed.

57 His letter of 5 September 1696 (in the Darien Papers I 83.7.4. No. 33 NLS) is chiefly concerned to make the case for the East Indian trade. It shows Douglas was a man of much experience and good business sense.

58 *Letter of Robert Douglas to an Edinburgh director*, 5 September 1696, Darien Papers I. 83.7.4. No. 33 NLS.

59 *Letter of Robert Douglas to an Edinburgh director*, Darien Papers I.83.7.4. No. 33 NLS. Douglas claimed that, when in London, Paterson had brought several English East India Company shareholders into the Scottish Company in a plot to bring it down. This seems malicious nonsense.

60 Prebble, *Darien*, op. cit. p. 82.

61 Quoted in Prebble, pp. 78–9.

62 R. Savile, *The Bank of Scotland, a History*, op. cit. p. 49 and Appendix 6, p. 861.

63 Herries was later to allege that Paterson had too much to drink here and blurted out his plans to all and sundry. This is unlikely since Paterson was a strict teetotaller.

64 Simon Schama, *Rembrandt's Eyes*, London, 1999, pp. 312–13.

65 Instructions of the Court of Directors of the Company of Scotland, The Royal Bank of Scotland Group Archives, 23 June 1696.

66 See for example Letter from Francis Stratford Snr, Agent in Hamburg, to Committee of Foreign Trade, Edinburgh, 5 October 1696, Darien Papers MS 1914, National Library of Scotland: '...Mr Gibson hath bought a ship belonging to the City of Amsterdam which is known to us and we think he hath her a pennyworth for it cost the owners who built her a considerable sum more'.

67 The ship was to be named *The Rising Sun* and was to become Gibson's flagship on the second big Darien expedition.

68 *Letter from Haldane, Erskine and Paterson to Committee of Foreign Trade*, Edinburgh, 22 January 1697, Darien Papers, MS 1914, National Library of Scotland.

69 See Chapter 2.

70 Darien Papers, NLS. MS 1914. Stratfords to Committee of Trade, Edinburgh, 16 February 1697.

71 Like London, much of Hamburg had been burnt down in a fire and rebuilt.

72 *Letter from Paterson and Erskine to the Committee of Trade*, Edinburgh, 5 March 1607, Darien Papers. MS 1914, National Library of Scotland.

73 Ibid. *Letter from Paterson and Erskine to the Committee of Foreign Trade*, Edinburgh, 5 March 1697.

74 Ibid. *Stratford Senior and Junior Agents in Hamburg to Committee of Foreign Trade*, Edinburgh, 19 February 1697.

75 Ibid. *Letter from Paterson and Erskine to the Committee of Foreign Trade*, Edinburgh, 5 March 1697, Darien Papers, MS 1914, National Library of Scotland.

76 *Letter from Sir Paul Rycaut to Sir William Trumbell Secretary of State for Trade*. Quoted in Prebble, op. cit. p. 87.

77 *Letter from Sir Paul Rycaut to Sir William Trumbell Secretary of State for Trade*. Quoted in Prebble, op. cit. p. 87.

Chapter 7

1 See Chapter 4.

2 Quoted in I. G. Doolittle, *Origins and History of the Orphans' Fund*, in British Institutional History Research, vol. LVI No. 133, May 1983, p. 51.

3 Macaulay, *History of England*, op. cit. vol. 5, pp. 14–15.

4 I. G. Doolittle, *Origins and History of the Orphans' Fund*, in British Institutional History Research, vol. LVI No. 133, May 1983, p. 51.

5 Smith and Nowis were interviewed before the House of Commons in January 1695. They revealed that they had been promised 5 per cent commission by the City Corporation on the money disbursed. They claimed most of their work had involved gathering names for a Petition on behalf of the 'Orphans'. They denied bribing MPs. See *Journal of the House of Commons* Vol. XI, pp. 269–70.

6 The records refer to 'assignments and certificates' rather than to bonds, but they amount to the same thing.

7 Quoted in William Marston Acres, *The Bank of England From Within*, London, 1931, Chapter X, p. 59.

8 That was not exactly the end of the affair, since Aubrey Price proved to be a serial counterfeiter and was hanged on the Tyburn gallows in 1698. See William Marston Acres, *The Bank of England From Within*, London, 1931 (two volumes in one), Chapter X, p. 59.

9 So it would appear from the entry in the Edinburgh records of the company. Darien Papers I. 83.7.4 No. 31. Abstract of Court proceedings 3 August 1696, National Library of Scotland. Paterson, Smith and Lodge (who had already honoured their promise to subscribe) must be added to the number.

10 For an explanation of 17th century bills of exchange and how the system worked see Parker, *The Emergence of Modern Finance in Europe, 1500–1730*, Fontana History of Europe in the 17th Century, London, pp. 540–7.

11 Court of the Company of Scotland Minute Book, 16 September 1696, The Royal Bank of Scotland Group Archives.

12 *Letter from Haldane to Committee for Foreign Trade in Edinburgh*, Edinburgh, 3 November 1696, Darien Papers, MS 1914, National Library of Scotland.

13 Sir Robert Blackwood and William Dunlop cross-examined Paterson and found him blameless. Interestingly, Paterson explained how his decision to switch the Company funds into bills of exchange forwarded to London was based in part on his belief that the Scottish currency was about to fall by up to 20 per cent against other currencies. Blackwood and Dunlop accepted that 'the design was rational had not the intervening accidents made it ineffectual'. By this they presumably meant the fall in the value of the pound against the Dutch florin. The full report can be found in Saxe Bannister, *The Writings of William Paterson*, London, 1858, vol. I, pp. l–lv.

14 Of course £25,000 was a lot of money, a quarter of all the subscription money gathered in during June 1696.

15 It is notoriously difficult to translate 17th-century prices into today's values, if only because the pattern of consumption has so changed. £8,000 was certainly enough to pay for three ships.

16 Darien Papers, National Library of Scotland, MS 1914. Letter to Committee for Trade in Edinburgh from Haldane in Amsterdam, 4 May 1697.

17 See Chapter 5. Christopher Wren, John Locke and William Lowndes, Secretary of the Treasury, all contributed to the call for the reform the currency in 1695. William Paterson had already produced his own plan for the restoration of the coin as early as 1691.

18 See Hopton Haynes, *Brief Memoirs Relating to the Gold and Silver Coins of England 1696–1699*, Lansdowne MSS 801, fol. 78v British Library.

19 The figure comes from Stephen Quinn, 'Gold, Silver and the Glorious Revolution; International Bullion Arbitrage and the Origins of the English Gold Standard', *Economic History Review* 1996, Part 3.

20 Stephen Quinn, op. cit. *Economic History Review*, 1996, Part 3.

21 William Lowndes, *Essay for the Amendment of Silver Coins*, London, 1695.

22 Sir Thomas Gresham was a considerable London merchant whose thoughts on the state of the currency in Elizabethan times had moved the queen to reform the then currency.

23 Even this would still have faced the problem that any notice of the changeover would have opened the gates to a last-minute orgy of coin clipping.

24 This is an estimate. Newton calculated the mint could produce £3,000 of coin in a day when he started but it was notoriously inefficient. See Michael White, *Isaac Newton, the Last Sorcerer*, paperback edition, London, 1998, pp. 260–2.

25 The Correspondence of Isaac Newton, vol. 4 p. 195, quoted in Michael White, *Isaac Newton, the Last Sorcerer*, paperback edition, London, 1998, p. 253.

26 Narcissus Luttrell, the contemporary observer, reported that a total of £4,706,003 in old coin was taken in by the Treasury up to 24 June 1696. Thus around 5 million coins needed replacing. See Michael White, op. cit. p. 261.

27 Mints were set up in Exeter, Bristol, Chester, York and Norwich.

28 See Robert A. Mundell, 'Uses and Abuses of Gresham's Law', *Zagreb Journal of Economics*, Volume 2, No. 2, 1998.

29 Both quotes taken from Macaulay, op. cit. vol. 5 p. 155.

30 Macaulay, op. cit. vol. 5 p. 155.

31 Charles Montagu intervened to support the bank by issuing Exchequer Bills. See W. Marston Ayres, op. cit. p. 19.

32 Macaulay, *History of England*, op. cit vol. 5, pp. 156–7.

33 Richard Saville, *The Bank of Scotland, a History*, op. cit. p. 37.

34 See the *Correspondence of the Four Dutch Factors and of Francis Stratford Snr and Jnr with the Committee for Foreign Trade in Edinburgh*, in the Darien Papers MS 1914, National Library of Scotland.

35 The slump in the value of the pound sterling was directly related to the export of silver to pay for the war. The silver was replaced by 'bills of exchange' issued by the Amsterdam merchants payable in London. The value of these in sterling terms fell dramatically through heavy discounting. See Stephen Quinn, op. cit. Also D. W. Jones, *War and Economy*, op. cit. on use of bills of exchange to finance William's armies in Europe.

36 The pound was devalued against the Dutch florin by over 17 per cent, to which had to be added the discount on paper transactions. See D. W. Jones, 'London Merchants and the Crisis of the 1690s', in Clark and Slack, *Crisis and Order in the English Towns 1500–1700*, London, 1972.

37 *Letter from James Smith to Committee for Foreign Trade*, Edinburgh, 21 November 1696, National Library of Scotland, MS 1914, Darien Papers.

38 Smith's problems in keeping abreast of his accounts – the point picked up by Daniel Lodge in September – would have produced a nightmare scenario, one that Haldane was certainly not qualified to sort out. And it would be some time yet before the full extent of the losses became clear. When they were finally tallied up, was it not easier for the board to blame Smith for the shortfall, rather than accept that it was their own panic decision to convert paper to gold and silver that had done a major damage to the company's balance sheet?

39 Ibid. *Letter from Haldane to Committee for Foreign Trade in Edinburgh*, 3 November 1696, Darien Papers, MS 1914, National Library of Scotland.

40 Ibid.

41 Ibid. *Letter from Haldane to Committee for Foreign Trade in Edinburgh*, 7 November 1696.

42 Ibid. *Letter from Haldane to Committee for Foreign Trade in Edinburgh*, 21 November 1696.

43 Ibid. *Letter from James Smith to Committee for Foreign Trade*, Edinburgh, 21 November 1696.

44 Even as late as May 1697 the discount on English paper bills was sky-high, at 19.5 per cent. Richard Saville, *The Bank of Scotland, a History*, op. cit. p. 36.

45 Darien Papers, National Library of Scotland MS 1914, *Letter of Stratfords to Committee for Trade in Edinburgh*, 3 November 1696. See also Stratford letters of 6 November, 16 February 1697, 19 February, 23 February, 5 March and 30

March. There was no recovery in the value of the pound until 28 May.

46 *Letter from Haldane to Committee for Trade in Edinburgh*, 7 November 1696, Darien Papers, MS 1914, National Library of Scotland.

47 Ibid. *Stewart and Stewart to Committee for Trade in Edinburgh*, January 1697.

48 Ibid.

49 Ibid. *Letter from Haldane to Committee for Foreign Trade*, Edinburgh, 21 November 1696.

50 Ibid. *Letter from Paterson, Erskine and Haldane to Committee for Foreign Trade*, Edinburgh, 22 January 1695.

51 Ibid. *Letter from Stewart and Campbell to Committee for Foreign Trade*, Edinburgh, 20 February 1697

52 Ibid. *Letter from Stewart and Campbell to Committee for Foreign Trade*, Edinburgh, 23 February 1697.

53 It is of course possible that messages had been sent to various Dutch provinces indicating Dutch King William's disapproval of the Company of Scotland's plans.

54 *Letter from Sir Paul Rycaut to Secretary William Trumbell*, 3 March 1696, Landsowne MSS 1153 E. fol. 40 British Library.

55 Quoted in Prebble, *Darien*, op. cit. p. 87.

56 *Letter from Francis Stratford Snr to Committee for Trade in Edinburgh*, 30 March 1697, Darien Papers, MS 1914, National Library of Scotland.

57 Quoted in Prebble, op. cit. p. 89.

58 Rycaut heard of his arrival, but by then the damage was done. See Prebble, op. cit. p. 87.

59 Quoted in Prebble, op. cit. p. 88.

60 See Prebble, op. cit. p. 89.

61 *Letter from Straford Snr and Jnr to Committee for Foreign Trade*, Edinburgh, 16 February 1697, Darien Papers, MS 1914, National Library of Scotland.

62 See the fractious correspondence between Stewart and Campbell and the continental agents in Darien Papers, MS National Library of Scotland, MS 1914.

63 *Letter from the four factors in Amsterdam to Committee for Foreign Trade*, Edinburgh, 11 June and *Letter from Haldane and Erskine to Committee for Foreign Trade*, Edinburgh, 4 May 1697, Darien Papers, MS 1914, National Library of Scotland.

64 *Letter from Paterson, Haldane and Erskine to Committee for Foreign Trade*, Edinburgh, 24 May 1697, Darien Papers, MS 1914, National Library of Scotland.

65 Prebble, op. cit. p. 89.

66 R. Saville, *The Bank of Scotland, a History*, op. cit. p. 37 'William Paterson had the ill-considered idea to pay for supplies and ships in Holland by bills drawn on London – if this were done in house it would save on the costs of commission.'

67 Waldemar Westergaard, *The Danish West Indies Under Company Rule*, New York, 1917, pp. 110–11. Smith was rumoured to have been the Treasurer of the Scotch Darien Company 'when its trade had been ruined by the English he escaped with the Treasury's money'.

68 See W. R. Scott, *The Constitution and Finance of English, Scottish and Irish Joint-Stock Companies to 1720*, Cambridge, 1910–12, vol. 1 pp. 141ff.

69 See *Humble Proposals of William Paterson to Court of Directors* sent from Caledonia in Darien 1698, University of London Archive MS 63.

70 Prebble, op. cit. p. 90.

71 This can be inferred from Paterson's letter to the company, dated February 1699, asking for half the original sum promised to be paid, University of London Archive MS 63.

72 *Letters from Secretary Orth to Sir Paul Rycaut* (forwarded to London) 21 April 1697 in the Landsdowne Manuscript Collection, British Library (ref: Ms 1153E, fol. 40).

73 *Letters from Secretary Orth to Sir Paul Rycaut* (forwarded to London) 12 October 1697 in Landsdowne Manuscript Collection, British Library (ref: Ms 1153E, fol. 40).

Chapter 8

1 In these early days of the book trade booksellers and publishers were often the same people.

2 William Dampier, *A New Voyage Round the World*, London, 1697.

3 Ibid.

4 *Letter from James Vernon to the Board of Trade and the Plantations*, MSS of John Locke at the Bodleian Library, Oxford University, MS Locke c.30, f. Quoted in Ignacio Gallup-Diaz, *The Doors of the Seas and the Key to the Universe*, op. cit. New York, Chapter 4. Available as an electronic book: Gutenberg-E.

5 Quoted in Ignacio Gallup-Diaz, *The Doors of the Seas and the Key to the Universe*, op. cit. Chapter 4.

6 The Royal Society had appealed for help to produces guides for mariners to little-known parts of the world. Dampier and Wafer had set out to do this. See Ignacio Gallup-Diaz, op. cit. Chapter 4, Note 18.

7 Lionel Wafer, *A New Voyage and Description of the Isthmus of Darien*, London, 1699. Paterson had been given a copy of Wafer's manuscript in 1695. Such sentiments could only have reinforced his view that a base in Darien could be the making of the Company of Scotland.

8 Maureen Waller, *1700, Scenes from London Life*, London, 2000, p. 293.

9 Wafer's testimony appears in The Darien Papers, MS item 50 NLS. See Gallup-Diaz, op. cit. Chapter 4, Note 31.

10 The Earl of Tankerville was most famous – notorious indeed – for having eloped with his wife's sister, scandalising even the unshockable court of Charles II. See Cecil Price, *Cold Caleb: The Scandalous Life of Ford Grey*, London, 1956. See also Macaulay, *History of England*, op. cit. vol. 1, p. 519, vol. 5, p. 143.

11 In the 1850s a Scots Engineer, Dr Edward Cullen, surveyed a route from ocean to ocean that was only 39 miles long. See E. Cullen, *The Isthmus of Darien Canal*, London, 1853.

12 Board of Trade Journal 2 July 1697. Reproduced in Saxe Bannister, *The Writings of William Paterson*, 1858, vol. II, pp. 258–61.

13 Ibid. Summary of Evidence given by Dampier and Wafer.

14 Ibid. Report of Committee to Lord Justice 10 August 1697.

15 See *John Locke*, by Maurice Cranstoun, cited in David Armitage, *The Origins of the Darien Scheme*, in J. Robertson, *A Union for Empire*, Cambridge, 1995. Armitage writes that Locke bought Wafer's book at St Paul's in 1697 but this cannot be the case, since the book was not published until 1699. It is more likely that he bought Dampier's book.

16 Board of Trade No XX State Paper Office 1697. Reproduced in Saxe Bannister, op. cit. vol. II, p. 261.

17 In the course of that year Barcelona was over-run by a French army and the great South American port of Cartagena was sacked by a French fleet.

18 In fact in 1698 Richard Long, an English sea captain, was given a commission by the Lord Justices of England – who acted as the king's regents when he was away

fighting his wars in the Low Countries. Long interpreted it as giving him the power to claim Darien for England. See Chapter 9.

19 *Letter from Haldane to Committee for Foreign Trade*, Edinburgh, 19 March 1697, Darien Papers, MS 1914, National Library of Scotland.

20 Francis Russell Hart estimated the costs at £70,000 in his book *The Disaster of Darien* but this seems high, since the accounts held in the Darien Papers in Edinburgh suggest that the costs came to no more than £3,000 a ship, plus the costs of cannon and ordnance, plus agents' fees. Even if the financial crisis of 1696 added 20 per cent to these final costs the total bill is unlikely to have been more than £50,000.

21 See Prebble, op cit. p. 97. He quotes the figure as £18,413.

22 He received nothing for his work on the Bank of England, and had seen his share allocation in the Company of Scotland snatched away in London in November 1695. See Chapter 3 (p. 73) and Chapter 5 (p. 118).

23 Letter from William Paterson to Thomas Drummond 1699. Quoted in Saxe Bannister, *William Paterson, His Life and Trials*, London, 1858, Introduction p. xc.

24 William could claim a victory of sorts, since Louis had agreed to retreat from some of his conquered lands in Europe and to recognise William as the rightful king of England, Scotland and Ireland.

25 John Evelyn, Diary 3 October 1697: 'So greate were the Storms all this weeke that there were here 1000 poore men cast away going into the Texell & and many other disasters.' (The Texel is one of the Dutch islands at the mouth of the Zuider Zee.)

26 *Letter from Alexander Stevenson, Hamburg, to Committee for Foreign Trade*, Edinburgh, 20 October 1696, Darien Papers, MS 1914, National Library of Scotland.

27 Prebble, op. cit. pp. 95–6. St Andrew is of course the patron saint of Scotland.

28 Sir Paul Rycaut reported after meeting Paterson, that: 'he was always well-affected towards the English nation and looked on them as one people with theirs under one denomination of Brittains.' Letter from Rycaut to Trumbull, reproduced in J. Hill Burton, The Darien Papers, Section XIII, p. 13.

29 The Latin translates as 'No one meddles with me and gets away with it' – the Scots more directly as 'Who dares meddle with me?'

30 The orders had been to have built ships that matched the size of East India Company ships. A specification of a ship of about 550 tons appears in The *Darien Shipping Papers*, Edinburgh, 1924, pp. 267 *et seq*. See F. Russell Hart, *The Disaster of Darien*, Boston and New York, 1929, p. 54. The Spaniards reported that the flagship of the second expedition, *The Rising Sun*, had 62 cannon.

31 G. P. Insh, *The Darien Scheme*, Historical Association Pamphlet, London, 1947, p. 17.

32 Macaulay, *History of England*, op. cit. vol. 5, p. 472.

33 'He was one of the very few of his countrymen who never drunk wine'. Sir John Dalrymple of Cranstoun, *Memoirs of Great Britain and Ireland*, 1771. Part III, Book VI, p. 128.

34 Oakum was a material made from unpicking old ropes. It was used for caulking.

35 G. P. Insh, *The Darien Scheme*, Historical Association Pamphlet, London, 1947, p. 17. The *Ledger kept at Glasgow by Peter Murdoch for the African Company* lists the cargoes taken on the second expedition, and put the wild statements of Herries in perspective. A cargo check-list, possibly for the first voyage, is found in the manuscript collection held by University of London Archive. The date of 1699 seems to have been added later.

36 *Letter from William Paterson to Robert Chiesly*, 9 July 1695, Darien Papers, MS 1914, National Library of Scotland.

37 This is probably an underestimate. In some parishes 50 per cent of people died as a result of famine. See William Ferguson, *Scotland – 1689 to the Present*, Edinburgh, 1968, pp. 78–9.

38 Sunny warm climates were regarded as healthy by those who first experienced them. The scourge of malaria and of yellow fever were little understood. In *Historians Odyssey*, pp. 235 ff., G. P. Insh argues that yellow fever had not yet arrived in Central America at this time. But since it had reached Barbados by 1647 this seems unlikely. See Macfarlane, Burnet and White, *Natural History of Infectious Disease*, Cambridge, 4th Edition, 1972, p. 242.

39 In 1688 William III had accepted the 'Bill of Rights' drawn up by parliament. It specifically stated that the king could keep a standing army in time of peace only with the consent of parliament. Memory of the excesses of the absolutist ambitions of Charles I and James II meant this army would be kept as small as possible. William was so angry at the cuts in the size of his army that he contemplated abdication. See Pieter Geyl, *History of the Low Countries*, London, 1964, p. 135.

40 Macaulay, *History of England*, op. cit. vol. 5, p. 371.

41 England and Scotland remained separate countries constitutionally, but they shared the same king. The raising of an army was long seen as the prerogative of the king. Since 1660 the armies of England and Scotland had therefore been combined as one in the command structure, although separately funded.

42 *Seafield to the Rev William Carstares*. Quoted in Prebble, op. cit. p. 92.

43 His father died earlier in 1697.

44 Meaning 'Expedition'.

45 Prebble, op. cit. p. 100.

46 G. P. Insh, *The Darien Scheme*, Historical Association Pamphlet, London, 1949 pp. 15–16.

47 Quoted in Prebble, op. cit. p. 118.

48 It is generally argued that Paterson had never been to Darien before the expedition, but this is put in doubt by the extraordinary grasp he had of its geography, displayed in the new proposal of 1700. If indeed he had lived on Old Providence Island it is likely that he would have at least sailed along the coast.

49 Court of Directors instruction to a person being sent to London, 30 January 1698. Quoted in G. P. Insh, *The Darien Scheme*, op. cit. Historical Association pamphlet, p. 16.

50 MSS Journals of the Courts of Directors, The Royal Bank of Scotland Group Archives, vol. 1, pp. 447–8. His letter was dated 19 April 1698. Quoted in I. Gallup-Diaz, op. cit. (Chapter 4, Note 37). Gallup-Diaz suggests he travelled to Edinburgh in the spring of 1698. A letter dated 30 June 1698 and sent to London by an informer in Edinburgh, quoted by Gallup-Diaz, (Chapter 4, Note 38) rather supports the view that Wafer was in Scotland in June 1698 as Herries maintains. See Walter Herries, *A Defence of the Scots Abdicating Darien*, 1700, pp. 97–8.

51 Andrew Fletcher of Saltoun had dined with Wafer a few weeks before and reported the young man was happy to discuss terms. See Prebble, *Darien*, op. cit. p. 105.

52 Prebble, *Darien*, op. cit. p. 106.

53 Wafer's account of the trip, quoted in Prebble, *Darien*, op. cit. p. 107.

54 Ibid.

55 Ibid. p. 108.

56 Ibid. p. 108.

57 It was not published in the end until 1699. The fact that it took so long to appear rather militates against the conclusion that the Scots were trying to delay the publication of his book using underhand tactics.

58 Future research may settle this question one way or another.

59 Ibid. p. 118.

60 The character of the seven men is sketched out by Prebble, op. cit. pp. 109–12.

61 Prebble, op. cit. p. 59.

62 Walter Herries, *A Defence of the Scots Abdicating Darien*, 1700.

63 G. P. Insh, *The Darien Scheme*, Historical Association Pamphlet op. cit. p. 13 and p. 18. See also *Letter from Paterson and Erskine to Committee of Trade in Edinburgh*, 19 March 1697, Darien Papers, MS 1914 NLS. They wrote from Hamburg: 'The seamen who are sent hither on Acc^{ott} of the company tell us they are only hired to come to Leith whereas we humbly conceive that it is uncertain if there will be time for the ships at all to come to Leith.'

64 Sir John Dalrymple of Cranstoun, *Memoirs of Great Britain and Ireland*, Part III, Book VI, p. 133, London, 1771.

65 Paterson's Report to the Directors, March 1699. Quoted by John Prebble, op. cit. p. 123.

66 Prebble, op. cit. p. 124.

67 The contrast between the exaggerated respect shown to Paterson when he arrived in Edinburgh in 1696, and the appalling disrespect shown by his fellow councillors on the expedition (with the exception of Pinkerton) is quite astonishing.

68 Manuscript Sailing Orders, University of London Archive, MS 63.

69 James Smith's father, Peter Smith, was the factor for the Elector of Brandenburg on St Thomas Island. Captain Kidd, the notorious Scottish pirate was to call at St Thomas in April 1699. Peter Smith was sent out to find out why he was there. His presence did not help the Scots in securing Darien. See Chapter 10. See Waldemar Westergaard, *The Danish West Indies Under Company Rule*, New York, 1917. On the internet as www.mapesmunde.com/books/danish-west-indies/danish_bok.pdf.

70 Manuscript Sailing Orders, op. cit.

71 The Board of Longitude was established by the British Government in 1714 offering a prize of £20,000 for any method of defining longitude to within half a degree. The prize was won by John Harrison many years later.

72 See Chapter 1 for details.

73 *Journal of Hugh Rose*, Darien Papers National Library of Scotland. Reproduced in F. Russell Hart, *The Disaster of Darien*, Cambridge, Mass, 1929 Appendix II.

74 Letter from Darien, written by Colin Campbell, who appears to have been close to Captain Robert Pinkerton. The letter contains his journal of the voyage. In the Darien Papers, National Library of Scotland. MS 846.

75 Ibid. Entry for 2 November 1698.

76 See Chapter 1.

77 He was part owner of the cargo (to the value of £2,000) carried in the hold of Richard Moon's sloop. See Chapter 9.

78 See Waldemar Westergaard, *The Danish West Indies Under Company Rule*, New York, 1917. On the internet as www.mapesmunde.com/books/danish-west-indies/danish_bok.pdf p. 69 Footnote 50. Crab Island had also been claimed at various times by the English, the Spanish, and the Brandenburgers. The Danes acted to keep all of them off.

79 *Journal of Hugh Rose*, 2 November 1698, Darien Papers, National Library of Scotland. Quoted by F. Russell Hart, *The Disaster of Darien*, op. cit. Appendix II.
80 Ibid.
81 Ibid.
82 *Caledonia or the Pedlar turn'd Merchant*, London, 1700. The author in unknown.

Chapter 9

1 See Waldemar Westergaard, op. cit. p. 30.
2 See Chapter 1.
3 New Spain comprised Mexico, much of present-day New Mexico and Texas, Florida, the Central American provinces of Guatemala, Honduras, El Salvador, and Costa Rica, and the Spanish-held islands of the Caribbean.
4 He was related to Diego Sarmiento de Valladares, Inquisitor in Chief for the Spanish Inquisition. Although devoutly religious Jose Sarmiento returned to his native Galicia a very rich man in 1704, narrowly escaping capture by the British Admiral George Rooke at Vigo.
5 The dispatch was dated 8 November 1697. It mentioned that Chile also featured in the Scottish Company's plans. The source of the information may have been Rycaut himself. See Ignacio Gallup-Diaz, op. cit. Chapter 4, Note 19.
6 In fact the Scots never settled there, but Golden Island had a particular notoriety in Spanish circles as a base for piracy.
7 *Letter from Sarmiento to Zavala*, 28 March 1699. Archives of the Indies, Seville. Reproduced in translation in F. Russell Hart, *The Disaster of Darien*, Appendix XV, p. 258, op. cit.
8 *Letter from Sarmiento to the King of Spain*, 14 July 1699. F. Russell Hart, op. cit. Appendix XXI, p. 302. In this letter Sarmiento outlines the steps he had taken since he first heard the news of the Scots colony in January 1699. The exact date he received such news cannot be established, but a letter was sent from Cartagena as early as 11 November. It should have reached Veracruz before the end of December.
9 *Letter from Sarmiento to Zavala*, 28 March 1699. Archives of the Indies, Seville. Reproduced in translation in F. Russell Hart, *The Disaster of Darien*, p. 258, op. cit. Although dated in March Sarmiento tells us that he had already sent orders in January.
10 'Act of Parliament Constituting the Company of Scotland, Trading to Africa and the Indies 1695'. Reproduced in F. Russell Hart, op. cit. p. 186.
11 In the papers of the Council of the Indies in Seville appears the following minute: 'Reflecting on the possible, and today, imminent, danger which today menaces, the Council proposed and your Majesty [i.e. Carlos II] resolved that a fortification should be erected at Darien, *to settle that country* and to protect it against occupation by foreign nations.' Madrid, 12 February 1699. (Author's emphasis.) Reproduced in F. Russell Hart, op. cit. Appendix XIII.
12 The research of Ignacio Gallup-Diaz reveals that the Spanish had long attempted to administer Darien through the Carrizoli family.
13 Ignacio Gallup-Diaz, op. cit. Chapter 4, Note 20.
14 *Report by William Paterson to the Directors of the Company of Scotland* 19 December 1699. In The Darien Papers, reproduced in J. Hill Burton, *The Darien Papers*, Edinburgh, 1849, pp. 178–98. The original is in the National Library of Scotland.

15 *Journal of Hugh Rose*, in F. Russell Hart, op cit. p. 199.

16 See Note 28 for the bitter quarrel between Ambrosio and Diego.

17 *Journal of Hugh Rose*, Darien Papers, NLS. Reproduced in F. Russell Hart, op. cit. p. 202.

18 Ibid.

19 Ibid. p. 201.

20 Since 1688 the Spanish had had a policy of leaving the Darien gold mines undeveloped. See Proceedings of the Council of the Indies 12 February 1699. In F. Russell Hart, op. cit. p. 253.

21 *Journal of Hugh Rose*. Reproduced in F. Russell Hart, op. cit. p. 202. The original is in The Darien Papers, NLS.

22 Ibid.

23 This remark is reported by Walter Herries in *A Defence of the Scots Abdicating Darien*, 1700, and quoted by Gallup-Diaz, op. cit. Chapter 4, Note 101.

24 A pinnace is a small two-masted vessel with oars as well as sails.

25 *Journal of Hugh Rose*, op. cit. p. 208.

26 Ibid.

27 Walter Herries, *A Defence of the Scots Abdicating Darien*, 1700, p. 54. In fact Herries says it was Androae who died but he is clearly confused on this point. Ignacio Gallup-Diaz, who quotes this part of Herries account, is surely right in his assumption that a decision was made to gloss over the event.

28 The disappearance of Ambrosio from the accounts is noted by Ignacio Gallup-Diaz, op. cit. Chapter 4, p. 80, Note 106.

29 *Paterson's Report to the Directors*, 19 December 1699. Quoted in F. Russell Hart, pp. 165–6.

30 *William Paterson to Thomas Drummond*, 6 February 1700. In J. Hill Burton, *The Darien Papers*, op. cit. Section XXIX, p. 259.

31 See Prebble, op. cit. pp. 183–4.

32 *Letter of the Council to the Edinburgh Directors*, December 1698. Darien Shipping Papers, G. P. Insh, op. cit. Edinburgh, 1924. Quoted in F. Russell Hart, *The Disaster of Darien*, op. cit. p. 75.

33 'A Letter from a Person of Eminency and Worth in Caledonia', 18 February 1699. Reproduced in F. Russell Hart, *The Disaster of Darien*, op. cit. pp. 237–8. The Diary of Samuel Sewell, op. cit. (Chapter 3) confirms that this letter was from Paterson. Sewell indicates that the letter was read out at the Boston Town-Meeting on 9 May 1699. It is interesting to note that letters of this type were often used to promote new colonies, projecting a rather unrealistic picture of the conditions the pioneers faced. Thus in 1649 *The Moderate Intelligencer* in London published a letter from an anonymous 'well-willer', describing Carolana in similar terms to Darien, a land full of natural riches and with a soil 'of a black mould about two feet deepe'. In fact life in early Carolina was tough, see History of Albemarle County http:/www.ah.dcr.state.nc/sections/hp/colonial/Bookshelf/countie/countapp1.htm.

34 Despite having an exact description from Lionel Wafer as to the whereabouts of this treasured commodity, Pennicuik and his search-parties were never able to find it.

35 Despite having been written by the Pennicuik's secretary, Hugh Rose, the Declaration seems to have been largely, but not exclusively, the work of Paterson. See the full draft in F. Russell Hart, op. cit. pp. 226–9.

36 To avoid confusion, the colony has customarily been referred to as New Caledonia in history books.

37 *The Declaration of the Council Constituted by the Indian and African Company of Scotland*, 28 December 1698. Darien Papers, National Library of Scotland. Reproduced in F. Russell Hart, op. cit. pp. 226–9.

38 Ibid. See Chapter 2 for the practice of religious toleration in Amsterdam.

39 'The Declaration of the Council for the Indian and African Company of Scotland', 28 December 1698. Darien Papers NLS. Reproduced in F. Russell Hart, op. cit. pp. 226–9. It has been argued by Prebble that the Freedom of Conscience was not meant to apply to Roman Catholics. But Paterson believed in religious toleration in its broadest sense. Anything else was inimical to trade.

40 See 'A Letter from a Person of Eminency', F. Russell Hart, op. cit. p. 238.

41 The real nature of Richard Long's mission will be considered later, in Chapter 10.

42 We assume here that Duvivier Thomas was the same Petit-Goave sailor who is recorded as a close colleague of Admiral Du Casse, Governor of French Hispaniola. See website article 'L'admiral Du Casse de la marchandise à la Toison d'Or' at http://margaux.ipt.univ-paris8.fr/~aceme/toison_dor.html.

43 Duvivier Thomas had also tried to convince the Spanish authorities in Portobello that he had come to root out the French buccaneers lurking on the coasts of Darien. They never quite believed him. Recent research by Ignacio Gallup-Diaz has thrown much light on Duvivier Thomas's mission, and on his duplicity. See I. Gallup-Diaz, *The Door of the Seas and the Key to the Universe*, op. cit. Chapter 5 *Spanish Chaos*.

44 The *Journal of Hugh Rose* says it was the *Zantoigne*, but this sounds like a French version of a Spanish name.

45 The Windward or Barlovento Fleet was used to escort the Spanish treasure fleet sailing from Portobello to Cadiz early in the year. A convoy system had long been the best guarantee that the wealth of Peru and Mexico would get safely carried to Cadiz.

46 The opinions of Duvivier Thomas are recorded in some detail by Hugh Rose. See his journal reproduced in F. Russell Hart, op. cit. pp. 211–12. This quote comes from there.

47 Carlos II of Spain, and his state of health, will be dealt with in more detail in Chapter 10. It is sufficient to say that in December 1698 his death was considered imminent.

48 The Scots fleet had sailed with the authority of King William's Letters Patent, issued in 1695, and never withdrawn.

49 *Journal of Hugh Rose*, 16 December 1698, in F. Russell Hart, op. cit. p. 213.

50 The prevailing wind was east to north-east, but on this part of the Darien coast the mountains to the east forced it to take a more northerly direction in the dry season. See Francis Borland, *Memoirs of Darien*, Edinburgh, 1715.

51 *Journal of Hugh Rose*. The original is in the Darien Papers, National Library of Scotland. Reproduced in F. Russell Hart, op. cit. p. 216. Most histories say the ship was wrecked on the rock in mid-channel, but this account suggests this was not the case.

52 *Journal of Robert Pennicuik*, in the Darien Papers, National Library of Scotland. Quoted by Prebble, op. cit. p. 158.

53 *A Letter from a Person of Eminency in Caledonia to a Friend in Boston*. Reproduced by F. Russell Hart, *The Disaster of Darien*, pp. 235–6.

54 From 3 November to 25 December there were 32 deaths, out of 1,100 settlers. The rate of mortality increased rapidly afterwards. A further 170 were dead by

the beginning of March. But even this death-rate did not compare with that of the English East India Company post on the Hoogli River, the future Calcutta, where in the 1690s there were '1,200 English inhabitants of whom 460 were buried between the months of August and January in one year'. See Angus Calder, *Revolutionary Empire*, op. cit. p. 249.

55 *Paterson's Report to the Directors of the Company of Scotland*, December 1699. Reproduced in *The Darien Papers*, edited by J. Hill Burton, Edinburgh, 1849.

56 In practice crops such as maize had to be planted during the rainy season and harvested during the dry. This meant planting could not take place until late in the year. In any case the initial settlers were expected to take a year to lay out New Edinburgh and build the fort. Some tobacco was, however, planted. See *Letter from a gentleman now living in Darien* in the University of Glasgow Spencer Collection.

57 Report of Conde de Canillas, Presidente of Panama, to Spanish Crown 6 May 1699. Reproduced in F. Russell Hart, op. cit. p. 275.

58 Quoted by Prebble, *Darien*, op. cit. p. 184.

59 *Letter from Robert Douglas to a Board Member*. Darien Papers, Folder A. p. 159, NLS.

60 Quoted in G. H. Guttridge, *The Colonial Policy of William III in America and the West Indies*, London, 1922, p. 156. The source is PRO, Commissioners for Customs, 1696–7, 615.

61 Allison was actually aboard Moon's sloop when Paterson talked him into taking the Scots to Golden Island.

62 See *Paterson's Report to the Directors of the Company of Scotland*, 9 December 1699. Darien Papers, NLS. Reproduced in J. Hill Burton, *The Darien Papers*, Edinburgh, 1849, pp. 178–98.

63 *Paterson's Report to the Directors*, J. Hill Burton, op. cit. section XXII, p. 180.

64 'They should have our Goods as they cost in Scotland, and we were, in lieu thereof, to have the sloop's cargoe of provisions as it cost in Jamaica, and, as I remember, ten per cent advance.' *Paterson's Report to the Directors*. Reproduced in *The Darien Papers*, edited by J. Hill Burton, Edinburgh, 1849, p. 182.

65 Prebble, op. cit. p. 221.

66 Ibid. p. 183.

67 One of the other councillors threw the jibe of 'Your friend Mr. Wilmot' at Paterson at a later council meeting. Prebble, op. cit. p. 182.

68 It is unclear exactly what. But it was not enough.

69 Since the destruction of Port Royal by the earthquake of 1692 Port Morant had risen to new importance in Jamaica.

70 Quoted in Prebble, op. cit. p. 171. Prebble supposes that Wilmot and Moon had come merely to take the provisions supplied by Sands back. But a month had passed since he left and they surely would have been consumed. It seems much more plausible that they had come with fresh supplies and it is these they refused to part with.

71 *Paterson's Report to the Directors*, in J. Hill Burton, *The Darien Papers*, op. cit. p. 182.

72 *Paterson's Report to the Directors*, J. Hill Burton, op. cit. p. 183.

73 List of goods all taken from the hand-written cargo list to be found in University of London Archive MSS collection. The spices and silks had been brought from the East to Europe and carried from there to Scotland. Robert Douglas in his letter to a member of the Court of Directors in September 1696 had recommended this sort of cargo. See Darien Papers, Folder A, National Library of Scotland, Edinburgh, Letter of Robert Douglas.

74 Both extracts from *Paterson's Report to the Directors*, December 1699. J. Hill Burton, op. cit. p. 183.

75 Pinkerton gave his version of the story to the Court of Directors two years later. See J. Hill Burton, op. cit. pp. 123–4. Also testimony of James Graham, pp. 103–4.

76 A Letter from Pinkerton, written in the Seville gaol, is preserved in the University of Glasgow Spencer Collection. MS. Gen 502 (19).

77 *Letter from William Paterson to Rev Alexander Shields*, 6 February 1700, in J. Hill Burton, op. cit. p. 261.

78 Adam Smith in the *Wealth of Nations* estimated that the total capital possessed by Scotland around 1700 was 'not less than' £1 million. See *The Wealth of Nations*, Everyman Edition, London and New York, 1957, vol 1. p. 262d.

79 And then only with the help of a few wealthy shareholders offering to advance their next tranche of subscriptions.

80 J. Hill Burton, *The Darien Papers*, Edinburgh, 1853. The letter is dated February 1699.

81 Paterson's advice against using Leith as a base, sent from Madeira, had not yet reached Edinburgh. For sending of *The Dispatch* see *Letter from Court of Directors to the Council of Caledonia 24th February 1699*. Darien Papers. J. Hill Burton, op. cit. pp. 121–3. The other ship mentioned in this letter was presumably the *Olive Branch*, which did not eventually sail until May – see *Letter from Court of Directors to the Council of Caledonia 15th April*. Darien Papers. J. Hill Burton, op. cit. pp. 124–8.

82 *Board of Trade Journal*, 2 July 1697, p. 139. Reproduced in Saxe Bannister, *The Writings of William Paterson*, London, 1858, vol. 2, pp. 238–9. Dampier and Wafer suggested a force of 250 men would be enough to hold off the Spanish.

83 It had actually been founded by English settlers but was passed to Holland in 1667 as part of the package that gave England control of New Amsterdam, then renamed New York.

84 *Gen. Zavala to the Spanish Crown*, 28 July 1699, Appendix XXIV, in F. Russell Hart, op. cit. p. 313.

85 See *Letter from Viceroy to the Crown of Spain*, 14 July 1699. Reproduced in F. Russell Hart, op. cit. Appendix XXII, pp. 301–5. He suggested the king should send orders direct to Zavala since his had been ignored (p. 305).

86 Ignacio Gallup-Diaz, op. cit. Chapter 5 *Spanish Chaos* and note 35.

87 *Letter of Conde de Canillas to Spanish Crown*, 6 May 1699. Reproduced in F. Russell Hart, op. cit. Appendix XVI, p. 262.

88 Ibid.

89 *Letter of Conde de Canillas to Spanish Crown*. Reproduced in F. Russell Hart, op. cit. Appendix XVI, p. 263.

90 The story is told by Montgomerie in his report to the council, 6 February 1699, in J. Hill Burton, op. cit. pp. 85–6. He warned that a new and serious attack was being planned. The Spanish account of the incident is summed up in Ignacio Gallup-Diaz, op. cit. Chapter 5. See also note 55.

91 *Letter of Conde de Canillas to the Spanish Crown* 6 May 1699. Reproduced in F. Russell Hart, op. cit. p. 264.

92 There were easier, less arduous routes, but the Spanish attempted a direct assault from Toubacanti.

93 *Letter from Andres de Pez to the King of Spain*, 10 June 1699. In F. Russell Hart, op. cit. Appendix XIX, p. 294.

94 Ibid. p. 295.
95 See the testimony of Don Juan Martinez Retes de la Vega, Appendix XVI, in F. Russell Hart, op. cit. p. 279.
96 Each gave an affidavit recounting just why they had decided to abandon the planned attack on the Scottish positions. Presumably, they were guarding their backs from possible charges of incompetence, or of cowardice in the face of the enemy. See F. Russell Hart, Appendix XVI, pp. 261–82.

Chapter 10

1   William Dampier, *A Voyage to New Holland, etc*, London, 1703, Chapter 1.
2   As well as Dampier's, *A New Voyage Round the World*, 1697, the account of the voyages of the Dutch Explorer, Abel Tasman, had just been published in English for the first time in 1694.
3   Dampier was to reach New Holland and sail north of New Guinea (then thought to be part of Australia) to discover the island he named New Britain (part of the Solomon Islands) before being forced to turn back by sickness and an increasingly unseaworthy vessel.
4   It was left to Captain Cook to clear up the mystery by his voyages that began in 1768 and ended with his death at Hawaii in 1780.
5   See Chapter 9.
6   See Chapter 3 for Phips.
7   Long's proposal is reproduced in G. P. Insh, *The Darien Shipping Papers*, Edinburgh, 1924, pp. 97–9.
8   See Chapter 6. Dampier told the committee that: 'Upon the North Sea [coast of Darien] the Spaniards have no settlement at all. All the inland country is in the hands of Indians.' PRO, *Board of Trade Journal*, 2 July 1697.
9   PRO ADM 1/2033 f.2: Quoted by Ignacio Gallup-Diaz, op. cit. Chapter 4, p. 38, see Note 47.
10 It is unlikely. But it should be noted that the 'Partition Treaty' agreed with Louis XIV was not agreed until September 1698. Before the signing of the treaty William III did not have his hands tied quite so firmly.
11 Public Record Office. MS, PRO ADM 1/2033.
12 *Long's letter from Jamaica to the Admiralty*, 1699. Quoted in F. Russell Hart, *The Disaster of Darien*, op. cit. p. 219.
13 For example, one of the chiefs, known as Corbet, agreed to Long's suggestion that colonists from Jamaica should come and settle in his land. For an exposition of how the Indians of Darien went along with such suggestions, not because they agreed, but because it was not customary to argue with strangers, see Ignacio Gallup-Diaz, op. cit. Chapter 4, 'The Scots and the Tule'.
14 Public Record Office, MS PRO ADM 1/2033.
15 *Letter from Richard Long to Lord Justices*. Reproduced by F. Russell Hart, op. cit. pp. 219–23.
16 The word used by Long is 'Pelliar', which is loosely translated as 'most desirable'.
17 *Report of Richard Long to the Lord Justices*, in F. Russell Hart op. cit. pp. 219–23. See Ignacio Gallup-Diaz, *The Doors of the Seas and the Key of the Universe*, op. cit. Chapter 4, for a full description of Long's dealings with Diego. Long discussed the building of homes for the English settlers.
18 See Chapter 9 (p. 220). Was the Spanish fleet a threat, or did Long invent the story to scare the Scots? Perhaps one day the truth will be established.

19 It should be remembered that Spain also maintained a claim to North America, and had settlements in Texas and what is now New Mexico as well as in Florida.

20 According to Macaulay through loose talk in Holland. See his *History of England*, op. cit. vol. 5, p. 399.

21 *Letter from Sir William Beeston to Don Diego de Rios*. Quoted in translation in F. Russell Hart, *The Disaster of Darien*, op. cit. Appendix XVII, p. 291.

22 *Paterson's Report to the Directors*, in J. Hill Burton, op. cit. p. 184.

23 There is surprisingly little in the records about the nature of the weather during the rainy season. But a BBC programme shot in 2001 in Honduras – *Ray Mear's Extreme Survival, Honduras* – gives a vivid impression. I am indebted to Danny Cane for bringing my attention to it. Darien does not lie in the hurricane zone, but deep depressions are common. For a description of the rainy season on the north-east coast of Madagascar, a land with a climate similar to Darien, see Kevin Rushby, *Hunting Pirate Heaven*, Robinson Paperback edition, London, 2002, pp. 256–7, 260, 274–5.

24 Paterson wrote at least one letter that has survived in the records, a letter sent to John Borland in Boston. It is referred to in Samuel Sewell's diary. This letter was written at Fort St Andrew in Darien on 18 February 1699. It must have been carried first to Jamaica and from there to Boston. It took just over two months to get from sender to receiver. See *Diary of Samuel Sewell*, Entry for 27 April 1699, op. cit. pp. 496–7. The work he did on planning his new Darien Scheme is discussed in Chapter 12.

25 One of these books was *Phaenomena*, written by Samuel Sewell. In the letter Paterson writes: 'I have read the two books you sent, for which I thank the author and you; and am glad to see the Spirit and Hand of Almighty God at this time in so eminent a maner.' He also referred to his honour in being involved in the Darien project: 'this great Work, that we, though unworthy, are made the hapy instruments to begin.' See *Diary of Samuel Sewell*, op. cit. p. 497.

26 *Letter to Rev. Alex. Shields*, 6 February 1700. J. Hill Burton, op. cit. p. 261.

27 The Treaty appears to be in Hugh Rose's handwriting, but the sentiments and phrases are undoubtedly Paterson's.

28 A copy of the full treaty is to be found in F. Russell Hart, *The Disaster of Darien*, op. cit. Appendix V, pp. 224–5.

29 For a discussion of the rather casual approach adopted by the Cuna Indians of Darien to European colonial aspirations, see Ignacio Gallup-Diaz, op. cit. Chapter 4, 'The Scots and the Tule', p. 75. He writes: 'Trust and allegiance could not be finalized through testimonies recorded for all time on paper. These relationships, and the benefits of trade and defense that they brought ... could never be taken for granted. The exchanges that formed their base needed to be continually reenacted, and alliances, therefore, continually needed to be renewed.'

30 They offered to lease their vessels to the colony. They expected to be paid.

31 For the facilities in New York, see Chapter 11 (p. 270). As for Boston, Paterson had friends there. Sir William Phips and John Borland would have done all they could to help.

32 Turtling required special nets and ropes. Unless Sands had come with that intention, he would not have normally carried them.

33 *Paterson's Report to the Directors*, December 1699, in J. Hill Burton, op. cit. p. 185.

34 He confessed to the Rev. Alexander Shields that: 'the difficultyes I had met with in Scotland were turned into browbeatings in Caledonia.' *Letter to Rev. Alexander Shields*, 6 February 1700, J. Hill Burton, op. cit. pp. 260–1.

35 Prebble, *Darien*, p. 179.

36 Prebble, *Darien*, op. cit. p. 180. The words were reported by Lt Alexander Maghie, the man chosen by the council to carry their protest to Cartagena.

37 Their arrival angered Pennicuik in particular. He accused Moon of abducting a cabin boy from the colony against his will, and it was left to Paterson to try to smooth things over. See Prebble, op. cit. p. 181.

38 *Paterson's Report to the Directors*, December 1699, in J. Hill Burton, op. cit. p. 188.

39 Ibid.

40 Ibid.

41 Ibid.

42 Macaulay, *History of England*, op. cit. vol. 5, p. 444.

43 Note from the *Council of the Indies to the court of Carlos II of Spain*, communicating a message from His Britannic Majesty's Envoy, 16 May 1699. Reproduced in translation in F. Russell Hart, *The Disaster of Darien*, op. cit. Appendix XVIII, p. 290.

44 The Spanish records show that there was much scepticism as to William's real intentions. Was he using the Scots as a Trojan horse to gain a foothold on the Isthmus for himself? On 16 May the Spanish Council of the Indies reported to Madrid that: 'No matter how they [the English] may seek with plausible appearance to disguise their intentions, these are revealed in the manner and the purpose in which Secretary Vernon delivered the note, for the purpose is no other than the crown of England shall occupy new provinces in America.' *Report of the Council of the Indies to Carlos II*, 16 May 1699. Reproduced in F. Russell Hart, *The Disaster of Darien*, op. cit. p. 283.

45 Acts of Parliament of Scotland. King William III, Parl. I. Session 5.

46 There is no direct documentary evidence that the Scots foresaw such a role for Benbow. But Maghie had encountered Benbow at Cartagena and was given some encouragement by the Admiral. Some of the Scots must surely have thought along these lines.

47 One more than his previous plan in order to make up for the loss of Mackay.

48 In early March he and Montgomerie were at loggerheads according to Paterson. See *Paterson's Report to the Directors*, December 1699, in J. Hill Burton, op. cit. p. 186.

49 They sailed in Henry Patton's captured sloop to Jamaica, and from there travelled on a Bristol-bound ship.

50 The story is told in Francis Borland, *The History of Darien*, Glasgow, 1715. Quoted by Prebble, op. cit. pp. 298–9.

51 Some historians have suggested that Paterson and Drummond did not get on, but the enthusiastic and friendly letter Paterson sent to Drummond in February 1700 suggests the opposite, that they had worked well together and shared common aims. See *Letter to Thomas Drummond*, 6 February 1700, in J. Hill Burton, op. cit. pp. 258–60.

52 *Paterson's Report to the Directors*, in J. Hill Burton, op. cit. p. 190.

53 *Letter to Rev. Alexander Shields*, 6 February 1700, in J. Hill Burton, op. cit. p. 260.

54 Ibid. p. 262. He seems to have meant that 'petty officials' had not the breadth of view needed on the council. Sea captains he particularly railed against.

55 *Paterson's Report to the Directors*, in J. Hill Burton, op. cit. p. 190.

56 Although there had been heavy rain in March, the rainy season proper did not set in until mid to late April.

57 Prebble, op. cit pp. 183–4.

58 Patrick MacDowall's description of his illness, National Library of Scotland, *The Darien Papers*, quoted by Prebble, op. cit. p. 183.
59 See Burnet and White, op. cit. pp. 235–6.
60 This is despite the fact that some sailors of the time, such as the French privateer Tristian, swore that Darien was much healthier than say Hispaniola, see *Paterson's Report to the Directors*, in J. Hill Burton, op. cit. p. 190.
61 Mortality in all colonies was high – as indeed it was in London. As tropical colonies went Darien was not particularly unhealthy. Calcutta was far worse, while Portobello was so unhealthy that most inhabitants chose not to live there in the rainy season.
62 Walter Herries jokes that Spense was not much good at languages. See *A Defence of the Scots Abdicating Darien*, 1700, p. 52.
63 J. Hill Burton, *The Darien Papers*, op. cit. p. 27.
64 Ibid., p. 27.
65 *Paterson's Report to the Directors*, in J. Hill Burton, op. cit. p. 190.
66 *Paterson's Report to the Directors*, December 1699, in J. Hill Burton, op. cit. p. 189.
67 Ibid. p. 191.
68 Prebble, op. cit. p. 186.
69 Quoted in Prebble, op. cit. p. 196.
70 Quoted in Prebble, op. cit. p. 197. The proclamation had been issued on Sunday 9 April.
71 Charles Lisle, *A New and Exact Account of Jamaica*, London, 1740. Quoted in F. Cundall, *The Darien Venture*, New York, 1926.
72 *Paterson's Report to the Directors*, December 1699, in J. Hill Burton, op. cit. p. 192.

Chapter 11

1 As already pointed out, this was not a worm at all but a greatly elongated mollusc with a taste for wood.
2 The sudden overwhelming wish to leave was so strong that the cannons mounted in the redoubt of Fort St Andrew would have been left behind had it not been for the insistence of Thomas Drummond that such an armoury could not simply be abandoned.
3 Prebble, op. cit. p. 202. *Paterson's Report to the Directors*, in J. Hill Burton, op. cit. p. 195.
4 Prebble, op. cit. p. 204.
5 Paterson tells us that: 'We lost all our masts, except the main and mizzen masts, by a squall and want of hands to the saills. This was not all; but the leakes of our ship that were great before encreased to that degree that we were hardly able to keep her above water.' See *Paterson's Report to the Directors*, in J. Hill Burton, op. cit. pp. 195–6.
6 See Ignacio Gallup-Diaz, op. cit. Chapter 5, 'Spanish Chaos'. He tells us that 'The record of his questioning is an extraordinarily rich source for the history of the settlement, and merits transcription, translation, and publication so that it might be more widely consulted by historians.'
7 *Letter from John Borland, John Campbell, and John Maxwell, to Hugh Fraser*, Edinburgh, 23 September 1699. See J. Hill Burton, op. cit. p. 159.
8 It was captured by an English force in 1664, and was ceded to England in 1667. It was recaptured by the Dutch briefly in 1672.
9 See Prebble, op. cit. p. 216 and numerous Internet entries e.g. www.friendsof

clermont.org/history/. Livingston's family became the leading family in early colonial New York. His son, Philip Livingston, endowed the first professorship at Yale from the profits of the Slave Trade.

10 Prebble, op. cit. p. 216.

11 See *Letter from Adam Cleghorn to Sir Robert Blackwood*, 14 August 1699 in J. Hill Burton, op. cit. p. 49.

12 *By His Excellency Richard Earl of Bellomont Captain General and Governour in Chief of His Majesties Province of New York. Proclamation forbidding correspondence with the expedition from Scotland to Callidonia*, 15 May 1699 (New York, 1699). Available on Library of Congress website.

13 *Letter from Bellomont to Nanfan*, 4 September 1699. P.R.O. C.O./ 1043 2 XXII. Quoted in Prebble, op. cit. p. 210.

14 Prebble, op. cit. p. 213.

15 His first name was Etienne, changed to Stephen when he adopted English ways.

16 Prebble, op. cit. p. 213, and numerous website entries.

17 He lived in a riverfront mansion in Pearl Street and owned a house at 58 Wall Street.

18 Pirated goods should by rights have been returned to their owners.

19 For evidence of this, see *Letter from John Borland, John Campbell, and John Maxwell, to Hugh Fraser*, Edinburgh, 23 September 1699. See J. Hill Burton, op. cit. p. 159.

20 See *Letter from Adam Cleghorn to Sir Robert Blackwood*, 14 August 1699, in J. Hill Burton, *The Darien Papers*, op cit. Edinburgh, 1853, p. 149.

21 Prebble, op. cit. p. 214.

22 *Court of Directors to Council of Caledonia*, 15 April 1699, in J. Hill Burton, op. cit. p. 197.

23 In fact the two ships did not leave until 12 May. J. Hill Burton, op. cit. p. 132.

24 He was to marry Margaret Livingston in 1700 and take up residence in a fine mansion on Pearl Street. See G.M. Waller, *Samuel Vetch, Colonial Enterpriser*, Chapel Hill, North Carolina, 1960.

25 There were many Scots settled in the district then known as East New Jersey around the capital, Perth Amboy. Some of the survivors crossed the Hudson estuary to join them. See, for example, the case of John Christie of St Ninians near Stirling. His story can be found on http://homepages.rootsweb.com/~windmill/html/caledonia.html.

26 There is no definite evidence pointing to the funding of the six weeks of supplies taken on board by the *Caledonia*. But Wenham and de Lancey had financed the *Ann* and Adam Cleghorn certainly had the ability to raise funds. See J. Hill Burton, *The Darien Papers*, op. cit. p. 149.

27 Quoted in Prebble, op. cit. p. 215.

28 Quoted in Prebble, op. cit. p. 269.

29 But all voyages were subject to the weather. When the main part of the second expedition left Greenock that August it was held up for six weeks unable to leave the Firth of Clyde because of contrary winds.

30 The Spanish captain Juan Delgado had visited the site in July and was to claim that many of the huts had already been burnt. Had the Scots set them on fire, or were they destroyed by French sailors who had called at the port in June, just as the Scots left? The Spanish credited the Indians with their destruction, but this seem unlikely, given the good relations the Scots had with the local chiefs. See F. Russell Hart, op. cit. pp. 308–9 for the Spanish account. Delgado certainly finished the job.

31 The tale of Jameson and Stark's misadventures in Darien is told in Prebble, op. cit. p. 7.
32 See Chapter 6, p. 151.
33 The *Caledonia* reached Greenock on 20 November 1699. Paterson himself tells us that he arrived in Edinburgh on 5 December, F. Russell Hart, op. cit. p. 96. *Paterson's Report to the Directors* in J. Hill Burton, op. cit. p. 197.

Chapter 12

1   G.M. Trevelyan, *English Social History*, London, 1944, p. 420.
2   Ibid. p. 420.
3   P. W. J. Riley, *King William and the Scottish Politicians*, Edinburgh, 1979, p. 132.
4   News of the proclamation reached Edinburgh in the first week of August. See Prebble, *Darien*, op. cit. p. 223. The first definite news of the abandonment of the colony arrived on 9 October in a letter from George Moffat, who had reached New York aboard the *Caledonia*. The letter came via London. Prebble, op. cit. pp. 232–3.
5   Philo-Caledon (Fletcher of Saltoun), *A Defence of the Scots Settlement at Darien*, London, 1699, p. 21.
6   Prebble, op. cit. p. 266.
7   *Paterson's Report to the Directors*, in J. Hill Burton, op. cit. pp. 178–98.
8   The famine made supplies difficult to obtain and hugely expensive. In a letter of February 1699, intended to keep the colony informed of the situation in Scotland, the directors had written: 'We have a scarcity of corn and provisions here since your departure, even to a dearth...'. This letter never reached Darien. Quoted in J. Prebble, op. cit. p. 218.
9   *Letter from Cleghorn to Robert Blackwood*, 14 August 1699, in J. Hill Burton, *The Darien Papers*, op. cit. p. 148.
10 Ibid. p. 149.
11 Walter Herries, *A Defence of the Scots Abdicating Darien*, 1700, p. 1.
12 Herries memorably suggested he mixed with buccaneers and 'other such vermin'. I think it is fair to assume he included brothel keepers in that category! See Walter Herries, op. cit. p. 1.
13 Ibid. p. 1.
14 Prebble, op. cit. p. 275.
15 It was entitled *An Enquiry into the Causes of the Late Miscarriage of the Scots Colony at Darien*, Edinburgh, 1700. For the order for it to be burnt, see Prebble, op. cit. p. 276.
16 The story comes from Colin Campbell's letter in *The Darien Papers*, NLS, Edinburgh. It is retold in Prebble, op. cit. p. 205. Some of the survivors made a name for themselves on the island, especially Colonel Dowdall who had fought in the army of King William at the Battle of the Boyne with distinction. He and several other survivors became landowners in Jamaica. See Lisle, *A New and Exact Account of Jamaica*, London, 1740.
17 Macaulay, op. cit. vol. 5. Macaulay clearly states he was not dishonest (p. 454) but he portrays him as a 'false prophet'. He wrote that Paterson: 'after the fashion of all the false prophets who have deluded themselves and others, drew new faith from the credulity of his disciples' (p. 455). Prebble's first mention of him is as 'the original Scots Pedlar'. Prebble, op. cit. p. 10.
18 For the status of the 'pedlar' see *The Diary of Samuel Pepys*, 20 October 1660.

Referred to in Claire Tomalin, *Samuel Pepys – the Unequalled Self*, London, 2002, p. 116.

19 Quoted in Prebble, op. cit. p. 86.

20 He was quite explicit about how the benefits of trade would flow through the entire economy. See an interesting essay published by him in 1708 under the pen name of Philopatris (Lover of my country). See p. 308. The essay is to be found in *The Works of William Paterson*, ed. Saxe Bannister, London, 1858, vol. I, pp. liii–lix. The title is 'An Essay concerning Inland and Foreign, Publick and Private Trade...showing how a Company or national Trade, may be established in Scotland, with the advantages which will result therefrom'.

21 There had been wars between Scotland and England in every century between 900 and 1600.

22 For evidence to show that people linked catastrophe and good fortune to God's Will see, for example, the diaries of John Evelyn and of Samuel Pepys. The Calvinist tradition to which Paterson belonged questioned the assumption that the doing of 'good works' would guarantee a place in paradise. All depended on God's Grace.

23 *Letter from Paterson to Thomas Drummond*, 7 February 1700, in J. Hill Burton, op. cit. Section XXIX, p. 259. The view that God operated in strange ways and determined the success and failure of all enterprises was shared by the Church of Scotland. Following the 'Great Fire' it ordered several days of fasting and humiliation. See D. Armitage, *Origins of Darien Scheme*, in J. Robertson, *A Union for Empire*, Cambridge, 1995, p. 111.

24 *Letter from Paterson to Thomas Drummond*, 7 February 1700, in J. Hill Burton, op. cit. pp. 259–60.

25 *Letter from William Paterson to Rev. Alexander Shields*, in J. Hill Burton, *The Darien Papers*, op. cit. p. 261.

26 University of London Archive, Petitions by William Paterson to the directors of the Darien Company 'requesting a remuneration for money spent during a visit to Holland and Hamburg on Company business'. Undated but written in 'Caledonia'. The title is misleading.

27 See Chapter 9.

28 Frances Borland, *Memoirs of Darien*, Glasgow, 1715. Quoted in Prebble, op. cit. p. 238.

29 Indeed, Sir William Beeston had feared the opposite effect – that many of the Scots in Jamaica would choose to go and seek their fortune in Darien. He would be happy to see the Scots colony effectively abandoned. See F. Cundall, *The Darien Venture*, New York, 1926, p. 35.

30 Later a rumour that Benbow was on his way was brought to the colony by a visiting Jamaican sloop. It was untrue, but the joy that spread through the colony suggests that the colonists had cast him as a potential saviour. See Prebble, op. cit. p. 258.

31 Named in honour of the Company's great noble shareholder.

32 We know observers were placed on high hills, since the Spanish troops discovered their posts. See *Diary of Don Juan Pimento* in Hart, op. cit. p. 372.

33 Quoted in Prebble, op. cit. p. 252.

34 The river Chugunagua.

35 *Diary of Don Juan Pimienta*, reproduced in F. Russell Hart, op. cit. p. 361.

36 12 February 1699 quoted in Dalrymple of Cranstoun, op. cit. Vol. III Book VI, p. 139.

37 As recently as 1695 the whole idea had been thrown out decisively by the House of Lords when it had been suggested that such a union might be a way out of the developing row over Paterson's Anglo-Scottish company. See P. W. J. Riley, *The Union of Scotland and England*, Manchester, 1978, p. 8.

38 See T. C. Smout, *The Road to Union*, in Geoffrey Holmes (ed.), *Britain after the Glorious Revolution*, London, 1969, p. 177.

39 Queensberry arranged for Paterson to receive an annuity of £100 a year as a token of thanks. He was in the habit of thinking money could cement all political loyalties. He was given a fund by London of £20,000 to smooth the passing of the Act of Union. He put £12,000 of that in his own pocket. See Arthur Herman, *The Scottish Enlightenment*, London, 2003, p. 39.

40 Paterson refers to the colony as 'Your Settlement in Darien'. This dates it to before the news of the final surrender of the colony, which reached Edinburgh on 28 June 1700, even if there is no record of Paterson having met directors of the Company until August. See *Carstares Papers* p. 631. The document appears in full in Sir John Dalrymple of Cranstoun's *Memoirs of Great Britain and Ireland*, London, 1771, Part III, Book VI, Appendix, pp. 154–66.

41 Sir John Dalrymple of Cranstoun, *Memoirs of Great Britain and Ireland*, London, 1771, Part III, Book VI, p. 156. The 'American Isles' he refers to are the West Indies.

42 See Macaulay, op. cit. vol. 5 p. 458.

43 Sir John Dalrymple of Cranstoun, *Memoirs of Great Britain and Ireland*, London, 1771, Part III, Book VI, pp. 162–3.

44 Strictly speaking there was to be a very small duty, not exceeding 5 per cent, to begin with. This would help pay for the costs of the harbours and any link – by road or by canal – across the Isthmus, and for defence. But eventually custom duty would be replaced by a blanket excise duty 'upon sugar, tobacco, wine, salt and such like' in England and Scotland to meet King William's expenses in the colony. Ibid. p. 165.

45 Sir John Dalrymple of Cranstoun, *Memoirs of Great Britain and Ireland*, London, 1771, Part III, Book VI, p. 163.

46 It is worth noting that Paterson talks nowhere of 'empire'. The greatest period of British industrial expansion came in the mid-19th century when the very notion of empire was frowned upon by free traders like William Cobden and John Bright.

47 Child died in 1699. The 'New East India Company' had been set up in 1698, with the support of Charles Montagu.

48 Sir John Dalrymple of Cranstoun, *Memoirs of Great Britain and Ireland*, London, 1771, Part III, Book VI, p. 164. Paterson uses the phrase.

49 Sir John Dalrymple of Cranstoun, *Memoirs of Great Britain and Ireland*, London, 1771, Part III, Book VI, p. 163.

50 Prebble, op. cit. pp. 283–6.

51 Prebble, op. cit. p. 286.

52 In December 1698 Ambrosio had warned the Scots that Andreas was not to be trusted, since he was in the Spanish camp.

53 *Letter signed by James Gibson and two others*, 28 March 1700, reproduced in F. Russell Hart, op. cit. p. 379.

54 There is some confusion over the exact date. The original Spanish document is dated 31 March, but Pimienta's diary is clearly marked 11 April. This was of course 31 March under the old Julian calendar.

55 *Diary of Don Juan Pimienta*, reproduced in F. Russell Hart, op. cit. p. 388.

56 See entry in *Diary of Samuel Sewell*, the Boston judge, op. cit. 23 October 1699.

57 A descendant of Stobo married into the Roosevelt family.

58 Prebble gives an account of the voyages home, op. cit. pp. 300–7.

59 There is no clear estimate of the death toll on the second expedition. More than 500 were sent to Jamaica. Three ships made it home, and there were survivors who stayed on in Charleston. John Prebble's estimate that 1,000 out of the 1,300 died seems excessive.

60 P. W. J. Riley, *The Union of Scotland and England*, Manchester, 1978, p. 218.

61 *Letter from John Stewart, King's Secretary to Carstares*, 3 September 1700, *Carstares Papers*.

62 William Paterson, *Memoir upon Expeditions against the Spanish West Indies, 1701*. Reproduced in Saxe Bannister, *The Writings of William Paterson*, London, 1858, Vol. 1 pp. 107–62.

63 Prebble, op. cit. pp. 312–14.

64 *Letter from Scotland*, London, 1705. Quoted in Prebble, op. cit. p. 9.

65 William Ferguson, *Scotland – 1689 to Present*, Edinburgh, 1968, p. 47.

66 P. W. J. Riley, *The Union of Scotland and England*, op. cit. p. 170.

67 The figure is taken from a file in The Royal Bank of Scotland Group Archives in Edinburgh concerning a claim by a Toronto law firm that the Bank owed money to a then living heir to a share of Paterson's fortune. The bank politely wrote back to indicate that Paterson had not been a shareholder in the Company of Scotland and no money was paid to him under the Equivalent. The Royal Bank, therefore, owed Mr Paterson's alleged heir nothing.

68 The letter is quoted by G. P. Insh in an article, 'William Paterson and the Dumfries Election of 1708', he wrote for the *Transactions of the Dumfries and Galloway Natural History and Archaeological Society*, 1952–3, Series III, Vol. 32, pp. 124–31.

69 The 66 Scottish Burghs were grouped into 15 constituencies each representing four or five of them. The electorate averaged just 23 persons per borough. There was no secret ballot and landowners like the Earl of Annandale could expect to exercise much influence over any result. See Tom Devine, *The Scottish Nation, 1700–2000*, p. 187, London, 1999.

70 The details come from the article by G. P. Insh, cited above.

71 It is unlikely Smith every received the bonds, since he had gone to live on St Thomas Island. We must remember also that Smith was a common name.

72 Information from The Royal Bank of Scotland Website, www.rbs.com.

73 The quotation is from *An Essay on Inland, Foreign, and Publick and Private Trade, etc*, by Philopatris, Edinburgh, 1708 – attributed to William Paterson by Saxe Bannister. It is reproduced in Saxe Bannister, *The Writings of William Paterson*, London, 1858, vol. 2, pp. liii–lix. The selected quotation is on p. liv.

74 Philopatris Essay, reproduced in Saxe Bannister, *The Writings of William Paterson*, London, 1858, vol. 2, p. liii.

75 See J. H. Shennan, *Philippe, Duke of Orleans*, London, 1979, pp. 91–125 passim. And Janet Gleeson, *MILLIONAIRE, The Philanderer, Gambler, and Duellist Who Invented Modern Finance*, New York, 1999.

76 From a tract reproduced by Saxe Bannister in *The Writings of William Paterson*, op. cit. vol. 1, pp. xlviii–lii.

77 See G. P. Insh, *William Paterson and the Dumfries Election of 1708*, op. cit. p. 126.

78 W. Marston Ayres, *The Bank of England from within 1694–1900*, London, 1931,

vol. 1 p. 17. The information derives from a guidebook published in 1887. It should be treated with caution.

Epilogue

1 *Message from King William III to the Scots Parliament*, 29 October 1700. Quoted in G. P. Insh, *The Darien Scheme*, Historical Association pamphlet, London, 1947, p. 20.

2 For a detailed narrative of the complicated twists and turns on the diplomatic front between the death of Carlos II of Spain and the death of William in March 1702 see Sir Winston Churchill, *Marlborough, His Life and Times,* London, 1967, vol. 1, pp. 440–66.

3 Dr Edward Cullen, *The Isthmus of Darien Canal*, London, 1853, p. 21.

4 For years the route through Nicaragua had been the one most favoured. The choice of the present route was as much driven by politics as economics. In 2003 the plan to build a canal in Nicaragua was revived.

Bibliography

1. Manuscript Sources

The Darien Papers in the National Library of Scotland, Edinburgh
The Minute Book of the Company of Scotland, The Royal Bank of Scotland Group Archives, Edinburgh
Papers Relating to The Darien Scheme in the University of London Archive, London
The minutes and other records of the Bank of England held in the Bank of England Archives and the Bank of England Museum
Public Record Office, Kew Admiralty records.
The Spencer Collection, University of Glasgow

2. Printed Documents

The Darien Papers J. Hill Burton, Edinburgh, 1949
The Darien Shipping Papers, G. P. Insh (ed.), Edinburgh, 1924
The Journal of the House of Commons, Vol. XI
The Journal of the House of Lords, Vol. XV
Appendix to F. Russell Hart, *The Disaster of Darien*, New York
House of Lords Manuscripts, New Series, London 1903
Dansk Saml., Copenhagen
Guildhall Folio Pamphlet 896, Guildhall Library London.
Acts of the Parliament of Scotland (APS)
Lansdowne Manuscript, British Library, London
The Diary of Samuel Sewell, Boston Historical Society, 1878
Carstares Papers
The Spencer Collection, University of Glasgow holds many contemporary pamphlets

3. Books, Pamphlets and Articles

Anonymous, *Some seasonable and modest thoughts partly occasion'd by and partly concerning the Scots East India Company*, Edinburgh 1696
Anonymous, *An Enquiry into the Causes of the Late Miscarriage of the Scots Colony at Darien*, Edinburgh, 1700
Anonymous, *Caledonia or Pedlar Turn'd Merchant*, London, 1700
David Armitage, *The Ideological Origins of the British Empire*, Cambridge, 2000
William Marston Ayres, *The Bank of England from Within*, London, 1931
Emerson E. Baker and John G. Reid, *The New England Knight*, Boston, 1999

Saxe Bannister, *William Paterson, Founder of the Bank of England, His Life and Trials*, Edinburgh 1858

Saxe Bannister, *The Writings of William Paterson*, London, 1858

James Samuel Barbour, *A History of William Paterson and the Darien Company*, London, 1907

Violet Barbour, *Capitalism in Amsterdam in the 17th Century*, Baltimore, 1950

Francis Borland, *A History of Darien*, Glasgow, 1715

P. Hume Brown, *Early Travellers in Scotland*, Edinburgh, 1891

Angus Calder, *Revolutionary Empire* (Pimlico Paperback), London 1998

Edward Chancellor, *Devil Take the Hindmost*, New York, 1999

K. N. Chaudhuri, *The Trading World of Asia and the English East India Company, 1660–1760*, Cambridge, 1978

Sir Josiah Child, *Selected Works*, London and Farnborough, 1968

Sir Josiah Child, *A Discourse on Trade*, London, 1994

Winston Churchill, *Marlborough, His Life and Times*, London, 1967

Sir John Clapham, *The Bank of England, a History*, Cambridge and London 1944

Sir John Clapham, *A Concise Economic History of Britain*, Cambridge, 1949

G. N. Clark, *The Later Stuarts, 1660–1714*, 2nd edn, Oxford, 1956

Peter Clark and Peter Slack, *Crisis and Order in the English Towns 1500–1700*, London, 1972

Edward Cullen, *The Isthmus of Darien Canal*, London, 1853

Frank Cundall, *The Darien Venture*, New York, 1926

Sir John Dalrymple of Cranstoun, *Memoirs of Great Britain and Ireland*, Part III, London, 1771–6

William Dampier, *A New Voyage Round the World*, London, 1697

William Dampier, *A Voyage to New Holland*, etc, London, 1703

Daniel Defoe, *The Advantages of Scotland in a Corporate Union with England*, Edinburgh, 1706

Daniel Defoe, *The Anatomy of Exchange Alley*, London, 1719

Daniel Defoe, *An Essay on Projects*, London, 1797

Gary DeGrey, *A Fractured Society*, Oxford, 1985

Tom Devine, *The Scottish Nation*, London, 1999

G. M. Dickson, *The Financial Revolution in England 1688–1756*, London, 1967

I. G. Doolittle, 'Origins and History of the Orphans' Fund', in *British Institutional History Research*, Vol. LXI, no. 133, May 1983, London

John Evelyn, *The Diary of John Evelyn*, Oxford, 1955

Niall Ferguson, *The Cash Nexus* (paperback), London, 2001

W. Ferguson, *Scotland – 1689 to the Present*, Edinburgh, 1968

Peter Gieyl, *History of the Low Countries*, London, 1964

J. Giuseppi, *The Bank of England, A History*, Chicago, 1966

Janet Gleeson, *Millionaire*, New York, 1999 (life of John Law)

Michael Godfrey, *A Short Account of the Bank of England*, London, 1695

H. Guttridge, *The Colonial Policy of William III in America and the West Indies*, London, 1922

Francis Russell Hart, *The Disaster of Darien*, Boston and New York, 1929

Arthur Herman, *The Scottish Enlightenment* (paperback edition), London 2003

George P. Insh, *Scottish Colonial Schemes*, Glasgow, 1922

George P. Insh, *The Company of Scotland Trading to Africa and the Indies*, London, 1932

George P. Insh, *Historian's Odyssey*, Edinburgh and London, 1938

George P. Insh, *The Darien Scheme*, Historical Association, London, 1947

George P. Insh, 'William Paterson and the Dumfries Election of 1708' in *Transactions of the Dumfries and Galloway Natural History and Archaeological Society 1952–3*

Jonathan Israel, *Dutch Primacy in World Trade, 1585–1740*, London, 1989

D. W. Jones, *War and Economy in the Age of William III and Marlborough*, London, 1988

John Keay, *The Honourable Company*, London, 1991

David Landes, *The Wealth and Poverty of Nations*, Abacus Edition, London, 1999

Robin Law, 'The First Scottish Guinea Company, 1634–1639', *Scottish Historical Review* Vol. LXXVII, Edinburgh, 1997

Charles Leslie, *A New and Exact Account of Jamaica*, London, 1740

William Letwin, *A Brief Life of Josiah Child*, London, 1959

Christopher Lloyd, *Dampier*, London, 1966

William Lowndes, *Essay for the Amendment of Silver Coins*, London, 1695

Narcissus Luttrell, *A Brief Historical Relation of State Affairs*, Oxford, 1857

Michael Lynch, *Scotland, a New History*, London, 1992

Thomas Babington Macaulay (Lord Macaulay), *A History of England* (in five volumes), New York, 1899

Patrick McGrath, *The Merchant Venturers of Bristol*, Bristol, 1975

W. C. Mackenzie, *Andrew Fletcher of Saltoun*, Edinburgh, 1935

John Macky, *Memoirs*, London, 1733

Arthur Percival Newton, *The Colonising Activities of the English Puritans on Providence Island*, London, 1914

William Pagan, *The Birthplace and Parentage of William Paterson*, Edinburgh, 1865

J. H. Parry, *Europe and a Wider World, 1415–1715*, London, 1949

J. H. Parry, *Trade and Dominion: the European Oversea Empires in the Eighteenth Century*, London, 1971

Philo-Caledon (Andrew Fletcher), *A Defence of the Scots Settlement at Darien*, London, 1699

Philopatris (William Paterson), 'An Essay Concerning Inland, Publick, and Private Trade', Edinburgh, 1708

John Prebble, *Darien, the Scottish Dream of Empire*, Edinburgh, 2000 (reprint of *The Darien Disaster*, 1968)

Cecil Price, *Cold Caleb, The Scandalous Life of Ford Grey*, London, 1956

Stephen Quinn, 'Gold and Silver in the Glorious Revolution', *Economic History Review*, Vol. XLIX

R. S. Rait, *The Parliaments of Scotland*, Glasgow, 1924

P. W. J. Riley, *The Union of Scotland and England*, Manchester, 1978

P. W. J. Riley, *King William and the Scottish Politicians*, Edinburgh, 1979

J. Robertson, *A Union for Empire*, Cambridge, 1995

John Robertson, *Selected Writings of Andrew Fletcher of Saltoun*, Cambridge, 1997

Jan and Annie Romein, *Erflaters van Onze Beschaving*, Amsterdam 1979

Kevin Rushby, *Hunting Pirate Heaven* (paperback edition), London, 2000

Simon Richard Saville, *The Bank of Scotland, a History*, Edinburgh, 1997

Simon Schama, *The Embarrassment of Riches*, New York, 1987

Simon Schama, *Rembrandt's Eyes*, London, 1999

William Robert Scott, *The Constitution and Finance of English, Scottish and Irish Joint-Stock Companies to 1720* (in three volumes), London, 1910–12

J. H. Shennan, *Philipe, Duke of Orleans*, London, 1979

A. J(ames) S(mith), *Some Account of the Transactions of Mr William Paterson, etc*, London, 1695

Adam Smith, *The Wealth of Nations* (Everyman Edition), 1957

T. C. Smout, *Scottish Trade on the Eve of the Union*, Edinburgh, 1963
T. C. Smout, 'The Road to Union', in G. Holmes (ed.) *Britain after the Glorious Revolution*, London, 1969
Joseph Taylor, *A Journey to Edenborough in Scotland in 1705*, London, 1706
Hugh Thomas, *The Slave Trade*, London, 1997
Newton Thorpe, *The Federal and State Constitutions, Colonial Charters, etc*, Washington DC, 1906
Claire Tomalin, *Samuel Pepys – the Unequalled Self*, London, 2002
G. M. Trevelyan, *English Social History*, London, 1944
Jan de Vries and Ad Van der Woude, *The First Modern Economy*, Cambridge, 1997
Lionel Wafer, *A New Voyage and a Description of the Isthmus of Darien*, London, 1699
G. M. Waller, *Samueal Vetch, Colonial Enterpriser*, Chapel Hill, N.C., 1960
Maureen Waller, *1700, Scenes from London Life*, London, 2000
Edward Ward, *A Trip to Jamaica*, etc., London, 1698
Emily F. Ward, *Christopher Monck, Second Duke of Albemarle*, London, 1933
Eliot Washburton, *The Merchant Prince, a Historical Romance*, London, 1852
Waldemar Westegaard, *The Danish West Indies Under Company Rule*, New York, 1917
James Whiston, 'England's Calamities Discovered', in *Harleian Miscellany*, Vol. 6, London, 1745
Michael White, *Isaac Newton the Last Sorcerer* (paperback edition), London, 1998

4. On the Internet

Ignacio Gallup-Diaz, *The Doors of the Seas and the Key to the Universe*, E-Book published by the Gutenberg Project
Steven C. A. Pincus, *Whigs, Political Economy and the Revolution of 1688–89*, http://www.src.uchicago.edu/politicaltheory/Pincus02.pdf

Index

About TEXERE

TEXERE seeks to become the most progressive and authoritative voice in business publishing by cultivating and enhancing ideas that will illuminate the global business landscape. Our name defines the spirit of our vision: TEXERE is the ancient Latin verb "to weave". In an increasingly global business community, we seek to create an intersection where authors and readers can share the best thinking and the latest ideas. We want to leverage the expertise and insights of leading thinkers by weaving them with TEXERE's capability to deliver them to the marketplace. To learn more and become a part of our community visit us at:

www.etexere.com

and

www.etexere.co.uk

About the typeface

This book was set in 10.5/14pt Baskerville. The Baskerville typeface was created in the 1750s by John Baskerville of England. Credited with originating the English tradition in fine printing, John Baskerville was appointed printer to Cambridge University in 1758. This typeface is known for its delicate and simple style.